Gullah

ENTRANCE TO TOMOTLEY PLANTATION, PRINCE WILLIAM PARISH, NEAR BEAUFORT, SOUTH CAROLINA

Gullah

NEGRO LIFE *in* THE CAROLINA SEA ISLANDS

Mason Crum

COMMONWEALTH BOOK COMPANY
St. Martin, Ohio

Copyright © 1940 by Mason Crum
Copyright © 2024 by Commonwealth Book Company

All rights reserved. No part of this book may be reproduced in any form or by any means without the prior written consent of the publisher, excepting brief quotes used in reviews. Printed in the United States of America.

ISBN: 978-1-948986-88-5

COVER IMAGE: O'Sullivan, Timothy H, photographer. *Cabins for enslaved workers on a plantation, Port Royal, South Carolina.* Port Royal South Carolina, 1862. [April] Photograph. Library of Congress

TITLE PAGE ILLUSTRATION:
Gullah Fanner Basket, Smithsonian Institution

TO FLORA, CHARLES, AND ALEX, SLAVES OF MY GRANDFATHER, WHOSE AMIABLE LIVES, TYPICAL OF THE BEST IN NEGRO CHARACTER, HAVE LEFT IN ME AN ABIDING AFFECTION FOR COLORED PEOPLE EVERYWHERE

PREFACE

I WAS BORN and reared in the coastal plain of South Carolina and have known Negroes intimately from my youth up. My social inheritance, speaking broadly, was that of the average youth in the Deep South near the turn of the present century. In this atmosphere I imbibed all the emotional attitudes and prejudices regarding the Civil War and the dreadful years of Reconstruction that followed. From the cradle I learned of the horrors of this conflict: indeed, I got it firsthand, for a part of Sherman's army passed through my grandmother's house.

The early recollections of my childhood are of the friendly colored people who lived in little white-washed cabins in the cotton fields near my home and the scores of black folk who flocked to the village store on Saturdays to buy bacon and grits and calico. I remember them as kindly, earnest people, who shared with my father in confidence the vicissitudes of their simple lives and sought his advice, especially when cotton was low and "rations" high. The names and personalities of many of them stand out in my own mind as vividly as do prominent names in history. There were the ever amiable Charles and Alex, boyhood playmates of my father; Peg, their sister, who had a penchant for receiving gifts; and Jane, the rotund, camp-meeting cook, handy with the skillet. Among the patriarchal types were Uncle Eli, white haired and of placid countenance, who looked for all the world like Uncle Tom in Harriet Beecher Stowe's great novel; and Uncle Ephraim, who never told a lie except when the Yankee soldiers took him with Sherman's army and tried to put him too near the front. He was always welcomed in the kitchen, where he invariably interested the children, who listened attentively to his homely philosophy and tales of the long ago. Uncle Ephraim was my hero, for he slew a nine-foot alligator, singlehanded, with a woodman's axe. I saw the reptile, and I stood by with bulging eyes as it was measured and weighed in the flickering light of a kerosene lamp. This old man lived in the swamp and decorated the outside of his cabin with coon hides and skins of various "varmints." His little son Noog and I hunted birds together, using one gun, a diminutive muzzle-loader, with powder horn, sack of shot, and a box of caps. Other colored boys were Sunny, Archie, Duk, and Ting. Unforgettable in the list is Shagood, the village idiot, who had fits. Near the big swamp was a solitary cabin in a cotton field—a place of mystery. A Negro woman lived there, a widow, who had a demented daughter. I sometimes saw the mother ploughing in the field.

Then, there was Mary McCormick, the cook, a willing soul, who stood over the big hot stove in the unceiled kitchen, which was separated from the house by a small porch. When her baby came, she accepted the family fountain syringe in order to have some medical equipment for the event. Later, in dismay, she reported that her little boys had cut it up and made it into slingshots! Rosalind Summers, who was the soapmaker for the family, made lye-soap in the big black pot in the back yard. She was a woman of kindness, and, when my mother went away for the day, Rosalind suckled at her black breast my baby brother as well as her own baby. I have never known a colored person who would let a child white or black go hungry.

Among my earliest memories is the benign, sweet-faced Negro woman named Julia, my nurse. My mother told her that, when I grew up to be a man, I would give her a pretty dress. This promise I fulfilled and I only wish that I might have done more for her. However anomalous it may seem, my grandfather was both a slaveholder and a good man. When his slaves were told that they had been set free, they rejoiced, but most of them stayed with him. They visited my family frequently, and we were always glad to see them. When old Mammy died, my father placed a monument over her grave.

In this environment I grew up. When in college I became aware of the difficult position of the Southern Negro before and after slavery, I felt that a grave responsibility rested upon the shoulders of Southern white people and wished that I might lend a hand. This desire has not diminished, yet I have done little about it.

With this sort of background I am led to make the following observations: (1) One of the most pressing social needs in the South today is the discovery of some rational basis for a better understanding of racial problems. It appears that we need to establish some procedure by which the two races may cultivate attitudes which will lead to a mutually sympathetic understanding of the desires and purposes of each; (2) it is obvious that such an understanding cannot develop from the conventional patterns of thought and the emotionalized attitudes which each group has inherited: these new attitudes must be built upon the solid foundation of knowledge and the appraisal of facts. Too long have both groups, resorting to sentiment and emotion, received as a reward the host of irrational prejudices which easily follow. The theorist and the fanatic have had their day; it is now time to take stock and view the problems in their wider historical perspective. Young people of both races need to know more about the social history of the American Negro and his interesting and often intimate and friendly relationships with the white people of the South. Southerners white and colored are acquainted only with the present difficulties and antagonisms and know little of the finer relationships which have existed all along. They might profitably take time to know more fully the interesting story of Negro progress and the Negro's contribution to American life in economics, in letters, and in art. Such an approach will do more to establish mutually helpful relations than all the loud protestations of the theorist and impatient idealist.

I have tried to give a faithful picture of the life of these people, not only in their present status, but also under slavery and during the trying years that followed. The frequently quoted letters and other sources speak for themselves. My own opinion of this material has been reduced to a minimum. The rather long quotations are justified on the ground that they give a far more vivid and accurate picture of events than any comment could possibly give. They are fraught with the stress and emotion of the times and convey both the humor and pathos of the people.

This study is purposely limited in its scope: it deals with the social history of one of the most interesting groups in the South—the Gullah Negroes, who live among the sea islands and in the coastal region of South Carolina. In a very true sense the history of these people furnishes a key to the whole racial situation in America. In their isolation the Gullahs provide materials for an interesting social study. It is significant that nowhere on the continent can a purer African culture be found. Until recent years this whole area has been cut off from the rest of the world. The cultural and geographical isolation of these Negroes offers an absolutely unique situation for the student interested in human relations. Socially, relatively few changes have taken place in their mode of living and their outlook upon life since Emancipation. The plantation pattern still exists and provides an interesting laboratory for the study of conditions which have long since disappeared in other sections.

Perhaps something should be said at this point in explanation of the term *Gullah*. The word is almost certainly a corruption of the African *Gola* or *Gora*, names of African tribes living in Liberia, east of the city of Monrovia. For a long time *Gullah* was considered a modification of the African *Angola*, but this belief is hardly tenable now. Many of these Gola or Angola Negroes were brought to Charleston and sold as slaves; thence they were shipped to the rice and cotton plantations along the coast. Whether this particular group perpetuated its name because of a certain racial dominance and strength of character or whether by chance the name was retained is not known, but the fact is that in recent years all the native Negroes of this region are known as Gullah Negroes.

The most distinctive characteristic of these people is their unique form of speech. It constitutes one of the most curious dialects to be found anywhere in America. Amiable in disposition, courtly in manner and with a gentility exceedingly rare today, the Gullah Negroes of the Carolina sea islands are a delight to know, and to the student of human affairs an interesting reminder of a day that has gone.

M. C.

Duke University
June 6, 1940

ACKNOWLEDGMENTS

THE AUTHOR wishes to express his thanks to the following publishers and writers for permission to quote from their publications: The Macmillan Company, The State Company, Oliver Ditson Company, D. Appleton-Century Company, Little, Brown and Company, Peter Smith, Publisher, Hampton Institute Press, The Cokesbury Press, Charles Scribner's Sons, R. L. Bryan Company, Dr. I. Jenkins Mikell, Mr. Harold Vinal, Miss Rossa B. Cooley, Professor Henry C. Davis, Mr. Augustine T. Smythe, Mr. S. C. Murray, the Reverend Robert W. Barnwell, and Judge M. S. Whaley.

Lines from the spirituals which introduce Chapters IV, IX, XI, XIII, and XIV are (excepting IV) modifications of lines from the collection of William Francis Allen, *Slave Songs of the United States*. Those introducing Chapters I, III, V, and VII, while not exact quotations, were suggested by the collection in *The Carolina Low-Country*. The verse appearing at the head of Chapter X is from a poem of Charles Roundtree Dinkins, and that in Chapter VIII is by an author unknown to the writer. The lines were used in an article by St. Julian Ravenel in *The State*, Columbia, South Carolina, in 1936. The line beginning Chapter VI was recorded by Mr. John Bennett of Charleston. Mr. Bennett's articles in *The South Atlantic Quarterly* have been most useful. Professor Reed Smith's monograph on *Gullah* was quoted in several instances, and excerpts from an article of Mrs. Stephen Elliott Puckett were gratefully used.

The three collections of spirituals most widely drawn upon for illustrative purposes were the *St. Helena Island Spirituals*; "The Society for the Preservation of Spirituals," *The Carolina Low-Country*; and the Civil War collection of Allen, *Slave Songs of the United States*.

CONTENTS

Preface	vii
Acknowledgments	xi

CHAPTER

I. The Carolina Low Country	3
II. The Sea Islands	19
III. Plantations	34
IV. The Gullah World of Nature	55
V. The Black People	77
VI. The Gullah Dialect	101
VII. Spirituals of the Sea Islands	132
VIII. The Cultural Background of the Gullah Spirituals	146
IX. Religious Instruction of the Slaves	173
X. The Plantation Missions	198
XI. Negro Life in the Rice Community	232
XII. Hardships of Slavery	266
XIII. Thunder Over Port Royal	282
XIV. The Port Royal Experiment	308
Bibliography	345

ILLUSTRATIONS

Entrance to Tomotley Plantation, Prince William Parish, Near Beaufort, South Carolina	*frontispiece*
Edisto Island, Once Celebrated for Its Sea-Island Cotton	16
At Peace with the World on Its Own Terms	48
A Sea-Island Boy	48
Uncle Sam, the Netmaker	112
They Work in the Oyster Factory	112
Understanding Hearts	176
Negro Cabin Near Port Royal	240
A Tidal River, Dawhoo	240
Negro Church, Edisto Island	304
I Look Down de Road and de Road So Lonesome	304

GULLAH

CHAPTER I

THE CAROLINA LOW COUNTRY

> Oh, I got a mansion up on high;
> Well, 'e ain' mek wid han',
> No—'e ain' mek wid han'.

A STRIP of low-lying pineland about a hundred miles wide running parallel with the white sandy beaches of the Atlantic constitutes what is known as the Carolina coastal plain. Its interior limit is marked by submerged sand dunes bearing unmistakable evidence of having once been sea beaches; and what is now the fertile sandy-loam of a part of the Cotton Belt was once the bed of an ancient sea. Excavations in many areas to-day reveal fossilized fish bones. The nether strip of this level plain is the Carolina low country. Its maritime fringe is the "black border," land of the Gullah Negro. The Carolina low country is bounded on the north by the village of Georgetown, with its hinterland of deep swamps, and on the south by Port Royal and the shimmering waters of St. Helena Sound. The country is cut across with many rivers and streams which bring down their wine-colored waters to mingle with the salty tides from the sea. As the coastal rivers approach the sea, their slow-moving waters are halted twice each day by the tide, which ascends, in some of them, to a distance of twenty miles, making the dark streams brackish and permitting finger mullet and sea bass to swim along the decaying banks of the deserted rice fields.

The Carolina low country is bordered by a fringe of fertile islands made by the tedious work of rivers depositing their silt into the lap of the sea. They are in reality but a part of the mainland, but are given the name of islands merely because they are cut off from the mainland by wide marshes, deep tidal rivers, and arms of the sea. About these modest islands there is a serene beauty almost beyond description. One who visits them with a view to finding sophisticated pleasures or, indeed, anything modern meets nothing but disappointment. No signs of progress are evident. The islands are like lavender and old lace; and he who does not love old things and the mellowing processes of time should not visit them. The Carolina sea islands are backward looking; they have no interest in the future. They tell a story of a romantic and glorious past. The stately live oaks, draped in Spanish moss, are reminiscent of plantation days in the Old South and seem to express a disdain for the noise and claptrap of modern life and progress. The long avenues leading up to the clearing where once stood a white house seem to bespeak peace. In this silent country the intrusion of gasoline stations and speeding cars suggests impudence and a boorishness out of harmony with the prevailing tone.

The islands were once wealthy, deriving their opulence from silky sea-island cotton and Negro slavery; rice and indigo also contributed to their affluence. There was a genuine culture, unhappily based upon the enforced labor of the enslaved Negro, but accompanied by a degree of contentment even among the slaves. They flourished until that fatal day in April, 1861, when Fort Sumter fell and Charleston Harbor belonged to the Confederacy. But this achievement was no guarantee for Confederate possession of the whole length of coast, and before many months Federal strategists were laying plans to occupy ports of secondary importance. On November 7, 1861, the Federal fleet moved proudly into Port Royal Harbor, and the Union flag was raised over Fort Walker.[1] Meantime the white residents of these island regions had fled before the invader, leaving behind crops, mansions, and Negroes to an alien who scarcely knew what to do with any of them.[2]

From that day until this the islands have sat in sackcloth and ashes and have hardly lifted their heads. The tragedy of war and the sudden snapping of a social and economic order apparently secure have left their marks upon every aspect of life, and one feels on every hand an ineradicable touch of pathos and the sense of moving through a great house whose master has departed. These invaders were themselves moved by the pity of the scene and the desolation that stalked through the homes of the island planters. One of the first, E. S. Philbrick, of Boston,

[1] Robert Underwood Johnson and Clarence Clough Buel (eds.), *Battles and Leaders of the Civil War* (4 vols.; New York, 1884-1887), I, 685 f.

[2] Elizabeth Ware Pearson, *Letters from Port Royal* (Boston, 1906), pp. v-ix.

who occupied one of the planter's homes, recorded his impressions during a sojourn at Beaufort, South Carolina:

> There is something very sad about these fine deserted houses. Ours has Egyptian marble mantels, gilt cornice and centre-piece in parlor, and bath room, with several wash-bowls set in different rooms. The force pump is broken and all the bowls and their marble slabs smashed to get out the plated cocks, which the negroes thought pure silver. Bureaus, commodes, and wardrobes are smashed in, as well as door-panels, to get out the contents of the drawers and lockers, which I suppose contained some wine and ale, judging by the broken bottles lying about. The officers saved a good many pianos and other furniture and stored it in the jail, for safekeeping. But we kindle our fires with chips of polished mahogany, and I am writing on my knees with a piece of flower stand across them for a table, sitting on my camp bedstead.[3]

The military invasion was followed almost immediately by the vanguard of "missionaries," those zealous Northerners whose sense of duty brought them south to "elevate" the Negro race. Here in the sea islands of Carolina they obtained their first foothold. A young woman of New England who came to Port Royal with the band of "missionaries" early in the war to minister to the slaves lived in the beautiful old plantation house on Coffin's Point, St. Helena Island, overlooking the blue waters of the Sound. Writing back to friends in New England, this young lady vividly described the spoliation which followed the flight of the planters and the occupation of the area by Union troops. Much of the damage was done by the slaves, who, like children, knew not how to govern their impulses in new situations. They walked brazenly in and out the plantation houses, appropriated whatever struck their fancy, and ignorantly destroyed articles of beauty for which they had no appreciation or sense of value. They fraternized with their newly made friends and liberators and enjoyed a brief but ecstatic experience of being set free. The tragedy lay in their inability to envisage the long and dreary road of Reconstruction and the deadening years that followed. The intoxication of freedom which seized some of the more erratic Negroes was voiced in the pathetic ejaculation of those who, in frenzied de-

[3] *Ibid.*, p. 8.

light, cried: "I free, I free! I free as a frog! I free till I fool! Glory Alleluia!"[4]

A description of the Coffin Point house, in a letter written during the early period of the war, is as follows:

> It was built in good style originally, but it is very old, and has been so abused by the negroes in the first place, and then from having had soldiers living in it for so many months, it is very shabby. It must have been handsomely furnished, to judge from the relics, for they are nothing more—rosewood tables, sideboards and washstands with marble tops, drawers and doors broken in and half gone, sofas that must have been of the best, nothing left but the frame; no one can conceive of the destruction who has not seen it. The rooms are twelve feet high, and the lower story is more than that from the ground. The air is delicious, and we shall find the blinds which are on the second story a luxury. I have my own little bed, bureau, marble top washstand, three chairs and a large wardrobe, to say nothing of a piano, in my chamber, which I should think eighteen feet square.[5]

The deep humiliation and the sense of resentment which seized the planters of the Port Royal area were accentuated by the brazen manner in which the religious teachers from the North and the agents of the Federal government took possession of their homes. They not only lounged in parlor chairs and slept in beds, but read private letters stored away in attics and old drawers. Three excerpts from letters in the Port Royal correspondence describe the insatiable curiosity of the "missionaries":

> July 10. William has been overhauling the old letters and papers in the garret and has come across many very interesting bits of information among them. They are mostly very old. Old plantation books of Mr. Eben Coffin, the first proprietor of this estate, dated 1800, containing lists of the slaves of former generations, in which some of the oldest here now, like Uncle Sam, are mentioned as two years old; estimates for this house and the building in the yard, etc.
>
> Aug. 5. C. has found a spike of papers in the old overseer house, on which he and Mr. Soule are now expending their eyesight. Letters from Mr. Coffin to Mr. Cockloft, etc.

[4] Elizabeth Waties (Allston) Pringle, *Chronicles of Chicora Wood* (New York, 1922), p. 273. [5] Pearson, *op. cit.*, pp. 59 f.

Aug. 6. I entertained myself today reading over these same letters. It made me feel very queerly—they were mostly written during the summer of 1860, from Charleston and Newport. It seemed so short a time ago, and everything and person spoken of about the plantation was so familiar.[6]

The diary of Mary Ames, of Boston, who came to Edisto Island during the war as a teacher of the slaves, gives many interesting glimpses of conditions in this particular area: "We walked down the road to a church, which bore marks of destruction similar to those of our house. The frame of the organ remains, the windows are gone, doors off their hinges, and pews mutilated, but we decided that it would serve our purpose well as a schoolhouse."[7]

I have seen at the home of Edward Jenkins on Edisto Island a large pulpit Bible and prayer book with the name of the Episcopal Church embossed in gold, which had been taken from the church during the Federal occupation of the island. The books had been returned from the North by an officer in the United States Army, together with a letter explaining the circumstances under which they had been removed. Perhaps the officer had removed the books to save them from the hands of souvenir hunters among the more unscrupulous soldiers.

The Presbyterian Church on Edisto Island was taken over by the freedmen, incited thereto by the false hopes of the Northern people then inhabiting the island. Jenkins Mikell, of the same island, relates the experience of the congregation in repossessing the Presbyterian Church after the close of the war:

Our venerable church, whose charter of corporation was near two hundred years old, was firmly held by colored members of the ante-bellum congregation, who refused to vacate, claiming right of possession, and as being a large majority of the former congregation. Considerable work and red tape was necessary to obtain the order for their dispossession. At last the coveted paper came from Washington. The following Sabbath our old pastor, with a small number of his white congregation, who had returned to the Island from their exile, assembled at the door of the Church. Services were then being held by the colored minister and his flock, which numbered

---

[6] *Ibid.*, pp. 205 f.
[7] Mary (Clemmer) Ames, *From a New England Woman's Diary in Dixie in 1865* (Norwood, Mass., 1906), pp. 17 f.

hundreds. Waiting until the end of the hymn they were singing, our venerable pastor, Wm. States Lee, whose pastorate extended back fifty years without a break, save the four years of the war, dressed in his black silk Geneva gown, and followed by those of us who were present, marched up the aisle, with Bible in one hand and the order for possession in the other, to the foot of the pulpit, a very tall mahogany one, reached by two long spiral stairs, and, raising his arm for silence, said: "In the name of God, and by the authority of the United States Government, I demand possession of this building!"

For a moment, the strain was intense. All were on their feet. No one could tell what the next move might be. No one could guess what might happen. A loud word, an impatient gesture, an angry exclamation would perhaps precipitate a riot. The two ministers eyed each other. The colored minister from above gazed down on the feeble white man standing below. "Pass me up the order for possession!" broke the silence. This order was read, examined, and handed back. "Your titles, sir, are clear, so far as might and power makes [sic] them so. We will vacate." He left the pulpit, marched towards the door, his congregation following, singing as they went.[8]

Traveling south through the coastal plain to the sea, one passes through the pinelands, once the backwoods of the aristocratic coast colonists. From the village of Orangeburg southward is the most typical pine country, vestibule of the glorious islands. The early settlers' approach to the coast country was different from that of the traveler by land today. The Spanish adventurers saw chaste Santa Elena first from the sea and were hardly aware of the rich sandy-loam pinelands lying back of the islands on the main, destined to become one of the rich agricultural regions of the New World. Even the keen-eyed English, who settled Charleston and rested snugly in the velvet pews of St. Philip's and St. Michael's on Sundays, were unaware of the possibilities of the pinelands of the "po' buckra" and the razorback hog. Their approach was from the sea, and they pitched their tents and their hopes along the rich tidal creeks of the low country.

But to the traveler today the country lying back of the coast furnishes an interesting contrast to the islands he is about to enter. For in this area are the wide swamps, with their strong,

[8] Isaac Jenkins Mikell, *Rumbling of the Chariot Wheels* (Columbia, S. C., 1923), pp. 124 ff.

tall cypress trees, druidlike, knee-deep in water. Four Hole Swamp is solemn and dark, with an air of mystery lurking in its deep recesses, and so are Cypress Swamp and innumerable other swamps, which have kept the people isolated in the past. The low-country swamp is the home of the dreaded cottonmouth moccasin, a vicious water snake whose peculiar name is derived from the white, cottonlike lips exposed when he coils to strike. His venom is as deadly as that of the diamondback rattler, which inhabits the sunny upland as well as the shady areas of the swamp. Throughout these deep swamps the water seems always inky black. Held in a glass, it reveals a slightly reddish tinge, caused by the vegetable matter suspended therein. These still, ebony waters of the Southern swamp constitute the distinguishing charm of the deep woods, especially when the waxy petals of the fragrant bay fall upon their surfaces or when the flaming azalea is reflected in their depths. In early spring yellow and green pollen cover the quiet eddies and lend brilliant contrasts of color to the somber hue of the water. These dark streams, locally called lakes, are the delight of the fisherman, and abound in game fish, redbreast and trout, whose progeny have ample chance for survival among the wide shallows of the flat swamp. Most interesting of swamp trees is the cypress, a wise old tree. Standing in water, it reinforces itself with buttressing protrusions as neatly executed as those of the most expert architect's plan. In order to get air for its root system, it sends up above the water's surface numbers of "cypress-knees" —one of the cleverest tricks in nature. All over the swamp are these "knees" poking comically above the water like old men's shins.

In early spring blue and white violets add variety to the floor of the swamp, while the air is heavy with the odor of bay blossoms and sweet myrtle. The calls of the shy swamp birds are of peculiar sweetness. There is something liquid in their notes. The yellow swamp canary is a delight to the eye. But by night the deep wood becomes alive with the vibrant life of the nocturnal tribe. These night sounds are different. The frogs open with their orchestra, the big booming bass of the bullfrogs mingling with the finer treble notes of the smaller ones up to the high falsettos of the little fellows. The quiet pauses of the night are disturbed with the terrifying cry of the big owl, who talks to his mate across the river. So startling is this weird sound that for a moment one thinks he has heard the scream of an hysterical woman in distress. The screech owls are more modest; their call is plaintive and delicately shuddery. The screech owl is an unwanted creature at the farmhouse; according to the Negroes, it is a sign of death in the family when he sits near the window and calls; consequently, he is always shooed off. And he is likely to come at the gloomiest time of night, those eerie hours that precede the breaking of day.

A few years ago one traveled over rough, bumpy, sandy roads with deep ruts. After rains, mud puddles dotted the highway. The sound of grinding sand under the wagon wheels was familiar to dwellers in this region. Life was slow and easy. One absorbed nature and felt himself a close brother to the soil and trees. Now smooth ribbons of concrete lie across the pinelands. They are straight and level, and make the out-of-the-way places accessible in a very brief period of time. The beauty of the low country, however, is not to be found along the paved highways, but in the sequestered places approached only by inconspicuous side roads or waterways. The plantations of the low country were developed along the waterways, their means of transportation. Highways into the interior were a second thought. The chief factor in the development of the upcountry was the South Carolina Railroad, running out of Charleston. For years it was the chief artery of transportation leading into the crude and undeveloped interior. Then came the modern hard-surfaced road, which is now carrying the burden of traffic and the curious tourists into the hitherto quiet and unmolested haunts of the rice planter.

Cotton and corn grow luxuriantly in good seasons along these highways. The crop is always a little better near the road because of the pride of the farmer. He puts his last ounce of fertilizer under those rows which greet the eyes of his passing neighbor.

In July the cotton fields are in full bloom. Creamy white blossoms, turning deep pink and red, lovely blooms as delicate as orchids, they, like all wild flowers, are beautiful only in their

THE LOW COUNTRY

native habitat. Cotton in long straight rows, thriving in the semitropical sun, likes dry, hot weather. When the corn is parching for lack of water, cotton flourishes in its hot sandy-loam beds. Next in beauty to cotton in full bloom is the period of its maturity, when, in late September, the white locks hang from open bolls, giving the appearance of a field swept with snow. The smell of a cotton field late in the afternoon at picking time stirs memories of youth in all who have lived in the South. Negroes with their peculiar racial odor, burlap sacks and cotton sheets, sweating mules, yellow flies, the light, bantering conversation of Negroes, steelyards, and one white man weighing the bundles while another writes something in a book —all these make up the scene. Critical eyes watch the beam to see that a just weight is given. Then Saturday afternoon at the country store is pay-off day. So much a hundred pounds. Nickels and dimes flash in abundance, and a few bright silver dollars. And back into the white man's hand go the earnings in exchange for grits, "butt meat," bright calico, and tobacco. Cotton-picking time is a bright spot in the economic treadmill of the Deep South. The Negro makes a bare living or less; the white tenant, except in rare instances, does little better. The millstone round the neck of the agricultural South is tenancy and the one-crop system.

The crop of the tenant farmer is usually poor, for his land is depleted of its fertility. Since he does not own his land, there is little incentive to improve it; anyhow, since he may have to move next year, he gets all he can and gives little, just as his predecessors have done. He has a crop of "bumblebee" cotton, so named because a bumblebee can sit flat on the ground and suck the blossoms. His landlord does not let him have much fertilizer because he is not a good risk. He is fortunate if he is able to pay for his supplies, including his food at "time" prices. His share of the crop must stand for the debt, and when the cotton is sold, he is exactly where he started at the first of the year. He has no capital, he has nothing, lives in debt, and is a slave. His wife and numerous children are most to be pitied. The cards are stacked against them. They live in poverty and have no ray of hope. Their rations are cornbread, molasses, and fatback. The white tenant shares no better fortune than the Negro in this respect; if the condition of one of these is the more deplorable, it is that of the white tenant because the Negro is more used to hard times and has from the days of his slavery built up a resistance to hardship that the white man does not have.

The wide swamps of the low country, once barriers to transportation and progress, have been in recent years spanned by smooth strips of concrete, laid upon high causeways securely built above the line of high water. Great holes resulting from the removal of earth for making the roadways are now minor lakes along the causeways. Filled with still water, they are fertile breeding grounds for fish, cooters, and water snakes. In early spring snakes crawl out of their cool depths to sun themselves on the warm pavement. Black snakes and other fast runners worm their lithe bodies across the highways. Cooters crawl out on logs to sun themselves, and, with necks protruding, remain undisturbed by passing cars. Approach too near, and they slide off among the green lily pads in the dark water out of sight.

A depressing scene in the low country is the cutover timberland. For mile after mile the traveler sees pine saplings, a few scraggly hardwoods, great stumps, and burnt-over land—residue of the lumberman and the turpentine "still." These two agencies have laid low and prostituted the beauty of the low country. The land of the longleaf pine has been stripped and denuded of its once lovely garments. Only here and there does one see glimpses of its former woodland glory. Towns like Summerville and Pinopolis and hallowed places like Magnolia and Middleton Gardens have preserved something of the original beauty.

Old piles of decaying sawdust mark the spots of carnage where the great logs were collected and sawed into yellow boards. The second-growth pine is still exploited by the turpentine industry. Great loblolly pines are scarified with sharp steel instruments, and bleed into small tin buckets. The sap is gathered and distilled at the near-by distilling plant, and for the sake of trade the magnificent forests of the pinelands are laid waste.

The cutover timberland is the range for scrub cattle and

bony hogs. The tenant's cow is staked out on long, tough grass growing in swampy places. Her udder is shriveled and she is of a brindled color. Those running loose wear a bell. Of all lonesome sounds the most lonesome is the tinkle of a cowbell in the dreary cutover timberlands of the low country.

Adolescent Negro boys pause and stare as the traveler passes along the silent roads. Accompanying them, is the inevitable dog, bony and full of fleas. Every Negro cabin has its dog or dogs, for poverty never becomes so acute that the dog must be relinquished. He is usually a sly and sulking animal to strangers, looking quite abashed until one turns to go; then he lets out an unearthly yelp and with much noise and commotion tries to drive the stranger from the premises. He is usually a cur without a pedigree worth mentioning, and enjoys the freedom of one who has no reputation to maintain. His chief accomplishments are his vigilance at night and his ability to tree a coon or trail a rabbit, requisites of all dogs worth having round a tenant farm.

The pineland is the home of the partridges. Frequently they run across the road ahead of one's car. In the spring and summer in pairs, in fall and winter in coveys, they startle the pedestrian with a sudden fluttering of wings as they rise above the broomsedge and sail away to cover. Their nests are built on the ground like miniature hens' nests, with small, white eggs, twelve or fifteen in number. Their worst enemies are floods and fire.

Crows are everywhere—the smartest of all the birds. A scarecrow stands in every cornfield, a greater indictment of the farmer's good sense than of the crow's, for he is too smart a bird to be deluded with such a ruse. His "caw-caw" is heard throughout the still days of the long summer, and, in keeping with his provident nature, he stores up his full share of the farmer's peanuts, a supply which will last till far into the winter. The succulent roots of young corn constitute his chief delicacy in spring, and in his raids he is utterly without conscience.

Doves in pairs rise startled from the roadside during the warm months. As autumn approaches, they gather in droves and hover over pea fields. Hunters take delight in surrounding these fields and shooting the doves that are startled into flight by the booming of the guns.

Turkey buzzards circle lazily in the still summer sky. The presence of carrion flesh immediately strikes their keen sense of smell, and they descend gracefully to earth in narrowing circles until, with great flaps of wings and distended legs, they clutch the dead limbs of a lonely pine, balance themselves, and settle down to survey the scene. A dead horse will bring hundreds of buzzards from miles around, and there is great jubilation as they hop gingerly over their prey and tug at the flesh of the carcass. A buzzard feast is a familiar sight in the low country. In former times these birds were valued as scavengers, and they enjoyed an immunity from the wanton hunter and would-be sportsman that few birds were privileged to have. A few decades ago they walked leisurely and undisturbed about the market of Charleston. Much of their prestige faded when they were accused by the Department of Agriculture of carrying hog cholera from one farm to another. By and large they are still unmolested and profit by the long tradition which has been so much in their favor. At dusk hundreds of them gather in the tops of tall pines to roost for the night. The only sounds coming from their lofty rookery are the ceaseless flapping of wings and the creaking of the pine limbs as the birds settle on the branches as thickly as they can sit. The buzzard is silent and, in many respects, the most austere of all Southern birds. He is almost an aristocrat, and probably would be but for his inexcusable taste and "ornery" habits. The young buzzards are white, strange as that may seem. Brer Rabbit, in *Uncle Remus*, once said: "Old Miss Turkey Buzzard got some likely looking chillun, *if* you can call buzzards likely."

In traveling through the coastal plain one is impressed by the lack of paint. House after house is unpainted. Occasionally a house of more than usual size, occupied by a landowner, is painted white, with green blinds, a sort of hangover effect of the "big house" of the plantation. But paint, the sign of prosperity, adorns very few dwellings in the low country. The tenant house is almost never painted: sometimes a progressive farmer will whitewash his outbuildings with lime and incidentally whiten the Negro cabins on his premises, but in the last decade even that is rare.

So, all along the highways and the unfrequented side roads, the drab, unpainted Negro tenant houses sit in open fields, unadorned and bare, the symbol of a decrepit economic system which takes its annual toll of human hope and aspiration. Nature does a little for these tenants, and an occasional chinaberry tree of the umbrella type will spring up to shade the black children from the midsummer sun. Cosmos and sunflowers grow readily, and often adorn the front yards of Negro cabins. One sees, occasionally, a row of potted plants on the front porch, a bright red geranium here and there, set in ugly tin lard-buckets. All summer long, children of all sizes and ages hover round the front door. The windows and doors are not screened. Flies swarm and crawl everywhere; they breed in the manure of the stables and scatter their spawn far and wide, lighting upon bits of food and the faces and lips of children, who patiently brush them away and do not complain. Adolescent girls spend many hours on the sunny side of the house, exchanging bits of romance and industriously combing each other's hair. Nothing is more characteristic of Negro life than these mutual hair-combings; it is the inevitable substitute for the beauty parlor patronized by their more sophisticated sisters of the city.

There are no grass lawns, for grass does not grow well in the sand country. White sandy yards are swept clean on Saturday afternoons: young girls with large eyes stoop over homemade brush brooms and sweep away every particle of trash, an important bit of tidying-up for Sunday.

If the Negroes own their land, they exercise greater care over trees and decorative shrubs. Pink crape myrtles as well as pecan trees grow about the front porch; in the back yard a fig tree or perhaps a beautiful live oak, festooned in moss, often hovers lovingly over a shanty.

In the majority of these houses there is no running water, no adequate facilities for sewage disposal, no bath. The toilet, if there is one, is found in the back yard; it rarely meets the requirements of sanitary regulations, and is a breeding place for filth and disease. Often no such limited provision as a "house" is made, and the members of the family resort to the woods.

The more progressive Negroes have a sugar-cane patch, a sweet potato patch, and a small garden. Most familiar in these limited gardens are a half-dozen rows of green collards, plants which stand the winter's frost and are eaten throughout the winter. The sweet potatoes are dug in autumn and "banked" for the winter's use. The sugar-cane mill is found in each community, where everyone brings his cane for grinding. The long, blue stalks of cane are placed between the rollers, and the juice flows into a large barrel. From the barrel it is transferred to an open copper kettle, where it is fired and evaporated until the residue of golden syrup stirs happy anticipations of cornbread and molasses on frosty mornings. The sugar-cane grindings are great social occasions. The process of cooking the syrup, of skimming and placing it in jugs and bottles, extends into the night. Anybody is welcome to a drink of cane juice. No one accepts pay; it is just not done.

In July watermelons are found in abundance, rows of them on the front porches, and chickens walking around among them. The tenant farmer during harvest time piles his seed cotton on the veranda or stores it away in a spare room until twelve or fourteen hundred pounds are picked, sufficient for a bale. When this amount is gathered, it is packed on a two-horse wagon and taken to the gin. If the tenant is a share-cropper, he takes his bale to the landlord for a division of the proceeds. Usually the share-cropper's half is taken in payment for supplies obtained during the months of production, and with the exception of small change to buy a few of the "shiny" things of life, he has little left. Nothing is accumulated for next year's crop production. He goes into debt again and repeats the vicious cycle of time-prices, hard work, and a bare living. Thus a species of slavery persists in the South, a type of bondage even worse than that of ante-bellum days, for now it stalks in the guise of freedom and holds both white and black in its clutches. The plight of the white cotton tenant is even worse than that of the Negro.

Familiar sights round the premises of the low-country tenant farmer are the well sweep and the gourds for martins. Some of the old wells have been modernized with pitcher pumps, and some with two buckets and a chain on an iron pulley above the well. The old well sweep is the most picturesque of all sights, with its long wooden beam of thirty feet, supported by an upright serving as a fulcrum; the bucket on one end dips down

EDISTO ISLAND, ONCE CELEBRATED FOR ITS SEA-ISLAND COTTON

into the well, and a few old plowshares counterbalance the other. The old oaken bucket has definitely passed, and has been superseded by a metal one, galvanized.

The gourds for martins are suspended on an upright resembling a tall telephone pole with its cross-pieces. Ten or a dozen empty gourds with holes cut for doors house martins for a part of the year. The martin is the arch-enemy of the chicken hawk, and, though a mere mite beside the big-pinioned bird, will drive him away from the premises. Chicken hawks watch the spring brood of baby chicks with hungry eyes, and will swoop down without warning and carry away one by one a whole crop of broilers. The martin is the farmer's friend, especially of those farmers who live near the swamps, where the depredations of the big hawk are greatest.

In the back yard, near the well, is the wash pot. This is the spot also for butchering the one or two hogs with the first winter's cold. A tilted barrel, whose base is partly buried in the ground, is filled with boiling water from the big black pot, this for scalding. The animal is either struck in the head with an axe, or "stuck," and the carcass is immediately thrown into the barrel of scalding hot water to loosen the hair. All gather around and scrape the hair off with heavy case knives. The carcass is then hung under a tree, disemboweled, dressed, and cut up. Spareribs, hogshead cheese, pudding, and sausage are enjoyed for days. Greasy mouths and lean stomachs full of fat pork represent happy thoughts of one of winter's happiest occasions. Fresh pork is the most highly valued meat to the Negro of the low country.

In the near-by horse-lot, the small barn, formerly of logs but now of boards, houses the corn; the more spacious barns have lofts for storing a minimum of hay or fodder. The Southern cotton tenant still buys hay and feed from the West. The cotton mule on the small Carolina farm is familiar with the taste of timothy hay, corn, and oats grown on the prairie lands of the West.

The live-at-home program of farming has not been generally followed by renters and share-croppers of the Cotton Belt. They are still slaves to cotton, the one sure money crop of the South. There is little time or energy left for producing home supplies. The problem is further complicated by the banker or lien merchant who finances the crop. When a farmer enters a bank and timidly applies for a loan, the first question asked by the cashier is "How many acres of cotton are you going to plant?" If the applicant does not plant a sufficiently large acreage in the fleecy staple, the loan is declined, and the horny-handed man of the sun goes dejectedly from the glass enclosure of the big chain bank. The banker is not wholly to blame, for he, too, is a part of the awkward economic system which grinds the poor. Cotton must be produced because it means cash money in the autumn. Southern tenant farming is a long, tedious grind from fall ploughing to fall harvesting, when the fruit of one's labor goes to pay for the sustenance of one's body, and that sustenance is consumed in advance. The one-crop system persists in the South for another reason: little intelligence is required for producing a tolerably fair crop of cotton. Almost any Negro brought up in the Deep South can grow cotton. Seaman A. Knapp, prophet of Southern agriculture, once declared that farming in the South consisted of a few motions handed down from Adam. This was no exaggeration, for the majority of poor whites and Negro renters still live from hand to mouth. They were caught in the backwash of the poverty and destruction which dogged the South throughout the dark years following the Civil War. And to this day the marks of that tragedy are still to be seen in the rural South.

CHAPTER II

THE SEA ISLANDS

> The gentle peace of a quiet beach,
> A lonely sea and sky,
> Where only wild sounds fill the air,
> And never a sail goes by.

TRAVELING southward through the pine and swamplands of the coastal plain, one comes rather abruptly to the island country. Contrasted with the shaded areas of the mainland is the sudden brightening of the landscape. The atmosphere is heavy with the mellow odor of the marsh. A fresh breeze from the sea, distant horizons, acres of mud flats at low tide, and an air of mystery which invariably hovers about the sea—all conspire to impress the traveler that he is in a different land. To one whose childhood has been stirred by the sights and sounds of the coast region there is always the feeling of entering a land of enchantment. Its rich past crowds upon the imagination, and every shaded road has a thousand tales to tell of romance, war, slavery, and a departed glory. The saddest spots in this region are the old plantation sites, marked only by the long avenues of venerable oaks, draped in grey moss, standing in perpetual mourning. Walking down the nave of one of these cathedral-like avenues, such as that at Tomotly plantation, the visitor is constrained to speak in whispers. Nature seems gentle here, even kind; the climate is mild. Subdued sounds prevail; the croaking of frogs in the rice fields, the timid barking of squirrels in the tall hickories, the ruddy hue of the cardinal, more than normally brilliant against the perennial green of the lordly oaks—each in its own way contributes to the unique "atmosphere" of the coast country. The sea islands of South Carolina, as heretofore stated, extend roughly from the small sandy islands above Georgetown on the north, to Hilton Head and Port Royal on the south. But the richest of these insular lands are located south of Charleston. They are larger and more fertile, and from the days of the earliest settlers were best adapted to agriculture and the plantation regime. Chief among them are John's Island, James Island, and Wadmalaw, near Charleston; Edisto, forty miles to the south; Port Royal, St. Helena, and Hilton Head, the last-named not far from the mouth of the Savannah River.

In the early days of the settlement of the South Atlantic coast "Carolina" was made up of a part of Florida, Georgia, and the present Carolinas. On a quaint old map of "The Province of Carolina" published in 1730 is inserted "ye most improved part of Carolina."[1] This "most improved part" was Charleston and its neighboring parishes. Charleston, a virtual city-state, then exerted a wide influence culturally and economically throughout the Province. Henry Laurens, writing about the year 1780, declared: "Before the war, about four hundred sail of vessels were usually employed in the trade of South Carolina, one-tenth of which were owned in the State, since which time most of the trade has been carried on by their own vessels. The marine consisted of two large fleets purchased from Count D'Estaing, three or four armed brigs, four galleys; and they sent Commodore Gillon to Europe to build or purchase three frigates."[2]

A picture of this capital among the islands has been left by an English historian, John Oldmixon, in his *History of the British Empire in America*, written in 1708. He described the infant city, less than forty years after its settlement:

'Tis fortify'd more for Beauty than Strength. It has 6 Bastions, and a Line all round it. Toward Cooper River are Blake's Bastion, Granville Bastion, a Half Moon, and Craven Bastion. On the South Creek are the Pallisades, and Ashley Bastion; on the North a line; and facing Ashley River are Colliton Bastion, Johnson's cover'd Half-Moon, with a Draw-bridge in the Line, and another in the Half-Moon, Carterett Bastion is next to it.

Neither is its Trade inconsiderable; for it deals near 1000 Miles into the Continent: However, 'tis unhappy in a Bar, that admits no Ships above 200 tuns. Its situation is very inviting, and the Country about it agreeable and fruitful: The Highways extremely delightful, especially that call'd Broad-way, which for three or four Miles makes a Road and Walk so pleasantly green.

[1] David Humphrey, *An Historical Account of the Incorporated Society for the Propagation of the Gospel in Foreign Parts* . . . (London, 1730).
[2] Henry Laurens, *Correspondence*, ed. Frank Moore (New York, 1861), p. 186.

There are several fair Streets in the Town, and some very handsome buildings; as Mr. Landgrave Smith's House on the Key, with a Drawbridge and Wharf before it; Col. Rhett's on the Key; also Mr. Boon's, Mr. Loggan's, Mr. Schinking's, and 10 or 12 more, which deserve to be taken notice of. As for publick edifices, the Church is most remarkable.[3]

Speaking of its cultural trend, the same writer added:

There's a Publick Library in this Town, and a Free-School has been long talk'd of: Whether founded or not, we have not learn'd. The Library is kept by the Minister for the time being. It owes its Rise to Dr. Thomas Bray; as do most of the American Libraries, for which he zealously solicited contributions in England.

There are at least 250 Families in this Town, most of which are numerous, and many of them have 10 or 12 children in each; in the whole amounting to about 3000 souls.

In Charles Town the Governour generally resides, the Assembly sit, the Court of Judicature are held, the Publick Offices are kept, and the Business of the Province is transacted.[4]

Charleston was not only the "Capital" of the Carolina low country, but in less than a hundred years it was destined to be one of the chief centers of culture in the Colonies. As early as 1732 *The South-Carolina Gazette,* a combination magazine and newspaper, was published in the city. This early literary attempt was the forerunner of many publications of a literary, religious, and miscellaneous nature.[5] As evidence of the remarkable literary activity in Charleston at the beginning of the nineteenth century, William Stanley Hoole calls attention to the fact that between 1795 and 1864 seventy magazines were actually published in the city: "Thirty-eight of these 70 published magazines were devoted to Literature and the Arts; 19 to Religion; 4 to Medicine; 2 to Historical Societies; and 1 each to Agriculture, Temperance, Masonry, Commerce, Politics, Chess, and Insurance. . . . Over the entire period, 1800-1864, Charleston's white population averaged less than 15,000, a fact which

[3] John Oldmixon, *History of the British Empire in America* (1708), quoted in Alexander Samuel Salley (ed.), *Narratives of Early Carolina, 1650-1708* (New York, 1911), p. 363.
[4] *Ibid.,* pp. 364-365.
[5] William Stanley Hoole, *A Check-List and Finding-List of Charleston Periodicals, 1732-1864* (Durham, N. C., 1936), p. 4.

makes more outstanding the many attempts to create mediums of expression."[6]

This classification does not include newspapers published during the same period. It should be added, however, that regarding many of them it is difficult to distinguish between magazines and newspapers; hence some of the above may be classified as newspapers. Certainly this great literary activity would indicate that Charleston and its plantation community ranked among the outstanding cultural centers of the nation.

Traveling out of Charleston a little west of south, one follows the coastal highway, running just inside the island fringe, toward Savannah. Dirt roads lead from the main highway into the islands. Until recent years the islands have been accessible only by water, separated as they are from the mainland by wide marshes and deep tidal creeks; now drawbridges span the waterways, and high causeways of oyster shell have been thrown across the wide expanses of marshland, making accessible these formerly isolated areas.

One of the largest and most interesting of the islands is Edisto, named by the Indians who inhabited the country when the Spanish, French, and English first looked upon its shores. Its southeastern extremity dips into the sea, and its main area is fortified by several long barrier islands, cut off from the main body by small tidal creeks. Most of the so-called barrier islands are hardly more than beaches and sand dunes, which serve as breakwaters between the tenable lands of the inhabited areas and the ever-encroaching sea. These alluvial islands, as has been observed, were no doubt formed by the slow work of rivers as they brought down their silt throughout the centuries. Consequently, they are very rich, and for nearly two hundred years have formed the basis of a profitable agriculture. Upon rice and cotton and the plantation regime, a culture arose which for a long time was unexcelled in any part of America. A Southern historian several years ago described this culture as follows:

> The rice coast community was a small one. Even as measured in its number of slaves it bulked only one-fourth as large, say in 1790, as the group of tobacco commonwealths or the single sugar island of Jamaica. Nevertheless it was a community to be reckoned with. Its people were awake to their peculiar conditions and prob-

[6] *Ibid.*

THE SEA ISLANDS

lems; it had plenty of talented citizens to formulate policies; and it had excellent machinery for uniting public opinion. In colonial times, plying its trade mainly with England and the West Indies, it was in little touch with its continental neighbors, and it developed a sense of separateness. As part of a loosely administered empire its people were content in prosperity and self-government. But in a consolidated nation of diverse and conflicting interests it would be likely on occasion to assert its own will and resist unitedly anything savoring of coercion. In a double sense it was of the southern South.[7]

Of the productivity of the soil in 1925, even after decades of depletion and abuse, the late James Henry Rice, a resident of the coastal area, declared: "Permanent pastures are easily made and silos easily filled. Five acres will pack a silo capable of keeping 30 cows fat all winter. Most crops are abundant. Some of our big live oaks will yield 100 bushels of acorns. Pine, beech, chinquapin, and haws are great yielders of mast. Berries, wild fruits, and roots exist in profusion."[8] Since the coastal plain and particularly the islands offer every inducement to the small farmer, one wonders why this region is not more generally settled. Instead, however, it is very much a deserted land, and almost the only signs of progress are the investments of Northern men who have bought up large tracts to be used as hunting preserves. Rice further observed: "Over forty years ago the late N. G. Gonzales called my attention to the opportunities for small farmers on the coast, showing how easy it was to get food, wood, water and make a comfortable home. Long after I confirmed these things by observation. The soil, everywhere fertile, is easily brought up by tilth and rotation, the growing season is long, rainfall abundant and climate genial. Fish, game and shellfish are to be had anywhere in season—something all the year round."[9]

The decline of this section and the general lethargy which has fallen upon it since the Civil War, Rice attributed to certain very definite factors. Among them were the discovery of phosphate rock, turpentine operators, lumbering, and the pineland "bushmen" of the "cattle belt." The phosphate mining operations drew thousands of laborers from the fields. Small shop-

[7] Ulrich Bonnell Phillips, *Life and Labor in the Old South* (Boston: Little, Brown and Co., 1929), p. 97.
[8] James Henry Rice, *Glories of the Carolina Coast* (Columbia, S. C., 1925), p. 22.   [9] *Ibid.*, p. 19.

keepers set up stores around the mines and swindled the Negroes out of their money.

Turpentine operators from North Carolina came just after the Civil War, buying turpentine rights and destroying millions of beautiful trees. The trees were "boxed" by simply cutting in the side a receptacle, into which the sap flowed. The sap was then carelessly dipped out, and much of it wasted. Rice asserted: "By 1880 nearly 400,000 barrels of turpentine were exported and by 1903 the last boxes were cut (except in a few localities) . . . leaving desolation and ruin behind. Soon the industry moved to Florida with its devastating methods."[10]

Rice planting was tried again, but the storm of 1893 dealt it a staggering blow. Besides, it could now, under altered conditions, be more economically raised in Louisiana, Arkansas, and Texas. It then passed from South Carolina. Lumbering, in its turn, drew from the plantations more labor, creating an industry which devastated the great longleaf forests, making them now scarcely more than a memory. Sea-island cotton was eliminated as a money crop by the boll weevil in 1918.

Exploitation has marked every economic development since the Civil War. The people have been left poor. "The most casual observer notes," wrote Rice, "the absence of out-buildings, barns, stables, cribs common on every up-country and Mid-Western farm. Up to a few years ago, there was not a smokehouse on the coast. There are precious few now."[11] Because of their isolation and lack of opportunity, the most promising members of the younger generation have moved away and sought fortune in other sections. The "po' buckra" of the pinelands also exploited the region, according to Rice: "Bushmen from the cattle belt raided the plantations after they had forced their abandonment by the owners, turned in cows and hogs and set fire to millions of acres each spring and winter. Cows trampled the sacred resting places of the dead. Hogs rooted up rose gardens, once the pride of their possessors and the envy of travelers. Burial vaults were not respected but often violated and the bones of the dead scattered, out of wanton deviltry."[12] The islands have been drained of their best.[13]

Riding one day over the main road which traverses Edisto

[10] *Ibid.*
[11] *Ibid.*, p. 13.
[12] *Ibid.*
[13] *Ibid.*, pp. 12-13.

Island and leads to the sea, I paused on one of the recently constructed bridges spanning a tidal creek. At this slight elevation in so flat a country, I could see for miles. It was summertime, and the long, waving spartina, or marsh grass, covered innumerable acres of mud flats. I saw low-lying islands cut into segments by the intrusion of creeks, which in the olden time furnished convenient modes of transportation about the country.

Silhouetted against the green spartina was a snowy heron fishing. Standing knee-deep, he waited with watchful eye patiently for his catch. Presently he fixed himself into a slightly squatting posture, poised his long neck, and shot his bill forward into the water like a flash. A gulping movement, a few steps forward where the water rippled slightly from the movement of a school of fingerling, and the silent fisherman was ready to repeat his simple technique. All day long these herons, blue and white, little and big, ply their trade in the quiet recesses of the marshlands. They are peaceful creatures and move slowly, as does everything in this restful country. No one is in a hurry; the tempo of life is slow and easy. The upcountry man is impressed with the slow movement of the big rivers; they flow leisurely to the sea. The silent and powerful tides affect profoundly the life of the islands. The pelicans fish on the wing, flying majestically in military formation, groups of three or five, just beyond the breakers. They are awkward-looking birds on land, with their ponderous pouches and ugly legs, but beautiful in flight. Their wing movement is slow and graceful. From my vantage point on the bridge I saw various sorts of birds feeding upon small shellfish. There was a veil of silence over the landscape. The only sounds audible to me were from reed birds chattering, as their small bodies swayed among the seed clusters of the tall grass. Now and then the peculiar bassoonlike squawk of the waterfowl was heard. Breaking the silence occasionally, was the impertinent croaking of the marsh frog, ducklike in timbre, and impudent. A great white gull swept by with a fish in its mouth.

A common sight in the coast country is the fishing habits of the osprey, or fish hawk. The osprey hovers over water in which schools of fish play, flying cautiously, with keen eyes alert for the slightest movement of the water's surface. Suddenly he drops perpendicularly into the water like a shot, and with a splash rises with his prey. He does not always enjoy the benefit of his catch, however, for the bald eagle, which inhabits this region, dominates the fish hawk. As the osprey flies inland with his fish, the eagle, watching from afar, sees his chance to get something for nothing and makes straight for the enemy. There is no battle, for the osprey drops his catch and the eagle swoops beneath him and takes the fish in mid-air. Yet at certain seasons of the year, when the fish hawk is in migration southward, the bald eagle has to seek his own food. The eagle lives principally on catfish, and observers have discovered that the young eaglets are fed this species of fish. The eagle's nest is usually built in the top of a tall pine, underneath which are found great numbers of catfish heads, the refuse from his feedings.

Roads traverse the islands in all directions—sandy roads with deep ruts, so deep in dry white sand that motor cars pass through them with difficulty. They wind in and out among the sweet-scented myrtle and hardy cassena, going everywhere and making the most remote cabins accessible. Many of them were made by the heavy cartwheels of slavery days and have remained until this day as they were. These minor roads are never worked (there is nothing to be done for them), for they are simply two deep ruts winding tortuously through the sand. In wet weather these sandy stretches absorb moisture like blotting paper, and there are few mudholes like those common on the mainland. The State Highway Department maintains the principal road across the larger islands. On Edisto this driveway is known by the Negroes as "de high-ball pike," or, in true Gullah dialect, "de hoigh-ball."

In the island country retail trade is conducted in the country stores found at every crossroad. A touch of modernity has been added to these rural establishments in recent years by the presence of brightly painted gasoline pumps. Inside, on long counters, are flat showcases from which the customer may purchase anything from red stick-candy to a ball of thread. The proprietor is usually a white man though some stores are operated by Negroes. The store buildings, old and weatherworn, give evidence of having been whitewashed in a more prosperous time. Windows, well barred, have solid board shutters painted blue. In front of these stores, on benches or boxes, Negroes sit and whittle. What they talk about few white people know, for they are timid among strangers. But there they sit in winter or in summer, as carefree as their forefathers were two centuries ago in the tropical shades of Africa. The island country store serves as drygoods, grocery, and drug establishment, all under one roof. Chewing tobacco is generally used, and on Saturday afternoons it is quite proper to carry in the hip pocket a big plug of "Brown Mule." Chill tonic, always on sale, is the first prescription when chills and fever come on. One can buy blue jeans overalls or yards of green, yellow, and red calico. In the grocery department "butt meat" is the chief delicacy, for it is the seasoning for the island Negroes' "greens." Nothing is more valued by the Negro than his cabbage or collards cooked with "butt meat." When broccoli was introduced in the coast country by commercial truck growers, the Negroes looked upon it with considerable suspicion. Two Gullah boys, who were discussing the situation in a country store on one occasion, argued that broccoli was very good greens, for all one had to do was to boil it like cabbage, putting the cheap bacon into it. The other boy looked at the bunch of broccoli dubiously, shrugged his shoulders, and said, "I woudn't resk my meat in dem ting."

Not only is the island store a place for trade, but to the Negro it ranks also next to the church as a social agency. From far and near Negroes come to the store. Here the latest news is exchanged, a can of sardines purchased, and a bag of sweet crackers. In the summertime Negro women bring pans of ripe figs to be sold to visitors. Colored boys come up from the creek with a string of whiting or croakers. They are always ready to sell, for fish are plentiful nearly all the year; the only hindrance to more and better fish is the lack of will to get them. It is delightful to strangers to stand in earshot of these amiable people and listen to their banter and good humor. The island Negroes laugh much. They have a lively sense of humor, are quick at repartee, and enjoy the keen thrusts of ridicule and satire directed at some despondent brother of their group whose cotton crop is devoured by the boll weevil, or whose "taters an' ting" are caught by the drought.

Modes of transportation among the Negroes have changed very little in a hundred years: a few of them own automobiles, usually secondhand cars worn out by the "buckra," and spend the greater part of the Sabbath repairing tires by the roadside. This labor they do with infinite patience, while their women wait with equal composure; for the greater part, the island Negroes still walk. At any time of day or night they walk the roads, going nowhere in particular, but always, on summer evenings, "breshin' 'skeeters." Oxcarts lumber along over bumpy stretches of shell road. When traveling for social purposes the women sit in chairs placed in the body of the cart. Negroes frequently ride astride their oxen, without saddle or bridle. One such rider who came under my observation presented a perfectly ludicrous picture as he sat upon his sleepy ox with hands folded, both man and ox a picture of perfect contentment and repose. At St. Helena Island I pulled up by the roadside and awaited the tedious approach of a man with his ox and cart. I asked him whether I might make a picture of his ox. With some apology he explained that he was in a hurry and would not have time! But this is the tempo of island life. No one is in a hurry. Time makes little difference. There is nothing in particular to do but to enjoy life. There is little struggle. Everyone seems to have made peace with the world on its own terms. To hurry is to lose step and to be out of harmony with everything. The visitor to this region who cannot catch the leisurely stride that prevails will be unhappy and ill at ease. To be happy here one must float with the tide and find pleasure in its ebb and flow. One must wait to go fishing, for the tide must be right. Of all things, the great sacrilege is to hurry. I once asked a Gullah Negro boy why I had to wait for the tide before fishing. He explained: "You always fish on de last o' de ebb tide or de fust o' de flood, suh. Nebber fish on de flood tide. When de tide is at de flood de fish out in de ma'sh feedin'. Dey does bite on de low tide."

I asked a Negro youth one warm September day to tell me where the colored Methodist minister lived. He told me accurately in his delightful dialect and offered to accompany me the three or four miles to the house. I was a little puzzled to know how he would get back after doing this courtesy. Presently he suggested that if I were coming back that afternoon he would return with me then. It appeared that one place in the island was as good as another for him. The fact that it was harvest time did not seem to weigh upon his conscience or to interfere with his leisurely habits.

As stated before, the early mode of travel in this region was by boat over the water lanes, which form a network of passages over the low alluvial islands. Today, flat-bottomed boats are seen everywhere. They are used for fishing in the "creeks" and for hauling oysters. In ante-bellum days every plantation had its fleet of boats—boats for tending the rice trunks, freight boats with sail, and pleasure boats oared by muscular boatmen. Jenkins Mikell describes the large canoe in which his family took flight upon the approach of the Union soldiers in 1861: "One side of her was hewn out of an immense cypress log, likewise her other side, a third log furnished the bottom and keel—the three pieces most deftly and artistically joined and fashioned by experts trained for that purpose. In the stern was a collapsible cabin of wood with seats and berth room for a large family. The middle portion—'amid-ships'—contained seats for twelve oarsmen. In the prow or 'foreward' was stored the luggage. The negroes called her 'Nellie Fier' (Nullifier)."[14]

It was not until 1918 that Edisto Island was connected with the mainland by a bridge over Dawhoo River and a road across the salt marshes. Before that time there was little passing from the island to the mainland, and that little was by the slow way of the ferry and miles of bad roads. The preferred mode of travel to Charleston was by water, and today "Steamboat Landing" marks the spot where happy parties embarked for a trip to the city. Until the building of the bridge very few Negroes ever left the island, for pressure was brought to bear upon them by the whites to prevent their leaving. In truth, in some of the isolated islands the Negroes were held in a state of semi-slavery, their labor and destiny being controlled by the "buckra." Now nearly all the larger islands are connected with the mainland by bridges and highways, and their isolation and, incidentally, much of their charm, are passing. After the bridges were built, many Negroes, feeling that the barriers were down, mi-

[14] Mikell, *op. cit.*, p. 28.

grated to other sections, particularly the North. Many have come back, but great numbers have stayed in the cities. Some of those who went away have desired to be buried under the peaceful oaks in the Deep South. At a Negro church on one of these islands not long ago I saw the casket in which lay an island woman who had migrated to New York and died there. She had wished to be buried in the beloved islands, among her own people, in the quaint and much respected graveyard of the black people, and her friends had sent her body home.

Of primary interest in the island country are the old plantation sites. Many of them have been abandoned, and only the venerable live oaks and domestic shrubs mark their place. A few of the original houses still stand, but during the period of the Civil War and that following the vast majority of them fell into disrepair and neglect and became the certain victims of careless fires. In the vicinity of Port Royal and Savannah scores of them were burned by Sherman's army. During the occupation of Port Royal and its neighboring islands Union troops made adventurous raids up the big rivers and destroyed many plantations. These raids were presumably of military importance and at the time were presumed to rescue hundreds of slaves from the sinister influences of their owners; but a candid review of their operations furnishes every evidence that they were, for the most part, sporting expeditions, planned by adventure-loving young officers who enjoyed the role of soldiers of fortune. Colonel Higginson's romantic account of *Army Life in a Black Regiment*, in which he relates his exploits in and about Port Royal, and especially the raid up Edisto River, is evidence in point:

We left Beaufort, S. C., on the afternoon of July 9th, 1863. In former narrations I have sufficiently described the charm of a moonlight ascent into a hostile country, upon an unknown stream, the dark and silent banks, the rippling water, the wail of the reed-birds, the anxious watch, the breathless listening, the veiled lights, the whispered orders. To this was now to be added the vexation of an insufficient pilotage, for our negro guide knew only the upper river, and, as it finally proved, not even that, while, to take us over the bar which obstructed the main stream, we must borrow a pilot from Captain Dutch, whose gunboat blockaded that point. . . . Thus accompanied, we steamed over the bar in safety, had a peaceful ascent, passed the island of Jehossee,—the fine estate of Governor Aiken, then left undisturbed by both sides,—and fired our first shell into the camp at Wiltown Bluff at four o'clock in the morning.

The battery—whether fixed or movable we knew not—met us with a promptness that proved very shortlived. After three shots it was silent, but we could not tell why. The bluff was wooded, and we could see but little. The only course was to land, under cover of the guns. As the firing ceased and the smoke cleared away, I looked across the rice-fields which lay beneath the bluff. The first sunbeams glowed upon their emerald levels, and on the blossoming hedges along the rectangular dikes. What were those black dots which everywhere appeared? Those moist meadows had become alive with human heads, and along each narrow path came a straggling file of men and women, all on a run for the river-side. I went ashore with a boat-load of troops at once. The landing was difficult and marshy. The astonished negroes tugged us up the bank, and gazed at us as if we had been Cortez and Columbus. They kept arriving by land much faster than we could come by water; every moment increased the crowd, the jostling, the mutual clinging, on that miry foothold. What a scene it was! With the wild faces, eager figures, strange garments, it seemed, as one of the poor things reverently suggested, "like notin' but de judgment day." Presently they began to come from the houses also, with their little bundles on their heads; then with larger bundles. Old women, trotting on the narrow paths, would kneel to pray a little prayer, still balancing the bundle; and then would suddenly spring up, urged by the accumulating procession behind, and would move on till irresistibly compelled by thankfulness to dip down for another invocation. Reaching us, every human being must grasp our hands, amid exclamations of "Bress you, mas'r," and "Bress de Lord," at the rate of four of the latter ascriptions to one of the former. Women brought children on their shoulders; small black boys carried on their backs little brothers equally inky, and, gravely depositing them, shook hands. Never had I seen human beings so clad, or rather so unclad, in such amazing squalidness and destitution of garments. I recall one small urchin without a rag of clothing save the basque waist of a lady's dress, bristling with whalebones, and worn wrong side before, beneath which his smooth ebony legs emerged like those of an ostrich from its plumage. How weak is imagination, how cold is memory, that I ever cease, for a single day of my life, to see before me the picture of that astounding scene.

Yet at the time we were perforce a little impatient of all this piety, protestation, and hand-pressing; for the vital way to ascertain what force had been stationed at the bluff, and whether it was withdrawn. The slaves, on the other hand, were too much absorbed in their prospective freedom to aid us in taking any further steps to secure it. Captain Trowbridge, who had by this time landed at a different point, got quite into dispair over the seeming deafness of the people to all questions. "How many soldiers are there on the bluff?" he asked of the first-comer.

"Mas'r," said the man, stuttering terribly, "I c-c-c—"

"Tell me how many soldiers there are!" roared Trowbridge, in his mighty voice, and all but shaking the poor old thing, in his thirst for information.

"O mas'r," recommenced in terror the incapacitated witness, "I c-c-carpenter!" holding up eagerly a little stump of a hatchet, his sole treasure, as if his profession ought to excuse him from all military opinions.

I wish that it were possible to present all this scene from the point of view of the negroes themselves. It can be most nearly done, perhaps, by quoting the description given of a similar scene on the Combahee River, by a very aged man, who had been brought down on the previous raid, already mentioned. I wrote it down in tent, long after, while the old man recited the tale, with much gesticulation, at the door; and it is by far the best glimpse I have ever had, through a negro's eyes, at these wonderful birthdays of freedom.

"De people was all a hoein', mas'r," said the old man. "Dey was a hoein' in the ricefield, when de gunboats come. Den ebry man drap dem hoe, and leff de rice. De mas'r he stand and call, 'Run to de wood for hide! Yankee come, sell you to Cuba! run for hide!' Ebry man he run, and, my God! run all toder way!

"Mas'r stand in de wood, peep, peep, faid for truss (afraid to trust). He say, 'Run to de wood!' and ebry man run by him, straight to de boat.

"De brack sojer so presumptious, dey come right ashore, hold up dere head. Fus' ting I know, dere was a barn, ten tousand bushel rough rice, all in a blaze, den mas'r's great house, all cracklin' up de roof. Didn't I keep for see 'em blaze? Lor, mas'r, didn't care notin' at all, *I was gwine to de boat.*"[15]

From a military point of view it appears that the expedition up the Edisto River was a failure. Higginson thus continues his narrative:

All our previous expeditions had been so successful it now seemed hard to turn back; the river-banks and rice-fields, so beautiful before,

[15] Thomas Wentworth Higginson, *Army Life in a Black Regiment* (Boston, 1870), pp. 170 ff.

seemed only a vexation now. But the swift current bore us on, and after our Parthian shots had died away, a new discharge of artillery opened upon us, from our first antagonist of the morning, which still kept the other side of the stream. It had taken up a strong position on another bluff, almost out of range of the John Adams, but within easy range of us. The sharpest contest of the day was before us. Happily the engine and engineer were now behaving well, and we were steering in a channel already traversed, and of which the dangerous points were known. But we had a long, straight reach of river before us, heading directly toward the battery, which, having once got our range, had only to keep it, while we could do nothing in return. The Rebels certainly served their guns well.

Thus we glided down the river in the waning light. Once more we encountered a battery, making five in all; I could hear the guns of the assailants, and could not distinguish the explosion of their shells from the answering throb of our own guns. The kind quartermaster kept bringing me news of what occurred, like Rebecca in Front-de-Boeuf's castle, but discreetly withholding any actual casualties. Then all faded into safety and sleep; and we reached Beaufort in the morning, after thirty-six hours of absence. A kind friend, who acted in South Carolina a nobler part amid tragedies than in any of her early stage triumphs, met us with an ambulance at the wharf, and the prisoners, the wounded, and the dead were duly attended.[16]

A raid up Combahee River in 1863 dealt equal damage in that locality. Two Federal boats tied up in the rich plantation area and began their destruction. Seventy-three Negroes from one of the plantations aided in the destruction of their own and three neighboring plantations. They burned the "big house" containing a library of thirty-five hundred volumes, destroyed the rice mill, rice barn, corn house, kitchen, storeroom, mule stable, and three Negro houses. From the plantation barn they took six thousand bushels of rice, as many pigs and chickens as they could carry, while men, women, and children scrambled upon the boats.[17]

[16] *Ibid.*
[17] *Charleston Mercury,* June 19, 1863, quoted in Guion Griffis Johnson, *A Social History of the Sea Islands* (Chapel Hill, N. C., 1930), pp. 158-159.

CHAPTER III

PLANTATIONS

I'm gwine eat an' nebbuh git hongry
Some o' dese days, Hallelujah!
I'm gwine to drink an' nebbuh git thirsty
Some o' dese days, Hallelujah!

No COMPLETE understanding of the social history of the Gullah Negro is possible without some knowledge of his plantation experience. One of the most interesting ante-bellum plantations on Edisto Island is Peters Point. Driving past the post office and general store, center of social and commercial interest of the island, I took a road to the right marked with a faded sign, "To Peters Point." The distance is several miles over a pleasant sand road, bordered with fields of cotton, corn, and sweet potatoes, with patches of woodland here and there. "The Point," as it is locally known, is formed by the convergence of two bold tidal rivers. The big house was occupied by Northern teachers during the war. Expansive fields of cotton and corn now give an air of prosperity to the place. As I traveled along the way, a score of Negroes were chopping cotton under the bright June sun with a white man directing their labor as in slavery days.

I was shown about the place by a scion of the family, a very courteous gentleman who lived in a smaller house near the mansion: it is not practicable now for island planters to maintain these big houses; they were built for a slave economy, and only the wealthy can maintain them in their former grandeur. As we walked through the great halls and high-ceilinged rooms, we were impressed with the fact that the Old South had passed. The great fireplaces, the handsomely carved furniture, the chandeliers, the quaint pictures of bearded grandsires in old-fashioned frames hanging on faded walls, and the musty odor of a great house closed for years, all impressed us indelibly with the sense of departed glory.

Pictures of festive occasions, which were a prominent part

of plantation life, crowd upon the mind: beautiful Southern girls in hoop skirts and lace; ante-bellum youth steeped in the traditions of the Old South; courtship upon the broad piazzas; hopes, fears, and the whole gamut of human emotion. These old houses, if they could reveal their secrets, could tell a dramatic story of human life. There was struggle in the Southern aristocrat: on the one hand, his conscience warned him of the diabolic influence of slavery and his common sense told him that the whole economic system of the South rested upon the insecure foundation of a race in subjection; on the other hand, he attempted to justify slavery and to bring it in line with the principles of religion. He was troubled by the distant rumblings of war and the sudden flash in Charleston Harbor which brought on the conflict with a swiftness undreamed of; then followed the humiliating experience of flight from home, the horrors of war, and the devastation, more horrible, of Reconstruction. Thus nowhere on the American continent have human emotions run a wider gamut than in the hearts of the aristocratic planter folk of the Carolina sea islands. Their suffering was far keener than the suffering of the carefree black people whom they held in bondage.

Mikell, who lived in the Peters Point house as a boy, describes his home: "I see before me, the home of my childhood, with its twelve great rooms, with white and colored marble for its inside adornment; the spiral 'flying stair'; its brown-stone front steps; its double piazzas; its groves of oranges, its figs, its pomegranates, its jujubes; with its extensive grounds of ornamental shrubs and imported cedars, trimmed into fantastic shapes, done by a master hand—all enclosed with moss-covered live oaks, a point where two rivers meet on their journey to the sea three miles away, with not a tree to obstruct the view."[1]

The plantation houses were almost invariably located on rivers or tidal creeks, a necessary circumstance because the only medium of transportation was water. This location added greatly to the landscaping possibilities, and brought into existence the fish pond, one of the luxuries of the larger plantations. These fish reservoirs served a dual purpose: they not only met a utilitarian need, but were often rare beauty spots. A slave was charged with the responsibility of keeping the

[1] Mikell, *op. cit.*, p. 163.

pond well stocked with fish during the summer months in order to have an abundant supply during the winter.

The fish pond at Peters Point on the Mikell plantation is vividly described by Mikell, who enjoyed its offerings as a boy. I saw it in its decadent, abandoned state. It had been a large parallelogram some hundreds of feet long, with the land side built of brick. The other three sides were dikes, which kept the pond from the river:

> The pond was of sufficient depth to maintain its briny inhabitants at all stages of the tide, and the water was renewed twice daily by the rise and fall of the tides of the ocean, three miles away. There were several Venetian bridges thrown across it and small islands covered with fancy shrubbery scattered at intervals over its area, each island about the size of a medium dwelling-room, on which diminutive Chinese "tea gardens" were built, reached only by a little skiff. There was built out from the outer side of the pond, into and over the river, a small house on palmetto logs, connected with the shore by a bridge, from the piazzas of which one might fish in the river with hand line or pole. And in the floor was a trap door, through which, in case of rain, one might catch sheepshead in satisfying quantities.[2]

This utilitarian aspect by day in no way marred the lush tropic splendor, which was even more enhanced by night:

> The dreamlike beauty of it passes description. In the moonlight of a late spring evening, one might wander over its banks under the evergreen live oaks and hear our Southern mocking bird singing its song of Spring, making up, it would seem, for its silence of the winter. One might hear the splash of the channel bass and see its phosphorescent pathway as it darted at its prey beneath the surface of the lake. One might hear the "boom, boom" of the drum-fish, as it signals to its mate; the sharp angry snap of the trout as it takes its prey, a shrimp, in its mouth; the clear silvery leap and splash of the mullet, as it rises from the water in sheer ecstasy of living, and if very still, one might get a swift glimpse of an otter as it steals along the bank in its nocturnal depredations on the finny tribe within. In the bright moonlight, one might see rise, almost directly beneath, a little black spot on the water not there a moment before. A sound, and it would vanish. It was the head of a diamond-backed terrapin. . . .[3]

[2] *Ibid.*, pp. 164 f. [3] *Ibid.*, pp. 165 f.

PLANTATIONS

The two great enemies of the pond were animals of wide extremes in their relative size: the alligator and the little "fiddler" crab. The alligator devoured the fish; the fiddler was the bane of the dike builder. The fiddler's chief occupation, besides running nervously over the marsh, was to dig holes in the dikes, letting the ever-restless sea reclaim its own.

Another of the old houses on Edisto which has withstood the ravages of time and war is that on the William Seabrook plantation. The residence has been restored to something of its former beauty by its present owner, a Northerner, who now uses the estate as a hunting preserve. It has the usual approach, a long avenue of big live oaks draped in Spanish moss. This grand setting bespeaks the large agricultural operations once conducted there. A shaded gravel walk leads from the house to the river, which served long ago as the chief artery of transportation and communication. Glossy-leaved magnolias and swamp trees provide an almost impenetrable shade in the wooded area to the rear. Through this mass of green a vista affords a pleasing glimpse of the shining water of the river beyond the green expanse of marshland.

The Seabrook place was used as headquarters for Union Army officers stationed on Edisto Island during the Civil War. In her diary Mary Ames left a description of the Seabrook place and a portrayal of military life then so much in evidence: "At the end of a shady walk back of the house are the fish and terrapin ponds. Around the fish pond is a broad carriage drive shaded by immense oak trees. A lovely grove of large trees beyond was approached by an avenue of tall laurels, planted so closely that they formed a thick hedge on either side, and met over our heads, shutting out completely the rays of the sun. At four o'clock we went out to see the dress parade of the colored soldiers."[4]

The planters on Edisto Island spent their summers on the beach fronting the ocean. Here they were relatively free from the dreaded chills and fevers. At that time the process of transmitting the malarial parasite by the anopheles mosquito was unknown. Edingsville Beach was the popular ante-bellum summering place. Beaufort and Charleston also were favorite resorts. Many of the more opulent masters sent their families

[4] Ames, *op. cit.*, pp. 36-37.

to the North Carolina mountains, some to New England, and some even abroad. A long row of pretty summer houses fronted the sea at Edingsville. Today only their old foundations remain. The beach was abandoned years ago because of the gradual encroachment of the sea. It is now a lone, solitary spot where one hears only wild sounds and the somber thunder of the turf.

During the Civil War this resort, like the remainder of the region, was also deserted, and left open to the curious eyes of Northern "missionaries." One "missionary" wrote:

> No school. The morning being fine and the roar of the ocean plainly heard, we decided to drive to the bay. I cannot describe our conveyance. There were large spaces between the floor boards of the cart; both horses were skeletons, one large and the other small. The harness was of ropes and small cords, with twine for reins.
>
> The road was much overgrown, flowers of all kinds lined the way, and turkey buzzards were sitting in solemn conference. Within a quarter of a mile of Edingsville—as the bay is called—we reached a creek, which we crossed on a flat-bottomed raft and walked to the long row of houses on the beach. Once this was a famous summer resort, and some of the houses are very pretty. The beach is broad and hard, and the surf was grand. We went to several houses, looking for one that suited us for a summer home.[5]

Even in 1824 the island was famed for its beauty and for the leisurely and spacious life of its residents, among whom Lafayette tarried briefly in his tour of America. A. Lavasseur, Lafayette's secretary, recorded his impressions: "We then rapidly traversed the Island in carriages to join our steamboat, which awaited us on the side next to the ocean. What we saw of the Island in this short ride, appeared to us enchanting. The vegetation was particularly striking because of its variety. Odoriferous shrubs of the most elegant forms were agreeably interspersed among large forest trees, and on the downs which border the seashore we saw some beautiful palm trees, which gave to the small dwellings they shaded an aspect altogether picturesque."[6] The "small dwellings" were the summer cottages of the planters on the seashore. Their plantation homes were pretentious, spacious dwellings.

The planters' tables must have been bountifully supplied

---

[5] *Ibid.*, pp. 41-42. [6] Mikell, *op. cit.*, p. 224.

with every good thing that field and woodland could produce, if one may judge from a letter of a New Englander who was doing duty "within the lines" as a government plantation superintendent. Writing back home from the war zone, he described some of the products of the land as follows: "I should like to look in upon you and bring you some of the delicacies of this tropical clime; watermelions, as the 'inhabitants' call them, rich and red; huge, mellow figs, seedy but succulent; plump quails, sweet curlew, delicate squirrels, fat rabbits, tender chickens. We fare well here. If the wretched country only had more rocks and less sand, better horses, more tolerable staff officers, and just a little more frequent communication with New England, I should perhaps be content to make quite a long stay, if I were wanted."[7]

Miss Botume, who like Mary Ames came as a "missionary" to the freedmen, wrote interestingly of Old Fort plantation, on Parris Island. This plantation derives its name from the ruins of old Fort Charles, built by Jean Rebault in 1562. As was the custom, the invaders occupied the plantation homes of those who were in the Confederate Army:

The plantation house at which we stopped, and which was to be my future home, was one of the oldest on the island. It was a low, two-storied mansion, built in a wonderful grove of live-oaks and water oaks, which covered an area of sixty acres. All these trees are heavily draped with the long gray moss, which is never found in greater luxuriance than on and around the sea-islands.

It hung dank and heavy from the recent rains; and as we entered the grove, this bright summer afternoon, the place seemed like a solemn, grand old cathedral. . . .

It seemed indescribably pathetic to me, thus to walk into a stranger's house and take quiet possession. There was nothing within to remind one of the original owner. It was only when I walked around and saw the carefully arranged grounds, with fine shrubs and vines and gravelled walks bordered with flowers, that I realized what the place had been. In spite of years of neglect,—for it was first left to the care of the negroes, and then taken by the Union troops and used for soldiers' barracks and hospitals,—in spite of all this, there was much beauty left. As I walked around I was more and more overwhelmed by a realization of the cruel necessities of a civil war. . . .

[7] Pearson, *op. cit.*, pp. 74-75.

The house was stripped of all furniture. The windows were without curtains, and had only board shutters to protect us from the sun by day and unwelcome intrusion at night. When these shutters were closed we were in absolute darkness. When they were open the windows were so shattered there was nothing to protect us from the wind and the weather. There were no domestic utensils. A few articles of household furniture had been gathered together for our immediate use. This place was first deserted by its owners, and then entirely devastated by the soldiers.[8]

Bleak Hall, on Edisto, has lost much of its former grandeur. Situated on one of the large tidal creeks leading out to sea, it is a pertinent reminder of more opulent times. All that remains of its former dignity is the "tabby"[9] foundation on which a new house stands, an old smokehouse, an ice house, and a few "tabby" buildings. The old place is now being restored by its owner, a New England college professor, it having passed from the lineal descendants of its original owners during the recent financial depression.

Mikell recalls vividly some boyhood recollections of a Christmas "oyster roast" given by the proprietor of Bleak Hall. Invitations were sometimes issued at church and given in plenty of time so that there would be no conflict of engagements. Most elaborate preparations were made for these entertainments. The Bleak Hall party was given at "Botany Bay," a small island of the plantation which faces the sea. This island is about five miles long and a half mile wide, and, with the exception of the strand, was at one time covered with an impenetrable jungle of palmettos, live oaks, and cedars. Cords of oak, hickory, and cedar, the latter for its aroma, were hauled to the island for making live coals and furnishing warmth through the mild winter afternoons. The island was uninhabited, except for half-wild cattle, wild hogs, and "marsh tackeys." Deer were there in abundance, and, chief of all, the "white foot" oysters, named for the "White Foot" Indians, a subdivision of the Edistoes. Mikell says:

[8] Elizabeth Hyde Botume, *First Days Amongst the Contrabands* (Boston, 1893), pp. 36-39.
[9] "Tabby," a corruption of "tapia," Spanish, meaning a concrete mixture made of lime and oyster shells. The lime was made by burning quantities of shells, particularly oyster shells.

By sunrise wagons were moving, containing everything pertaining to an elaborate feast, from the humble oven to drinking water . . . from the ancestral silver and the table napery to the aristocratic champagne glass, accompanied by a host of household and kitchen servants.

The first course, oysters, was served at one o'clock. As the guests were seated, and wooden platters placed upon linen mats before each diner, the butler came with a silver pitcher of steaming hot punch. Then the toast: "To our kinsfolk, our guests, welcome!" Immediately a dozen little picaninnies rushed from the fire with platters filled with hot, sputtering oysters and placed one before each person, and for a time nothing was heard save the knife struggling with an obdurate oyster. The trimmings to this course were also in evidence. Not too much—they were purposely limited, dinner was only one hour off.

A rest. Then came the embarrassing, and to the men the amusing disentanglement of the young women from the stationary benches on which they were seated . . . with their long, balloon-shaped gowns and the hoops of the day, it was some job getting out. . . . No sooner had the guests retired to the beach than a rapidly driven wagon came up with the dinner from the home kitchen, packed in extemporized "fireless cookers". . . .[10]

Among the vegetables served was palmetto cabbage, but one must never associate such a humble viand as "cabbage" with this delectable dish: "Every 'cabbage'—or heart, more correctly,—used, means the death of the palmetto tree. It has the combined taste of cauliflower, burr artichoke, and asparagus, with a most fascinating predominant taste of its own."[11]

David Doar, of St. James Parish, Santee, speaking before the local agricultural society in 1907, gave some glimpse of social life among the Santee Huguenots of the Carolina rice country. Referring to an earlier period, he explained:

. . . the planters on river, and around, also had a clubhouse on River Road, where they met, once a month, during winter for social intercourse. Each man took his turn to furnish dinner and all necessaries. It was found at first that there was great rivalry amongst members, as to who should have the best spread. So, to put the richer and poorer contributors on the same footing and prevent competition, only a certain number of dishes of a certain class were to be provided. . . .

It was not, with these old parishioners, all work and no play,

[10] Mikell, *op. cit.*, pp. 170-177.   [11] *Ibid.*, pp. 175-176.

for they had amusements in abundance, they had their fishing parties, and judging from the ball-rooms in some of the old houses, they could not have disdained dancing.[12]

Jehossee Island is in reality part of greater Edisto. Its insular character is due to the circumstance of small creeks and the Edisto River, which surround it and cut it off from the parent island. It was one of the most unusual of all the plantations of the rice coast community. In the ante-bellum period it was owned by William Aiken, one-time governor of South Carolina. An Iowa farmer named Solon Robinson visited the plantation in 1850 and wrote a complete account of its operations at the time. Jehossee now shares with many other old plantation sites an air of desolation and abandonment, but in 1850 it was alive with human interests—slaves, the best of slave quarters, the kindly treatment of a benevolent owner, and hospitality unbounded. Robinson's account, originally written for the *American Agriculturist* and reviewed in *De Bow's Review*, describes in glowing terms the ideal ante-bellum plantation:

> There are 1,500 acres of rice lands, divided into convenient compartments for flooding, . . . Besides this, Gov. Aiken cultivates 500 acres in corn, oats and potatoes; the balance is gardens, yards, lawns, and in woods, pasture and unreclaimed swamp. . . . Corn, upon the low or rice land, does not yield well, though it makes very large stalks. With sweet potatoes, on the contrary, the low land produces nearly double, and of better quality, averaging 200 bushels to the acre, and frequently 400 bushels. The average yield of rice is 45 bushels to the acre, and upon one eighty-acre lot the average yield is 64 bushels. . . .
>
> The average annual sales of the place do not vary materially from $25,000, and the average annual expenses not far from $10,000, of which sum $2,000 is paid the overseer, who is the only white man upon the place, besides the owner, who is always absent during the sickly months of summer. All the engineers, millers, smiths, carpenters and sailors, are black. A vessel, belonging to the island, goes twice a week to Charleston and carries a cargo of one hundred casks. The last crop was 1,500 casks; the year before, 1,800, and all provisions and grain required, made upon the place. . . .
>
> Like nearly all the lower-country plantations, the diet of the

---

[12] David Doar, *A Sketch of the Agricultural Society of St. James, Santee* (Charleston, 1908), p. 23.

PLANTATIONS

people is principally vegetable. Those who work "task work" receive, as rations, half a bushel of sweet potatoes a week, or six quarts of corn meal or rice, with beef or pork, or mutton occasionally, say two or three meals a week. As all the tasks are very light, affording them nearly one-fourth of the time to raise a crop for themselves, they always have an abundance, and sell a good deal for cash. . . .

The number of negroes upon the place is just about 700, occupying 84 double frame houses, each containing two tenements of three rooms to a family, besides the cockloft. Each tenement has its separate door and window, and a good brick fireplace, and nearly all have a garden paled in. There are two common hospitals and a "lying-in hospital," and a very neat, commodious church, which is well filled, every Sabbath, with an orderly, pious congregation. . . .

Now, the owner of all this property lives in a very humble cottage, . . . making no show, and is, in fact, as a dwelling for a gentleman of wealth, far inferior, in point of elegance and convenience, to any negro house upon the place, for the use and comfort of that class of people.

He and his family are as plain and unostentatious, in their manners, as the house they live in. . . .

Nearly all the land has been reclaimed, and the buildings, except the house, erected new, within the twenty years that Governor Aiken has owned the island. I fully believe that he is more concerned to make his people comfortable and happy, than he is to make money.[18]

Another significant account of this plantation has been left by one of the Methodist circuit riders, the Reverend M. L. Banks, in whose pastoral charge the slaves of this plantation were included: "Jehossee was separated from Edisto by a small creek spanned by a bridge. That, to me, was the most interesting part of the work. Ex-Governor Aiken lived there, and was sole owner of the island. He owned hundreds of negroes, and few slaves had a kinder master. His negro quarters looked like a little village, and much whiter and cleaner than many villages I have seen. The large building he had erected for his people to worship in was generally crowded at the hour of preaching. The worshipers appeared in decent apparel, and not a few were dressed like ladies and gentlemen. What a

[18] *De Bow's Review*, IX, 201-203 (Aug., 1850). Robinson's account of the plantation is also cited in U. B. Phillips, *American Negro Slavery* (New York: D. Appleton-Century Co., 1918), pp. 251-253.

privilege it was to hear them sing! I have sat in the pulpit and listened until I would weep for joy."[14]

The greatest rice planter in South Carolina, and perhaps anywhere, was Nathaniel Heyward. The fact that upon his death, just prior to the Civil War, he owned more than two thousand slaves on fourteen rice plantations, places him in the big business class of his day. A manuscript in the possession of Mrs. Hawkins K. Jenkins, of Pinopolis, South Carolina, contains information concerning this remarkable man. Upon this document Phillips based the following interesting comment:

That the tide when taken at the flood on the rice coast as elsewhere would lead to fortune is shown by the career of the greatest of all rice planters, Nathaniel Heyward. At the time of his birth, in 1766, his father was a planter on an inland swamp near Port Royal. Nathaniel himself after establishing a small plantation in his early manhood married Harriett Manigault, an heiress with some fifty thousand dollars. With this, when both lands and slaves were cheap, Heyward bought a tide-land tract and erected four plantations thereon, and soon had enough accrued earnings to buy the several inland plantations of the Gibbes brothers, who had fallen into debt from luxurious living. With the proceeds of his fallen crops at high prices during the great wars in Europe, he bought more slaves year after year, preferably fresh Africans as long as that cheap supply remained available, and he bought more land when occasion offered. Joseph Manigault wrote of him in 1806: "Mr. Heyward has lately made another purchase of land, consisting of 300 acres of tide swamp, joining one of his Combahee plantations and belonging to the estate of Mrs. Bell. I believe he has made a good bargain. It is uncleared and will cost him not quite £20 per acre. I have very little doubt that he will be in a few years, if he lives, the richest, as he is the best, planter in the state. The Cooper River lands give him many a long ride." Heyward was venturesome in large things, conservative in small. He long continued to have his crops threshed by hand, saying that if it were done by machines his darkies would have no winter work; but when eventually he instituted mechanical threshers, no one could discern an increase of leisure. In the matter of pounding mills likewise, he clung for many years to those driven by the tides and operating slowly and crudely; but at length he

[14] Reverend M. L. Banks, *Sea Island Slave Mission Work*, quoted in William Pope Harrison, *The Gospel among the Slaves* (Nashville, Tenn., 1893), p. 266, in a chapter entitled "Notes from the Pioneers," which is a series of short accounts written by various ministers who participated in the mission work among the slaves.

PLANTATIONS

built two new ones driven by steam and so novel and complete in their apparatus as to be the marvel of the countryside. He necessarily depended much upon overseers; but his own frequent visits of inspection and the assistance rendered by his sons kept the scattered establishments in an efficient routine. The natural increase of his slaves was reckoned by him to have ranged generally between one and five per cent annually, though in one year it rose to seven per cent. At his death in 1851 he owned fourteen rice plantations with fields ranging from seventy to six hundred acres in each, and comprising in all 4,390 acres in cultivation. He had also a cotton plantation, much pine land and a sawmill, nine residences in Charleston, appraised with their furniture at $180,000; securities and cash to the amount of $200,000; $20,000 worth of horses, mules and cattle; $15,000 worth of plate; and $3000 worth of old wine. His slaves, numbering 2,087 and appraised at an average of $550, made up the greater part of his two million dollar estate. His heirs continued his policy. In 1855, for example, they bought a Savannah River plantation called Fife, containing 500 acres of prime rice land at $150.00 per acre, together with its equipment and 120 slaves, at a gross price of $135,600.[15]

It is to be deplored that there are not more written records from the slaves themselves recounting their plantation experiences, their hardships and joys. Negro life on the slave plantation was not altogether one of hardship and discontent. A very useful and talented Negro of Columbia, South Carolina, the late Reverend I. E. Lowery, has left some graphic pictures of the more pleasant aspects of slave life. That he emphasized the brighter side of his life as a slave is evidence of his tolerant, forgiving spirit. Lowery wrote:

But how shall I begin to describe this wonderful old plantation?[16] As I write, the scene comes fresh before my vision. I imagine I can see the old farm house, where the white folks lived, nestled in the midst of a clump of stately old water oaks. There was a front and back piazza and there was a brick chimney at each end. It was a one-story building, with an ell running back, in which was located the dining room. About thirty feet east of the building was the kitchen, and about the same distance in the rear of the dining room stood the smoke-house and the store-room. That smoke-house was never without meat and lard, and that store-room con-

[15] Phillips, *American Negro Slavery*, pp. 249-250.
[16] This plantation was located in Sumter County, S. C., not on the coast, but in the coastal plain.

tained barrels of flour, barrels of sugar, barrels of molasses and sacks of coffee from one year to another. And the corn, oh, there was no end to that. There were several barns, some big and some little, but when the corn was gathered and the "corn-shucking" was over and the crop was housed, the barns were full to overflowing.[17]

Lowery continued:

On the east side of the white folks' house was the orchard. It occupied a space of about five or six acres and contained a large number of fruit trees of every description. There could be found the apple in variety, the peach, the pear, the apricot and the plum. On the west side was a large vegetable garden, which contained, in addition to the supply of vegetables for the table, several varieties of grapes. The arbors built for these grapes were large, strong and well cared for. And the slaves got their portion of all these delicious fruits. Of course, they were not allowed to steal them (but this does not mean that they never resorted to this method of obtaining fruit), but they could, and did, get fruit by asking for it.[18]

A diary of Charles Cotesworth Pinckney, written in 1818-1819, brings one close to the commonplace routine of an island plantation and gives some insight into the manner in which the life of the Negro was woven into the very warp and woof of the white man's experience. Such commonplaces as the number of fish caught, the names of the Negro fishermen, the quantity of milk an old cow gave, and the notation of issuing tobacco and fishhooks to the slaves put the reader into the very heart of Carolina plantation life in the early part of the nineteenth century. Some of the notations in the diary are as follows:

April 6th. Left Charleston in the steamboat with my daughters at 6 o'clock this morning.

April 7th. Arrived at the Island about 9 o'clock this morning. Sent the boat a Drum fishing and caught 5 Drum. Gave a Drum to each of the overseers, and one among the fishermen.

April 8th. Sent the small yawl fishing with George, and Handy and little Abram from the Old Place, and York & Dagr from the Crescent; they caught 4 dozen Shrimp for bait last night & 14 Drum Fish today. Gave two to fishermen.

April 11th. Gave to the Negroes of each Plantation 14 heads,

[17] Irving E. Lowery, *Life on the Old Plantation* (Columbia, S. C., 1911), pp. 29 f. [18] *Ibid.*, pp. 31-32.

19 back bones & 37 sides of Drum fish. Mr. Cannon sent one dozen and eight eggs.

The Fishermen caught 15 Drum. Gave the Fishermen two Drum.

April 13th. The Fishermen caught 10 Drum Fish. Gave one to the Fishermen and one to each of the overseers.

April 14th. Gave to the Negroes of each plantation six heads 17 sides and 6 Back Bones.

April 21st. The fishermen caught 5 drum none with roes. The steam boat did not pass from Charleston today.

April 22nd. Gosport & Quash from the Crescent & January & Bob from the old place are the Fishermen for the ensuing week.

April 29th, 1818. Gave to the Negroes of each plantation this morning 10 heads, 11 Backs and 23 sides of Drum Fish. Cuffie & Sambo from the Crescent and Adam & Caesar from the Old Place begun fishing today. The 2 fed cows gave 6 quarts, and a pint. Mr. Cannon sent 1 dozen eggs. James brought two chickens. The Fishermen caught 8 drum. Gave One to Capt. Rogers, one to themselves and one to each of the overseers. . . .

Sweet potatoes, 10 acres; Irish do., 2 do.; Oats planted & slips to be planted, about 23 do.: (Total,) 35 acres . . . Total crop at Old Place, 268 acres.

May 10th. Gave tobacco, pipes, salt and Fish Hooks to the Negroes of both Plantations, and at the Point. My Brother's carriages and Horses were sent over to Mr. Robertson's.

May 12th. The Fishermen did not go for shrimps last night, and therefore only caught today two drum fish.

Caught no drum today, & gave up fishing for the season.

Drum fish caught in 1818: Drum fish, 219; Hard roes, 38.[19]

Port Royal is deserted, but in spite of man's abandonment of it, nature and time are bestowing touches of beauty that are ineradicable. There is still the great, deep harbor, described by an early French explorer as sufficient to float the navies of the world. The live oaks are probably more beautiful now than in former and more prosperous times because their gnarled trunks and branches are touched with age. Nature has done more for its main street than for any city in that section, for its evergreen trees are festooned in grey moss and their venerable dignity adds a touch of loveliness that is beyond the skill

---

[19] Ulrich Bonnell Phillips, *A Documentary History of American Industrial Society* (Cleveland, 1910), I, 203-208.

of the landscape gardener. Wandering through its silent streets is like thumbing the pages of an old yellow-stained book.

The town is inhabited principally by Negroes. Their homes and yards are carelessly kept, but touches of beauty are to be seen everywhere. Late of an afternoon in early summer one is overwhelmed with the heavy odor of the bay blossoms. In the warm sun creamy white magnolia blossoms stand out against glossy green leaves, and the giant yucca sends up a spike of immaculate blooms eight and ten feet high. Crape myrtle trees, white and pink, grow in unsuspected places, and the sweet myrtle with its tantalizing odor is at home everywhere. In the winter the cassena (yaupon) is laden with red, waxlike berries. The Negroes call them "Christmus berry" and use them to decorate their houses at Christmas time.

About 1870 Port Royal was a thriving town.[20] Then it had the largest cotton compress in the world, was an active lumber port, shipping lumber to all parts of the globe, and was a thriving center for phosphate dredging. In those days the harbor was full of ships and the town was one of considerable importance commercially in South Carolina.

Many of its once prosperous business houses are closed, while residences are dilapidated and in a state of decay. Many of the old houses are leaning and will soon be prone upon the ground. Negroes walk the streets aimlessly, for there is no business to occupy them. A few people enter the post office. I went into a store; the proprietor was out. Nothing was going on. A Gullah Negro who was eating crackers assured me that the owner would be back after a while. The docks, once bustling with trade, are now silent, and the big warehouses are empty, for there are no ships in the great harbor. Not even a catboat was to be seen on the placid waters of the bay. Only a woebegone gasoline fishing boat spluttered at her mooring as I stood on the lonesome docks. Life here is without purpose. The only matter of interest on the water front now is that speckled trout are running. On cold December nights fishermen gig them as they lie in the shallow edges of the river. The hungry porpoises chase them out of the main current into the shallows, where they are easily seen with the flashlight.

[20] Information from Dr. M. G. Elliot, of Beaufort, S. C.

A SEA-ISLAND BOY

AT PEACE WITH THE WORLD ON ITS OWN TERMS

PLANTATIONS

Here they are "stuck," hundreds of them, and brought in and sold for from four to ten cents a pound.

But to the "missionaries" who came to Port Royal during the Civil War this strange new country presented a remarkable contrast to their native New England. One of them, Edward S. Philbrick, an engineer from Brookline, left a description worth reproducing: "The shore is as flat as flat can be, sandbanks and beaches being the only variety, backed by long green masses of foliage of the pitch pine, reminding me forcibly of the coast of Egypt, with its sand and palm forests." In Beaufort he wrote: ". . . I can't find any place over ten feet above tide-water, and no hill over six feet high. . . ." The town presented to him a dilapidated appearance with its "desolated houses surrounded by heaps of broken furniture and broken wine and beer bottles which the army had left after their pillage. Quantities of Negro children lay basking in the morning sun, grinning at us as we passed."[21] These first "missionaries" and teachers (of the Negroes) were soon to be followed by plantation superintendents, cotton agents, land speculators, soldiers of fortune, and carpetbaggers. Among the first of the teachers to come to Port Royal was a young New England woman, who recorded her impressions on approaching Beaufort: "The sail up was very beautiful, the green beyond description brilliant, and now and then the deeper shade of palmetto or live-oak. Some of the plantations were very picturesque. Roses and azaleas were plainly visible." The party came up the river, docked at the wharf at Beaufort and, after landing, was sent to headquarters of one of the Federal officers, "whither we walked a long half-mile, a sentry at the street-corners, darkies bowing in every direction, birds and the scent of flowers filling the air, everything like a June day after a shower."[22]

In 1664 William Hilton recorded his impressions of Port Royal in a pamphlet entitled *A Relation of a Discovery:*

> Now our understanding of the Land of Port-Royal, River Jordan,[23] River Grandie, or Edistow, is as followeth: The Lands are laden with large tall oaks, walnut and bayes, except facing on the Sea, it is most Pines tall and good: The Land generally, except

---

[21] Pearson, *op. cit.*, pp. 5, 7. [22] *Ibid.*, p. 16.

[23] River Jordan was the present Combahee. Grandy was the name given the forks of the Edisto, near the sea.

where the Pines grow, is a good Soyl, covered with black Mold, in some places a foot, in some places half a foot, and in other places lesse, with Clay underneath mixed with Sand; and we think may produce any thing as well as most part of the Indies that we have seen. The Indians plant in the worst land because *they cannot cut down the Timber in the best,* and yet have plenty of Corn, Pumpions, Water Mellons, Musk-mellons: although the Land be overgrown with weeds through their lazinesse, yet they have two or three crops of Corn a year, as the Indians themselves inform us. The Country abounds with Grapes, large Figs, and Peaches; the Woods with Deer, Conies, Turkeys, Quails, Curlues, Plovers, Teile, Herons: and as the Indians say, in Winter, with swans, Geese, Cranes, Duck and Mallard, and innumerable of other water-fowls, whose names we know not, which lie in the Rivers, Marshes, and on the sands: Oysters in abundance, with great store of Muscles; A sort of fair Crabs, and a round Shel-fish called Horse-feet; The Rivers stored plentifully with Fish that we saw play and leap. There are great Marshes, but most as far as we saw little worth, except for a Root that grows in them the Indians make good Bread of. The Land we suppose is healthful; for the English that were cast away on that Coast in July last, were there most part of that time of year that is sickly in Virginia; and notwithstanding hard usage, and lying on the ground naked, yet had their perfect healths all the time. The Natives are very healthful; we saw many very Aged amongst them. The Ayr is clear and sweet, the Countrey very pleasant and delightful: And we could wish, that all they that want a happy settlement, of our English Nation, were well transported thither, etc.[24]

Today the Negroes of St. Helena Island, near Port Royal, fare better economically than do those of the other islands, partly on account of the constructive work of the Penn School for Negroes, whose chief concern is to adapt its educational procedure to the needs of the people. Since St. Helena is wholly a rural community, the curriculum of instruction centers about agriculture, better home conditions, and the training of boys and girls in domestic arts. Formerly the Negroes depended upon cotton almost entirely as a money crop. In recent years they have diversified their crops, produced only the necessities for living at home, and have even begun to ship truck to Northern markets, by express, in single crate lots.

[24] William Hilton, *A Relation of a Discovery* (London, 1664), quoted in Salley, *op. cit.,* pp. 44-45.

PLANTATIONS

Many of the Negroes in the Port Royal area own their land—small farms usually of ten or more acres. Many of these tracts came into the possession of their fathers through confiscation proceedings during the Civil War. A very courteous old Negro woman informed me that she owned her land, had inherited it, and that she had in the tract "t'ree acres and a tass."[25] She was hoeing cotton, seemed perfectly contented, and was a reminder of an age that had passed.

On some of the other islands the conditions of home life are deplorable. One cabin which I visited illustrates the situation. The owners were absent, but I made a photograph from the vegetable garden situated in the front yard. Underneath the house was tethered a grunting pig. The chimney was of the typical clay-and-stick type. The kitchen was a miniature building, not much larger than a doll's house, attached to the rear of the dwelling and connected by a short board walkway. A graceful tree palmetto grew in the front yard.

Another cabin near the beach was occupied by an amiable Negro islander, about sixty years old. He was not suspicious of my intentions, probably because of the nearness of his place to the beach, which for the last few years has been a summer colony for whites. He plants a little cotton, and owns about five acres of land, with a few other scattered tracts; this land he inherited from kinsfolk on each side of his family. The usual "hard times" talk was offered, but he readily agreed that the creek furnished food in emergency. There were crab, "swimp, and eyesters." A baby of crawling age sat in the doorway and bawled at the top of his voice. He was "jist crying cause his mammy over to the beach, and he's hongry."

The poorer houses are usually very small, with two or three rooms. Occasionally a cookroom is attached to the house. Chimneys are made of brick or of clay and sticks. Windows generally are without glass and rarely screened. Each window has a board shutter, and if painted at all is blue. Roofs are of varied materials. Originally they were shingled, but since the advent of the boll weevil and the consequent increasing poverty, every sort of improvised covering is used: an old sheet of tin, a bit of tar paper, boards, or anything that will turn water.

---

[25] "Tass," meaning *task*, a slavery term. In this instance a task is a quarter of an acre.

There is usually a small, insignificant porch. In hot weather, doors are stretched wide open and one sees clear through the house. There is no attempt at beautification save the occasional sunflower, a chance crape myrtle, oleander, or tree palmetto. The chief impression one gets is that of dilapidation. In summer children of all sizes loiter on the steps and in the sandy yards.

Here, on the other hand, is a better sort of home owned by an island farmer and built by his own hands. It has dormer windows and a front porch, painted white with lime whitewash; blue solid board shutters; no screens. This man has eight children living and four dead. He owns his home, together with a few rude outhouses and ten acres of land. When I asked him if he would let me take a photograph of his home, he wanted to know if that would have anything to do with the raising of his tax rate. A little boy of twelve was plowing in a near-by cotton field. The father gave very peremptory commands and showed all signs of being the power in the household. He, too, complained of hard times. He said that there was no market for his produce; therefore only those food crops were planted which could be used at home. A few acres were planted in short staple cotton. No control over the boll weevil was attempted. The gift of a few toy balloons to the children enabled me to make photographs of them and to do almost anything else I cared to do.

It is interesting to compare Negro houses today with those of slavery times. Miss Botume, a Northern teacher, found on Cat Island and on Cane Island that the home conditions of the slaves were better than those of the neighboring islands. She discovered that their houses were built better and had a more pleasing arrangement than any she had seen elsewhere. Around each yard she observed pigs and poultry and a piece of ground fenced in for a garden. Their superior condition was partly due to the fact that the military establishment had not had access to these areas. She explained: "The negro quarters consisted of two rows of very small houses, built on each side of a very narrow road, which was not much more than a foot-path. The quarters the negroes called 'a town,' and the paths a 'street.' "[26]

Edisto Island was at one time the wealthiest and most in-

---

[26] Botume, *op. cit.*, p. 88.

PLANTATIONS 53

fluential community south of Charleston; its condition today is in striking contrast to its former importance. For the last fifty years it has been an almost forgotten region; cut off from the main currents of life, it has passed its sleepy, idyllic existence all alone. The island was settled early in the eighteenth century, principally by emigrants from Scotland and Wales. Their first agricultural efforts were rice culture. Finding that this crop could be better grown along the rivers and in the swamp country, they turned to the production of indigo and sea-island cotton, the latter to the great profit of the proprietors. The island is twelve miles long and, in its widest part, four or five miles broad.[27] McLeod estimated its acreage in 1800 as 28,811, or 122 acres for every white person, and nearly eleven for every slave, a fraction of more than ten acres for every inhabitant. About three fourths of it was cleared at that early date, and even then firewood and fencing timber were scarce on some plantations.[28]

The census of 1790 lists seventy heads of families living on Edisto, and thirty-nine individual family names. Nearly everybody owned slaves, whose numbers were published in the census report.[29] The number of slaves held by each family ranged from two or three to seventy. The day of large holdings had not yet come, for

> Out of the thirty-nine individual names only those of Bailey, Jenkins, Mikell, Murray, Pope, Seabrook, Wescott, and Whaley are found on the island today. The Jenkins family, one of the most numerous of the families, are represented now by two heads of families, and the Seabrooks by five. Twelve Seabrook families were noted in 1790. Only one Murray appeared in 1790, but at the present time there are six Murray groups on Edisto, all descendants of Joseph Murray. There is one Wescott on the last census rolls, three Mikell families, two Pope groups, one Whaley and two Baileys.

A strip of woodland is named after the Flinn family; a plantation after the Crawfords; a settlement bears the name of "Clarks"; "Parmenter" has been corrupted by the negroes to "Palmetto," for which numerous fields are named; Hanahan, now called "Hynyan,"

---

[27] Account of Donald McLeod, in David Ramsay's *History of South Carolina, from Its First Settlement in 1670, to the Year 1808* (2 vols.; Newberry, S. C., 1858), II, 278.   [28] *Ibid.*

[29] Article by C. S. Murray, of Edisto Island, in the Charleston, S. C., *News and Courier*, Sept. 9, 1935.

is a well known fishing drop, and McLeod is blended with Seabrook to form the name "Seacloud," a plantation in Seaside.

Cotton still was being seeded by hand in 1790. It was before the days of the cotton gin, so there were no large slave holders then. Daniel Jenkins owned 106 and Ephraim Mikell, eighty, but most of the planters found that between thirty and forty slaves were enough to cultivate their crops. Big cotton crops were out of the question until machinery was substituted for the "hand gin."

The days of the great slave holders were to come later. At the time of the War Between the States, one planter on the island was reputed to have owned 1,000 slaves.[30]

In regard to the population of Edisto during the first decade of the nineteenth century, McLeod wrote: "A census of the Island, taken at this time, 1808, would rate the white population at 236 inhabitants. Of these 111 are males, and 135 females. Of the males 37 are married, 4 are widowers, 9 natives of Europe, and 2 of the middle States; of the females 37 are married, 12 are widows, and all are either natives of the Island or the adjacent parts of the State. The births are to the deaths annually as 13 to 11. Nevertheless, the white population decreases in consequence of the numbers who leave the island."[31] At that time the ratio of Negro to white appears to have been something more than ten to one: "From the return made to the tax-collector of the district for the year 1807, it appears that the black population of the Island exceeds by a few infants and newly bought Africans, 2,609 slaves."[32] On St. Helena Island today there are approximately twenty-five Negroes to one white person.

[30] *Ibid.*
[31] Account of Donald McLeod in Ramsay, *op. cit.*, II, 279-280.
[32] *Ibid.*

CHAPTER IV

THE GULLAH WORLD OF NATURE

> I know moonlight, I know starlight,
> I'm walkin' troo de starlight;
> Lay dis body down.

THE LIFE of the Gullah cannot be fully understood without some knowledge of the world of nature with which he is familiar. The ante-bellum plantation offered few attractions in the way of entertainment which are common in modern times, and the Negro was perforce thrown upon his own resources in devising means of recreation. Much of his pleasure he found in field and stream as fisherman and hunter, living close to the creatures of the woods. The coastal Negro today has an intimate acquaintance with the deep swamp and the denizens of its shady recesses: he is at home in a boat, is an accomplished fisherman, a good hunter, and with a single-barrel shotgun can in a year's time bring home more game than the most expert sportsman at the club. A common sight in the low country throughout the fall and winter months is the ever-present Negro with his gun and dog. Together they roam the countryside, chiefly in search of rabbits and squirrels. In ante-bellum days Negroes were never permitted to carry guns. Their eagerness to own a firearm today would appear in some measure a reaction against the prohibition brought to bear so stringently upon their forefathers. Denied the use of a gun under the slave regime, they became expert at trapping and other means of securing game which did not require the use of powder and shot. With a long hook they mastered the dangerous alligator: they entered his holes at low water, and at considerable risk of life and limb dragged him out and dispatched him quickly. 'Gator meat is still a delicacy among the low-country Negroes. They claim it has the peculiar quality of tasting like any kind of meat: if you think about pork, it tastes like pork, and "ef you t'ink 'bout beef, it taste like beef."

The stories of Uncle Remus, by Joel Chandler Harris, the

perfect representation of the Gullah speech by Ambrose Gonzales, of Pon Pon, South, Carolina, the exquisite tales of C. C. Jones depicting Negro life of the Georgia coast, and the folklore of the Negroes round Port Royal and Beaufort as told by Mrs. M. H. Christensen—all reveal how profoundly the Negro's personality has been influenced by the "critters" of the woods. Buh Rabbit, Buh Fox, and Buh 'Coon are as close as brothers, and among some of the South's greatest students of nature and the ways of living things are the black people of the coast country. They do not know the scientific names of the animals, but they know their habits and ways of living.

A complete story of the social history of these people can never be told without some record of their participation in the white man's sports. Even today the Negro is an essential part of every fishing or hunting expedition. He always drives the deer or paddles the boat and quite often contributes much of wisdom in the ways of the woods. Like the caddy who laughs at many a cocksure golfer, the Gullah has many a secret chuckle over the ignorance of his white employer on the hunt. At times his patience is sorely tried as he tries to enlighten a novice in the marsh. On one occasion a Northern sportsman was hunting ducks. He had had poor luck and had brought down only one, and, because that one was only stunned, it got away in the tall marsh grass. He was sure, however, that he had killed the duck and made his Negro oarsman paddle over the area time and again without success. The Negro grew hotter and hotter and, realizing the futility of further looking, at last said in exasperation: "Cap'n, dat duck aint huh: one o' dem scragglin' shots hit 'im in de head and jist knocked him ign'ant for aw'ile."

The Carolina coast, with its swampy hinterland, comprises one of the greatest bird and game sanctuaries in eastern America. The deep, impenetrable swamp has been the refuge of deer and other animals for years, and the wide rivers spreading into innumerable "lakes" have furnished unexcelled breeding places for fish. Here they have been able to survive and multiply in spite of the pothunter and illegal trapper. These swamps are so extensive that every year a few persons are lost within their depths, and for days at a time have had to await the searching parties which eventually lead them out. The sparsely settled islands and the wide expanse of marshland furnish abundant refuge for many animals and for the great flocks of waterfowl that migrate southward each autumn to feed upon the wild rice and succulent swamp grasses.

One sees the great wood ibis fishing knee-deep in the brackish waters of the marsh, standing for long periods on one leg, the very personification of patience. Redwings chatter in the tall marsh grass, while coots and gallinules race across the lily pads. Nonpareils, the most gaudily dressed birds of the South, cling to swaying reeds and rob them of their rich seed-clusters. One sees gulls, terns, shearwaters, skimmers, and the huge pelican.[1] In August rice birds (rice "buds" to the Negro) swarm the rice fields. In slavery days Negro boys "minded" the rice fields during harvest time. They were furnished with black gunpowder, but no shot, which was fired from muzzle-loading guns to scare the birds away. As stated above, the law forbade slaves to carry firearms, but they were permitted to protect the rice fields with this bombardment of blank charges. James Henry Rice, of Chee-Ha plantation, tells of a resident of the Waccamaw section who used to ship sixty thousand dozen rice birds a season picked at a dollar a dozen. "Rice bird pie" was once a favored dish among Negroes and whites. The destruction of these birds was so complete that the species has been almost exterminated, and now stringent laws have been enacted to protect them. These birds were slaughtered by Negroes and whites, who hunted them at night as they roosted in low shrubbery growing along the cross-ditches of the rice fields. They were easily seen with a torch, then plucked from the branches as they slept, and their tiny necks were crushed between thumb and forefinger. Thousands were taken in this way every season.[2]

The rice fields and marsh lands in autumn are alive with grackles, redwing blackbirds, and the unlovely cowbird.[3] The marsh hen, or, clapper rail, noisy and fat, feeds on snails and slugs.[4] In August the air is filled with migrating swallows, the forked-tailed barn swallow, the white-bellied tree swallow,

---

[1] The names and descriptions of birds in this section, taken largely from James Henry Rice's book, *Glories of the Carolina Coast*, pp. 121-126, have been supplemented by the author's own observations.
[2] Rice, *op. cit.*, p. 55.
[3] *Ibid.*, p. 56.   [4] *Ibid.*, p. 51.

and others. The purple martin is also a swallow. The chimney-swift, more like the nighthawk, migrates also.[5] As one travels along the shell roads of these islands in late summer, one may see thousands of swallows sitting in endless rows on telephone wires, like giant strings of beads, miles long.

Of the water birds the most impressive in point of numbers are the wild ducks, which, like royal tourists, seek out the balmy marshes of the South at the first sign of winter. I have stood in wonder near a wide expanse of marsh on a cold December day and watched them come in. When the sea is stormy, they fly inland in search of quieter feeding grounds. On this day the wind blows hard and cold; the big birds come in with lightning speed, for they are strong of wing. High in the air at first, they then drop low and turn to light gracefully upon the water. With heads down and tails up, they feed all day long. Some bask in the warm sunshine against the mud banks of the marsh; others move ceaselessly from place to place in search of the tender wild rice, which grows in abundance.

Of the large ducks, usually found in the marsh, are the mallard, the black duck or dusky mallard, and the pintail. On open water one usually finds the large canvasback and redhead. Among the small ducks are the teal, blue and green winged, the widgeon, gadwall, spoonbill or shoveler, lesser scaup, ruddy duck, and ring-neck.[6]

Other water birds are loons, grebes, mergansers, and the Florida cormorant. Among the heron family are the American egret, snowy heron, little blue heron, little green heron or "shike poke," and the great blue heron.[7]

In the higher places round fields and orchards are sparrows, myrtle warblers, gold-and-ruby-crowned kinglets, warblers, nuthatches, and woodpeckers. Of the last named there are the great pileated, red-headed, hairy, downy, red-bellied, and flicker or golden-winged—all of the woodpecker tribe. In springtime one sees vireos, kingbirds, wood thrushes, summer tanagers, and others.[8]

Of the pigeon family there are the mourning or Carolina dove and the ground dove.[9] The famous passenger pigeons are

---

[5] *Ibid.*, p. 58.
[6] *Ibid.*, p. 120.
[8] *Ibid.*, p. 73.
[7] *Ibid.*, p. 69.
[9] *Ibid.*, p. 58.

THE WORLD OF NATURE 59

now extinct; at one time they swarmed through the low country as in other parts of America. Mr. A. S. Salley, of Columbia, South Carolina, writes: "In December 1885 or 1886, the editor saw a passenger pigeon in Orangeburg County, South Carolina. Since that time very few have been seen in the state."[10]

The beautiful Carolina paroquet, which for a long while added a touch of beauty to the deep swamps of the low country, is now extinct in South Carolina. One of the most beautiful sketches of this species was done by Audubon. The distinguished ornithologist of Charleston, Sayne, wrote in 1910: "As its name implies, the beautiful Carolina Paroquet was formerly exceedingly abundant in the state, but it has become extinct within the past fifty years on or near the coast, as well as in the state at large. . . . There were, in the Charleston Museum, many mounted specimens of this bird that had been taken near the city, but as they were dust-stained and moth-eaten they were thrown away many years ago."[11]

The birds of the Carolina coast were described by Thomas Ashe in 1682 as follows: "Birds the Country yields of differeing kinds and colours: For Prey, the Pelican, Hawk, and Eagle, etc. For Pleasure, the red, copper and blew bird, which wantonly imitates the various Notes and Sounds of such Birds and Beast which it hears, wherefore, by way of Allusion, it's call'd the mocking Bird; for which pleasing Property it's there esteemed a Rarity. Birds for Food, and pleasure of Game, are the Swan, Goose, Duck, Mallard, Wigeon, Teal, Curlew, Plover, Partridge, the Flesh of which is equally as good, tho' smaller than ours in England. Pigeons and Parakeittoes. In Winter Huge Flights of wild Turkies, often times weighing from twenty, thirty, to forty pounds."[12]

The deep swamps back of the islands abound in deer. As the upcountry was gradually settled, the deer were forced to take cover in the wide and unexplored woodlands of the low country. Here they had many hiding places and a never ending supply of food. Until recent decades there was a steady decrease in their numbers, but the establishment of many hunt-

[10] Salley, *op. cit.*, p. 151 n.
[11] Wayne, *Birds of South Carolina*, p. 85.
[12] Thomas Ashe, *Carolina, or a Description of the Present State of that Country* (London, 1682), quoted in Salley, *op. cit.*, pp. 150-151.

ing preserves since has increased their numbers in a most gratifying manner.

In the early days during the first settlements the elk, or wapiti, ranged over the state, as did the bison or buffalo. The puma, sometimes called panther by the early inhabitants, prowled over the coastal region, taking toll of many sheep and hogs. Although harmless so far as his activities toward man were concerned, he was despised because of his forays upon domestic animals and was soon wiped out of the country. The last known puma was killed in Newberry County during the middle of the last century. The wild cat or bay lynx, found on the coast, furnishes exciting sport for coon and 'possum hunters who accidentally run into him on the regular hunts.[13]

The explorers of the seventeenth century were impressed with the quantity of game which roamed through the coastal section; one of them described its variety:

> Deer, of which there is such infinite Herds, that the whole Country seems but one continued Park, insomuch that I have often heard Captain Matthews, an ingenious Gentlemen and Agent to Sir Peter Colleton for his Affairs in Carolina, that one hunting Indian has yearly kill'd and brought to his Plantation more than 100, sometimes 200 head of Deer. Bears there are in great numbers, of whose Fat they make an oyl which is of great Vertue and Efficacy in causing the Hair to grow, which I observed the Indians daily used, by which means they not only kept their Hair clear and preserved from vermine, but by the nourishing faculty of the Oyl, it usually extended in length to their middles. There are Bevors, Otters, Foxes, Racoons, Possums, Musquasses, Hares and Coneys, Squirrels of five kinds, the flying squirrel, whose delicate Skin is commended for comforting, if applied to a cold Stomack, the Red, the Grey, the Fox and Black Squirrels. Leather for Shoes they have good and well tann'd: The Indians have also a way of dressing their skins rather softer, though not so durable as ours in England.[14]

Jenkins Mikell, of Edisto, as a youth hunted deer in the islands after the Civil War and has left such an excellent account of one of his experiences that it seems appropriate to give it here in part. Not only is this an account of a hunting expedition, but a vivid picture of the island country, giving glimpses

---

[13] Rice, *op. cit.*, p. 70.
[14] Ashe, *op. cit.*, quoted in Salley, *op. cit.*, p. 150.

THE WORLD OF NATURE

of Gullah Negroes as they are, with their charming dialect and their relationships to the whites, and, in all, a bit of Southern life that is rapidly passing.

The Hunting Island, immediately on the ocean, was the paradise of deer hunters and duck shooters, and may be now. It is about six miles in length from north to south, and averages about three-quarters of a mile across, is uncultivated, uninhabited, a jungle of saw palmettoes, tropical undergrowth, of pines, live oaks and cedars, that need fear no comparison with many a jungle in Africa. Only a deer path bisects it from the front beach to the back beach, a distance of three-quarters of a mile, trackless, lengthwise. It was the property and game preserve, in ante-bellum days, of a few planters in lower Beaufort County, more particularly of St. Helena's Island and the Town of Beaufort. They hunted there in October, November, and December. It could only be reached by the row-boats of the planters, from four oars to ten oars in size, manned and propelled by the slaves of the respective owners. . . .

This sportsman's paradise is separated from Edisto by a stretch of water, "grand, gloomy (at times) and peculiar"—St. Helena's Sound. It was as though a prehistoric monster had come out of the sea and with a Gargantuan mouth had bitten out of Carolina a jagged mouthful of some eight miles in length by four in width, leaving the wound ever raw, resentful, treacherous and dangerous. The waters of the Edisto, Ashepoo, Coosaw and Morgan Rivers, with their sand and silt, levied from a thousand miles of territory, emptied themselves into this unsettled inland sea. Their outgoing tides meeting the incoming flood from the ocean cause swirls, currents and counter-currents that deposit the sand brought down in shallow, banks and quicksands a few feet beneath the surface. However harmless and inviting to the mariner may appear these long, sensuous swells rolling in from the ocean, and suggesting the perpetual baths of the mermaid, death and destruction await the boat and crew who here may get aground, and not speedily release themselves. These smooth and deceptive swells, opposed by any obstacle to their onward motion, break into combers, white-crested and cruel, at their mercy. . . .

On Monday morning our medium-sized, six-oared family boat was brought to the landing. We thought it necessary only to have four oarsmen. . . .

The miserable hounds were to blame. As usual, when wanted, they could not be found, and when found, were so suspicious of something out of the ordinary run of their lives—sleeping and eating—that they could not be caught. Two of them we fooled over a plate. . . .

At length our load of men and beasts were aboard, the landing lined with spectators, white and colored, to bid us goodbye. The oars had made the first dip, the boat started, the song began, when old Flora, her suspicions still unallayed, made a spring overboard, swam for shore and made a dash for liberty. Overboard Jim had to follow, waded to shore and pursued the unwilling hound.

"Wer mex dawg lub ter do dat ting, ebery time we go for hunt coon an' ting haffer tu'n back fer dawg!" soliloquized one. At length Flora was captured and slammed down in the bottom of the boat under the seat. According to dog nature, she stood up and shook herself, when a cascade of spray deluged the man on the seat near. . . .

At length we started in earnest. The men gave their cleanest stroke, their most lugubrious "spiritual." In all my experience with colored oarsmen, I have never heard them sing (and singing is their chief inspiration) any but religious songs. True, these may be distorted, almost unrecognizable, and far of the mark, but nevertheless they are meant to be sacred hymns. To the waving of handkerchiefs and aprons on shore, the boat sprinted ahead. Turning a bend in the river, we moved out of sight. All "frills" were now cast aside and we settled down to the business of the day—reaching the promised land. In a half hour's time we were at the very outer mouth of the Edisto River. We began to feel the long, deep water swells rolling in from the ocean. The head of the boat would gently rise and as gently go down and meet the next incoming swell following. Having reached Bay Point, the most southern point of Edisto and immediately and directly opposite the most northern point of Hunting Island, we turned at right angles to the course we were running and faced the eight miles of water intervening, realizing that we would experience many an anxious thrill before we crossed it. The tide was very low, though the Sound was smooth, which lowness of the tide made it necessary to go farther out in the ocean than usual. We had to go outside some banks on which the swells were showing their teeth—shallowness of water the cause. We were about half over, the more numerous of the submerged banks had been left behind toward the Edisto side. Mostly deep waters were ahead of us. The mercury in the negro nature had begun to rise— danger always sobers them. They now began to pick at Kim, to kick the dogs under their feet, and to jolly each other. Bright visions of a big fire with oysters and "tetter" in abundance swam before their warmed up fancy, when, without warning, came the dreaded grating of the keel on sand, the boat quivering in every timber and coming to a standstill. "Overboard all!" was the immediate command, which none for an instant hesitated to obey. Overboard we went, up to our knees, seizing and pushing the boat, which, thus lightened, soon slid across into deeper waters, none too soon. One swell had broken over her, another may have swamped her. Pushing until the water reached our waists, we scrambled in as best we could, having "the devil take the hindmost" to hasten us. We were three miles from land. . . .

But the worst was over, deep water the rest of the way and the sun leaning toward the west hastened us toward our destination. . . . On the grating of the keel on shore, each oarsman grabbed a dog and tied him before anything else was done. Then came the joy of making camp. Jim was dispatched for wood, and to make a fire some hundred yards from the landing, and what with getting oysters and moving the stuff, night had settled down on us before we knew it. . . .

We were being tortured into a state of insensibility, when our sleepy senses were startled into wakefulness by "You Flora! Tex you mouf outen my bittle, you teifen debbil, you! Huccome you loose, meddle wit turrer man tings—you'se too gutlin!"[15] Then came a thud and a howl from Flora as she precipitately fled and hid under some bush. An unopened bunch of "coon" oysters is about the only article of food that a hound dog will not attempt to steal.

In the stillness that followed, one might hear the "plunk-plunk" of a coon's foot in the mud as it stole along the shore seeking its food, and the hard scratchy sound of its grinning mouth as it met a fellow coon on the same errand; then the sound of many waters as a number of porpoises succeeded in "cutting out" a school of mullet from its only protection—an oyster bank—driving them, frantic with fear, into a kind of cul de sac—any mud flat—and rushing them with such vim and impetuosity that their very momentum caused the projection of their whole body out of the water on to the soft surface of the mud, fish in mouth. With a shake of the head, like a sea lion, they swallowed the fish and slid back into the water, and repeated the charge again and again until the now frenzied fish, leaping high in the air over the drum fire of living artillery, scattered into deep water.

The night wore on, the fire burned down to coal and ashes, and as the small hours of the night arrived there encompassed the camp

[15] This Gullah dialect translated is as follows: "You Flora! Take your mouth out of my food (vitual), you thieving devil, you! How did you get loose? You meddle with another's thing's—you think too much of your guts!"

an atmosphere so cold, so cruel, so deadly that its effect was immediately felt by the sleepers, as shown by their restless movements and by the fact that they moaned in their sleep, particularly those of the race that revels in heat. None but those dwelling on the ocean can understand this phenomenon of nature. A mist seems to arise from the surface of the sea, is carried to land by a gentle breeze and paralyzes the functions of the body. It continues its benumbing work until near sun-up. If the night is comparatively warm, all its cold seems to concentrate in that period. If the night is cold, it grows intensely colder at that time.

This period of the night had arrived, and all began to feel it, particularly the negroes. One more sensitive than the others arose and started the fire, and, following his racial habit, looked at the eastern sky, then cried out, "Git up, Jim, and sta't buckra coffee. 'Seben Star' done rise an' he only two hour to sun. Dey hab only time fo git to duck pon, fo' he too late." By now we were all awake. The celestial timepiece of the negro was the constellation of the Pleiades. At certain hours, and practiced observation enables the negro by this means to approximate the time sufficiently for practical purposes.

Our first day on Hunting Island had begun. Having partaken of coffee, our first march was to the duck ponds, timing ourselves to arrive there just as day was breaking. We returned to camp after sun-up to find our breakfast awaiting us. Having partaken of this, the business of the day began, the deer drive. . . .

When we reached the beach, we saw four little objects in the distance barely visible. It proved to be the dogs near the edge of the water, occasionally giving a howl as they looked towards the sea. As we came near, we found the tracks of the deer as it entered the surf, but saw none coming out. After close inspection, we finally located a small object some two hundred yards beyond the breakers, sometimes stationary, sometimes moving about. Its movements were erratic, swimming straight away and then, rapidly, in a circle. Our "Paladin" of the hunt remarked softly to himself, "Its motions are very unusual. Deer generally keep still, and are not desirous of attracting attention. There must be something annoying it."

This proved to be only too true. Shortly after the deer was seen to spring partly out of the water and come down with a splash. Then followed such a commotion as caused quite an area to be whipped into foam. The deer soon sank. The waters quieted. Dr. Hazel simply remarked, "A shark got him!" then turned away toward camp.[16]

[16] Mikell, *op. cit.*, pp. 247-265.

THE WORLD OF NATURE

Among the most interesting visitors to the island shores are the great sea turtles (loggerheads) that come to the islands once each summer to lay their eggs. These great reptiles, weighing two and three hundred pounds, may be seen on the sandy beaches on moonlight nights in June. Sometimes their dark, rotund backs are visible above the water as they come bobbing over the swells and through the breakers. Then, scrambling up the smooth sandy strand, they laboriously work their way into the dry sand, where several hundred eggs, like ping-pong balls in size and shape, are deposited. The big female with her heavy flipper digs a hole about eighteen inches deep, crawls directly over it and deposits the eggs. Once they start laying they are not deterred by even a large gallery of onlookers armed with flashlights. Curious boys catch the eggs in their hands or hats as they drop from the big animal to the nest. After laying, the hole is carefully covered and tamped with the huge plastron; and then, having done her duty for a year, the loggerhead with much groaning and blowing pushes her way back into the foaming surf. I stepped upon the back of a large turtle one night on Edisto Beach, and she walked away as though I weighed nothing.

The sea turtle is protected by law, but unhappily the law is not observed. Thousands of eggs are destroyed annually by wanton hunters. They are sometimes boiled and served at table or used in baking cakes. Their taste is slightly fishy and unpalatable.

One resident on Edisto Beach, with the help of his children, gathers the eggs before destructive hunters find them and "plants" them in the deep warm sand in his front yard facing the sea. Here the young turtles hatch out unmolested and scramble back into the water.

The watchful eye of Thomas Ashe beheld these animals years ago as he explored the Carolina coast. His comments are interesting in this connection:

> The Tortoise, more commonly call'd by our West Indians the Turtle, are of three sorts, the Hawks-bill, whose Shell is that which we call the Turtle or Tortoise Shell; the Green Turtle, whose shell being thin is little regarded; but its Flesh is more esteemed than the Hawks-bill Tortoise: The Logger head Turtle, or Tortoise has neither good shell or Flesh, so is little minded or regarded. They

are a sort of creatures which live both on Land and Water. In the day usually keeping the Sea, swimming on the surface of the Water, in fair Weather delighting to expose themselves to the Sun, oftentimes falling asleep lying, as I have seen several times, without any Motion on the Waters, till disturbed by the approach of some Ship or Boat, being quick of hearing, they dive away. In the Night they often come ashore to feed and lay their Eggs in the Sand, which once covered, they leave to the Influence of the Sun, which in due time produces her young ones, which dig their passage out of the sand immediately making their way toward the Water. At this Season, when they most usually come ashore, which is in April, May and June, the Seamen or Turtlers, at some convenient distance watch their opportunity, getting between them and the Sea, turn them on their Backs, from whence they are unable ever to rise, by which means the Seamen or Turtlers turn 40 or 50 in a night, some of 2, 3, 400 weight; if they are far distant from the Harbor or Market to which they design to bring them, they kill, cutting them to pieces, which Salted they Barrel.[17]

Frogs have a wide geographical distribution, of course, and they are familiar objects almost everywhere, but in the coastal plain they seem to hold a place of dominance and to monopolize the otherwise quiet evenings with their noisy concerts. Every low place of the upland, every ditch or cypress pond is alive with them. There is little doubt that they are more boisterous and more in evidence in the low country than in the interior. As intimated before, the marsh frog strikes one with surprise with his impertinent, broad-open-daylight croaking, and is famous for his long leap.[18] The giant bullfrogs render their arias in deep bass notes, and are outrivaled in volume of sound only by the big horned owl, whose sudden outcry, startling in the extreme, reminds one of the shriek of an hysterical woman. No one can fall completely in love with the Carolina low country until he has secluded himself in some towering cypress swamp and listened to the innumerable wild voices of the night.

Colonel Higginson, of the Union Army, penned a graphic picture of the "magic of those haunted nights" near Port Royal when he served in 1863 as officer on picket duty along the banks of the Coosaw:

[17] Ashe, *op. cit.*, quoted in Salley, *op. cit.*, pp. 152-153.
[18] Rice, *op. cit.*, pp. 44 f.

THE WORLD OF NATURE 67

Night brought its own fascinations, more solitary and profound. The darker they were, the more clearly it was our duty to visit the pickets. The paths that had grown so familiar by day seemed a wholly new labyrinth by night; and every added shade of darkness seemed to shift and complicate them all anew, till at last man's skill grew utterly baffled, and the clew must be left to the instinct of the horse. Riding beneath the solemn starlight, or soft, gray mist, or densest blackness, the frogs croaking, the strange "chuck-will's-widow" droning his ominous note above my head, the mocking-bird dreaming in music, the great Southern fireflies rising to the tree-tops, or hovering close to the ground like glow-worms, till the horse raised his hoofs to avoid them; through pine woods and cypress, swamps, or past sullen brooks, or white tents, or the dimly seen huts of sleeping negroes; down to the glimmering shore, where black statues leaned against trees or stood alert in the pathways;— never, in all the days of my life, shall I forget the magic of those haunted nights.[19]

The hours of the night in a Southern swamp present a world entirely different from that of the day. Nocturnal animals, who shake off their sleep with the setting sun, constitute a race of beings which is little known to urban dwellers. The Negroes say, "De big 'possum walks jest fo' day." All night long 'coons range through the oozy marsh in search of mussels and small shell fish. The swamp is also the home of the muskrat, the alligator (especially in fresh water or slightly brackish marshes), cooters, innumerable birds, and, in the creeks, which rise and fall with the tide, many species of fish, not to speak of the big blue crabs, shrimp, and oysters. A lover of nature can spend many days observing the varied and vibrant life of a strip of apparently prosaic marsh. Among the frog family of the coast country are the giant bullfrog, previously referred to, the Southern bullfrog, leopard frog, tree frog, and marsh frog.[20] Of lizards, or skinks, there are the red, blue, and striped ones, erroneously called "scorpions."[21]

There are many stories which reveal the perennial interest of the Negro in the alligator. Much of Southern folklore and many charming stories of Negro life have "Buh Alligator" as a leading character. The Negroes' unusual interest in the 'gator is doubtless due to the hazards connected with his capture, for

---

[19] Higginson, *op. cit.*, pp. 140-141.
[20] Rice, *op. cit.*, p. 45.   [21] *Ibid.*, p. 46.

he is considered a "dang'us beast." They haunt all low-country streams and may be seen in summertime lying near the surface of the water with only their eyes and nose protruding. In former times their inroads upon hogs and other animals of the plantation were so frequent that they were considered a common enemy, and every effort was made to destroy them. The alligator has been so much in evidence in the swamp areas of South Carolina that, lowly and secretive as they are, they were observed and noted by early visitors to the coast. An early account states:

> There is in the mouth of their Rivers, or in Lakes near the Sea, a creature well known in the West Indies, call'd the Alligator or Crocodile, whose scaly Back is impenetrible, refusing a Musquet Bullet to pierce it, but under the Belly, that or an Arrow finds an easie Passage to destroy it; it lives both on Land and Water, being a voracious greedy Creature, devouring whatever it seizes on, Man only excepted, which on the Land it has not the courage to attacque, except when asleep or by surprize: In the Water it's more dangerous: it sometimes grows to a great length, from 16 to 20 foot, having a long Mouth, beset with sharp keen Teeth; the Body when full grown as large as a Horse, declining toward the Tail; it's slow in motion, and having no Joynt in the Vertebraes or Back Bone, but with its whole length is unable to turn, which renders it the less mischievous; yet Nature by Instinct has given most Creatures timely Caution to avoid them by their strong musky Smell, which at a considerable distance is perceivable, which the poor Cattle for their own Preservation make good use of: their Flesh cuts very white; the young ones are eatable; the Flesh of the older smells so strong of Musk, that it nauseates; their Stones at least so called, are commended for a rich, lasting perfume.[22]

The island region is noted for its excellent fishing, yet there has been very little commercial fishing among the island people, especially those of the islands lying south of Charleston. This fact is due, doubtless, to their former isolation and inaccessibility to markets. An early account gives a rather glowing description of varieties of fish found in this vicinity:

> Sturgeon, of whose Sounds Iceing-glass, of whose Roes Caviare are made: Mullet, a delicious sweet Fish, of whose Roes or Spawn Botargo is made: Whale, Salmond, Trouts, Bass, Drum, Catfish,

---

[22] Ashe, *op. cit.*, quoted in Salley, *op. cit.*, p. 155.

whose Head and glaring Eyes resemble a cat; it's esteem'd a very good Fish; it hath a sharp thorny Bone on its Back, which strikes at such as endeavor to take it: which by Seamen is held venemous; yet I saw one of our Seamen, the back of whose Hand was pierced with it, yet no poysonous Symptoms of Inflammation or Rancor appear'd on the Wound, which quickly heal'd, that I concluded it was either false, or that of this Fish there were more kinds than one: Plaice, Eels, Crabs, Prawns twice as large as ours in England: Oysters of an Oblong or Oval form; their number inexaustible; a man may easily gather more in a day than he can well eat in a year; some of which are margiritiferous, yielding bright round Oriental Pearl.[28]

On February 20, 1863, a Northern teacher in the Port Royal area wrote home of her observations of Negroes who were seining off one of the islands. The planters had all left this region because of the occupation of Union troops, and the only whites present, other than the soldiers, were the teachers from New England and the government agents. Part of the letter is as follows:

Feb. 20. Today all the people were on the Bay "drawing seine" when I came out of morning school, and as that is a process I have wished to see I ran down to the beach myself between whiles. Here was a droll enough scene indeed. They had made one "drawing" and were just casting the seine again as I walked along for half a mile toward the drum-hole. The shell-banks, which are exposed at low tide, were fringed with small children with baskets and bags which they were filling with oysters and conchs. Rose followed me as guide and protector, jabbering away in her outlandish fashion to my great entertainment, and was very much afraid that the oyster-shells, over which she walked with impunity with bare feet, would cut up my heavy leather boots. I could go out to the very edge of one of these curious shell-banks, and the seine was drawn up almost at my feet. The net was laid on a boat which was hauled out into the water by the men, who were up to their waists, then dropped along its full length, which is very great, and gradually hauled in shore again with two or three bushels of fish in it, and any number of crabs, which the children pick up very carefully and fling ashore. There were about thirty men, and you would have thought from the noise and talking that it was a great fire in the country, with no head to the engine companies and every man giving orders. They were good-natured as possible, but sometimes their gibberish

[28] *Ibid.*, p. 152.

sounds as if they were scolding. The boys, with their pantaloons, or what answer for such, rolled up to their knees, were hauling at the rope or picking up the crabs and making them catch hold of each other till they had a long string of them. Another mode of proceeding with them—for a crab-bite is a pretty serious thing—is to hold an oyster-shell out, which they grab, and then with a quick shake the claw is broken off, and they are harmless. A large bass having been taken in the haul I witnessed, it was laid at my feet for my acceptance, and then, the girls following, most of the boys staying to see the third drawing, I wended my way back to school.[24]

An apparently accurate account of the great variety and quantity of sea food around Edisto Island is given by a Reverend Mr. McLeod, who was a resident minister there in 1800 and who wrote an account to Dr. Ramsay of Charleston, the distinguished historian of South Carolina:

The creeks, rivers, and seas which indent and surround the Island, furnish at different and appropriate seasons of the year, a great variety of excellent fish—as the larger drum, the small black drum, bass, rock-fish, sheephead, cavallie, bonnetta, salmon-trout, yellow-tail, yellow-fin trout, whiting and mullet in great profusion, blackfish, ale-wife, croaker, plaice, flounder, skate, pike, shad, and catfish, and many others, suitable for the table. Porpoise and sharks frequent the creeks and surrounding waters. Some of the latter are seen and caught of an enormous size. They are considered as just objects of terror by the negroes. And yet, although the fishermen continue hours together waist deep in water, and have often the misfortune of hooking them, they escape with impunity. Of shellfish, the turtle is sometimes to be met with, but not in any considerable number of variety. Terrapin, land, stone, and sea crabs, muscles, clams, conchs, shrimps, are common and abundant; and the oysters of the creeks that intersect the sea-bays, below described, are equal in flavor, perhaps to any found on the American shores.[25]

Perhaps the greatest fisherman and sportsman South Carolina ever produced was William Elliott, a planter of note, living near Port Royal. He was born in Beaufort in 1788, was graduated from Harvard College, managed large estates in his home district, wrote fluently and brilliantly on political and agricul-

[24] Pearson, *op. cit.*, pp. 156-157.
[25] Ramsay, *op. cit.*, II, 279, Appendix No. 1, "A Statistical Account of Edisto Island, by Donald McLeod."

THE WORLD OF NATURE

tural subjects, and became widely known. He died in Charleston, South Carolina, in 1863.[26] His most beloved publication is a volume entitled *Carolina Sports by Land and Water*, published in Charleston in 1846, being in the main a collection of articles written over a period of years for a Charleston newspaper. Included, also, are excerpts from his journal describing hunting and fishing exploits in this region.

The most thrilling incidents of this volume are the descriptions of the capture of devilfish in Port Royal Harbor. In the 1840's this was a favorite sport in that particular vicinity. The big devilfish, of the ray family, weigh from three to five tons and annually come in schools off Bay Point and Hilton Head. Dr. J. O. La Gorce, associate editor of the *National Geographic Magazine*, who assisted in capturing a large devilfish near the Isle of Bimini in the Gulf Stream a few years ago, has a story of its capture in *The Book of Fishes*,[27] in which the technique used is remarkably similar to that used by the planters a hundred years ago. The modern fisherman goes after his quarry in a motor launch, while in the past oared boats, propelled by slaves, were employed.

The sport has been likened to miniature whaling: harpoons are used, and when these strike, the big fish takes everybody for a ride out to the open sea. Negroes evidently enjoyed these exciting diversions. They had a part in everyone of them, and, when they got back to the slave quarters, they must have given vivid accounts of their exploits to eager listeners.

In contrast with this recent account of an almost extinct sport, is the record made by William Elliott on "Monday, 24th June," 1844:

Wind very fresh at northeast. Mr. W. Cuthbert came on board, and we sailed for Hilton Head, and reached the avenue an hour before high water. Saw a devil-fish at the landing and gave chase, but to no purpose—he was apparently feeding, and would show his wings only at long intervals, and for a few seconds at a time; so that before the boat could reach the spot he was gone. He sometimes came very close to the beach (I should say in five feet water), but would sheer off at the approach of the boat. After a

---
[26] Maurice Garland Fulton, *Southern Life in Southern Literature* (Boston, 1917), p. 19.
[27] *The Book of Fishes* (Washington: The National Geographic Society, 1924), pp. 186-194.

fruitless pursuit of an hour, we gave him up, and cruised up to the mouth of Skull Creek. Saw nothing—returned to the landing, and visited the cotton-field. It was now four o'clock, P. M., and a full quarter ebb. In a last hope to see them, loitered a while on the beach, when, just as we were making ready to get on board, a shoal of devil-fish came sweeping along the beach, travelling rapidly downward with the tide, and showing themselves more freely than any I had seen this year. I pushed at one that showed his back fairly above water, as he swam; but he sank just before I reached him, and I drove down the harpoon at a venture. He had a narrow escape, for the staff struck him. At this moment, three showed themselves below and one above. I pushed for the latter, and when I approached the spot, I saw the water boiling up like a caldron—from which sign I knew that the fish was throwing his somersets below the surface (in the way which is so peculiar to them). Making the oarsmen check the headway with their oars, I looked anxiously for a view, when, unexpectedly, I saw the white of his belly far beneath the water, and quite away toward the stern. He was thus behind me, but wheeling suddenly toward the right, I pitched the harpoon at him, across the oars, and felt a sensation of surprise, as well as pleasure, in finding that I had struck him. The fish dashed out violently for the channel, and we payed him out thirty fathoms of rope, until, headway being given to the boat, we brought him to a dead pull: and now his motions were very erratic; unlike some that I had before struck, he did not take a direct course for the sea, but sometimes drew the boat against the tide—then suddenly turned and ran directly toward us, so as to give slack line. I inferred from these signs, that he was mortally hurt. As often as he approached the Middle Bank, and shoaled the water, he drew off in alarm, and would not cross it until he had got to its tail; his course was then for Paris Bank, which suiting well with our intention to land him, if we could, at Bay point, we did not interrupt. About this time he came to the surface without being pulled, and showed great distress —and we resolved, then, to draw upon him and get a second harpoon planted. It was after various fruitless efforts, and by shortening the rope as far as we prudently could, that we at length drew him so far up, that the dark shadow of his body was indistinctly seen beneath. The second harpoon was now driven, and the gush of blood to the surface, showed that it had done its work. We now drew mainly on this second, leaving only a moderate strain on the first—and after a few convulsive runs, brought him up helplessly to the surface, and with a spear dispatched him outright. With a hatchet we now cut a hole in one of his feelers, and inserting a rope, passed it to the stern, drawing solely on this, so that the resistance of the fish through the water should be as small as practicable. The wind was now due east, and moderately fresh; we raised both sails, and, helped at the same time by the oars, made some way in our tedious progress of towing our prize to land. At this time, espied a boat beating down from Beaufort, and on signalizing her, she proved to be that of Col. De Treville, then on his way to Bay Point. His offer of assistance was accepted, and a tow line being passed to his boat, we landed our fish at the Point exactly at sunset. This fish measured sixteen feet across, which I suppose to be the medium size of those that visit our waters. The first harpoon had struck it near the centre of the belly—had pierced the liver, and passed nearly through to the back. The second had passed from the back into his lungs or gills—so that the full power of so large a fish was never fairly exerted against us. Had the same fish been struck in the wings, or other parts not vital, his capture would have been uncertain, and would at any rate have cost us the work of many hours.

I suppose the shoal of devil-fish was a large one; the third which appeared we struck at—the fourth we harpooned—and as we were rapidly drawing off from the shore, a fifth was seen. How many were still behind us, we had not leisure to observe; but conjecture this was the advance guard of the column.[28]

I made no further notes of my excursions at the time, but will add that prior to my departure for the North, in July of this year, I had struck seven of these fish, and captured four.

In 1845, these sports were renewed; but under aspects that offer but little novelty to the reader. The devil-fish were reported to be in force in Broad River, during the month of June; but no expeditions were planned against them during that month. Early in July, E. B. M., already known to the reader of these "sports," made a cruise after them, and, on the second day's search, succeeded in capturing one. On Wednesday, the 16th, I made my first venture—saw five and captured one. On the next day, being joined by Mr. M., we sallied out in our respective boats, and found them in force. I think we could not have seen fewer than fifteen. But the weather was unpropitious, and though we struck five, and probably killed the greater part of them, we could not affirm with certainty that we had captured one. Once, during the day, I enjoyed a solitary run, and twice a run in company—both boats being engaged at the same time, and the fish running in the same parallel. Two hours before nightfall, each boat then having a fish in tow, we were overtaken by a perfect tempest. A black and fearful-looking thunder-cloud lay brooding over the bay, and seemed to descend to the

[28] William Elliott, *Carolina Sports by Land and Water* (Charleston, 1846; London, 1847), pp. 68-72.

very waters, and be commingled with them. It was extreme rashness, in our undecked boats, to brave the anger of the storm; and, by a simultaneous movement, we resolved to force up our fish, so as either to lose or capture them before it should burst upon us. The harpoon of my consort tore out when the fish was drawn to the surface, and almost in "articulo mortis." In my own case, the fish, struck through the branchial processes, and evidently at his last gasp, snapt asunder the harpoon and escaped, leaving the barb in his body. Thus released from our fish (for in all my service I have never severed a rope or voluntarily disengaged myself from a devil-fish), we lifted a hand's breadth of canvas to the gust which was now upon us, and made our escape to the shore. We had capital and very exciting sport; but considered our victory somewhat incomplete, because we had not carried off the body of the slain.[29]

Of Dr. M. G. Elliott, a physician of Beaufort and a direct descendant of William Elliott of sports fame, I recently made some inquiries in regard to the possible presence of devilfish in Port Royal waters at the present time. He does not think that they visit these waters any more. He informed me that the last devilfish caught in the waters thereabout was taken in 1883 by his two brothers. It was on this wise: there were several long piers extending out into the river, having been built in connection with his father's phosphate works. A great devilfish entangled itself among the pilings of one of the piers and was securely fastened. The huge fish created a great commotion and soon attracted the attention of near-by workmen. The boys took an old saber which had been especially sharpened for stabbing shark and drove it into the body of the devilfish. With a great lunge it disentangled itself and for a moment was free. In its frenzied effort to escape the great fish drove into the other pier and became again ensnared in its pilings. It was there that repeated stabs of the saber finally conquered the giant. The water was crimson with the great amount of blood which flowed from the wounds. The fish was then dragged ashore. Dr. Elliott, who was present, saw the fish after it had been landed.

Next in excitement to harpooning the devilfish was the sport connected with drumfishing. The drumfish, which abounded in island waters in the ante-bellum period, averaged three feet

[29] *Ibid.*, pp. 72-74.

THE WORLD OF NATURE 75

in length and weighed about forty pounds. Notations from the Pinckney journal, in a previous chapter, indicate their use on the slave plantations. They constituted a considerable source of food supply at certain seasons and must have added to the plain ration of the average slave, a relish which he deeply regarded.

An account of drumfishing explains that boats impelled by oars and sails were necessary and at least fifteen fathoms of rope to the grapnel. The line must be thirty fathoms long and furnished with two pounds of lead distributed in movable sinkers. For bait, crabs, clams, and prawn were used.[30]

> Generally speaking, you are occupied five minutes in taking a fish; but if the tide be strong and the fish large, your sport may last fifteen. . . . As a general rule, with five lines in your boat, you may count on fifteen or twenty fish as the result of a day's sport. Occasionally, you have memorable luck—sixty-three were taken during the present season, by a boat with seven lines, and I once knew a boat with ten lines to take as many as ninety-six; the best success I have met with personally was to take forty to three lines —eighteen fish fell to my share of the sport; my two oarsmen took the remainder. Thirty fish were all the boat could conveniently contain; her gunwale was but a few inches above the water, and we slung the ten (which were "de trop") alongside by a rope. In this situation we were attacked by sharks. These grim companions would range up alongside, and make a rush at them to cut them off, and we were compelled to beat them off with boat-hooks. A little more boldness in their attack, and we must have fallen victims; for a single blow from their tails would have filled our overloaded boat. . . . In the sport of this day, my gloves were torn into shreds by the friction of the line, and my fingers so blistered by the severity of the play that I was incapable of renewing my sport for several days.[31]

In closing this chapter I shall let an old resident of Beaufort speak: the Reverend Robert Woodward Barnwell, a retired Episcopal minister now living in the beautiful memories of a boyhood spent in this quaint village, has written a small volume of poems about boats and books of Beaufort, which gives a truer picture of its ante-bellum life than many pages of prose could possibly do. He says of his native village:

[30] *Ibid.*, p. 126.   [31] *Ibid.*, pp. 127-128.

A Town's Peculiarity

Books and the boats I sing:
And this old town of note.
Where each man had a library
And every man a boat.

Leisure and island homes!
For them old Homer wrote,
And oft they went to Odysseus
To learn about a boat.

They'd sit upon a balcony
With Gibbon, Hume, and Grote,
And then they'd take some exercise
With six oars and a boat.

Plantations all had muscled crews,
A landing and a boat.
Each lad was taught to sail and row,
But also how to quote.

On summer morns they loved to read;
On summer eves to float.
Woe to the man who had no books,
Or chanced to have no boat!

For Beaufort was a strange old town
In those days remote:
One had to have a library;
One loved to have a boat.[32]

---

[32] Robert Woodward Barnwell, Sr., *Dawn at Daufuskie and Other Poems* (Florence, S. C., 1936), p. 52. An enlarged edition of this book was published under the title, *Realities and Imaginations* (Florence, S. C., 1938).

CHAPTER V

THE BLACK PEOPLE

*Down in de valley on my praying knees,
Lawd I can't help from cryin' sometime.*

PERHAPS THE purest type of Gullah to be found anywhere is the Negro of Edisto Island. Edisto, one of the larger islands of the Carolina coast, harbors many descendants of slaves, who, because of their great numbers and the resulting social life, have been content to spend the years in almost complete isolation from the outside world. Edisto differs from St. Helena in that the latter, though with equal if not larger population, has been influenced by the presence of a Negro school which has kept its doors open to the children of the island since "freedom" and has influenced the people in ways which have lifted them from their former primitive estate to a higher culture. The Negroes of Edisto have in a peculiar way lived their own lives and have been little influenced by the few white people living on the island. Whatever influence the whites have had upon them since slavery days has been largely economic. In politics, in religion, and in social affairs, they have been and are as distant as the poles. In the light of this statement it may seem strange to outsiders that there should be many desirable contacts between the races, even agreeable and friendly in their nature; these fine relationships exist, but they must be conducted according to the code, and it must be remembered that a rigid pattern is set for the Negro's conduct. He must be "in his place," and, so long as this rule is observed, all goes well. Negroes and whites trade with each other in the stores, but they never sit down together at meals. That would be a violation of the code. Negroes never participate in the social affairs of the whites as companions, but in reality they bear a most intimate relation to all white social life. A colored cook, for instance, invariably prepares the food, colored men wait on table, and colored boys bring wood and tend the fires. But all of this is done according to the code: they are servants. It may seem strange, but the relationships are for the most part very agreeable. Each has respect for the other in his sphere. Again, it may be surprising to the outsider to find that between individuals, colored and white, there are feelings of genuine devotion —feelings which find expression in conduct of a high and praiseworthy nature; but this is true. Someone has said that the South loves the individual Negro and hates the race, while the North loves the race and hates the individual. There is at least some truth in the statement.

The Negroes of Edisto, as of most of the other islands, are almost all black. One rarely sees a mulatto. There is perhaps no place in this country where a purer African stock may be found. Their features are decidedly negroid, and they think less in terms of the white man than perhaps in any other section of the country. They have built up for themselves a culture of their own, and because of their separateness constitute one of the most interesting social groups in the United States.

There is something of mystery and elusiveness about Negro personality. A white man who tries to understand the Negro is constantly baffled by the unfathomable workings of the Negro's mind. Most Southern people think they understand the Negro; I am sure they understand him only in part. There are vast areas in the background of his thinking which are never revealed to the white man. Ambrose Gonzales, who perhaps knew the Gullah better than anyone who has undertaken to write about him, observed: ". . . of all the inscrutable peoples of the Eastern world, none is more secretive than the negro, nor any so puzzling to the psychologist, for while it is easy to know that deceit lurks behind the mask of engaging frankness with which he seeks to disarm those who doubt him, the exact nature of the deceit can seldom be discerned."[1]

Some students of Negro life feel that much of this enigmatic element of Negro personality is directly connected with his forgotten experiences in the jungles of Africa. It is passing strange that he should have left behind him much of the religion and language and the many customs of his tropical home and that he brought with him those subconscious elements which influence his life though he knows not from whence they come.

[1] Review of Charles C. Jones, *Negro Myths from the Georgia Coast*, quoted in Reed Smith, *Gullah* (Columbia, S. C., 1926), p. 12, n. 2.

THE BLACK PEOPLE 79

Even the Negro himself has not fathomed the depth of his soul. Students among the white race have undertaken this task, but it still remains for some black man to tell effectively and truly the vivid story of his people in their exodus from Africa to America.

The late Stanhope Sams, literary editor of *The State* (Columbia, South Carolina), wrote in regard to the Negro's past:

There is a dark region beyond the mind and soul of the Negro of the slave plantations that may never be explored. No trained and well equipped psychologist, so far as I know, has ever attempted this magnificent research. Certainly none of the Negro students of the race has seemed to get even so near as white students have approached. So far as I have ever seen in their writings or heard in their speech, Dubois and Booker Washington did not enter that primeval jungle. And it is not possible now, perhaps, to "restore" this primitive jungle race and lore. It would be a far more difficult task than the restoration of Kish or Ur, or to bring back to earth some semblance of the mysterious Sumerians. There we have at least a tablet or stele or monument to help; but we must decipher the Negro of the days of the Pharaohs and of Carthage and of the impenetrable backward and abysm of time that stretches like an uncharted sea behind the African Negro from the modern Negro in America or Africa.

At all events, as it seems, the contact he must have had with cultured Egyptians and Carthaginians left no enduring record. It is possible—despite some vague beginnings of civilization in certain parts of Black Africa—that the only lasting betterment in conditions the Negro has yet known or held had been received during and since he became a slave in the Southern States.

It remains an alluring, but a chimerical adventure—this attempt to learn what the Negro was before his contact with us.

On their own part, the Negroes seem to have formed a conspiracy of silence. Possibly they suffered too profoundly, were hurt too bitterly to tell us their own story. They preferred, doubtless, to leave it behind them in the engulfing and obliterating jungle. They must have known, must have remembered, those first slaves, and they have always had the genius for story-telling and singing. Yet they tell us no stories that reveal their previous march, sing no songs— except with borrowed music—and fill their mythologies with the animals and beings of the world that bound and enslaved them.[2]

[2] Smith, *op. cit.*, p. 12.

As has already been remarked, the white man does not know the Negro so well as he thinks he does. He knows the side the Negro turns to him, but this is not always the true Negro. It is only that side which the Negro wishes to reveal. This mystifying quality of personality is due, not only to the subtleties of his African background, but to the fact of slavery. Wherever one race dominates another, the subject people always cultivate attitudes of secretiveness and duplicity as protective measures.

As a result, the Negro in his relations to white people is a dual personality. He has two fronts, one for the white man and one for his own race. It is obvious that the real Negro is to be found in the latter. His most genuine self is that which finds expression among his own when no white men are around. It would doubtless be very revealing to many Southerners to know what is said and done in the lodges and secret societies of Negroes.

The Negro of the Deep South is a most tolerant and amiable fellow. He usually says what his white friend wants him to say, and he acts in a way that will be agreeable to his white friend. One of the ingratiating traits of the Negro is his desire to please; he has learned throughout the years of oppression the wisdom of being agreeable.

The people of the South can never forget the loyalty of the Negroes during the trying experiences of the Civil War. Reference has often been made to their devotion and chivalry toward white women and children whose husbands and fathers were in the army and away from home. This fact alone, if it were more generally known by white and colored youth, could be made one of the rallying points round which the races might get rid of some of their troubles. It may seem strange to people who do not know the Negro that he should not have turned his hand against the homes that enslaved him, but they do not know the innate kindness of the Negro heart. He is the most tolerant being on earth, and his good will knows no bounds. Many of them followed the Northern troops very reluctantly, and thousands returned to the plantations to take up the broken threads of living, with their former owners, in an attempt to rebuild the devastated South. Even during the trying experiences of the Reconstruction, the Negro's conduct for the most part was laudable. The minority, influenced by carpetbaggers and scalawags, tried to attain the impossible, complete citizenship and the control of government. Several years ago Ambrose Gonzales wrote: "But of one thing the white man of the slaveholding class has always been sure—in war or peace, under slavery or freedom, the good intent of the Negroes toward the persons of those to whom they once belonged. Even during the tense days of Reconstruction, in communities where they swarmed a hundred to one, the white man slept in absolute security with unlocked doors, however securely he nailed up his corn-crib and his smokehouse!"[3]

Not only did the wartime slave stand guard over the fortunes of his master's household during times of stress, but he was very close to the white family, of which he felt himself a part. This was not true, of course, of all the Negroes, for some of them had ungenerous masters, but there was a sufficiently large number of them to add strength to the foundation upon which a better racial understanding might be built. A Southern man, born and reared in the Gullah country, writes as follows: "Under the almost feudal system of the Low country plantations, the devotion of the old family slaves to their masters was comparable to, but even stronger than, that of servant to master in the great English families, wherein for generations the most cordial and confidential relations existed, for if the slave belonged to the master, the master likewise belonged to the slave, who prided himself upon his master's family and upheld its traditions so stoutly that old servants sometimes questioned the fitness of a match under consideration for a son or daughter of the 'Big House,' objecting to the alliance as unsuitable for a member of 'our family.' "[4]

Professor Joseph Le Conte, the eminent geologist, was at the time of the war connected with the University of South Carolina, then South Carolina College. His special service to the Confederacy was in the manufacture of medicines in the city of Columbia for the army. Upon the entrance of Sherman's army Professor Le Conte left the city to avoid arrest and imprisonment. Of his narrow escapes from Union soldiers he has left the following account: "I learned in the morning

[3] Ambrose Elliott Gonzales, *The Captain* (Columbia, S. C., 1924), p. xi.
[4] *Ibid.*, p. xii.

that three of the negroes, fearing that the Yankees might have heard of my being in the house, had patrolled the roads all night while I peacefully slept. The same faithful and affectionate fellows before daybreak conducted me to the hiding-place they had selected, a dry spot in the midst of a strip of thick, swampy ground surrounded by a ten-foot canal."[5]

In Fort Mill, South Carolina, there was set aside by the town authorities, years ago, a small park in memory of the Confederate soldiers. In it is the familiar monument to the Confederate dead, an object so typical of the South that it has become a part of the landscape of every county seat. But in this park there is another monument, doubtless unique—a monument to the Negro slaves. This stone was erected by Captain Samuel E. White, a Confederate soldier, "in grateful memory of earlier days," with the names of ten slaves engraved thereon. Carved in the stone on one side is an old Negro woman seated on the steps of a large plantation house, holding in her arms a white child; on another is a Negro man, laborer, scythe in hand, seated on a log in the shade of a tree, by the edge of a field of shocked grain. The inscription reads:

> Dedicated to
> The Faithful Slaves
> Who, Loyal to a Sacred Trust,
> Toiled for the Support
> Of the Army, with Matchless
> Devotion, and with Sterling
> Fidelity Guarded our Defenseless
> Homes, Women and Children, During
> The Struggle for the Principles
> Of Our Confederate States of America.

Strange as it may seem, the Negro is by nature an aristocrat. Evidence of this is found among his own people today in the social cleavages so rigidly adhered to. He has always been quick to sense real worth, and, when he finds it, he is willing to recognize it in either race. His chief aversion in ante-bellum days, as now, was what he very aptly termed "po' white trash," or, in the Gullah country, "po' buckruh." Mr. Gonzales comments on this as follows: "As long as the older Negroes lasted,

---

[5] Joseph Le Conte, *Autobiography* (New York, 1903), p. 192.

during the first twenty-five or thirty years of freedom, the *nouveaux-riches*—'the butcher, the baker, the candlestick maker,' and the corner-shopkeeper who had come into the ownership of landed property—while treated with respect, were held rather lightly by the old slaves, as interlopers, who, through the fortunes of war, or the misfortunes of Reconstruction, had come into plantations formerly owned by aristocrats, and between the old and the new—whom behind their backs the Negroes referred to as po'-buckruh—the line was sharply drawn."[6]

One of the interesting traits of the Gullah is his duplicity and kindly insincerity. He will frequently answer "Yes" when he means "No." If you ask him if he will mow your grass tomorrow, he will reply, "Yes, sir," when he knows full well that he is not coming. But it is better to be agreeable, not to offend. To decline to do so may stir up complications. The fact that you are sorely disappointed next day when he does not show up has little effect upon his conscience. This purely defense mechanism is a relic of slavery days.

I once met two diffident Negro boys on Port Royal Island at the old "tabby" fort, who were determined not to reveal themselves to the stranger who wanted to engage them in conversation. They were the personification of timidity and meekness and would reply only in agreeable monosyllables. The conversation was as follows:

"Are you all brothers?"
"Yaas, suh."
"Do you go to school?"
"Yaas, suh."
"Did you study about this old fort?"
"Yaas, suh."
"Is this a cassena bush?"
"Yaas, suh."

Then, turning to them, I said, "Every time I ask you a question you say, 'Yaas, sir' "; and their reply was a meek "Yaas, suh."

One of the cleverest instances of kindly duplicity and the Negro's instinct to conceal his inmost thoughts is given by Mrs. Stephen Elliott Puckette, formerly of Edisto Island. With keen insight into the mental workings of the island Negroes, she writes:

[6] Gonzales, *The Captain*, p. ix.

The black peasants of Edisto are all more or less mind-readers and born actors. They have self-preservation always in mind and will never commit themselves to more than they deem safe. They can be exasperating as well as subtle in withholding information that they think may get themselves or their friends into trouble. Not long ago I drove down a miserable side road over an almost trackless field, and, fatigued, I came at last to a little cabin. I soon found out it was not the house I was looking for, and I asked the man in the yard if he knew where Liza Bailey lived. The man looked dreadfully puzzled, as if I had certainly put a hard one to him that time.

"Liza Bailey? Lemme study hard. You mean you want to know if she live in dis house?" and as he asked this question he looked too stupid.

"No," I said, "I merely want to know if she lives down this way."

"No, Mam. Not as I knows of. I don't t'ink she live down dis way." And he looked even stupider.

"Surely you ought to know who your neighbors are," I said, rather put out by his pretense. Still most politely but with a wilful dumbness he continued to dodge my question. I realized I could get no further in this affair unless I revealed what my interest in Liza was, so I said:

"It is too bad you can't help me out. If I could have found Liza, I should have offered her a job. I need a good cook and I was told that Liza Bailey was just the person I needed." That was the key. The man's whole face took on understanding at once; he brightened up.

"Oh," he exclaimed, laughing at his mistake. "So it been Liza Bailey you want to talk wid, Mam, Liza Bailey what cook out. Lordy, Lordy, I reckon I does know where dat Liza live. I sho neber know, Mam, it been Liza Bailey what cook out dat you is want to find. You mus' 'scuse me, Mam. I's too heavy. Now all you's got to do is just keep on dis same road and right down yander on de far side of dat myrtle thicket, de fust house you come to as you pass de bresh, dat is Liza Bailey house, Mam."[7]

Traveling along any of the roads crossing the islands, one sees the landscape here and there dotted with small Negro houses. Many of these Negroes own their homes and the little tract of land adjoining. A kindly old Negro woman was hoeing grass out of her cotton patch, and with considerable grace

[7] *The State*, Columbia, S. C., Dec. 10, 1933.

and kindness answered all of my questions one day. She owned her farm, consisting of "t'ree acres and a tass," had "heired" it, but knew nothing else about its former ownership. Many of these small tracts came into the Negroes' possession through confiscation proceedings during the Civil War. On Edisto Island most of the houses are unpainted and present a drab, dilapidated appearance. Among the more prosperous Negroes one finds whitewashed cabins with blue board shutters. Some think that originally blue was used because it was a charm color and would keep evil spirits out of the house. I am quite sure that, even though this be true, many Negroes who thus paint their shutters do not know the origin of the custom; they do so simply as a matter of habit, and, as one told me, because it is pretty. The island Negro usually builds his house out in an open field. He seems to care little for shade and makes no effort to plant trees which would protect him from the vertical rays of the summer sun. Occasionally there is a live oak near his door, but it seems to be there by chance. The tall palmetto is found in his yard, and on occasion the giant yucca, with its tall spike of creamy-white blossoms, adds a touch of undesigned beauty to his humble abode. In front of the most unlivable huts I have noticed, growing near the rickety front porch, a graceful pink crape myrtle. Thus are beauty and shabbiness blended. Nature has done much for this country, but man little.

A queer custom among the Negroes is to stake out the pig. A rope is tied around his neck and he is put out to graze like the cow. Milk cows are scarce and those that are to be seen have shriveled udders and a lean and hungry look. Bull calves are valued, for the owner has in each a potential work animal. The patient ox serves both as mount and draft animal. Like the pig, the ox is staked out on tough grass and appears to subsist on a ration that would be wholly inadequate for the average respectable cow.

Sometimes an islander chooses to build his house on one of the many inlets that interlace the region. At low tide his boat is high and dry, but at the flood he paddles down the tortuous course in search of fish and oysters. Like the cave man, he is careless about the disposal of his waste. Oyster shells growing white with age, are found about all Negro yards, and piles of them under their houses.

A well, usually equipped with a hand pump, is found in the level sandy yard. Most of these wells are shallow, with water of doubtful purity. Ground-itch and hookworm are an abomination among the children.

There are no screens in the windows. It would be of little use to cover these openings, for many another hole would furnish ingress for the ever-present 'skeeters of the summer season. Instead of screens, smudge pots are used and kept burning all night. The familiar outdoor fire, luring to its blaze swarms of insects and sending off black smoke from pine knots, serves as another substitute for screens. Fortunately, many Negroes are immune to malaria because the law of the survival of the fittest operates among them. In the ante-bellum era, as has been stated, the white people of the plantation, except the overseer and his family, retired to the beaches or to the sand ridges of the pinelands for the dreaded summer period. Today it is the white man, largely, who buys the chill tonic, advertised on every barn and roadside fence.

On Edisto Island Negro children do not play games to any great extent. On St. Helena the teachers of Penn School found the same situation; one of the first things they did in dealing with the children was to teach them to play. On Edisto, children are nearly always found about the yards, but they just sit, and appear rarely to be engaged in games. Negro boys told me that they sometimes played baseball, but I saw no signs of it. Around the country stores boys are always found. There they sit and talk and whittle, engage in laughter, and enjoy the sharp thrusts of good-humored irony directed toward each other.

Aesthetically the Negro child of the sea-island country has little chance. The only pictures he sees are those from newspapers pasted on the wall, and their purpose is purely utilitarian: they keep the wind out. There is nothing that would stir him to a sense of the beautiful other than the sky, the sea, and the placid marsh; and these are not always available to little children who must stay about the house. The Negro cabin does not occupy artistically chosen situations like the big house of the plantation, but is usually in some unlovely spot.

The Gullah Negro is noted for his inborn courtesy. However queer his manners, and especially his dialect, he is always

THE BLACK PEOPLE

the gentleman. He has little use for grammar, but his language is that of courtesy. The only living slave of my grandfather is named Charles Baxter. He is one of the most "mannerable" men I ever knew. His snow-white hair, his ingratiating smile, and his courtly bearing would set him apart in any company. His use of the English language is very faulty, but is picturesque and delightful. I should be willing to place Charles in any social group; with his innate graciousness and human interest, he immediately wins his way into the hearts of those who meet him. On my last visit to him he impressed me with the fact that he had not been one of the field hands in the olden days, but was a house servant, my grandmother's waitin' boy. I was particularly amused at his recital of a fact I already knew, to-wit, that he had been my uncle's body servant or valet in the Confederate Army. It is amusing now to look back upon the romantic and sporting attitude that characterized many men who threw themselves into this most romantic yet horrible war. It should be said that the soldier referred to was a surgeon, and doubtless surgeons needed a servant. This old Negro, like the last leaf on the tree in the spring, proudly wears his Confederate Cross and collects from his white friends many a dime when he comes to town on Saturdays. His status in the Confederate Army has become a financial asset in his old age, for he not only reaps a reward because of the badge, but also draws a small pension from the state of South Carolina, along with the few remaining veterans of the Civil War.

It is worth a long trip to see this lovely old character on state occasions. State occasions are those times when he dresses up on Saturdays and Sundays. One would hardly think that a derby hat would go along with a cotton mule; but in this guise Charles comes to the village. His exact age has been lost in the limbo of slavery days; he can only estimate it. But one thing is certain, he was a body servant in the Confederate Army in 1861, and anyone can make his own computation of the years.

Negroes of the low country are very generous people. When a visit is made to their homes, they are nearly always disposed to make some little gift to their white friends. The most appropriate gift is a handful of eggs. I was once visiting the humble home of a Negro tenant in the Carolina coastal plain; after I received much advice and an extemporaneous sermon (this friend was a local preacher), he insisted that I accept a gift. The present was to be nice fresh eggs. He rummaged around through all the hen's nests in the yard, the lot, and the stable, and brought forth at least a dozen pearly white eggs. I thanked him as best I could and begged him to keep them, especially as I was several hundred miles from home and could not safely convey them. Against all my most polite protestations he prevailed upon me to take them. There was nothing else to do but accept. This I did with my best thanks and gave them away at my first opportunity.

This practice of giving eggs is evidently a very old one among the Negroes of the Deep South. I find a goodly number of references to this practice in the records dating back to Civil War days. An old letter, written to New England from the islands around Port Royal, says: "Louisa came up to give me two eggs carefully wrapped in her apron. This makes over a dozen brought to me by my faithful pupils."[8] Another reads: "I find I shall have to give up going to the quarters if they insist upon giving me so many eggs—I had two dozen and a half today.... Tira, Sims' wife, brought me three little fish fried."[9]

In the quaint village of Beaufort is an equally quaint old hotel, originally built as a summer residence by one of the wealthy rice planters before the war. Its rooms are colossal, with high fireplaces and large paneled doors. The halls are wide and high, and the great piazzas extend all the way across the front of the house. As was the custom, in order to protect the house from the spring tides, it was built high off the ground, at least eight feet. This under-the-house part has been enclosed and fitted up as a hotel lobby. The first floor, up to which great steps were originally constructed, looks easily like the second story of a modern small house. Its original owner, the richest planter of the Carolina rice community, owned over two thousand slaves, and must have kept a score or more to service the summer place. A high brick wall surrounds the back yard and its spacious verandas overlook the beautiful bay.

The only reminder of this retinue of servants in the olden days is a bright young Negro boy named Abraham. Few people were about the hotel this quiet June day; even the white pro-

[8] Pearson, *op. cit.*, p. 35. [9] *Ibid.*, p. 36.

prietor was absent and Abraham apparently was left in charge of the establishment. I was greeted with a pleasant smile and bow and in beautifully quaint English made to feel very much at home. In fact, Abraham's English was more truly "English" than the average "American" so generally spoken, for he used the broad "a" and in his accent betrayed many signs of seventeenth-century peasant English, which for over a hundred years has been preserved among the Negroes in the isolated islands. He stepped behind the long desk, pushed the big hotel register forward, and with marked courtesy explained the advantages and disadvantages of the many rooms in the great house. I selected a rather spacious one on the third floor, a part of the hall, now an improvised room made of wall board. Through the big doorway the fresh breeze blew in from the sea and reminded one of the glorious days of rice culture, when planters and their families left the plantations on the big tidal rivers—malarial regions—and retreated to the salt marshes and the health-giving winds that blow across the blue waters of St. Helena Sound.

Another character trait which makes the Gullah Negro an interesting person is his inveterate optimism. Few of them commit suicide—they refuse to war with fate. Their years of bondage and the following decades of inevitable race discrimination appear to have softened their natures and to have made them kindly and generous. They practice literally the beautiful Christian injunction not to be overanxious about what to eat or drink or to be clothed with, realizing that nothing is to be gained by taking anxious thought of tomorrow. So, in this mood of resignation and self-effacement, they have lived at peace with their world, and, while not many have laid up treasure upon this earth, they have as a race maintained an inner peace and composure which is without price. Historically they have never been aggressors, but have been the servants of mankind, a role which in the eyes of the world is despised; but in their slow struggle up the long road, with all odds against them, they have acquired a spiritual quality which might well be the envy of those who have outdistanced them. A subtle psychology works among aggressors; they generate within themselves turbulent forces. To the unjustly wronged the forces of heaven seem always near, thus it is with the island Negro.

The Gullah Negro refuses to worry. He is an extrovert and

views his affairs objectively. There are few neurotics among them, for they refuse to carry burdens of guilt. Mrs. Puckette, of Edisto, comments thus:

> They shed sin and dirt and wrong doing as neatly as a duck sheds water. Though they make big mourn on occasion, they do not grieve for long, but live according to the principle that what is past is over with; that each day is a new life. Against calamity they adopt an attitude of resignation; and death after all is hardly sad, for it means to those truly trusting souls the realization of all that life has denied. They have confidence that with them it will be as it was with Joseph:
>
> > "Joseph was a servant of de Lord, of de Lord;
> > Joseph was a servant of de Lord.
> > He had trials long and sore,
> > But his troubles now are o'er
> > And he's walking in de Promus Land."
>
> I know of no other people as a whole whose happiness is so independent of material blessings and whose spirituality triumphs so completely over trouble, want, sorrow, suffering. Nor is it that they do not desire things to be better than they are. To his very toenails, the black peasant thrills at the thought that he is "dressed up," and the satisfaction with which one of these humble folk will rear back in a big automobile and go flying down High Ball Pike is evidence of the importance and pleasure he attaches to such an experience.[10]

The islands are dotted with Negro churches, modest little frame structures, many of them with belfry and front porch. A gallery is nearly always provided, however small the structure; probably a suggestion from the white churches, in which galleries were frequently provided for the slaves.

The island Negroes take their church and their religion seriously. The parson is the most respected person in the community, and to his support they contribute liberally according to their means. On Sundays the roads are filled with Negroes going to church. All day long they travel the highways in twos, threes, and dozens. Dressed in their best bibs and tuckers, they present a varicolored procession, moving leisurely over shell and sand roads. Every color of the rainbow is presented

[10] Mrs. Stephen Elliott Puckette, in *The State*, Columbia, S. C., Dec. 10, 1933.

in their dresses, calicoes of blue, red, yellow, and green—garments simply made, and mostly homemade. They chat and laugh and enjoy the holiday spirit. Like the ancient Hebrews they have learned the happy art of combining religion and social life. A woman comes by with her large pocketbook balanced on her head—why, I do not know. A proud mother carries her baby in her arms, dressed in brilliant yellow. There are black adolescent girls dressed in snow-white frocks—jet black faces and large white eyes; pearly white teeth accentuated against the dark background. Nearly everybody walks, but a few ride in buggies or sit upon chairs placed in wagons. There is an occasional old automobile that laboriously makes its way to church.

On Edisto Island there are twelve Negro churches, Methodist, Baptist, and Episcopal. On St. Helena nearly everybody is Baptist.

A very important part of every church service is the collection, and much attention is given to it. No people are more liberal in giving than the Negroes. On this point Mrs. Puckette writes:

> It is interesting to note the procedure for taking up the offering carried out in some of these churches. During the singing of a soul-stirring selection of the choir, the elders come down from their high places and pass around the plates. They are very obliging and if someone has a nickel and wants to contribute only a penny (as is generally the case) the elders will gladly make change and collect the small offering with an encouraging smile. When the rounds have been made, the elders march up to the rostrum and empty their plates on a table and, before the congregation, count the offering. During this pause, those who have given all they can or will, slip out. But there are few shirkers. The great majority wait to hear the result and, later, the pocketbook-loosening appeals made from the pulpit in the event that the offering fails to come up to what is considered sufficient, and it usually fails. Quoting scripture and much that passes for scripture, the pastor pleads with his eloquence-loving flock to "do they utmost for de Lord, to cast they bread upon de water dat after many days it may return unto them." This goes on until by and by someone in the congregation is moved, some big fat sister, maybe, who will go waddling up the aisle proud in all her Sunday best. With due noise and display she will, perhaps, put down a quarter on the money table. Her generous donation will be at once handsomely acclaimed from the pulpit, and

quickly others are inspired to do likewise or even go the old soul one better. Sister Rinda may think it to her glory to drop three dimes upon the table and incidentally take Sister Riah down a peg or two. Competition and the promise of reward hereafter work wonders in increasing the collection. But after awhile not all the preacher's moving sentences can lure another soul from his seat, and everyone instinctively knows that it is time to bring the service to a close. The contributions are then added up, checked and double checked and the sum announced with proper gratitude to the patient flock. After the singing of a hymn the crowd breaks up. Some go out, some loiter in the aisle to pass the time of day with neighbors in fine grand Sunday style, not in the ordinary everyday manner of conversation, and some go up to shake hands with the parson. Everybody is happy. It is worth sweating through the week to enjoy this great Sunday experience.[11]

The services must be emotional, and every oratorical device is used to arouse feeling. Rhythm is essential and is used not only in the singing, but also in the preaching. The preacher on one occasion was speaking on lying, stealing, and deception, and managed to work his congregation up into a rhythmic response to every statement he made, as follows:

"You can deceive man," shouted the preacher, "but you can't deceive de Lawd."

"You can't deceive de Lawd," came the response.

"You can tell lie to man, but de Lawd will find you out."

"De Lawd will find you out."

"You can steal from your brudders, but from de Lawd you cannot steal."

"From de Lawd you cannot steal."

And so the sermon continued, and by and by it was only with an effort that one kept from making responses, so borne along was everyone by the intense fervor of the gathering, the wave of emotion and at least temporary conviction that was sweeping over the dark crowd.[12]

Visitors who attend these services are not moved to levity, and they are not inclined to interpret the proceedings as humorous. There is of course the perennial human interest and, naturally, the curiosity about the Negro's unique manner of religious expression, but he who comes to a Negro church to laugh is likely to go away to pray. The sweetness and genuine-

[11] *Ibid.* [12] *Ibid.*

THE BLACK PEOPLE 93

ness of their spirituals will brings tears to the eyes of the average man susceptible to the appeal of beauty and sincerity. Their courtesy extends to their churches no less than their homes. White visitors are always accorded privileges and considerations all out of proportion to their deserts. From the back seat of a colored church, into which I slipped as inconspicuously as possible, I was taken, in the midst of the service, to the pulpit, and was seated in the big armchair. There was nothing comical about that service. The prayers were genuine and from the heart, and the lovely spirituals were unforgettable. The pastor led the congregation in the old slave spiritual:

> Lawd, I want to be a Christian,
>   In my heart, in my heart;
> Lawd, I want to be a Christian in my heart.
>
> Lawd, I want to be more lovin'
>   In my heart, in my heart; etc.
>
> Lawd, I want to be like Jesus,
>   In my heart, in my heart; etc.
>
> Lawd, I don't want to be deceitful
>   In my heart, in my heart; etc.

The Northern teachers who worked among the slaves during the Federal occupation of the islands apparently never appreciated fully the genuineness and worth of the slaves' religion, as is evidenced in their correspondence. They always referred to the Negro's religion with a smile. Mary Ames has left the following account of a Negro religious service held on the back piazza of the Whaley house on Edisto Island:

> An Elder who could read led the singing. George held for him a lighted candle, which we supplied. The leader read one or two lines from the hymn-book; then they all sang, each man for himself. After the singing, the Elder prayed. He asked the blessed Lord to raise the window curtains this blessed night and let the poor sinners look in, and if it was the blessed Lord's will, would he this blessed evening send down his angels with a hammer and knife and knock at every sinner's heart, for many there are this blessed evening, weeping and tearing their hair and searching for religion, and not knowing how to get it. They sang again, then the sisters walked round in a circle with short, quick steps, swinging their arms and singing, "Oh! Lord, don't be offended. Oh! Lord, don't judge

me hard," and much more of the same strain. They kept this up a long time; the meeting lasted till long after midnight. One song was "Sister, you come too late, the Devil came and shut the gate and carried home the keys." Another, "When Gabriel blow his horn for Massa Jesus, would he please blow a little louder?"[13]

Death always made a profound impression upon the slaves. Their great pivotal points of experience, around which they wove all the sentiment of their natures, were birth, marriage, and death. To be sure, they are dominant areas of experience of all humankind, but the Negro, along with all primitive peoples, has always heightened the effect of these occasions and shrouded them in ritual and deep emotional expressions. Civilized man has ingeniously camouflaged the stark realism of these expressions, but not so with the Negro. He has magnified them and found in them a strong stimulus for his crude emotions. The art of the modern mortician has softened somewhat the reality and crassness of death by the introduction of the funeral home, professional service in handling the dead, the elimination of the harshness of filling the grave and of hearing the dull thud of earth as it falls upon the coffin, before the assembled group. But not so with the Negro; he finds satisfaction in emphasizing all the heart-rending situations, using as his aids mournful music, "wakes" for the dead, and every conceivable device for elaborating and intensifying the experience.

On some plantations it was the custom to bury the dead at night or on the Sabbath. A young slave named Mary was buried at night on the Frierson plantation.

The coffin, a rough home-made affair, was placed upon a cart, which was drawn by old Grey, and the multitude formed in a line in the rear marching two deep. The procession was something like a quarter of a mile long. Perhaps every fifteenth person carried an uplifted torch. As the procession moved slowly to the "lonesome graveyard" down by the side of the swamp, they sang the well-known hymn of Dr. Isaac Watts:

"When I can read my title clear
To mansions in the skies,
I bid farewell to every fear
And wipe my weeping eyes."[14]

[13] Ames, *op. cit.*, pp. 81-82. [14] Lowery, *op. cit.*, pp. 85 ff.

Mary's baby was taken to the funeral in the gloom of the night and passed over the coffin several times in order to make sure that it would survive and not be claimed in death by the spirit of its mother. Babies who were not passed over their mothers' dead bodies could not be "raised."

The body was then committed to the earth, and each member of the funeral party threw a handful of dirt into the grave as a final tribute of respect to the dead. While this was being done the leader announced the hymn:

> Hark from the tombs a doleful sound,
> My ears attend the cry;
> Ye living men, come view the ground
> Where you must shortly lie.[15]

The committal service was never read, as very few slaves could read at all. Its oral rendition, with the numerous interpolations which inevitably crept in and the curious dialect of the Negro of the Deep South must have added a human touch to the occasion which deeply impressed the outsider. A big funeral sermon was preached at a later date.

Miss Botume, stationed at "Old Fort" plantation during the war, has left an account of a midnight funeral near Port Royal. The usual procedure of torchlight procession and hymn singing was introduced to add a touch of horror to the occasion. In this case a muffled drum was used, as the deceased had been a soldier in the Union Army. The account follows:

A young colored sergeant just returned from the army died, and was buried at midnight. He had lived at the negro quarters not far from us. He died a little after dark. His friends immediately assembled and held a watch-meeting, which they call "a setting-up." All night long we could hear their solemn chanting and clapping of hands, as they beat the time. They had a praise-meeting before the house, as they believe the spirit remains with the body until daylight, when it takes leave and goes home to the heavenly Father as the morning stars go out.

The comrades of the young sergeant wished to bury him with military honors, so they waited until the next night at midnight. They had a long procession, with torches and a muffled drum. Then all the women and children straggled along, singing their spirituals.

[15] *Ibid.*

It was a sombre sight as this sable procession wound around throughout the grove.[16]

A Negro funeral on St. Helena Island has been described in a letter written by a young woman who was a teacher among the freedmen during the period of occupation. She says the little Negro children brought their schoolbooks and picturebooks and sang the ABC's to religious tunes. They were evidently confusing their New England education with religion, a mistake easily made when one considers the intense religious zeal which accompanied the occupation of the Port Royal area. No missionaries ever entered a foreign land more triumphantly or with a deeper sense of piety than did the curious wartime "missionaries" who swarmed into Port Royal and Beaufort. Continuing the description of the funeral ceremony, the writer says:

Uncle Sam took off his hat, tied a red handkerchief round his head and, adjusting his glasses, read the hymn through, and then deaconed out two lines at a time for the people to sing. He repeated the process with a second hymn, when Abel made a prayer; then Uncle Sam read from the Burial Service and began his exordium, apologizing for his inability to speak much on account of a sore throat, but holding forth for about half an hour upon the necessity for all to prepare for "dis bed," filling his discourse with Scripture illustrations and quotations aptly and with force, using the story of "Antoninus" and "Suffirus" as a proof that God would not have any "half religions"—that if anybody had "hid his Lord's money in de eart" he must grabble for it before "twas too late." He read from the services again, one of the men throwing on earth at the usual place. When they came to cover the grave, the men constantly changed hoes with those who had not handled them before, that each might aid, women and old men stooping to throw in a handful. Abel made another prayer, they sang again and dispersed.[17]

The sea-island Negroes not only emotionalized the occasion of the burial of their neighbors, but gathered in great numbers about the house of the dying and signalized his passing with a great shout. A sympathetic teacher who had been alarmed by the weird noise made during one of the "setting-up" celebrations made some inquiries of a Negro next morning. The reply

[16] Botume, *op. cit.*, pp. 222-223.   [17] Pearson, *op. cit.*, pp. 65-66.

was "I dunner if you yeardy de whoop when he gone."[18] Describing the "strange wild screaming wail," she says:

At first I thought it must be the mules; but it rose and fell again and again in such agony, as I thought, that Mr. Soule and William went out to investigate, while I opened the window to listen more distinctly. It seemed to come from Uncle Sam's house, and though now more subdued I thought it the sobbing of strong men, and that I could distinguish Titus' and Robert's voices. . . .

The night was wild and stormy, but above the tempest I could hear, as I woke from time to time, the strangely "solemn, wildly sad strains" which were continued all the night through. At sunrise they ceased and separated.[19]

A funeral takes precedence over every sort of religious exercise. It is an occasion of great pomp and ceremony. Usually the secret societies turn out in force with all members in full regalia. Neighboring churches dismiss their congregations that they may participate in the final rites of a neighbor. Mary Ames was impressed with this custom on Edisto Island, and wrote:

We started for church, but to our surprise met the congregation coming away. There was to be a funeral at a distance, and the minister had to omit the church service. Later we saw the procession, a long one. They were singing the melancholy dirge as they walked. As they passed, they spoke to us, the men touching their hats, and the women curtsying.[20]

Not only does the Gullah Negro give particular emphasis to funerals, but he is equally meticulous concerning the graves of the dead. The graveyard is an important place in the community. It is nearly always on the church lot and shaded with great oaks. Solemn spots they are, exhibiting the best care and artistic touches of a simple people. Only a few can have tombstones to mark the red clay mounds; the majority use a wooden head-piece and foot-piece, but as these soon rot and deteriorate, large conch shells of varied hue encircle the grave to give it clearer designation. Many of the graves are lovingly decorated with discarded vases or broken pieces of crockery. Sometimes an old lamp or clock, or a cup and saucer are placed upon the grave. I once saw an old soap dish on a grave on Edisto

[18] *Ibid.*, pp. 252-253.
[19] *Ibid.*, p. 252.
[20] Ames, *op. cit.*, p. 21.

Island. Bits of brightly colored glass are frequently used, and a large number of graves I observed had upon them blue milk of magnesia bottles. I asked a friendly Negro who accompanied me if he could tell why they placed a cup and saucer on the grave. I doubt whether he knew why, but his reply was, "It's just a little farewell gift to the dead, sir." Perhaps this custom had its origin in Africa. E. J. Glave, writing on "Fetishism in Congo Land," says: "The natives mark the final resting-places of their friends by ornamenting their graves with crockery, empty bottles, old cooking pots, etc., all of which articles are rendered useless by being cracked, or perforated with holes. Were this precaution not taken, the grotesque decorations would be stolen."[21]

In the latter statement I believe Mr. Glave is mistaken. The Carolina sea-island Negroes, who, for the most part, came from the West Coast of Africa, and many from the Congo, have great respect for the resting places of the dead and have a perfect dread of removing decorative articles from the graves. A striking instance of this is given in Du Bose Heyward's story, "The Half-Pint Flask." In this story a Northern man, whose hobby is collecting bottles, in visiting one of the Carolina islands, is fascinated with a very rare specimen, a half-pint flask decorating a Negro grave. He takes the bottle. His friend, a native, is alarmed at his audacity and pleads with him not to remove it because of certain evil consequences. But he laughs at the primitive credulity and superstition of his friend and adds the bottle to his collection. Soon he is beset with every sort of terror and begins to waste away—"plat-eye" got him—the dreaded "plat-eye." He has to flee the island to save himself.

By some Negroes graveyards are dreaded, especially at night. This is doubtless due to their firm belief in ghosts or "sperits." This fear and superstitious attitude are rapidly passing among many Negroes as they become educated, but much of it lingers in those of such isolated regions as the Carolina sea islands. The old Negroes believed profoundly in "sperits" and many were sure that they had seen them. A few of the Negroes who were "born with a cane" could see "sperits" and commune

---

[21] H. Carrington Bolton, "Decoration of Graves of Negroes in South Carolina," *Journal of American Folklore*, IV, 214 (July-Sept., 1891).

THE BLACK PEOPLE

with them. These few held no fear of the spirits, but prided themselves on their occult powers and were set apart among the Negroes of the neighborhood. One of the most delightful instances of this is given by Charles Colcock Jones in an intriguing account of his conversation with a fine old Negro who walked and talked with spirits. He asked the old man if he could recognize the spirits:

Yes, Mossa, ef I bin know dem befo dey dead, I kin know dem now. Me kin see dem dist es plain es me kin see you now. Only tarruh night me bin commin from Barnedo plantation. Dest es I cross de causeway an rise de hill by Shannul ole buryin-groun me see Miley,—wuh bin dead de year arter freedom,—duh lean up genst one oak tree sider de road. Day dis biggin fuh broke. Me gone up ter um an me try fur pass de time er day wid um, fuh me yent bin see um sense day rainy ebenin wen we bury um in Shannul. Miley look say eh bin want fuh ax me someting; and den, all ob a sutten, eh check isself, an eh tun roun an mek off fuh de grabe-yad. Me foller um, an wen eh come teh eh own grabe eh pit eh head down, an eh gie two er tree whul, an down eh gone. Me walk up en sarche de grabe. Me cant fine out how Miley git een. De grass yent mash. De groun yent broke; no hole day; an yet me see um, wid me own yeye, gone down, head foremose, een eh grabe.

Mrs. Puckette, of Edisto Island, tells of a Negro living there now who related to her a vivid tale of a ghost that walks the big road. Her account follows:

On High Ball Pike lives a colored man of more than average intelligence. He can read and write and served as a private during the World War. He thinks he knows "a heap of t'ing," yet this William Pinckney, with eyes bulging with excitement, related recently to me a hair-raising story about old Mr. Baynard's ghost. Mr. Baynard's grave lies in a lone thicket upon the hill not far from High Ball Pike. According to William's story, the ghost of this old gentleman "Don't rest easy but walk de big road night after night." A short while back one Ben Wright happened along the highway after dark and met old Mr. Baynard's ghost out for his nocturnal stroll. "It gone bery ha'd wid poor Ben Wright," for the ghost seemed in a disagreeable humor. It sprang upon poor Ben's back and rode him almost to death. After a wild and terrified race down High Ball Pike, Ben at last reached his door to fall weak and unconscious on the door step, as the ghost released his choking grip and glided swiftly away into the night. These superstitious fears fall, perhaps, as the darkest shadows athwart the lives of these naturally happy-hearted people.[22]

There is an old woman living on Edisto Island who claims to be a sister of Porgy, made famous in Du Bose Heyward's novel. Mrs. Puckette knows her well and has given such an accurate description of the old woman that it appears appropriate to close this chapter with her excellent characterization:

Last summer on Edisto Beach I ran across Florence Flud, born back in "Rebel days," but still spry and going strong. She takes in washing and ironing, does cooking and housecleaning and is handy at "nu'sing chillun." Her little cabin is, according to accounts, full of a "powerful mess of chillun, grands and great-grands." Florence, or Old Da as she is known, is one of the remnants of the Old Guard, that efficient, devoted, sturdy type of house-servant belonging to a past that will never return. Da is a worthy and quaint old soul, and so exaggeratedly African in appearance as to attract attention wherever she goes. But her chief distinction in life is that she claims to be the sister of Porgy, old crippled Porgy, who, with his goat cart, has been made known to the world through the pages of Mr. DuBose Heyward's delightful story, "Porgy." If you would listen to old Da you might hear something like this, "Ya, Porgy been a stiff cripple (meaning domineering) but he ain't been mad like he been powerful. Porgy had a way wid him when it come to white folks." And it might be observed that old Da also has a way with her when it comes to white folks. "The worst thing about old Da," said the lady on whose plantation Da lives, "is that her cabin is full to overflowing with children, grandchildren, and even great-grandchildren, and what is more, is getting fuller." At all birthdays in her family, Old Da seems to feel that it is her duty to be present to lend a hand. Too many such events have made Da a reluctant helper. Not long ago Da returning home from her visit to Edisto Beach, saw pouring out of her cabin those women in her community who are usually attendant upon the advent of a little pickaninny into the troubled world. Instantly Da knew that the expected great-grand had arrived, or, as she expressed it, that "Lola done cross." Da scrambled out of the automobile, and, dropping slowly to the ground upon her knees, murmured low and fervently as she clasped her tired old hands together, "T'ank Gawd I miss 'em. T'ank Gawd I miss 'em."[23]

[22] Puckette, *op. cit.*   [23] *Ibid.*

CHAPTER VI

THE GULLAH DIALECT

Dey use dem mout' so funny.

THE NEGROES of the sea islands and the coastal hinterland speak a dialect which is perhaps the most peculiar of all American forms of speech. This dialect, commonly known as Gullah, is spoken also by many whites in a more or less modified form. All low-country people, white and black, exhibit in their speech a tonal quality and accent peculiar to the region. The term *Gullah* has a vulgar connotation locally, and cultured parents try continually to steer their children away from this intriguing form of speech to purer English. And, it should be said in the beginning, as will be explained in detail later, that Gullah is predominantly English, a true English dialect; in fact, more truly English than much of the English spoken in America today.

To the outsider Gullah is as strange and incomprehensible as a foreign tongue. An amusing circumstance to people of the low country is the frequent perplexity of Northern tourists as they try to fathom the depths of a real Gullah's conversation. Mr. John Bennett, of Charleston, tells of the predicament of a Northerner who was placed on a deer stand with a Negro hunting companion. The visitor was ignorant of the habits of deer and proposed that they change positions, much to the dismay of the Negro. In astonishment the Negro protested: "No shuh-shuh! If 'e duh dey, de dee' duh no dey-dey; ef 'e no dey, de dee' duh dey-dey!"[1] I inquired of a kindly old Negro fisherman on Edisto Island concerning the health of the neighborhood. The reply was: "De oiland berry he'lt'y, suh. Yo' aint sick much, an' w'en yo' sick, yo' sick fo' ded." Mr. Hammond Bowman, a Charleston lawyer, relates that a Negro client from Johns Island spoke such extreme Gullah that he was unable to

---

[1] John Bennett, "The Comedie Humaine of the Gullah Darkey," in *The State*, Columbia, S. C., Dec. 17, 1922.

handle his case until another Negro, his neighbor, was retained as an interpreter.

The laugh, however, is not altogether on the side of the white man, for the Gullah Negro is just as much amused at the stranger's speech as the stranger is at his. After listening to the unaccustomed speech of an outsider a Gullah remarked, with a chuckle, "Dey use dem mout' so funny."[2]

The coast-country speech is peculiarly soft and musical. Even where it appears rapid and difficult to understand its musical quality is discernible. There are few if any guttural sounds in Gullah; it is a language spoken on the edge of the lips and with a tonal quality which sets it apart as a delightfully different form of expression. I have heard soft-voiced Negro school children reading from their books in attractive island brogue. Sophisticated teachers try to train them away from their local peculiarities, but always with great difficulty. A little colored girl on James Island was reading aloud from her Third Reader. As she read, she of course looked upon the standard English words on the printed page, but pronounced every one in Gullah. If one of these children is asked what d-a-r-k spells, he will say "daa'k" (if he forgets for the moment his teacher's instructions); and, similarly, l-a-r-k is "laa'k"; p-a-t-h is "paa'th." Gullah is also one of the most difficult dialects to imitate. One had better not try it unless he has spent the early years of his life in that region. There is a rare tonal quality in the coastal speech no one can imitate with any degree of accuracy.

Another quality of Gullah speech which must be mentioned in this connection is its quick rapid-fire enunciation, so often heard among Negroes where the Gullah is most pure and the English impure. One of the cultural objectives in the low country is to get away from the rapid staccato movement and the shortened, half-pronounced syllables of Gullah. Even this extreme form of the speech is not harsh; it is choppy, but nimble and pleasing.

Bennett, speaking of its phonology, refers to the "quick, crackling sounds," which, he adds, are "caused in part by excessive laxity of pronunciation, in part by the elision of every sound of which language may be shorn and still remain articulate."

[2] John Bennett, "Gullah: A Negro Patois," *The South Atlantic Quarterly*, VII, 332-347 (Oct., 1908).

Again: "Its peculiar intonation is that of the *Five and Six Stripes Coast;* its 'harshness,' that peculiar to the dialects of the West Coast south from Sierra Leone, is something comparable to the chatter of the coast-trading negro tribe, the *Jack-jacks,* who more than two centuries ago were denominated Qua-quas, because their speech resembled the gabbling of ducks."[3]

The most extreme form of the dialect is found in the neighborhood of Edisto Island and the Cumbahee section. On the islands near Charleston the dialect is less intense, probably because of the proximity of these areas to the city and to the outside currents that flow into urban centers. Round Port Royal and St. Helena Island a similar situation obtains, due doubtless to like causes, especially the presence on St. Helena of Penn School, which has been there since 1862. The dialect in the Georgetown area, while differing slightly and being easily distinguishable by low-countrymen, is of the same general tonal quality. Just how to account for this unique quality of voice is a difficult matter. The mild semitropical climate has probably had something to do with it; certainly, the English, Scotch, Welsh, and Irish emigrants, with their provincialisms and peculiar manner of speech, exerted a marked influence; and in spite of Professor Krapp's objection, I doubt not that the African West Coast through its human cargoes contributed something of distinctiveness and charm to the spoken word of the Carolina sea islands.[4]

The area in which the Gullah dialect is spoken is roughly the islands and littoral of South Carolina beginning at Georgetown and extending south through Charleston, Savannah, and the Georgia coast. Each section has its slight variation, and the difference is often detected by natives with keen ears. In fact, in the early days Negroes from the different plantations were known by the accent peculiar to that particular locality.

One finds Gullah in its most pleasing form spoken by the old Negroes, whose lives as well as their speech have been mellowed by time and circumstance. Old Aunt Hester, on James Island, is such a one. Benign of countenance and with a gentility and dignity characteristic of the island Negroes, she

[3] *Ibid.,* VII, 337.
[4] For a discussion on this point, see George Philip Krapp, "The English of the American Negro," *American Mercury,* II, 190-195 (June, 1924).

greeted the stranger. In the doorway she sat barefoot on the sunny side of her house, on a cold November morning. Among other things she told the writer that, when she was able to go to church on Sundays, she did not take the big road followed by crowds, but rather walked leisurely along "de paa't [path] down by de crick and talk to me Gawd all de way 'tel I git to de chu'ch." On another occasion an old Negro man, describing the beauty of the Magnolia Gardens, said, "Dis gyahden aint fo' sin—cause Gawd he done walk through heah."[5]

The meekness and submissiveness of the little children are expressed in their mellow, pleading voices. An unknown Northern observer, writing of his experiences on Edisto Island shortly after the Civil War, related that as the little Negroes sat in school, some among them would be taken with malarial chills. Quietly they asked, "Please, teacher, lem 'e sit in de sun, I hab chill." And at other times with sweet voices they sang "Weepin' Mary, weep no mo'."

Other examples of Gullah follow: "Ef you ent hab hoss to ride, ride cow" and "Dat buck a eye bigger dan 'e belley."[6] A Gullah Negro was explaining to another what a jackass looked like; he said: "'E look same like mule, only mo' so."[7] At a dinner in the low country a very eccentric old preacher was asked to say "grace" and in doing so made it very long. The Negro boy waiting at table was overheard to say as he left the dining room: "I nebber see a buckra teck so long to say e prays wen e gwine nyam [eat] like dis wun befo'."[8] An old Negro called to work before he had finished eating his victuals complained, "Dis berry hahd, dese buckra ent giv me time to nyam me bittle."[9]

Mr. John Bennett tells of a traveler who had lost his way among the sandy roads of one of the sea islands. He thought he had traveled the greater part of his journey, but was not sure. Upon inquiry of an old Negro he received this reply: "De furdes yo' gone yo' done 'em," which means, when translated, "You have gone the greater part of your journey."[10] A cook who was mildly upbraided for taking sugar, replied, "Me

[5] From Mr. James Derieux and others.
[6] The Reverend John G. Williams, article in *The Sunday News*, Charleston, S. C., Feb. 10, 1895.   [7] *Ibid.*
[8] *Ibid.*   [9] *Ibid.*
[10] Bennett, "Gullah: A Negro Patois," VII, 341.

DIALECT

yent tief um, me yiz des' tuck um fuh tas' een me mout."[11] A. E. Gonzales remarks that feminine gossip is called "she-she talk," and one of the choicest idioms the Gullah ever devised is an equivalent of Shakespeare's "Frailty, thy name is woman" —the coastal Negro says, "'ooman iz a sometime 'ting."[12] Other quaint expressions are the following:

De squinch owl light 'puntop de chimbly.
Deer hab long foot, him run fas'; cootuh hab shawt foot, him trabble slow.
Snake bite da' gal 'pun 'e lef' han' feet.
Uh lick da' gal good-fashi'n.
Da' gal him bin 'long de road en' 'e nubbuh study 'bout nutt'n.[13]

Mr. M. S. Whaley has compiled a list of Gullah idioms and expressions which give some insight into the nature of the dialect.[14] The following are selected from his list:

When one is worried or harassed—"Greebunce gottum."
To take an oath or "deposit your word"—"Possit your wud."
To go at an easy pace—"Saddlin' 'long."
Kitchen utensils—"Pot en piggin."
When one is off schedule—"Outtuh 'e runnin'."
When one talks too much and his words get ahead of his ideas—"Nuffuh wud ettup wuh yuh duh t'ink 'bout."
To signal one to stop—"Sign yuh down."
Early morning or first crowing of the cock—"Fuss fowl crow."
Good daylight—"Day-clean."
Afternoon—"Eb'nin."
Last July—"Dis July gone," or "Dis July munt gone."
Next July—"Dis July cummin'," or "Dis July munt cummin'."

Mr. John Bennett, of Charleston, who has spent many years in a study of the coastal Negro, and who as early as 1908 wrote the first scholarly account of the grammar and phonology of the dialect, thinks that unquestionably the name *Gullah* is derived from a group of West Coast Africans called Golas or Goras.[15] In a recent conversation, Mr. Bennett reiterated to the

[11] *Ibid.*
[12] Ambrose Elliott Gonzales, *The Black Border* (Columbia, S. C., 1922), p. 317.   [13] *Ibid.*, from the glossary.
[14] Marcellus Seabrook Whaley, *The Old Types Pass* (Boston, 1925), pp. 190-192.
[15] Bennett, "Gullah: A Negro Patois," VII, 332-347; VIII, 39-52 (Jan., 1909).

writer his conviction that the word had its origin with these particular tribes, Liberians, living inland east of the city of Monrovia. The general belief has been that the word *Gullah* came from *Angola*, a large province in southern Guinea, a thousand miles south of the equator. Speaking to this point, Professor Reed Smith says: "A small but positive bit of evidence to this effect is found in an entry of the Charleston City Council under the year 1822, in which reference is made to 'Gullah Jack' and his company of Gullah or Angola negroes. This indicates that rightly or wrongly, as far back as 1822 the official governing body of the City of Charleston regarded Gullah as a corrupted form of Angola."[16]

The Reverend John G. Williams, a native of coastal Carolina, born and reared in the Combahee rice plantation section, suggested as early as 1895 the probable Angola origin. He was not sure, however, and probably took his cue from the "Gulla Jack of Angola" statement in 1822, referred to above. He wrote:

"Gullah" is very probably a corruption of Angola, shortened to Gola, a country of West Africa, and a part of Lower Guinea, from which a great many negroes were brought to this country in the days of the slave trade. I remember hearing the old plantation negroes before the war speak of one as a "Gullah nigger" and another as a "Guinea nigger." In Appleton's "New American Cyclopaedia" the Guinea negroes are described as "black and having thick lips and flat noses," and the Angola or "Gulla" negroes as having "few of the negro peculiarities of form and feature. They are brown in color." These differences between negroes in the country have been often noticed and remarked upon frequently, the explanation of which difference is that the "thick lips" and "flat noses" point to Ashantee and Dahomey as the places from which their ancestors were brought and the "brown color" and features, more like the European in some negroes, very different from the Guineas, point to Angola or "Gulla," as the country from which their ancestors came. So deeply fixed are race and even tribal characteristics. "Uncle Jack" was a Gulla. There is history in the word "Gullah," as it is improperly spelt.[17]

[16] Smith, *op. cit.*
[17] John G. Williams, "Is Gullah a Corruption of Angola?" in the *Sunday News*, Charleston, S. C., Feb. 10, 1895.

DIALECT

Not until the last decade has much attention been directed in a literary way either to the dialect or to the people. Until recent years the Gullah Negro and his speech were almost unknown in literature except to those who lived in his immediate vicinity. As a literary character the coastal Negro was practically out of the picture until introduced by Ambrose Gonzales, Du Bose Heyward, Julia Peterkin, Stoney and Shelby, and others who have placed him prominently in current literature.

Early contributors to Gullah literature, those in the period before the Civil War, did little to introduce the coastal Negro to the American public. Professor Reed Smith lists three contributions to this early group: Mrs. Caroline Gilman's *Recollections of a Southern Matron,* Edgar Allan Poe's "The Gold Bug," and William Gilmore Simms's *The Wigwam and the Cabin.* These authors did little in popularizing Gullah speech or character.

Some of the best early work in Gullah was done by Northerners who were in the South during and immediately after the Civil War. It is true that they labored under difficulties inevitable for those not brought up among the Negroes, but they recorded the Negroes' speech with a fidelity that is amazing to one who examines the letters and writings of that day. The *Letters from Port Royal,* written during the Civil War from the islands by missionaries and teachers, are replete with Negro expressions. Mary Ames, a teacher on Edisto Island during this period, recorded in her diary many side lights on Negro character and dialect.[18] Some of the most faithful recording of Negro spirituals was done by Colonel Thomas Wentworth Higginson, a young Massachusetts colonel who was sent to Port Royal early in the war to recruit a regiment from among the plantation Negroes.[19] *Slave Songs of the United States,* by W. F. Allen and others, is the first serious attempt to make a collection of Negro spirituals. It is an excellent work and was first published in 1867.[20] Southern people apparently had taken the Negro as a matter of course and had seen nothing in him as a subject for literary effort. The Northerners very soon

---

[18] Ames, *op. cit.* [19] Higginson, *op. cit.*
[20] William Francis Allen (comp.), *Slave Songs of the United States* (1867). Collected mainly in the Port Royal area by Union Army officers and mission teachers between 1861 and 1865. Reprinted in 1929.

sensed his unique character, the charm of his speech, and the weird beauty of his songs; they set about immediately to record their impressions of these things. It is an interesting fact that the New England people for a number of years after the war knew more about the Carolina coastal Negro than was generally known by the people in the South. This is particularly true of the so-called "Port Royal Experiment," in which Northern emissaries undertook, during the war, to prepare the Negroes for citizenship and, depending upon the promise of the military authorities, to give to them a large area of coastal territory. These portentous events have been better known in Massachusetts than in South Carolina. Perhaps the reason is that the South wanted to forget.

In the literary background of Gullah speech the names of half a dozen storytellers stand out prominently. Their writings fall roughly in the two decades from 1880 to 1900. Most widely known and popular of them all is Joel Chandler Harris, of Georgia. One hastens to say that Harris's stories are not in pure Gullah, but a much modified form, a fact which accounts in large measure for their popularity and wide distribution. Pure Gullah is appreciated most by those who have known the coastal Negro at firsthand and who are acquainted with his oddities of speech and peculiar form of expression. To the outsider much of it is unintelligible without careful study and therefore will never be read very generally. The modern writers who portray the Gullah Negro "step down" their speech to such an extent that it is far from the original dialect. But such modification is necessary to make any Gullah writing acceptable to the general reading public.

As the Negroes moved inland from the large coastal plantations, their speech was modified to a great extent. In the interior, plantations were smaller and slaves had many more opportunities to come in contact with the whites. Therefore today, among the South Carolina and Georgia Negroes one finds the intensity of Gullah inversely proportional to its distance from the sea.

The "Uncle Remus" stories of Harris began to attract national attention in the early eighties and soon overshadowed all other Negro dialect, in spite of the fact that many excellent stories of Gullah Negroes had appeared previously.

In 1888 Charles Colcock Jones, Jr., also of Georgia, published his *Negro Myths from the Georgia Coast*,[21] but because of their accuracy in phonetics and the unfamiliarity on the part of the reading public with pure Gullah they were almost forgotten. These excellent stories deserved much more attention than they ever received.

Mrs. A. M. H. Christensen, of Beaufort, South Carolina, published in the same year a small volume, *Afro-American Folk Lore*,[22] in which she recorded eighteen stories or fables which she had learned directly from the island Negroes. Among them is the familiar "tar-baby" story, made famous by Uncle Remus. Some of Mrs. Christensen's stories antedate those of Harris, but, when "Uncle Remus" appeared, all other Negro dialect stories faded into insignificance. Mrs. Christensen states: "Two or three years before the advent of 'Uncle Remus,' the writer had published a South Carolina version of 'De Wolf, de Rabbit, an' de Tar Baby' in the 'Springfield Republican,' which was followed by several other similar tales in the 'New York Independent.' "[23]

A noteworthy series of Negro sermons in Gullah began to appear in the columns of the Charleston *News and Courier* in 1895, contributed by the Reverend John G. Williams. They were published later in pamphlet form.[24] The dialect is good and gives an accurate picture of the religious aspects of Negro thought under slavery and after attaining freedom. It is strictly a view of the old-time Negro. The venerable colored preacher, when marrying a couple, did more preaching than hearing of vows. He began a very long discourse with these words: "De berry fust commandiment dat de Lawd mek an' gin to man was to marry, and den full up de wul wid people. Marry fus and den multiply. De Lawd mek marry, an' de debul mek dultrify. Da ent bin no preacher wen Adam an' Ebe married, an' so de Lawd marry dem eself."[25]

[21] Charles Colcock Jones, Jr., *Negro Myths from the Georgia Coast Told in the Vernacular* (1888, reprinted by The State Co., Columbia, S. C., 1925).
[22] *Afro-American Folk Lore, Told Round Cabin Fires on the Sea Islands of South Carolina* (Boston, 1892).   [23] *Ibid.*, p. x.
[24] John G. Williams, *De Old Plantation* (Charleston, 1896), a pamphlet containing the "Brudder Cotney's Sermons."
[25] John G. Williams, article in *The Sunday News*, Charleston, S. C., Dec. 16, 1895; also in the pamphlet, *De Old Plantation*.

J. Jenkins Hucks, of Georgetown, South Carolina, published in 1899 a pamphlet containing Negro stories which are of considerable worth though little known.[26] A. E. Gonzales, commenting upon the narratives of Hucks, declared that they are "perhaps the most humorous example extant of Gullah undefiled."[27] Marcellus S. Whaley, of Columbia, published a group of stories in 1925, growing out of his experiences with Negroes on Edisto Island,[28] where he was reared; hence he knows the Gullah Negro intimately.

The most prolific and in many respects the greatest of all the writers of Gullah dialect was the late Ambrose E. Gonzales, of Columbia. Gonzales was able to portray the deep recesses of the Gullah Negro's mind in a manner unequaled by any of his contemporaries, and his ability to disclose the subtle wit and wisdom of the coastal Negro was most unusual. Unhappily, relatively few people will ever enjoy Gonzales's stories. They are so true to the life of that little-known people, and the dialect is so pure, that only those who have lived among the Gullahs can have a full appreciation of their meaning.

Among the few writers who have attempted to explain the dialect in its historical aspects, its grammar and phonetics, stands John Bennett, of Charleston, whose name heads the list. Not that his work is the most nearly complete, but in his scholarly articles appearing in *The South Atlantic Quarterly* in 1908 and 1909,[29] he laid the foundation for all subsequent studies. At that time there was little interest in Gullah dialect, and, as Mr. Bennett told the writer, the only journal in the United States that would publish his material was the one above mentioned; for his work he received not a penny. He now possesses a mass of unpublished data, which will be of inestimable value to future students of this dialect.

Professor Reed Smith, of the University of South Carolina, who published in 1926 a scholarly monograph on Gullah, has added considerably to a better understanding of its grammar and phonology. The most recent and perhaps the most complete study of the dialect has been made by Professor Guy B.

[26] *Plantation Negro Sayings on the Coast of South Carolina in Their Own Vernacular* (Georgetown, 1899).
[27] Gonzales, *The Black Border*, p. 17.
[28] Whaley, *op. cit.*
[29] Bennett, "Gullah: A Negro Patois," VII, 332-347; VIII, 39-52.

Johnson, of the University of North Carolina. This research was restricted largely to one of the Carolina islands, and appears in a small volume, *Folk Culture on St. Helena Island, South Carolina*.[30]

It should be understood that the Gullah speech is distinctly different from the ordinary Negro dialect of the South, that heard on the stage in the typical blackface comedy sketch or on the screen, the usual drawl, the inaccurate use of "you all," and the like. There is in our writing and thinking about the Southern Negro a rather distinct dialect pattern which is used in nearly all Negro situations. But the Gullah dialect does not fit this pattern. There are at least three distinct Negro dialects in the South, according to Bennett: (1) the French Creole of Louisiana and the Mississippi Delta, used by George W. Cable and others; (2) the familiar Negro dialect of Virginia, North Carolina, western South Carolina, middle and upper Georgia, as written by Thomas Nelson Page, Joel Chandler Harris, and others; and (3) the Gullah patois of the South Carolina and Georgia coast.[31]

In any discussion of Gullah speech the question of its origin immediately arises. Is it African or English? The answer is very positive: it is almost wholly English—peasant English of the seventeenth and eighteenth centuries, with perhaps a score of African words remaining. Very early the slaves picked up the dialect of the illiterate indentured servants of the Colonies, the "uneducated English." As Bennett continues: ". . . low-bred redemptioners, humble Scotch, Scotch-Irish, and Irish English deportations, the greater part of whom were peasantry, from whose tongue it gathered a wealth of dialectical peculiarities, still traceable to their remote spring in the shires of Britain, where many of them still persist."[32]

It may be said that, while the body of the dialect is English, its spirit is African. Certainly there is the flavor of the slave coast in its peculiar intonation, its pleasing inflection, and its unique tonal quality. Johnson has shown this admirably in a simple diagram in which the rapid speech and peculiar inflection

[30] Guy Benton Johnson, *Folk Culture on St. Helena Island, South Carolina* (Chapel Hill, N. C., 1930).
[31] Bennett, "Gullah: A Negro Patois," VII, 336.
[32] *Ibid.*, VII, 338-339.

of the Gullah is shown. For example, the white man says: "I don't know, mam," usually slowly, with little change in pitch. The Gullah says: "I ent know, mum." The speech is more rapid and there is a decided rise in pitch on the word "know." In the first instance the time elapsed is one second; in the second, only six tenths of a second.[33]

A. E. Gonzales, who knew the Gullah Negro well, wrote:

> Slovenly and careless of speech, these Gullahs seized upon the peasant English used by some of the early settlers and by the white servants of the wealthier Colonists, wrapped their clumsy tongues about it as well as they could, and, enriched with certain expressive African words, it issued through their flat noses and thick lips as so workable a form of speech that it was gradually adopted by the other slaves and became in time the accepted Negro speech of the lower districts of South Carolina and Georgia. With characteristic laziness, these Gullah Negroes took short cuts to the ears of their auditors, using as few words as possible, sometimes making one gender serve for three, one tense for several, and totally disregarding singular and plural numbers. Yet, notwithstanding this economy of words, the Gullah sometimes incorporates into his speech grotesquely difficult and unnecessary English words; again, he takes unusual pains to transpose numbers and genders.[34]

There are other factors which affected Gullah dialect besides the influence of the English peasant and the indentured servant of the days of Royal Government. First, there was the influence from plantation life in the West Indies from which the first slaves came to the Carolina coast.[35] Later, slaves came direct from Africa, but many were shipped from the sugar islands, seasoned workmen who had already picked up a modicum of language from the rich plantation barons of Barbados and Jamaica. One cannot say with any degree of certainty just how much these early slaves, many of them with some touch of Spanish influence, affected the dialect of the Negro of the Carolina and Georgia coast; doubtless they had some share in making it what it is.

[33] G. B. Johnson, *op. cit.*, p. 54.
[34] Gonzales, *The Black Border*, p. 10.
[35] The first slaves in South Carolina were brought over by Sir John Yeamans from Barbados Island in 1671 for his Ashley River plantation. Cf. Edward McCrady, "Slavery in the Province of South Carolina, 1670-1770," *American Historical Association, Annual Report, 1895* (Washington, 1896), p. 631.

THEY WORK IN THE OYSTER FACTORY

UNCLE SAM, THE NETMAKER
ST. HELENA ISLAND

And then, it has been suggested that an important factor in the development of Gullah was the "baby talk" or abbreviated English used by overseers in directing the new slaves who knew no English. In this simplified speech, tenses, genders, and numbers were reduced, and only a minimum of language retained to convey simple instructions, a device often used in communicating with foreigners.[36]

Doubtless another factor in the development of Gullah was the simple language concepts of the unseasoned slaves who came fresh from the barracoons of Senegal and Sierra Leone with their simple dialects, to meet in Carolina the language of the white man. The Negro's first impulse was to cut his speech down, use as little of it as possible, take every shortcut available, and acquire just enough to meet his elemental needs. In the process he made a perfect wreck of English, violating every rule of grammar, caring only to be understood; and while, in the language of the street, he "murdered the King's English," his meaning was always unmistakable. In the process he wrought out some of the most homely and at the same time piquant idioms in the language. When the Gullah preacher wanted to impress the bride and groom at the wedding with the thought that jealousy was an attitude of mind which would produce much unhappiness, he cut his language down to the bare idiom, "jellus a bad t'ing."[37] Another Gullah statement illustrates the point: "'E yent crack 'e teet'," meaning, he did not open his mouth to speak.[38]

The language is full of quaint usages. An interesting one is the odd use of the word *condemn*, meaning "guilty": "W'en uh ketch Joe wid he hog, 'e look so condemn."[39] Wishing to say that the preacher took a certain text from Scripture, we have: "'E ketch 'e tex f'um de fus' chaptuh een Nickuhdemus."[40] *Broad daylight* is "Day-clean," or "Sunnup"; *dawn* is "day-bruck," and well into the forenoon is "high sun."[41] For years after the capture of Port Royal the old Negroes thereabouts referred to the event as "Gun-shoot."

---

[36] Krapp, *op. cit.*, pp. 190-195.
[37] John G. Williams, "A Wedding on Combahee," *News and Courier*, Charleston, S. C., Dec. 16, 1894.
[38] Gonzales, *The Black Border*, p. 294.
[39] *Ibid.*, p. 295.
[40] *Ibid.*, p. 309. [41] Whaley, *op. cit.*, p. 190.

Mr. Bennett has very aptly referred to Gullah as "English along the line of least resistance," and says that "paradoxically, the part that the African has added to it is that which he has omitted, or deliberately taken from it and abandoned, by elision, by muting, by nuances of sound covering a multitude of strange omissions, by misapprehension of delicately shaded sounds, by ignorance, by indolence, and by a constant dissolution of language into a state of fluidity."[42] In another place he speaks of Gullah as "the residue of language literally worn away by use."[43]

Stoney and Shelby think of the very early beginnings of Gullah as a blending of dialects in barracoons of the African slave coast. To these slavepens were brought men, women, and children from provinces and districts where the slave traders and buccaneers plied their inhuman business, some of them kidnapped, some taken as prisoners of war, some sold on account of tribal lawlessness, others for trinkets and gunpowder—all huddled together awaiting the white sails of the slave ships which would transport them to Western seas and the rich alluvial islands of the Antilles. Most of these Negroes spoke some dialect of the Bantu, which covered half of Africa, but so diverse were the tongues that to many huddled in the pens the language of their neighbors was almost an unknown tongue. And the ship captains saw to it that not many from the same tribe traveled together. They were mixed into a Babel of tongues, for with slight means of communication there was safety from revolt and mutiny.[44] This blending of speech in transit was carried further upon disembarking in the West Indies, where the dialects of the Bantu met the dialect of the English planter, his bond-servitors and redemptioners. In this soil Gullah had its first roots. Transferred later to Carolina when the culture of rice and indigo was beginning to flourish, with its consequent demand for slave labor, the dialect took its second root and came to full flower in the speech of the rice-field Negro of the Carolina coast. Stoney and Shelby state further that "Gullah is the

---

[42] Bennett, "Gullah: A Negro Patois," VII, 337 f.

[43] *Ibid.*, VII, 337.

[44] Samuel Gaillard Stoney and Gertrude Mathews Shelby, *Black Genesis* (New York, 1930), p. xi.

DIALECT

strongest linguistic connection between America and the Antilles and Africa; it links two hemispheres and two eras."[45]

The persistence of Gullah has been commented upon by several writers with the implication that there is some ethnic basis for its peculiarity and uniqueness. Professor Reed Smith declares: "Whether originally from Angola or from Liberia, these Gullah tribesmen after their enforced immigration to our shores formed a distinct and peculiar group. Their resolute and persistent nature evidently assisted in impressing their dialectical characteristics on weaker and more plastic negroes from elsewhere brought in contact with them, and definitely fixed for two hundred years the tonality of the negro dialect of the Carolina and Georgia coast."[46]

Williams, writing in 1895, gave an example of the persistence of Gullah as follows:

It is wonderful with what tenacity this Gullah English of the low-country negroes holds on to life and refuses to become a "dead language," so completely has it become a part of them and ingrained, as it were, into their very nature. More perhaps than a hundred years ago certain negroes were carried from a rice plantation in Colleton County and put on a cotton plantation in Barnwell District, as it was called then, but to this day (1896) the older ones of that set of negroes, who grew up before the war, speak as pure Gullah as their grandfathers and grandmothers spoke on Ashepoo. They seem to have been scarcely affected in their low country Gullah speech by the white people that were numerous and all around them and the negroes native to that neighborhood, who talked so differently to themselves.[47]

Johnson, however, thinks that "it is not at all necessary to predict an ethnic basis for the survival of the low-country negro speech." He is sure that the low-country white speech shows the same persistence and that, when a Charlestonian or an Edistonian moves to the upcountry, several generations must pass before the coastal brogue is obliterated; he states further that "the persistence of Gullah is merely the persistence of a set of speech patterns in a more or less isolated cultural area."[48]

[45] *Ibid.*, p. ix. Reprinted by permission of the Macmillan Company.
[46] Smith, *op. cit.*, p. 8.
[47] *News and Courier*, Charleston, S. C., Feb. 10, 1895.
[48] G. B. Johnson, *op. cit.*, p. 61.

Of course, the isolation of the coastal Negro has been a predominant factor in preserving the dialect. This isolation obtained, not only before the Civil War, but for many years thereafter, indeed, in most of the islands, until a decade ago, when bridges and roads placed them in communication with the outside world. The overwhelming majority of Negroes as compared with whites, both before and since the war, has been another factor in keeping the dialect intact. Many Negroes on the large plantations rarely had the opportunity of conversing with white people. On many of the islands the ratio of Negroes to whites was and still is as great as ten to one. Even in the city of Charleston, in 1765, there were between seven and eight thousand Negroes to five or six thousand whites.[49] On Edisto Island the white population in 1808 was only 236, according to McLeod, who says: "It appears that the black population of the Island exceeds by a few infants and newly brought Africans, 2,609 slaves."[50] So it would appear that Gullah speech, with such overwhelming numbers and its attendant geographical isolation, could have easily retained its identity.

What is to be said of African influence upon Gullah? Relatively little has been done by philologists in this field. It remains an interesting pursuit for some students of literature, though a difficult task, to trace certain elements of the dialect back to the primordial haunts in Africa and to determine, not only the original jungle vocabulary, but the strange spirits and musical cadences which pervade the language.

As indicated before, relatively little survives of African inheritance, but that little is exceedingly interesting. If it had not been for the practice among overseers of distributing the fresh slaves among the seasoned ones, we should have had a much larger African element in Negro speech. But they were meticulously separated upon arrival and placed among their acclimatized fellow bondsmen, where they easily acquired the new language and methods of doing things in their new home. They had little use for their native tongue, and, as a result, Gullah is poorer because of the paucity of slave coast influence.

[49] Alexander Hewatt, *An Historical Account of the Rise and Progress of the Colonies of South Carolina and Georgia* (London, 1779), II, 291.
[50] Ramsay, *op. cit.*, II, 280.

DIALECT

Of course, up until the time of the Civil War the African element was much greater since fresh slaves were constantly being illicitly imported into Carolina while the life of the jungle was fresh in their minds. But when importations ceased and the years passed, many African words were dropped from their speech until scarcely a dozen are in actual use today.

Mr. Stoney thinks that about all elements that survive of African origin are a few rhymes, games, systems of counting, tricks of the tongue, and a few words in common use referred to. He is inclined to the view that, in so far as we can identify these words, they come from the Umbundu dialect of Angola.

Professor Joseph Le Conte tells of an old native African he knew named Philip, a slave on his father's plantation on the Georgia coast.[51] This old man, a Mohammedan, used to entertain the boys with many prayers and prostrations practiced in his native Africa. Le Conte remembered the system of counting as given by the old Negro, and has reproduced it in his autobiography. The numerals, which extend to twenty, are African, not Arabic, and run in series of fives, not tens, as do ours: "Go, dede, tata, nigh, ja, ja go, ja ded, ja tata, ja nigh, suppe, suppa go, suppe dede, suppa tata, suppa nigh, suppa ja, suppa ja go, suppa ja dede, suppa ja tata, suppa ja nigh."

Le Conte relates further: "During my boyhood there were on the plantation three very old negroes who were native Africans and remembered their African home. They were Sessy, a little old man bent almost double; Nancy, an old woman with filed teeth; and Charlotte, who left Africa, according to her own account, when she was about twelve. All of them, of course, were superannuated and taken care of without any remuneration."[52]

Mrs. Christensen, of Beaufort, South Carolina, records a few African words and phrases from the lips of slaves as they related to her stories from their native land.[53] One of the most interesting tales of unquestioned African origin is the story of "De Tiger an' De Nyung[54] Lady." The tiger " 'E holler to know who was dere,—Say: *Whoga, whoga, whogalor, da humbarnorta, sudundilly?*' " In the story "Cooter[55] and Deer," in

---

[51] Le Conte, *op. cit.*, pp. 29-30.
[52] *Ibid.*, pp. 28-29.
[53] Christensen, *op. cit.*, pp. 7, 12.
[54] "Young."
[55] Gullah for *turtle*.

which a footrace is the chief feature, the winner to get the "gal," the deer yells to the cooter, "Sarsy Bey cum blunda!" and the cooter replies, "Tung cum blunda!"

Smith gives a list of approximately twenty words which he thinks are of African origin.[56] Among them the following seem to have fallen out of use: "*dudu, cymbi, guffer, penepne, da, da-da.*"

Words most likely of African origin still used in certain sections of the coast (some are diffused over wide areas) are the following:

Ki, an exclamation, or used to express wonder.
Buckra, a white man; *po' buckra*, poor white trash.
Nyam, to eat; as "'e nyam 'e bittle."
Yam, probably related to *unyamo*, sweet potato.
Oona or *yoonah*, you or your.
Goober, peanut.
Pinder, peanut.
Cooter, turtle.
Okra, the vegetable.
Plat-eye, a prowling ghost or evil spirit.

Stoney and Shelby have arranged a very interesting table of Gullah words, showing both their English and African origin.[57] It will be noted that they list eight African dialects in the scheme, the Umbundu apparently furnishing the most words for Gullah. This table is shown on page 119.

These writers have emphasized the musical quality in many African words of the Bantu dialects. Examples are found in the diagram: "oonah," "ilou," "oluliso," "olongupa," and "fulcututu."

African music has touched Gullah deeply. The voice is pitched low, the tone is resonant, and the rhythm pronounced. What happens with all negro speech seems peculiarly easy in this dialect. In emotion, the quality of rhythm increases and the spoken word is intoned; then, as the feeling intensifies, it may at last be sung, so that a spiritual may grow spontaneously from the pulsing of a repeated phrase. This was one of the things that the African tongue did to English speech.[58]

[56] Smith, *op. cit.*, p. 32.
[57] Stoney and Shelby, *op. cit.*, p. xvii. Reprinted by permission of the Macmillan Company. [58] *Ibid.*, p. xxii.

DIALECT

English	Gullah	Umbundu	Kisikongo	Mangingo	Efik	Atam	Vai	Wolof	Ogwi
White-man	Buckra				Mbakara	Makara			
					Makara				
You		Oonah	Enu	Yeno	Ilou		Nye		
Ye		Yoonah	Yenu				Oya		
Your									
Eat (meat)	Nyam	Nyama (suckle)			Unam (meat)	Inyum Nyam (meat)			
Sweet potato		Unyamo					Jambi (wild yam)	Nyambi (yam)	
Yam	Yam	Inhame							
Turtle	Cooter	Fulcututu		Kouta	Ikut				
Peanut	Pinda	Olongupa	Nguba						
Ground-nut	Goober	Jinguba	Mpinda						
Louse	Oule	Ona							
		Oluliso (bedbug)							
Plenty	Toko								Joku (plenty)
									Toko (great)

Negro folk tales are, in part at least, a contribution from Africa. The characters, instead of human beings, are animals from the woods. It is interesting to note that in folk tales the cast of characters changes with the country in which the scene is placed. In Siberia, for instance, where there are no rabbits, the hero of the story is a little deer, round-eared, big-eyed, and nimble-footed, while among the Fang tribesmen the turtle takes the leading role, and in the West Indies, the spider.[59] Whoever the hero happens to be, he is always a small but wise creature who outwits his neighbors and attains his objectives through strategy and deceit.

The Gullah Negro makes Buh Rabbit the hero. And this mild and almost helpless creature represents the Negro himself in his fight against the humiliations of slavery, its attendant illiteracy, helplessness, and the constant dominance of the white race. His status of inferiority drove him to duplicity, deceit, and every imaginable protective device. There are no morals in the Negro folk tales. They are examples of weakness triumphing over strength and wit over the normal obtuseness of human beings. Stealing from their masters could hardly have been considered immoral by the slaves, for they were producers of the harvest. Misstatement of fact was hardly lying, for the master had no right to the truth. So these animal-folk stories reflect the life of discrimination and disadvantage experienced by the slave.

Mrs. Christensen records a conversation with an island Negro named Prince, in which the theory of strategy over strength is put forth and duly justified. Prince, in his own words, "ben born an' raise on de Nat Heywood place, a nice plantation on de Cumbee." He says: "You see, Missus, I is a small man myself; but I aint nebber 'low no one for to git ahead o' me. I allers use my sense for help me 'long; jes' like Brer Rabbit. 'Fo' de wah ol' Marse Heywood mek me he driber on he place, an' so I ain't hab for work so hard as de res'; same time I git mo' ration ebery mont' an' mo' shoe when dey share out de cloes at Chris'mus time. Well, dat come from usin' my sense. An' den, when I ben-a-courtin' I nebber 'lowed no man to git de benefit ob me in dat. I allers carry off de purties' gal, 'cause, you see, Missus, I know how to play de

[59] *Ibid.*, pp. xxii, xxiii.

DIALECT

fiddle an' allers had to go to ebery dance to play de fiddle for dem."[60]

As indicated before, Gullah speech is conspicuous for its short cuts. Its grammar, which is but an abbreviated and mutilated English grammar, knows no rule except to follow the line of least resistance, take its own tack, violate all rules of logic, and say just that which is natural and to the point. Often these cryptic sayings are exceedingly picturesque and pointed. For instance, feminine gossip is "she-she talk"; if a storm approaches, " 'e gwine to wedduh"; if the question is asked, "Did the woman whip the boy?" the answer is, " 'E lick 'um," or "Did the fire burn your house?" the reply is, " 'E bu'n 'um."[61]

Gonzales gives other examples: "De gal tayre 'e coat," meaning, the girl tore her petticoat. If anything does not measure up to expectations, " 'E cyan specify." When it is break of day, the phrase is shaved down to the crisp "crack-uh-day."[62]

Paradoxically, the coastal Negro occasionally takes the longest way around and complicates with additional words an otherwise simple statement. *Second, third,* etc., are seldom used, the more cumbersome "two-time," "t'ree-time," etc., being preferred, as in "Uh done tell oonah fuh de two-time fuh lef da' gal 'lone"; or "W'en uh look 'puntop de 'ooman en' see 'e yeye red, uh know him bex," meaning, "When I looked upon the woman and saw her eyes were red I knew she was vexed."[63]

The hyphenated *all-two* is peculiarly used. If the alligator has spots on both sides of his belly, the correct phraseology in Gullah is "De 'gator hab spot on all-two 'e belly."

The island Negroes use the word *task* in many interesting ways. It is a hang-over from slavery days, the "task" representing the amount of work assigned for the day, ranging all the way from a certain amount of wool to be carded to a portion of a rice field to be planted or harvested. On Edisto Island a "task of land" is a quarter of an acre, and a task of shrimp (or "tass o' swimp") is a plate of shrimp. Shrimp is still sold by the plate, even in the city of Charleston. Mr. Bennett says of this much used word: "A common unit of measure of area and distance is a *tass*—the allotted day's portion of labor, a *task*,

---

[60] Christensen, *op. cit.*, pp. 2-4.
[61] Gonzales, *The Black Border*, from the glossary, pp. 279, 284, *passim.*
[62] *Ibid.*, pp. 280, 283, 294.   [63] *Ibid.*, pp. 281, 284.

a *stent*; for a hoe-hand generally half-an-acre; for cotton-field hands, three-quarters of an acre; for the rice-field negro, usually a quarter of an acre; a man and his family can *cut a tass, tie an' carry a tass intuh de flat*. As a unit of distance, a *Gullah* black will inform you that his *two-time-one gun*, or his *one gun two-time*, that is to say, his *double-barrelled fowling piece*, can *t'row two tass, an' kill*. A tass is fifty compass, a compass being five feet (the possible connection between usage of compass, and passus, a pace—that is the geometrical, or great, pace, of 5 feet, is at once suggested) and *fufty compass* being fifty compass square; thus a fowling-piece that carries *two tass*, and slays, is effective over a good radius."[64]

Mr. Bennett points out other interesting expressions. For instance, the use of the word *soon*, meaning "early," as "soon brukwuss," an early breakfast, and "soon sta't," an early start. Expressions representing the various times of the day are "fus fowl-crowin'," "day-clean," "sun up," "fus' an' las' ho'n-blowin'," "fo' noon," "noon-res'," "attanoon," "de sun duh lean," "de sun duh lean fuh down," "sun-down," "deep dus'," "ebenin'," "can'le-lightin'," "night-time," "platt-eye prowl," and "hag-hollerin'."[65]

One of the most expressive short cuts is the use of the Gullah word *shum*, meaning "see them," "see him," "see it," etc. The writer asked a Negro boy on Wadmalaw Island where the colored Methodist Church was. He said, "W'en yo' tu'n da corner yo' shum."

Professor Reed Smith has arranged the following diagram, which reveals sixty-four possible meanings of the statement, "Uh yeddy 'um but 'uh ent shum":

		(it)				(it)
	(hear)	(her)		(didn't)		(her)
I		(him)	but I		see	(him)
	(heard)	(them)		(don't)		(them)

The Gullah has no respect for either tense, number, or gender. A man's wife is often referred to as "him" or even "it." One hears "'E hab chile" (of a woman), or "him been a bad 'ooman." Miss Botume, during the Civil War, was amused at this confusion of gender in her Parris Island school.

[64] Bennett, "Gullah: A Negro Patois," VII, 344.
[65] *Ibid.*, VII, 342.

DIALECT

She relates that a little Negro boy was trying to parse *sister*. After anxious deliberation over the gender of the word he exclaimed, "Him's feminine, Miss Ellen! Him's a gal!"[66]

It is usually thought that the Gullah Negro's confusion of gender is due to his ignorance and primitiveness. It is possible that his abuse of grammar in this respect is due not wholly to his naïveté but to English and Scotch dialectal influence through the unlettered bond servants who came among the slaves. Wright states that in Sussex *her* can refer to either a masculine or feminine noun and that in Scotland, Wales, and Gloucestershire the possessive *her* or *hers* is sometimes used where one would expect *his*.[67] In Cumberland *she* is used "familiarly or contemptuously of a man." The confusion in gender has been widespread among dialects in various sections of the British Isles.

Another characteristic practice of the South which may have been influenced by English is that of omitting the final *g*. It is never used by Gullah Negroes. The use of final *g* among Negroes is the hallmark of education. It would appear that one of the dearest objectives in most Negro schools is to change the Southern accent and simulate that of the North, especially emphasizing final *g* and rolling *r*'s, both of which are foreign to the Southern Negro's tongue. The omission of final *g* is not uncommon in English dialects. From Yorkshire and northwest Lincolnshire, Wright gives several illustrations: "They do tell me our Squire's for goin' to forren parts o' Setterday," and "I'm for goin', it's gettin' late."[68]

The very close relationship between Gullah and English is strikingly brought out by Johnson in a study of the Gonzales glossary.[69] Mr. Gonzales compiled a vocabulary of nearly two thousand words generally used in the Gullah dialect. Of them ninety-two per cent, says Johnson, are standard English words pronounced in standard way or as in English dialect of the eighteenth century; six per cent are corruptions and mutilations of standard English; two per cent are obsolescent English words; while only one half of one per cent are African.[70]

[66] Botume, *op. cit.*, p. 222.
[67] Joseph Wright, *English Dialect Grammar* (Oxford, 1905), p. 73.
[68] *Ibid.*, p. 73.　　[69] Gonzales, *The Black Border*, p. 277.
[70] G. B. Johnson, *op. cit.*, p. 42.

The task of tracing English paternity through the strange phonetics of coastal Negro speech is one for the philologist, but an interesting task it is. In the following list of illustrations I have merely touched the field. As one thumbs through the pages of English dialect dictionaries and grammars, one is impressed with the overwhelming influence of the English dialects upon early Carolina speech. There is evidence of considerable Scotch influence in the dialect of the Carolina coast, as will be noted in the illustrations; and in this connection it is significant that the Reverend Mr. McLeod, writing from Edisto Island about the year 1800, stated that the island was settled "principally by emigrants from Scotland and Wales."[71] The late I. Jenkins Mikell, of Edisto, writing in 1923, asserted that the Established Church of Scotland had a marked influence upon life and customs of island folk. One such instance was the old Covenanter practice of issuing tokens, little flat metal discs, on Communion Sunday to members of exemplary character. The minister collected one from each communicant before he was served, a practice which was continued by the colored members until the Civil War.[72] The great number of Anglican churches in the coast country bespeaks the predominance of English settlers. Most useful to the writer have been Joseph Wright's *English Dialect Dictionary* and the *English Dialect Grammar*, though the works of Skeat, Halliwell, Stratman, and others are of value.

The Gullah words listed below are found for the most part in the excellent glossaries of Gonzales and Whaley though many of them have been familiar to the writer from childhood. Not all of the words listed below are presumed to be exclusively Gullah words; some of them are widely diffused and are used by Negroes generally and by unlettered whites in many parts of the country:

Ax or *axt*, ask or asked. Has had general dialectal use in Scotland, Ireland, and England. Used by Chaucer. An old proverb from Yorkshire: "Ax and hev." From Lancashire: "Afore au've axt a blessin'," *E. D. D.*[73]

Balmoral skut, a long skirt or petticoat of the Victorian era.

---

[71] Ramsay, *op. cit.*, p. 278.   [72] Mikell, *op. cit.*, pp. 239-240.
[73] Where Wright's *English Dialect Dictionary* is referred to the letters *E. D. D.* will be used.

DIALECT

Bex or *wex*, vex. The Isle of Wight: "I wexed wery much about un." *E. D. D.*

Bile, boil. Has had various dialectal uses in Scotland, Ireland, and England; sometimes written "beil," "bile," or "bwile." An illustration from South Leinster, Ireland: "It is time to bile the dinner." From Shropshire, England: "Behappen they'n find it easier to get married than to keep the pot bwilin." *E. D. D.*

Bruck, broke. Used in Scotland and Ireland. Also written "bruck" in Shetland Islands. *E. D. D.*

Chaney, China. Wide dialectal use in England, varying as *cheeny, cheney, chaney*, etc. Illustration from Lancashire: "Tom had the old-fashioned chaney spread upon the table."—Brierley, *Waverlow* (1863), vi. *E. D. D.*

Chu'ch, church. In Lincolnshire written *chu'ch* and *chech:* "They tell'd me he were chu'chmester to-year." Also, "Bob went to Patrin'ton e' Yerksheer an' thaay maad him chech-maaister." *E. D. D.*

Critter or *creetuh*, creature, an animal, as "De critters in de woods," or "Ah got ten acre an' a critter," meaning a mule. From Lincolnshire: "Ye helpless critter, get out of the way . . ."; and from Leicestershire, "a creetur loike that," both suggestive of Gullah, and especially the pronunciation of "like" as "loike." *E. D. D.*

Cuz, cuzin, cousin. Used frequently in Shakespeare.

Cyaat, cart. Suggests Scotch usage of *cart*. "Dawvid was up b'cairts the streen."—Alexander Johnny Gibb, 1871, Aberdeen. *E. D. D.*

Dem, them. Used in Scotland and Shetland Islands, as, "Hits naethin' noo dae say, fur dem to treed (thread) oot da sax pakies wi' da sail, an dan huve der anchur." *E. D. D.*

Fo'punce, four pence. Used to indicate the size of a chicken in the Edisto and Combahee sections of South Carolina, as, "Dis a fo'punce chicken." Also *seb'n punce* used in the same way. Gonzales's Glossary, p. 302.

Hice, hoist. From Shetland Islands: "We'll heist up da sail."—Stewart, *Tales* (1892). Gloucestershire and Dorsetshire: "An heist his jacks."—Barnes, *Poems* (1879). *E. D. D.*

Peruse, to stroll or saunter. Used in Herefordshire, meaning "to explore the fields or woods." *E. D. D.*

Pit, put. From Scotland, County of Forfar: "Ye hae seen it pit its yal fit doon this w'y." *E. D. D.*

Shet, shut. South Oxfordshire: "I shu'n't like bein shet up all day." Norfolk: "A spring shet up." *E. D. D.*

Spile, spoiled. From Thomas Hacket's translation of Jean Ribaut's *Discovery of Terra Florida* (London, 1563): "Our victualles being perished and spilt. . . ."

Staa't-naked, stark-naked. Probably from the Anglo-Saxon word *steort,* meaning tail, therefore "tail-naked." For discussion see Johnson, *op. cit.,* pp. 45-46.

Swinge, singe. Johnson finds "swinge" used in many parts of England. Common in the Deep South among Negroes and illiterate whites. *Single-tree* (attached to plow-stock) is often pronounced "swingle-tree."

Tech, touch. In Cornwell, "tech." *E. D. D.*

Titty or *Tittie,* sister. Widely used in English and Scotch dialects. From Ayr, Scotland: "It's but your tittie,—Lass, dinna fright."—Fisher, *Poems* (1790). Dumbarton: "My *titty* Meg our joys had seen."—Johnson, *Poems* (1820). Cumberland: "My *titty* Greace and Jenny Bell are gangen bye and bye."—Anderson, *Ballads* (1808). *E. D. D.*

Tother, the other. Rather widely diffused. Frequently heard in the South and other sections from unlettered whites and Negroes. Was standard English once and is found in the Wycliffe Bible, Matt. 24:41, "Tweine wymmen schulen ben gryndynge in a querne, oon schal be taken and (the) *tother* left." Found generally among English dialects. An example from Nottinghamshire: "They're (the) *tother* side of the road." *E. D. D.*

Werry or *berry,* very. From the Isle of Wight: "I wexed *wery* much about un." *E. D. D.*

Wuk, work. In English dialects has various similar pronunciations. The one nearest "wuk" found in Wright's Dictionary is *wahk,* used in Yorkshire.

Wud, word. Found in the dialects of Westmoreland, Suffolk, and Devon. "Have you and Mark had *wuds?*"—Zack, *White Cottage* (1901). *E. D. D.*

Wussuh, worse. Wright finds in Oxfordshire dialect *wuss* used, and in Lancashire *wus. Worser* has common dialectal use in England.

Yit, yet. Wide diffusion in English, Scotch, and Irish dialects. "'E hanna bin theer *yit* as I know on," and "*yit* sall ye be as the wings o' ane dow."—Riddell, *Ps.* (1857). *E. D. D.*

Following are a few specimens of the dialect. Mr. Bennett records an instance which took place in the courtroom. Two boats had collided in a heavy fog. The defendant was a Gullah Negro. The plaintiff claimed that the Negro pilot rammed the plaintiff's boat without any warning of bell, horn, or whistle:

"That is not so," the plaintiff declared. "My lookout gave warning in ample time; he hailed you long before you struck, and ran us down, you had ample warning." The lookout was summoned, a black man, sphinx-like, silent. "You called out to the defendant the moment you saw him through the fog?" "Me yerre [heard] um; no shum [see them]; *too* long buffo' me shum, me yerre um." "And the moment you heard them you sang out; is that not so?" A grave nod assented. The plaintiff rested his case; the cross-examination began: "You hailed the sloop before you could see her; could they hear your hail?" A succinct nod. "How do you know?" "Me yerre dem; dem blan [obliged] fuh yerre we; yez yerre yondey senkah yerre yuh." [Ears hear yonder same as here.] "You hailed them then?" "Me duh holleh." "That is what I mean; you hailed the on-coming vessel?" "Me yent no sicarum [no such a thing]; me holleh one patty-augah [piragua]." "Very well. And what did you say?" "Me say, *'Oonah kounou oonah?'*" Which is equivalent, in *Gullah,* to *"Whose boat is that?"*[74]

The "Vision of Daddy Jupiter," by Charles Colcock Jones, is typical of the highly imaginative religious experiences of many old Negroes. It sounds not unlike the *Green Pastures, Black Genesis,* and other contemporary works of fiction depicting the religious life of the Negroes of two generations ago:

. . . Me bin study bout de time wen old Jupter hab ter meet him Lord and Master, and me berry happy een me bussum. Den me drap ter sleep. How long me bin ter sleep me dunno, but all ob er sutten pear like ebry shingle an boad hab er crack, and de light stream tru, an de room bin bright es day. Wile me duh wonder wudduh dat, four leely angel, wuh dress een wite an hab wing on eh back, fly een de room. Two light topper de foot er de bed, an one on arur side er me. My! but dem bin pooty! Me see heap er pooty wite chillun een me time, but me nebber bin see nutten teh come up ter dem, nur ter ketch nigh um. Dem look pon topper me so kind, and dey open an shet dem wing, an mek sich a cool breeze een de house. Bimby me retch out ma han fuh tell de one huddy wuh bin tan close me bed on de right side, but eh draw back, an eh say: "Jupter, we come fuh leh you know de blessed Jesus duh commin fuh cahr you up ter Hebben an show you de seat wuh eh hab ready fur you." Me dat glad me yent hab bref fuh mek ansur. Me hard fuh bleebe me own yez. Me harte rise up een me troat, and me yent duh say nutten, but me duh watch fur de Lord. Soon de blessed Jesus, wid de print er de nail een eh han an eh foot, an

---

[74] Bennett, "Gullah: A Negro Patois," VII, 340-341.

wid de star on eh head, drap right down tru de top er de house dout crack er shingle, an eh call me name, an he tell me fuh rise, an eh pit eh han onder me shoulder, an eh liff me up light es er fedder. Me ole cloze an me old body leff behine, an somehow narruh me sperit, him keep de shape er de body. Den eh pit eh han onder me arm, an eh cahr me way up eenter de element, beyant de sun an de moon and de star, an de leely angel duh foller we. We gone an we gone way up tel we git ter er big alabaster house, wid high piazza all roun an roun, wuh shine same luk de sun, buil in de middle er a beautiful garden wid flower, an fruit, an hummin-bud, an butterfly, an angel wid harp duh sing and duh joy ehself onder de tree. Dis es we git ter de big gate, wuh mek wid pearl, eh swing open dout tatch um, and de blessed Jesus lead dis poor ole nigger up de shinin paat to de big house way de Lord lib.

We gone up to step an enter de pahler, way de great God bin er set on eh golden trone. Den de blessed Jesus mek de good Lord sensible dat dis duh Jupter wuh him had sabe, an dat eh fetch um fuh show um eh seat wuh eh done prepare fur um. Wid dat de Lord, him call teh one angel, an eh tell um fuh bring one chair an set um down befo eh trone. Soon es dis bin done eh say: "Jupter, yuh you chair; set een um. Eh blants ter you." Mossa, you nebber bin see sech chair een all you life. Eh hab gold rocker ter um. Eh hab welwit cushin een en bottom. Eh hab high back, an eh arm stuff. Eh so soffe an easy. Eh look pootier den dat big rockin chair wuh ole Mossa bin gib Missy wen eh marry you farruh. Me shame fuh set een de chair, but de blessed Jesus him courage me, an me tek me seat, an me so tankful dat me hab one chair een de mansion een de sky.

Den de blessed Jesus tell anurruh angel fuh bring me some milk an honey fuh drink. Eh bring um een e nice glass tumbler, an eh gen me fuh drink. Me tase um, an eh sweet mone anyting me ebber drink een me life. Eh tell me fuh drink um down, an wen me drink all outer de glass, an me yeye ketch sight er de bottom er de tumbler, me see some speck. De ting trouble me, fuh me dunno wuh mek speck day een de bottom er dat clean tumber. Den de blessed Master notus me, an eh say: "Don fret, Jupter; dem speck duh you sin, but now dem all leff behine."[75]

The excerpt from Gonzales's "Noblesse Oblige" reveals the author's intimate acquaintance with the subtleties of the Gullah Negro's mind and speech. "Mass' Clinch" is former Governor Duncan Clinch Heyward of South Carolina. Joe takes great

---

[75] Jones, *Negro Myths from the Georgia Coast*, pp. 161-164.

DIALECT

pride in the fact that he belonged to the Heywards and gives a vivid account of his impressions of Mr. Heyward as he periodically visited the rice plantation on Combahee.

Hukkuh yo' maussuh plant all dat rice en' t'ing' ef 'e yent wu'k? Enty I tell wunnuh him lib een Walterburruh? Duh summuhtime 'e does dribe plantesshun now en' den fuh see how him crap stan'. Him dribe two hawss', en' de buckle on 'e haa'ness shine lukkuh gol'. One nigguh duh seddown behine 'e buggy wid alltwo 'e han' fol' befor'um lukkuh hog tie. Mass Clinch hab on one kid glub 'pun 'e han' wuh come to 'e elbow. W'en 'e git Cumbee, 'e light out 'e buggy. T'ree nigguh' run up fuh hol' 'e hawss' head. Mistuh Jokok mek'em uh low bow. Mass Clinch iz uh berry mannussubble juntlemun, alldo him *iz* quality, en' him 'spon' to de bow. Den 'e biggin fuh walk. Him hab shishuh rich walk! Den 'e cock 'e hat one side 'e head. You nebbuh see nobody kin cock 'e hat stylish lukkuh Mass Clinch. Den 'e onbutt'n 'e weskit. 'E pit 'e lef' han' een 'e britchiz pocket, en' swing 'e walkin' stick een 'e right han' en' biggin fuh quizzit him ob'shay. By dis time 'e git 'puntop de baa'nyaa'd hill en' look obuh 'e fiel'.

"Jokok," 'e say, "day de stretch flow you got on my rice, enty?"

"No, suh, dat de haa'bis' flow."

"De debble!" 'e say. "'E mus' be mos' time fuh ricebu'd!"

"Yaas, suh. We gwine hab some fuh dinnuh."

"Wuh else you got fuh eat?" Maussuh quizzit'um.

"We got one cootuh soup mek out'uh tarrypin' wuh bin een one pen duh fatten 'pun gritch en t'ing, 'en' one trout fish, en' summuh duck."

"You hab enny mint?"

"Yaas, suh, we hab 'nuf."

"Berry well, mek we a few julip," 'e say. "You got enny mo' 'pawtun' bisness dat 'quire my 'tenshun?"

"Yaas, suh; snake hole en' crawfish en' t'ing' spile one uh we bank, en' de trunk blow out, en' uh hab berry bad break, en' Cumbee ribbuh comin een de fiel'. You wantuh shum, suh?"

"No, I t'engk you," 'e say. "Leh de ribbuh tek 'e co'se. Let we eat."[76]

The story of the "Tiger and the Nyung Lady," heretofore referred to, is one of a group of stories faithfully recorded by Mrs. Christensen, of Beaufort, South Carolina. The dialect is not so true as that of either Jones or Gonzales, but the tales

[76] Gonzales, *The Black Border*, pp. 21-22.

come directly from the Negroes and constitute one of the early attempts to reduce the dialect to writing:

Well, de Tiger you know, him ben a Tiger.

Well, dere was a beautiful nyung lady, an' she said she wouldn't married a man what got a scratch on 'e back.

Well, de Tiger 'e tu'n himself to a man, an' dressed himself up bery nice, an' drive up ter de nyung lady house in a nice buggy. So de nyung lady came out an' saw him an' call to her mudder, say, "Mudder, dis is de man dat I'll married."

An' de Tiger did married de nyung lady an' carried her right off in 'e buggy. An' de mudder she 'greed, by lookin' at de man so smart, you know.

An' dey went 'way down in de swamp where de Tiger hab lib, an' 'e put her dere an' tell her to stay dere tel him come back, an' dere was nuttin' for her to eat in de worl'. An' 'e lef' her all alone wid a fly to min' her. An' ef anybody trubble dat lady de fly mus' go wherebber he is an' tell um. An' dere she stayed t'ree days. Nuttin' she had to eat, nuttin' she had to look on but de carcass an' ol' bone de Tiger done leabe dere befo'.

An' dere was a ol' man who was berry much acquainted wid de nyung lady's farmbly, an' 'e went out in de wood huntin'; an' 'e meet up wid her dere.

'E said to de nyung lady, "'Tis not a man did married you, 'tis a Tiger!"

An' in de mean time de fly gone to let de Tiger know someone here. Well, de Tiger him so bex him holler. 'E holler to know who was dere,—say: "Whoga, whoga, whogalor, de humbarnorta, sudundilly?"

An' 'e holler so loud de wood ring, 'cause 'e bery cross. 'E gone 'long furder, den 'e say same ting 'gain. An' 'e gone long tel 'e git ter um, stan' up ober de man an' holler 'gain to try de fait' ob de man.

An' den de man gi' um arnswer now, to le' um know dat 'e was a man dat didn't 'fraid nuttin'. (Dis old man went by de name ob Sambo.)

'E gib um arnswer. 'E said, "Coo me sormber norty sudundilly indelarum."

An' de Tiger, to try de man fait' gen run 'e spear in 'e side, an' den holler de same ting as befo', an' de man gi' um de same arnswer 'gain.

Tiger say, "Now den, Sambo, tek you nyung lady home. I ain't gwine hu't her. I only married um for le' um know dat a

DIALECT

woman isn't more dan a man, for de word dat she say, dat she 'Wouldn't married a man what gots a scratch on him back.'"

An' straightway dey tuk dey journey back home to de mudder.

An' de nyung lady she said, "Mudder, de man what married me de odder day, 'taint a man, 'tis a Tiger; an' 'twant for Uncle Sambo I would a dead!"

Den de mudder said, "Daughter, I tol' you so. I tol' you dat you always speak too venomous. God had nebber made a woman for be head of a man."[77]

Finally, a delightful bit of humor is recorded by Charles Colcock Jones. The story is too long in its entirety, but a few statements of Daddy Jack will convince the reader of the charm about these Negroes which is unique and unknown to outsiders: Daddy Jack, who had a few pairs of forceps and a lancet, did dental work for the slaves at twenty-five cents a tooth. Many Negroes had teeth which "hot um" and wanted Buh Jack "fuh pull um out fuh um." Uncle Jack would get his patient in the light where he could "git a fair sight at de teet." When his patient would howl in pain, Daddy Jack would comfort him with such expressions as: "Tan to um luk a man, me son. Eh yen gwine hot you much. Eh yen gwine tek long. Me mose done. Me soon git um out." After much pulling and twisting, when the tooth finally loosened, the black dentist would exclaim: "Haw boy! When I graff my han' on er teet, eh bound fuh come, er de jaw pop,—one er tarruh." He often boasted "dat no nigger teet' ebber yet did git de better er me."[78]

[77] Christensen, *op. cit.*, pp. 10-14.
[78] Jones, *Negro Myths from the Georgia Coast.*

CHAPTER VII

SPIRITUALS OF THE SEA ISLANDS

Moses down in Egypt land
You got to tek duh chillun out uh Pharaoh hand.

THE SPIRITUALS of the Gullah Negroes differ from the spirituals of other sections in the same degree as the Gullah dialect differs from Negro speech in other parts of the South. There is something unique about the religious songs of the sea-island Negro. Because of the geographical and cultural isolation of the island people, the Gullah spirituals have retained more of original simplicity and natural beauty than those of the interior, which have been subjected to various outside cultural influences. They are decidedly different from the usual published songs which have been reduced to musical notation, and are easily distinguishable from those excellent collections rendered by the Fisk Jubilee singers, the well-known choirs of Hampton Institute and singers of other institutions. Because of the peculiar situation of the South Carolina islands and the great preponderance of Negroes over whites before and since the Civil War, Gullah music, along with other cultural traditions of the Negroes, has remained almost in its original purity. The chief difference between the spirituals of the Carolina coast and spirituals in general is that the former are marked by their stark simplicity and naïveté, their freedom from the professional musician's influence, their wildness, and weird charm. One has but to read through the collection made by the Charleston Society for the Preservation of Spirituals, *The Carolina Low Country*,[1] and compare them with other collections, to be convinced that the Gullah Negroes in their music and in their modes of religious expression more nearly reflect the plantation slave culture which produced them than the Negroes of the interior. This difference is equally marked when comparing the Gullah spirituals with a collection made by Professor Newman I. White, in his *American Negro Folk-Songs*.[2] Professor

[1] Pp. 230-327.   [2] Cambridge, 1928.

SPIRITUALS

White has faithfully recorded over eighty songs under the title "Religious Songs," which he gathered principally in Alabama and North Carolina. These songs for the most part would be shocking to the island Negroes, especially if the suggestion were made that they be sung in their churches. Many of the songs there listed give every evidence of the white man's hand, the minstrel stage, and the college glee club. Nothing has so cheapened Negro spirituals as the white man who thought he saw something funny in them. Other deteriorating influences have come from sophisticated musicians, white and Negro, who have tried to express them in standard musical forms and have as a result squeezed out of them their native beauty and simplicity, making a new product, but an inferior one.

Like Negroes in other sections of the South, the coastal Negro does not restrict himself to religious songs. He has his secular songs, his popular music, drifting in from the mainland; his work songs and ditties; but, above all, he loves best and respects most the religious songs, the spirituals. Johnson, who made a special study of folk music on St. Helena Island (1930), says that secular songs are conspicuous for their scarcity and that a few out-of-date minstrel songs, a few songs brought back from the World War, some phonograph songs, and a dozen or more children's game songs of English descent compose the small body of secular songs found on the island.[3]

Spirituals are always sung without instrumental accompaniment. They must be free and unhampered. They had their birth in extempore composition and must always be rendered free of musical arrangement. Besides, musical instruments were held in considerable suspicion by the Negroes in earlier days, especially the violin, which was esteemed an instrument of the devil. Johnson finds that as late as 1930 banjos, guitars, and such instruments were considered not quite proper on St. Helena Island even though they were used by youngsters at ice cream parties and similar frolics.[4] A Northern teacher domiciled in the home of William Fripp, on Pine Grove plantation, St. Helena Island, during the Civil War, wrote: "I never fairly heard a secular song among the Port Royal freedmen, and never saw a musical instrument among them. The last violin

[3] G. B. Johnson, *op. cit.*, p. 63.   [4] *Ibid.*

owned by a 'worldly man' disappeared from Coffin's Point 'de year gun shoot at Bay Point.' "[5]

The spirituals have been adapted to a wide range of needs among the island Negroes. They are sung, not only in the churches and at the mid-week praise meeting, but in the rice and cotton fields, at the washtubs, on the rivers, as the Negroes tug at the oars of row boats, and in the homes of the white people where little children are crooned to sleep by their gentle melody. In a letter appearing in the *Boston Journal of Music* (1862), a visitor to the Port Royal area, writing of the Negro's ability to adapt his religious songs to various kinds of work, wrote: "Of course the tempo is not always alike. On the water, the oars dip 'Poor Rosy' to an even andante, a stout boy and girl at the hominy-mill will make the same 'Poor Rosy' fly, to keep up with the whirling stone; and in the evening, after the day's work is done, 'Heab'n shall-a be my home' (a line from 'Poor Rosy') peals up slowly and mournfully from the distant quarters. One woman—a respectable house servant, who had lost all but one of her twenty-two children—said to me: 'Pshaw! don't har to dese yer chil'en, misse. Dey just rattles it off,—dey don't know how for sing it. I likes 'Poor Rosy' better dan all de songs, but it can't be sung widout a full heart and a troubled sperrit!' "[6]

It is regrettable that the masses of the Negroes are still a little ashamed of the spirituals. In their minds they are associated with slavery and its humiliations. Ambitious Negroes, striving for an education, are looking always toward the white man's way of doing things, and particularly the ways of the North. There is of course a growing number of educated Negroes who have not only the tools of knowledge but a deep appreciation of cultural values, the genuinely educated; and it is they to whom we may look for the preservation of the best in Negro folk song and other cultural elements unique among them. In many of the island churches the "revival" songbook has supplanted the native religious songs of the Negroes, and their ministers in the main are striving to imitate city choirs and metropolitan modes of worship. The result is a great loss in native beauty of expression and the development of something

[5] Pearson, *op. cit.*, p. 29.   [6] *Ibid.*, p. 30.

SPIRITUALS 135

which is inartistic and cheap. In an ambitious little church in one of the sea islands they use a manila-back hymn book, play a whining organ, and have a choir which does most of the singing (as choirs do), and imitate as well as they can urban forms of worship. I do not feel that a plea for the retention of spirituals in the Negro churches is in any way detrimental to or an argument against Negro progress. The Negro will reach his highest by being himself, by cultivating his own peculiar gifts, and by making his distinctive contribution to American life—not through imitation of the whites but through his own genius. The Southern Negro needs nothing so much as a sincere pride in his race and its attainments and a faith in the great future which awaits a people so richly endowed. Such an outlook will tend to dispel the devastating sense of inferiority so common in the South and will inevitably command a mutual respect and a common justice too long delayed.

The spirituals of the Gullah Negro run the whole gamut of human emotion from the plaintive "Lawd, I Can't Help from Cryin' Sometime" and "Nobody Knows de Trouble I See" to the ringing shout, "Tell John Don' Call de Roll, Tell I Git Dere," as sung on Cooper River near Charleston.[7] Many of the Carolina spirituals reveal a keen sensitiveness to poetic beauty, and in their humble surroundings their authors have achieved a charm of expression unique in American literature. I think one of the choicest spirituals ever produced by the island Negroes was recorded by a Union soldier, Colonel Thomas Wentworth Higginson, during the Civil War.[8] Its inspiration was the starry sky and the innate poetry of the African slave.

> I know moon-rise, I know star-rise,
>   Lay dis body down.
> I walk in de moonlight, I walk in de starlight,
>   To lay dis body down.
> I'll walk in de graveyard, I'll walk through de graveyard,
>   To lay dis body down.
> I'll lie in de grave and stretch out my arms;
>   Lay dis body down;

[7] Cf. Society for the Preservation of Spirituals, *op. cit.*, pp. 268, 301.
[8] Higginson, *op. cit.*, p. 209.

> I go to de judgment in de evenin' of de day,
>   When I lay dis body down;
> And my soul and your soul will meet in de day
>   When I lay dis body down.

Colonel Higginson wrote: "I was startled when first I came on such a flower of poetry in that dark soil."[9] It would be difficult to express more poignantly the sentiment of a tired slave who could with resignation say, "I'll lie in de grave and stretch out my arms, when I lay dis body down." Other significant spirituals were recorded during the Civil War by Higginson: "Roll, Jordan, Roll," "Stars Begin to Fall," "Blow Your Trumpet, Gabriel," "Wrestle on, Jacob," and "I Build My House Upon de Rock."

The spiritual, "Many Thousand Go,"[10] doubtless had its inception in the hope of freedom occasioned by the occupation of Port Royal by Federal troops. The peck of corn referred to was the measure rationed out to the slaves:

> No more peck o' corn for me,
>   No more, no more,—
> No more peck o' corn for me,
>   Many tousand go.
>
> No more driver's lash for me, (Twice)
>   No more, &c.
>
> No more pint o' salt for me, (Twice)
>   No more, &c.
>
> No more hundred lash for me, (Twice)
>   No more, &c.
>
> No more mistress' call for me,
>   No more, no more,—
> No more mistress' call for me,
>   Many tousand go.

The "lonesome valley" and the "lonesome road" have been familiar figures in the spirituals. It would be interesting to know just what kind of mental picture the coastal Negro had of a valley. There is hardly a valley in a hundred miles of the coast. Certainly he borrowed this figure from the Bible, perhaps the valley of dry bones described in the prophecy of

---

[9] *Ibid.*, p. 208.   [10] *Ibid.* p. 218.

SPIRITUALS 137

Ezekiel, or the "Valley of the shadow of death" in the Twenty-third Psalm. He must have conjured up in his mind some weird place which was an appropriate setting for his melodramatic religion. Such a spiritual was recorded at Bluffton, South Carolina, with the first line, "Down een duh walley on my prayin' knees."[11] Higginson remarked that among the Port Royal Negroes the *valley* was synonymous with the "anxious seat" (mourners' bench) of the camp meeting. When one was seeking religion one was in the "lonesome valley": "When a young girl was supposed to enter it, she bound a handkerchief by a peculiar knot over her head, and made it a point of honor not to change a single garment till the day of her baptism, so that she was sure of being in physical readiness for the cleansing rite, whatever her spiritual mood might be. More than once, in noticing a damsel thus mystically kerchiefed, I have asked some dusky attendant its meaning, and have received the unfailing answer—framed with their usual indifference to the genders of pronouns—'He in de lonesome valley, sa'."[12]

Funerals have always been great occasions for Negro song. In the islands about Port Royal the Negroes devised a spiritual for use at the funeral of infants, "The Baby Gone Home." This is a pathetic song, with all the naïveté characteristic of the island Negroes:

> De little baby gone home,
> De little baby gone home,
> De little baby gone along,
>   For to climb up Jacob's ladder.
> And I wish I'd been dar,
> I wish I'd been dar,
> I wish I'd been dar, my Lord,
>   For to climb up Jacob's ladder.[13]

The Charleston Society for the Preservation of Spirituals has been particularly successful in its recordings of existing songs in that area. The songs as recorded have a peculiar charm and reflect accurately the native beauty and simplicity of Negro life in the isolated coast area. The delightful spiritual, "Welcome Table," stands out in the list. Like so many, it has the apoc-

---

[11] Society for the Preservation of Spirituals, *op. cit.*, p. 318.
[12] Higginson, *op. cit.*, pp. 205-206.
[13] *Ibid.*, p. 210.

alyptic hope of a better day, a glorious hereafter. A few of the lines follow:

> I'm gwine to sit at de welcome table, (twice)
> Some o' dese days, Hallelujah, etc.

Other stanzas begin:

> I'm gwine to drink en nebbuh git t'usty [thirsty].
> I'm gwine to eat an' nebbuh git hongry.
> I'm gwine to seddown [sit down] side my Jedus.
> I'm gwine to ride in duh glycerin cha'ayut [chariot].
> I'm gwine to see all duh 'Postles.
> I'm gwine to set een duh elbow chair.
> I'm gwine to rock from side to side.

And so this happy song goes on for twelve verses. It was recorded in the Santee River section.[14]

Another rejoicing spiritual of the same collection is the "Primus Lan'" (Promised Land). The first stanza opens with:

> Oh, uh got a mansion up on high
> Well 'e ain' mek wid han',
> No—'e ain' mek wid han', etc.[15]

Other titles in this group are the following: "Face duh Risin' Sun," "Chillun ob duh Wilderness Moan fuh Bread," "Blood Done Sign My Name," "I Look Down de Road and de Road so Lonesome," and "Grabe Sinkin' Down."[16] The dignity of these songs is very evident. There is not an iota of humor about them except as outsiders might consider them funny and read into them something that for the Negro does not exist.

From the standpoint of music the spirituals are simplicity itself. There is a wild swinging rhythm and the steady beat of feet and hands suggestive of the monotonous throb of the tom-tom. There are weird notes difficult of expression in conventional musical symbols, as difficult, some commentators have thought, as the notes of birds. Along with the simplicity of the music there is a multiplicity of rhythm. Robert W. Gordon noted the presence of three different rhythms in a single spir-

---

[14] Society for the Preservation of Spirituals, *op. cit.*, p. 298. Reprinted by permission of the Macmillan Company.
[15] *Ibid.*, p. 322.
[16] Higginson, *op. cit.*, pp. 232, 266, 270, 284, 296.

SPIRITUALS

itual: "One foot rested firmly on the heel and tapped with the toe. The other foot rocked back and forth, tapping alternately with heel and toe, and doubling the time. But the two feet were not precisely synchronized; there was a perceptible double tap when both would normally have come down together on the alternate beats. The hands meanwhile clapped a three against the two and four of the feet."[17]

Nathaniel Dett refers to the peculiar throbbing character of Negro religious song as follows: "For the most part, negro music consists of a series of pulses, all of which are alike. That is, the secondary beats are as strong as the primary, or perhaps it would be better to say that there are no secondary beats. The rhythm of the songs might very well be compared to that of the human pulse which is a series of throbs all of equal intensity."[18]

The spirituals reveal a strange blending of sadness and hope, expressed not only in the words but in the music as well. There is a peculiar quality in the Negro's voice and something in his personality which give to the spiritual a distinctive element. It is very difficult for white people to sing spirituals, and, when they try, they imitate poorly. C. W. Hyne says: "There is a distinctive mellow *timbre* to the Negro voice which in group singing makes possible a matchless effect of harmony. The white man cannot achieve this remarkable blending effect, nor can he imitate the quality of voice."[19]

As previously remarked, the Northerners who came to Port Royal during the Civil War were keen observers of Negro life and customs and, happily, they wrote down their impressions of spiritual singing in that area and related them in letters sent back home. In such a letter an observing New England woman gave an excellent impression of spiritual singing in that region. She was at the time living on Pine Grove plantation, St. Helena Island, in the home of William Fripp. She wrote:

The voices of the colored people have a peculiar quality that nothing can imitate; and the intonations and delicate variations of even one singer cannot be reproduced on paper. And I despair of

---

[17] Society for the Preservation of Spirituals, *op. cit.*, p. 220. Reprinted by permission of the Macmillan Company.

[18] Robert Nathaniel Dett, *Religious Folk-Songs of the Negro* (Hampton, Va., 1927), p. xv. Reprinted by permission of Hampton Institute Press.

[19] J. Rosamond Johnson (comp.), *Utica Jubilee Singers Spirituals* (Boston, 1930), p. v. Reprinted by permission of Oliver Ditson Company.

conveying any notion of the effect of a number singing together, especially in a complicated shout. . . . There is no singing in parts, as we understand it, and yet no two appear to be singing the same thing—the leading singer starts the words of each verse, often improvising, and the others, who "base" him, as it is called, strike in with the refrain, or even join in the solo, when the words are familiar. When the "base" begins, the leader often stops, leaving the rest of the words to be guessed at, or it may be they are taken up by one of the other singers. And the "basers" themselves seem to follow their own whims, beginning when they please and leaving off when they please, striking an octave above or below (in case they have pitched the tune too low or too high), or hitting some other note that chords, so as to produce the effect of a marvellous complication and variety, and yet with the most perfect time, and rarely with any discord. And what makes it all the harder to unravel a thread of melody out of this strange network is that, like birds, they seem not infrequently to strike sounds that cannot be precisely represented by the gamut, and abound in "slide from one note to another, and turns and cadences not in articulated notes."[20]

Another interesting echo of that period is to be found in the diary of Mary Ames, of New England, a young idealist working among the Negroes of Edisto Islands. She wrote: "In the evening the family sang for us, 'Heaven's bell ringing for believers.' Another was, 'Sister, you come too late, the Devil been and shut the gate and carried off the keys'; then 'Don't judge me, Lord, O Lord—don't be offended,' and 'Thar's rejoicing over yander'; 'Let me go, Jacob will not let me go,' this repeated over and over, and 'Oh, my Lord, help us.' "[21]

In the ante-bellum period and for a long time afterwards church members were forbidden to dance. The dance, that is, partner dancing, was looked upon as a device of the devil. Reference has already been made to the suspicion under which the violin fell. In the ballroom dance the feet are crossed, while in the "shout," a religious exercise, they are apart. The distinction between religious dancing (the shout) and crossing the feet was early made by the Port Royal Negroes. The shout was apparently used as a sort of safety valve for releasing the rhythmic energies of the plantation Negroes. This they could do in all good conscience and under religious auspices, but to "cross the feet" was sin. Gordon, in *The Carolina Low Coun-*

---

[20] Pearson, *op. cit.*, p. 29.   [21] Ames, *op. cit.*, p. 46.

try, recalls a spiritual which gives this word of warning: "Watch out, sister, how you walk on de cross! yer feet might slip an' yer soul got los'."[22] The Southern white missionaries who instructed the slaves looked with disfavor upon their ecstatic shouting performances, but on week nights it appears that the Negroes had more liberty in their plantation "praise houses." Here they shouted to their hearts' content, and after the evacuation of the islands by the white owners, it appears that they indulged unbridled intensity in these emotional exercises, so that the Northern benefactors saw slave religion in its most reckless phases. An excellent description of the shout as the Negroes did it around Port Royal was given by a correspondent to the New York *Nation*, in 1867:

> The true "shout" takes place on Sundays or on praise-nights through the week, and either in the praise-house or some cabin in which a regular meeting has been held. Very likely more than half the population of the plantation is gathered together. Let it be the evening, and a light-wood fire burns red before the door to the house and on the hearth. . . . The benches are pushed back to the wall when the formal meeting is over, and young and old, men and women, sprucely dressed young men, grotesquely half-clad field hands—the women generally with gay handkerchiefs twisted about their heads and with short skirts—boys with tattered shirts and men's trousers, young girls barefooted, all stand up, begin first walking and by-and-by shuffling around, one after the other, in a ring. The foot is hardly taken from the floor, and the progression is mainly due to a jerking, hitching motion, which agitates the entire shouter, and soon brings out streams of perspiration. Sometimes they dance silently, sometimes as they shuffle they sing the chorus of the spiritual, and sometimes the song itself is also sung by the dancers. But more frequently a band, composed of some of the best singers and of tired shouters, stands at the side of the room to "base" the others, singing the body of the song and clapping their hands together or on the knees. Song and dance are alike extremely energetic, and often, when the shout lasts into the middle of the night, the monotonous thud, thud of the feet prevents sleep within half a mile of the praise-house.[23]

In a letter written at this time from Port Royal we find that the Negroes used these all-night shouting occasions to examine "seekers," or probationers, who desired church membership.

[22] P. 201.   [23] Pearson, *op. cit.*, pp. 26-27.

The description is as follows: "They had had a 'Shout,' which I had heard distinctly at three o'clock in the morning when I happened to wake up. They come from all the plantations about, when these meetings take place for the examination of new members, 'prodigals and raw souls,' as 'Siah said, he being an elder and one of the deacons. They did not begin till about ten o'clock Saturday night, when the examinations commence and the other services, after which they keep up the shout till near daylight, when they can see to go home."[24]

Worship at the Praise House, Pine Grove plantation, St. Helena Island, was described as follows:

> In the afternoon, as I came out of school, Cuffy said, "You promise to jine praise with we some night dis week, Missus," so I told him I would go up in the evening if Mr. G. would go with me. When we went up after eight they were just lighting the two candles. I sat down on the women's side next a window, and one of the men soon struck up a hymn in which the others joined and which seemed to answer the purpose of a bell, for the congregation immediately began to assemble, and after one or two hymns, Old Peter offered a prayer, using very good language, ending every sentence with "For Jesus' sake." He prayed for us, Massa and Missus, that we might be "boun' up in de belly band of faith." Then Mr. G. read to them and made a few remarks to which they listened very attentively; then some one suddenly started up and pronounced a sort of benediction, in which he used the expression "when we done chawing all de hard bones and swallow all de bitter pills." They then shook hands all round, when one of the young girls struck up one of their wild songs, and we waited listening to them for twenty minutes more.[25]

One can hardly overestimate the value of song, especially religious song, to the Negro in his low estate. This value was sensed by Colonel Higginson, of the Union Army, who wrote: "These quaint religious songs were to the men more than a source of relaxation; they were a stimulus to courage and a tie to heaven. I never overheard in camp a profane or vulgar song. . . . By these they could sing themselves, as their fathers before them, out of the contemplation of their own low estate, into the sublime scenery of the Apocalypse."[26]

[24] *Ibid.*, p. 34. [25] *Ibid.*, p. 26.
[26] Higginson, *op. cit.*, pp. 221-222.

SPIRITUALS

Under the slave regime there were apparently no songs for children. When they wanted to sing, they patterned their music after that of their elders. A Northern teacher of the Civil War period wrote: "Then I let the children sing some of their own songs in genuine, shouting style, a sight too funny in the little things, but sad and disagreeable to me in the grown people, who make it a religious act. It is impossible to describe it—the children move around in a circle, backwards, or sideways, with their feet and arms keeping energetic time, and their whole bodies undergoing most extraordinary contortions."[27]

It is not altogether certain whether spirituals originated with individuals or whether they had a group origin. It is probable that we have songs from both sources. A classic example of the former is given by Colonel Higginson:

And I always wondered, about these, whether they had always a conscious and definite origin in some leading mind, or whether they grew by gradual accretion, in an almost unconscious way. On this point I could get no information, though I asked many questions, until at last, one day when I was being rowed across from Beaufort to Ladies' Island, I found myself, with delight, on the actual trail of a song. One of the oarsmen, a brisk young fellow, not a soldier, on being asked for his theory of the matter, dropped out a coy confession. "Some good sperituals," he said, "are start jess out o' curiosity. I been a-raise a sing, myself, once."

My dream was fulfilled, and I had traced out, not the poem alone, but the poet. I implored him to proceed.

"Once we boys," he said, "went for tote some rice and de nigger-driver he keep a-callin' on us; and I say, 'O, de ole nigger-driver!' Den another said 'Fust ting my mammy tole me was, notin' so bad as nigger-driver!' Den I made a sing, just puttin' a word, and den anudder word."

Then he began singing, and the men, after listening a moment, joined in the chorus, as if it were an old acquaintance, though they evidently had never heard it before. I saw how easily a new "sing" took root among them.[28]

It is likely that some spirituals began in the act of public worship. It is quite common for Negro congregations in the more isolated sections of the South to repeat after the preacher phrases that are particularly pleasing to them. Sometimes a

---

[27] Pearson, *op. cit.*, pp. 292-293.
[28] Higginson, *op. cit.*, pp. 218-219.

text, oft repeated, will be the spark to set off a song. Melody begins to clothe the words, and the simple pulsating rhythm gives it firmness, and before one knows it a new spiritual is born. An excellent example of this process is provided by Mrs. Murphy:

We'd all be at de Prayers House de Lord's Day and de preacher he'd 'splain de word and read whar Ezekial done say—

"Dry bones ter lib ergin."

and, honey, de Lord would come a-shinin' thoo dem pages and revive dis ole nigger's heart, and I'd jump up dar and den and holler and shout and sing and pat, and dey would all catch de words and I'd sing it some ole shout song I'd heard 'em sing from Africa, and dey'd all take it up and keep at it and keep a-addin to it, and den it would be a sperituals.[29]

Spirituals have been known to grow out of conditions of stress and anxiety, such as the fearful hurricane that swept the Carolina coast in 1911. Out of this circumstance, with its fearful loss of life and the obliteration of the meager possessions of hundreds of island Negroes, came the pathetic refrain to a St. Helena Island spiritual, "Lord, don' let de win' blow here no mo'."[30]

It is almost certain, as indicated above, that the spiritual of the Allen collection,[31] "No more peck o' corn for me," has its inception in the experience of freedom. The editors state it was a song "to which the Rebellion had actually given rise," and that "it was first sung when Beauregard took the slaves of the islands to build the fortifications at Hilton Head and Bay Point."[32]

It should be recalled that the true spiritual is always undergoing change; it is never static but always in a state of flux. It is true that many have been reduced to musical notation, but in the process they lose something of their original vitality. Musically, they may be superior, but their original freshness is lost. Like the fragrant yellow jessamine, which can be itself

---

[29] Jeannette Robinson Murphy, *Southern Thoughts for Northern Thinkers* (New York, 1904), p. 23, quoted in N. I. White, *American Negro Folk-Songs*, p. 54.
[30] Nicholas George Julius Ballanta (comp.), *St. Helena Island Spirituals* (St. Helena, S. C., 1925), p. 39.
[31] Allen, *op. cit.*, p. 48.   [32] *Loc. cit.*

only in its wild state and loses its simple beauty under cultivation, the spiritual is bereft of its peculiar charm when the musicians have done with it.

A spiritual may start out with a few simple stanzas and in time have many added to it. Carried to another locality, it may undergo further change and in the end become entirely different from its original. "Paul and Silas bound in jail" became "bounden Cyrus born in jail"; "Ring Jerusalem" appeared as "Ring Rosy Land," etc.[33]

Spirituals of the Carolina sea islands were never written, never read—they just grew up. Quite often they passed out of existence. Doubtless hundreds of them have been lost for all time. Johnson observes that of the fifty-five "Slave Songs" gathered in the vicinity of St. Helena Island just after the Civil War less than a dozen were heard on the island in 1929 when he made his investigations.[34] The transitory and fluid character of the spiritual is admirably represented by Gordon, who gives a definition passed on to him by a colleague, to-wit: "A spiritual is nothing but a tune—never twice the same—accompanied by not over two standard verses—not the same—followed by as many other verses from different songs as the singer happens at the time to remember."[35]

[33] Pearson, *op. cit.*, p. 29.   [34] G. B. Johnson, *op. cit.*, p. 71.
[35] Society for the Preservation of Spirituals, *op. cit.*, p. 198. Reprinted by permission of the Macmillan Company.

CHAPTER VIII

THE CULTURAL BACKGROUND OF THE GULLAH SPIRITUALS

> All we sinnuh dey deep een de wilderness, deep een de wilderness, deep een de wilderness.
> All we sinnuh dey deep een de wilderness,
> Fur frum Canaan sho'.

THE TRADITIONAL thought about Negro spirituals is that they are purely African creations brought bodily from the native land of the slave. Upon investigation it is found that many elements of the spirituals are of American origin. Whatever may be said on either side of the question, it is certain that in a very true sense the Negro has made the spiritual peculiarly his own.

The following diagram presents briefly those factors which have moulded the religious songs of the Negroes of the Carolina coast:

The African musical system and racial peculiarities in literary expression.	
The white camp meeting. The informal, unprinted revival songs and revival preaching.	The spirituals
The white churches where slaves sat in the galleries. The theology, doctrine, and Biblical material presented there. The standard hymns of Watts, Newton, the Wesleys, and others.	
The missions to the slaves on the plantations. Catechetical instruction, songs, and sermons of the missionaries.	

BACKGROUND OF THE SPIRITUALS

The most enigmatical element in the spiritual, and the factor most difficult to describe, is that which came from Africa. Those who claim that the spirituals are only white songs declare that the elusive character of the African element is evidence that it does not exist. But this is an unwarranted assumption. I find something of this difficulty in describing character and personality. The most real part of a person is that part which is most difficult to describe. Personality is something more than a collection of traits. Two men may acquire the same traits, use the same language, and in so far as we can measure them outwardly, be the same, but their personalities are obviously different. As Krehbiel pointed out, the peculiar quality of one's personality is revealed, not so much in what one says, as the way in which he says it. The tell-tale factors of personality find expression in pitch, dynamic intensity, and timbre of voice.[1] African music is different from Western music, and the Negro spiritual, in its purity, is different from the white man's revival songs.

The studies of N. G. J. Ballanta, a native of Sierra Leone, throw considerable light upon the problem of African influence upon Afro-American folk songs.[2] Since 1924 Ballanta has collected data on African music along the West Coast under the auspices of the Guggenheim Foundation. A careful scholar and student of music, he established the presence of a definite African musical system. True, in some tribes it underwent change through both Eastern and Western influences. The former he found emanating from Islamic culture characteristic of tribes skirting the western periphery of the Sahara Desert, while the latter was discernible along the coast. Between these points he discovered true African musical perception.

A brief quotation from Ballanta's article makes clear, to musicians at least, the difference between African and Western music:

> The two principles which govern tonal expressions are tone progression and tone combination; these are determined by perception of a principal tone and an interval of association. . . .

[1] Henry Edward Krehbiel, *Afro-American Folk Songs: A Study in Racial and National Music* (New York, 1914), p. 3.

[2] Nicholas George Julius Ballanta, "Music of the African Races," *Negro Yearbook 1931-1932*, pp. 441-445; a summary from an article first published in the *Journal of West Africa*, July 14, 1930.

This interval of association for all purposes is the perfect fourth in African music; as from "doh" to "fah," or "re" to "soh." This is the fundamental difference between African and western music. . . .[3]

This difference always makes it difficult for sensitive musicians to record the spirituals in conventional musical symbols. The difficulty was noted by members of the Charleston Society for the Preservation of Spirituals, who undertook to supply the deficiency in Western symbols with "legatissimo phrasing, slurs, pauses, and long grace notes." Even then singers were admonished to "use these effects more freely and with greater variety than the notation shows."[4] Ballanta wrote: "It is not easy to note down African music by existing musical notations, as the signs would convey a different idea from that they are intended to represent. A wholly different notation is necessary to do this properly."[5]

As regards perception of harmony, this authority was of the opinion that it is absent in the musical thought of the African: "What enters into a musical expression by way of a tone combination is a highly developed form of polyphony, which may embrace two, or at most three parts. This polyphonic form is the freest from the point of view of concords and discords and it is preponderantly rhythmic; that is to say each part preserves its individuality."[6]

Further comments of Ballanta on African music are of interest to those familiar with the unique quality of the spirituals of the Carolina sea islands. He pointed out that music is not cultivated among the natives for its own sake but that it is rather a means to an end, a necessary device for dancing or an aid to the laborer. Work songs are mainly rhythmic, composed of short phrases of two bars; "solo and chorus follow each other instantly; the chorus is in many instances composed of two or three ejaculatory words, answered by the workmen. Tempo moderate"[7]—an almost perfect description of Negro laborers doing heavy work in the Deep South.

[3] Ballanta, "Music of the African Races," p. 441.
[4] Society for the Preservation of Spirituals, *op. cit.*, p. 226, from "Notes on the Spirituals," by Katharine C. Hutson, Josephine Pinckney, and Caroline Pinckney Rutledge.
[5] Ballanta, "Music of the African Races," p. 442.
[6] *Ibid.*
[7] *Ibid.*, p. 443.

BACKGROUND OF THE SPIRITUALS 149

Play songs, described as more melodic, are accompanied by clapping of hands. The chorus is more prominent and overlaps solo parts.

Dance songs cover a wide range, "from the wild dances of the Bassas in Liberia to the highly artistic dances of the Yorubas in Nigeria. In the lower scale the solos are mostly ejaculatory sentences, but sometimes they are of great length and end after the chorus begins. Tempo fast; 2-4 time; simple rhythm."[8]

Another variety is the solo song, usually sung by women. There is no handclapping except as an accompaniment for dancing.[9]

The African element is noticeable in many of the pure spirituals in spite of the fact that several writers within the last decade have given the impression that all the words of the spirituals are taken directly from the revival songs of the whites. Certainly they borrowed freely from white songs, but there is more in the spirituals than borrowed materials. Even lines and stanzas that are unmistakable borrowings have usually been assimilated and clothed with a quality and form of expression which certainly belongs to the Negro. Robert W. Gordon, of Charleston, made the point that the clearest indication of Negro philosophy, psychology, and wit is found in the separate verses and couplets of their songs.[10] The unexpected turn in a spiritual reveals the Negro's contribution, even though it is embedded in a mass of borrowed imagery. The following couplet is given as an example by Gordon:

> Tremblin' woman, an' a tremblin' man,
> God gwine hol' you wid a tremblin' han'.[11]

This couplet simply does not sound like white people, and it does not square with common sense to claim that the white camp-meeting revivalist of ante-bellum days spoke these words.

Another example of Gordon's reveals the peculiar artistic bent of the Negro and shows how he takes the conventional religious imagery of the white man and makes it his own:

> One moment in glory
> To satisfy my min'

[8] *Ibid.*   [9] *Ibid.*
[10] Society for the Preservation of Spirituals, *op. cit.*, p. 218.
[11] *Ibid.* Reprinted by permission of the Macmillan Company.

> A settin' down wid Jesus
> Eatin' honey an' drinkin' wine!
> Marchin' round de throne,
> Wid Peter, James, an' John!!!—
>   But your body,
>   got to lie,
>   in de groun'.[12]

The last phrase appears to be characteristically Negro. Working through the conventional modes of religious thought, the climax comes with marching round the throne with the apostles, then, dramatically, the cold realism, "but your body got to lie in the ground." The Negro has always been much more prone to dramatize death and the grave than the white man. He makes a greater use of such stark imagery than does the white man in the most informal of his revival songs, as, for example, in "O graveyard ought to know me," "O grass grow in de graveyard," "O I reel and rock in de graveyard,"[13] and the pathetic

> O graveyard, O graveyard,
> I'm walkin' troo de graveyard.
>   Lay dis body down.[14]

So it appears that while the body of the Negro spirituals is drawn from the American environment, their spirit is African.

The camp meetings of the whites, and especially their technique of evangelization, had a marked influence upon the slaves' religious life and song. There were no Negro camp meetings until after "freedom," but the Negroes were permitted to attend in considerable numbers, as evidenced by the old records of these events. The Reverend Charles S. Walker, commenting upon the meeting at Beauty Spot, near Tatum, South Carolina (1838), declared that of the 195 persons received on probation, 96 were colored. He continued: "... the people flocked from every direction with their wagons and families ... the altar was crowded with mourners, weeping, struggling mourners."[15]

The camp meeting was the medium through which the religious revival, beginning about 1798, found its fullest expres-

---

[12] *Ibid.*, p. 218.
[13] Allen, *op. cit.*, p. 15.   [14] *Ibid.*, p. 19.
[15] W. A. Massebeau, *The Camp Meeting in South Carolina* (1919), p. 15. Quoted by Massebeau, but his source is not given. It is probably a report in the *Southern Christian Advocate*.

BACKGROUND OF THE SPIRITUALS

sion. This wave of religious interest apparently had its inception in southern Kentucky and in a very few years swept the entire country. Its influence continued for many years, and the camp meeting was the instrument which kept it alive and fostered its emotional phases. Massebeau recorded the names of fifty campgrounds in South Carolina and reckoned the list as being very incomplete since many sprang up here and there and, after continuing for a few years, were abandoned. In the Gullah country he mentioned Mt. Carmel, Green Pond, Union, Rehoboth, Black Swamp, Peniel, and Haddell's Point (Mount Pleasant).[16] In the latter half of the nineteenth century the camp meetings began to wane; now they are but a memory. Only three of the fifty or more survive in South Carolina: Indian Fields, near St. George; Cattle Creek, near Rowesville; and Cypress, in the vicinity of the village of Ridgeville. These have but a semblance of their former prestige. I have discovered no records of the Negro camp meetings though many were organized after the Civil War. There is now one in Orangeburg County, Prospect, conducted by the Negroes. It is a desolate spot, with a row of crude wooden structures on one side, a place for preaching, and a small church. Here the dying embers of a lost enthusiasm are fanned in the hope that the old-time religion will blaze forth in its former splendor.

In the beginning the camp meetings were conducted by several of the evangelical denominations in the state, especially Methodist, Baptist, and Presbyterian, but in time they became a distinctly Methodist institution. The Episcopalians looked upon them with considerable suspicion and some scorn, and at times condemned them heartily; but the Methodists defended the institution editorially and in public address and did everything to further its influence.

As a small boy I witnessed the latter years of the camp meeting in lower South Carolina. In the 1890's and earlier my father followed the precedent set by his parents and owned a "tent" (a small wooden structure) at Cattle Creek campground. Enthusiasm for the camp meeting at this time was at low ebb; it had already served its day. For sentimental reasons a relatively small crowd gathered during the hot month of July to stir memories of the olden days. The church still recognized

[16] *Ibid.*, pp. 8-9.

the institution as of value, and the presiding elder annually made plans for its services, inviting certain suitable preachers, who always stayed at the "preachers' tent."

There is no "great" preaching as in former times, no shouting or old-time singing. Many go out of curiosity, especially on Sundays, traveling long distances by automobile, but the old enthusiasm is gone. As early as forty years ago it was whispered by some of the older people that the camp meeting had become a social affair and that there was not much religion in it. Today, Indian Fields and Cattle Creek in their decaying state stand as silent reminders of a phase of religion which passed with the Old South. There is something pathetic about these old spots; like the deserted plantations, they, too, are looking back. The earnest people who once patronized them lie in the silent graveyards nearby. On a hot summer day the air is heavy with the pungent scent of pine needles that litter the white sandy ground so characteristic of these places, and the only sound is the soughing of the tall longleaf pines standing guard over these once hallowed places.

It is now appropriate to look in upon a camp-meeting service of ante-bellum days. F. A. Mood, in his little book, *Methodism in Charleston*, described a meeting on Goose Creek, near Charleston, in 1814, at which the preacher was speaking of Ezekiel's vision of the valley of dry bones:

From a silent wrapt attention, the throng was gradually melted to tears, and finally the speaker's voice was drowned amid the cries, and sobs, and shouts of the multitude. An invitation was extended for mourners to come to the altar, when a general rush was made in opposite directions, many hastening forward to obtain the prayers of the pious, and numbers endeavoring to make their escape from under the arbor. Many of these last, overwhelmed by their sense of guilt even in their flight, fell to the earth in every direction, as if smitten by the hand of death; and until the dawn of the Sabbath from under the arbor, the tents, and over the ground, the voice of weeping and intercession was heard.[17]

One of the most interesting exponents of camp-meeting preaching in South Carolina in the early days was a man named Lucius Bellinger, born in Walterboro, South Carolina, in 1806. He was known as the "Strange Preacher," the "War Horse,"

---

[17] *Ibid.*, pp. 25-26.

BACKGROUND OF THE SPIRITUALS 153

the "Wandering Arab," and by other names, all marking him as a unique character and perhaps a kind of genius. In 1870 he published his memoirs, *Stray Leaves from the Portfolio of a Methodist Local Preacher*, an invaluable work to students who desire a realistic picture of the spectacular and ecstatic phases of the camp meeting in the first half of the nineteenth century. Reading between the lines, one discovers the practical psychology used by these religious orators of the rural pulpit. To say that they were insincere is greatly to misrepresent them. Never were men more sincerely earnest about anything. Their religion was of the nineteenth-century fundamentalist type; they believed that the accompanying emotionalism and the strange conduct of their hearers were the direct results of divine influence, and without a knowledge of the laws of mind, they attributed to the Holy Spirit many things which are now known to be simple psychological manifestations. I am aware that in discussing the camp meeting at this distance, and with a considerable amount of psychological data at hand, it is easy to underrate the value of the camp meeting as a step in religious progress. Some contemporary writers see nothing but foolishness in this type of religious expression and describe its primitiveness in a very sophisticated manner. They overlook the fact that real values in character and renewed personality came out of the camp meeting in spite of the extra luggage it carried. After all, the chief function of religion is to make men good, and this it did in a significant way.

At any rate, we shall let the "Strange Preacher" speak for himself. In giving an account of a meeting at Cattle Creek campground he unwittingly included an excellent description of the preacher's psychological devices, especially the power of suggestion in moving his auditors to a desired goal. The subject of Bellinger's narrative is an influential fellow-preacher named Postell, who has established a reputation as an exhorter. Bellinger wrote as follows:

> The large and unpleasantly-situated congregation became very still when he rose. He observed, that he hoped to have the prayers and attention of all present, and exhorted the brethren to exercise faith, and to expect a large outpouring of the Spirit—that he looked for and expected it. He said, he was afraid there were several present who did not expect much, but that he hoped to see many

mourners and several conversions. I turned, and looked again, but saw no manifest signs of the great out-pouring which was expected. He hoped the mourners would not wait for singing to commence, as he wanted to see them coming up promptly. During his exhortation (which ought never to be forgotten) he several times requested us to pray, and not to fear, and said that we would have a glorious meeting. He looked round frequently, but saw no marked signs. He more than once gazed at me with his piercing black eyes, which seemed to say, "do not fear, Brother B., we will have a great revival."

He compared himself to an archer, with his quiver full of arrows, and said he was going to shoot them at the sinner, the backslider, and all cold-hearted Christians, and he hoped every one would feel a smart—that he had more than a score of them, and as he shot them off, he hoped the church would pray as they heard them whizzing through the crowd. In his very impressive manner he proceeded fixing the arrows. His soul-stirring words followed one another like a mighty torrent rushing down the mountain side. I soon forgot to turn again, for the last time I looked I saw the marked signs, not to be mistaken. If the rain continued to fall, that torrent would sweep everything before it—trees, houses, rocks, and all. He would every now and then, after some strong expression, tell us another arrow was shot off, and beg us to pray as we heard it flying from the string.

On, and still on, the archer of the cross went—getting at length to his last shaft. He then paused, as if to recover full strength for his last effort. O, my soul! what a pause was that! It seemed as if immortal souls were trembling in the balance, while angels and devils held their breath as they looked and listened. Before shooting the last arrow, he said he would put a new string on his bow, and he begged us, if ever in our lives we had prayed with faith, to do so now—and I doubt if a more general or fervent prayer was ever offered up in old Cattle Creek church. He then told us that an interesting young lady, whose parents loved the Lord, and were on their way to heaven, who came there with him, was very gay and fond of fashion, and he was afraid she would never meet her parents in glory. He said, he had begged her to try to get religion, and he would pray for her as long as he lived.

The last arrow went sounding from the string. As I turned round to look, I almost sprang to my feet; for I saw a young lady fall from her seat as if she had been shot through the heart; and now, from the outside of the crowd, came a young man, forcing his way, stepping from bench to bench, crying for mercy. And then a crowd

BACKGROUND OF THE SPIRITUALS 155

of mourners rushed up as if for their lives; and then Brother Postell came down from the pulpit, singing—

"Trouble's over, trouble's over;
A few more rounds of circuits here,
Then all our troubles will be over."

We had, indeed, a glorious old-time meeting. I remained until eleven o'clock, and then, not being able to reach the door, got out through the window. I hope to remember that night, in heaven, where all our troubles will be over for ever.[18]

The "Strange Preacher" also gave an account of a meeting at Black Swamp campground, in Hampton County, near the Savannah River. Some of the hymns they sang were "There is a Happy Land, Far, Far Away," "Our Bondage Here Will End By and Bye," and "I Would Not Live Always." Of a fellow-preacher named McPhail he wrote:

How he moved about, speaking suitable words to all; and then he prayed; and first one and then another was happily converted. And then the good man clapped his trembling hands together and passed through the throng, singing, with a voice that trembled too,
"O! brethren, will you meet me, in Canaan's happy land?"
And then, Brothers Lawton, Martin, Davis, Solomons, Blunt, Allen, Roberts, and others, all sung together,
"Yes, by the grace of God, we'll meet you, in Canaan's happy land."[19]

He continued:

In the intervals of service, the time was well spent in some of the tents—exhortations followed prayer, and song followed song. The holy feeling seemed to widen more and still more. I went into the woods with others, to pray for the trembling mourners who were still unconverted, unblessed. They cried for mercy, and entreated their friends not to leave them.[20]

The camp meeting at its height of emotional fervor made possible many interesting and strange manifestations of the preacher's power over his audience. I have heard my father say that when a boy he had seen Negroes who, after an orgy of emotionalism, were hauled off in wagons completely uncon-

---

[18] Lucius Bellinger, *Stray Leaves from the Portfolio of a Methodist Local Preacher* (Macon, Ga., 1870), pp. 58-59.
[19] *Ibid.*, pp. 74-75.
[20] *Ibid.*, p. 75.

scious, looking as though they were dead. Two incidents which occurred in South Carolina in the later period of camp-meeting history were recorded by Massebeau. They were the last manifestations of what Massebeau called "suspended animation": "About 1855 at Rehoboth camp meeting, in Berkley County, a Miss Emma Hucksford was stricken down apparently lifeless; and a ten-year-old boy, now an old man, wondered why her friends gathered about her and sang instead of weeping over her dead body."[21] The other instance was at Indian Fields in 1871: "A young man, kneeling at the altar, fell over and was stretched out on the straw. As he regained consciousness, he spoke the name of an idolized wife, who had recently died; and his friends believed that he had seen her."[22]

Lorenzo Dow (1777-1834), an eccentric Methodist itinerant from Connecticut, who preached in various parts of the country, recorded many instances of mysterious manifestations which accompanied the revival of 1800. While preaching in the coast section of Georgia he wrote in his *Journal* the following: "In a meeting a black woman belonging to General Steward . . . fell down and lay like a corpse for some time; and her hands seemed as cold as death; we were at prayer when she fell, and her falling had like to have knocked me over. After about an hour and a half she came to, and praised God."[23] Another instance, which occurred near Savannah, Dow described as follows: "Last night, as brother Cooke was preaching, a black woman was struck under conviction, with the power of God. Her body was cold as a corpse, and laid aside sixteen hours as in a sweet sleep or state of insensibility, and no symptoms of life, except a regular pulse. Some thought that she would never come to; however, she revived, praising God."[24]

Bishop William Capers, of Charleston, founder of the Methodist missions among the slaves, related in his autobiography his reaction to a South Carolina camp meeting in 1802. As a boy he was deeply impressed with the peculiar conduct of many in attendance, especially that affection known as the "jerks":

[21] Massebeau, *op. cit.*, p. 12.   [22] *Ibid.*
[23] Lorenzo Dow, *Life, Travels, Labors, and Writings* (New York, 1881), p. 97.   [24] *Ibid.*, p. 129.

BACKGROUND OF THE SPIRITUALS

In some instances persons who were not before known to be at all religious, or under any particular concern about it, would suddenly fall to the ground and become strangely convulsed with what was called the jerks; the head and neck, and sometimes the body also, moving backward and forward with spasmodic violence, and so rapidly that the plaited hair of a woman's head might be heard to crack. This exercise was not peculiar to feeble persons, nor to either sex; but, on the contrary, was most frequent to the strong and athletic, whether man or woman. I never knew it among children, nor very old persons. In other cases, persons falling down would appear senseless and almost lifeless for hours together; lying motionless at full length on the ground, and almost as pale as corpses. And then there was the jumping exercise, which sometimes approximated dancing, in which several persons might be seen, standing perfectly erect, and springing upward after seeming to bend a joint of their bodies. Such exercises were scarcely if at all present among the same people at the camp meeting of 1806. And yet this camp meeting was not less remarkable than the former ones, and very much more so than any I have attended in later years, for the suddenness with which sinners of every description were awakened, and the overwhelming force of their convictions, bearing them instantly down to their knees, if not to the ground, crying for mercy.[25]

Dow also encountered "jerks" in his preaching tours: "I had heard about a singularity called the *jerks* or *jerking exercise*, which appeared first near Knoxville in August last, to the great alarm of the people, which reports at first I considered as vague and false."[26] A little later he witnessed this strange phenomenon in a vast audience to which he was speaking: "I observed about thirty to have the jerks. Though they strove to keep still as they could, these emotions were involuntary and irresistible, as any unprejudiced eye might discern."[27]

But Dow was to see stranger things happen as the revival gathered momentum and the power of suggestion became more effective in the rural congregations. Near Knoxville, while speaking to an overflow congregation in and round the courthouse, he estimated that "about one hundred and fifty appeared to have the jerking exercise," among them a circuit preacher

[25] William M. Wightman, *Life of William Capers, D. D., One of the Bishops of the Methodist Episcopal Church, South; Including an Autobiography* (Nashville, Tenn., 1859), pp. 53-54.
[26] Dow, *op. cit.*, pp. 32-33.   [27] *Ibid.*, p. 23.

named Johnson. The Quakers, Dow added, although they attributed the jerking exercise to the excess praying and singing of the Methodists, were themselves seized in meeting with this strange bodily movement: ". . . about thirty of them [Quakers] came to the meeting, to hear one, as they said, somewhat in a Quaker line. But their unusual stillness and silence was interrupted, for about a dozen of them had the jerks as keen and as powerful as any I had seen, so as to have occasioned a kind of grunt or groan when they would jerk."[28]

Dow observed that it affected not only Methodists, but also Presbyterians, Quakers, Baptists, Episcopalians, and Independents. Its influence was felt by white and black, old and young, rich and poor. He wrote:

I believe that those who are most pious and given up to God are rarely touched with it, and also those naturalists who wish and try to get it to philosophize upon it, are excepted. But the lukewarm, lazy, half-hearted, indolent professor is subject to it; and many of them I have seen, who, when it came upon them, would be alarmed and stirred up to redouble their diligence with God; and after they would get happy, were thankful it ever came upon them. Again, the wicked are frequently more afraid of it than the small-pox or yellow fever; these are subject to it. But the persecutors are more subject to it than any; and they sometimes have cursed and swore, and damned it while jerking.[29]

It is not to be inferred that jerking, barking (which prevailed in some sections), suspended animation (hypnosis), and other peculiar psychic expressions were the norm of camp-meeting procedure. While such phenomena prevailed in many parts of the country, especially during the first decades of the revival movement, and were recorded by scores of eyewitnesses, they were, by and large, the exception and not the rule. Of course, the essence of the camp meeting was deep fervor and emotion, and the success of the preacher was judged by the amount of feeling exhibited and the number who threw themselves into the emotional current. Music was one of the chief techniques for arousing emotions, and the preachers themselves were frequently great singers and often burst into song in the midst of a fervent discourse. Camp-meeting procedure then was marked not only by highly emotionalized preaching and fervent singing, but also

[28] *Ibid.*, p. 134.   [29] *Ibid.*

BACKGROUND OF THE SPIRITUALS 159

by shouting, clapping of hands, hallelujahs, and amens. It is not surprising that the hundreds of Negroes who sat in special sections at the white camp meeting were deeply impressed by what happened. It is no wonder that in their attitudes of primitive credulity—little less primitive than some of their white friends—the Negroes, with their African mysticism and love for the dramatic, quickly seized upon the camp-meeting theology and wove it into the body of their religious songs.

What kind of songs did the Negroes hear in the camp meetings? Certainly they heard the standard hymns from the church hymnals; it is certain also that frequently the congregations would burst forth into some old-time songs—songs that were either never printed or else had been deleted from the hymnals because of their lack of dignity and literary quality. It is exceedingly difficult to lay hands upon these old songs, for the old hymn books do not contain the more rustic ones and it is only through the scant references made to them in the literature of that period and fragments of them referred to here and there that we have any adequate knowledge of their nature.[30] One of the richest sources for these rustic spirituals of the white camp meeting is that unique work already quoted, Lucius Bellinger's *Stray Leaves from the Portfolio of a Methodist Local Preacher*. The old "War Horse" as he recalled the vivid experiences of his camp-meeting ministry, frequently wrote down a brief line or a stanza from the old songs which burst forth with typical revival spontaneity. Some of them taken from his book are as follows:

> Give every fettered soul release
> And let us all depart in peace.

> Trouble's over, trouble's over;
> A few more rounds of circuits here,
> Then all our troubles will be over.

> There is a happy land far, far away.

> Our bondage here will end by and bye.

> I would not live always.

[30] For a fuller discussion see White, *op. cit.*, chap. ii, and G. B. Johnson, *op. cit.*, chap. ii.

O! brethren will you meet me,
   in Canaan's happy land?
Yes, by the grace of God, we'll meet you,
   in Canaan's happy land.

I've listed and I mean to fight
Till the warfare is over.

I feel the work reviving, I feel the work reviving,
   Reviving in my soul.
O! brethren will you meet me,
   In Canaan's happy land?

And hundreds of happy souls replied:

"By the grace of God, we'll meet you,
   In Canaan's happy land."

Come ye sinners poor and needy.

The warfare is over.

I want my friends to go with me.

I will join the army by and bye.

I want to be a Christian here,
I want to die a shouting,
I want to see my Savior near,
When soul and body are parting.

Where now are the Hebrew children?

Here we go rejoicing home,
From the banquet of perfume.

Other lines from the *Stray Leaves* give an idea of the part spontaneous song played in the camp-meeting services. The following are taken at random from Bellinger's book:

Someone then—Brother Holman, I think—sung a few lines of a beautiful hymn; and there was then a shout in the camp. I again glanced at Dr. S. who appeared so much excited that he could not keep still.

Another beautiful hymn was sung by Brother H., and we had another shout in camp.

There was another shout and clapping of hands, in which the preachers joined heartily.

BACKGROUND OF THE SPIRITUALS

If I had never clapped my hands and shouted "farewell world" before, I think I would have learned how, at that love-feast.

We now have old-time singing—clear loud and ringing.

There was a perfect jam, every place being filled with persons either standing or sitting. Such glorious old-time singing we had— even now in imagination I hear it.

I knew Brother Box Robinson would be there, and would sing his old song, beginning—

> "The richest man I ever saw,
> Was one that begged the most.
> And a begging I will go."

A common practice at the camp meeting and in the poorer rural churches was to "line out" the hymns, the preacher reading a line or two and the congregation responding in song. This was necessary because of the scarcity of hymn books, and because in the pinelands especially, many of the "po' buckra" could not read—and the slaves, of course, could not.

Then there was a type of antiphonal singing in which the preacher or some good member in the "amen corner" would sing a line, usually an interrogation, and the congregation would respond in loud chorus. Massebeau, writing about the early camp meeting, declared:

> Some saint with a good clear voice would begin,
>   "Where now is the good old Elijah?"
> The congregation would answer,
>   "Safe in the promised land."
>   "Where now are the Hebrew children?"
> And the response,
>   "Safe in the promised land."
>   "Where are now our good old fathers?"
>   "Safe in the promised land."
>   "Where now are our faithful pastors?"
>   "Away over in the promised land."[31]

It would appear that the Negro appropriated many elements of the camp-meeting songs: the clapping of hands, antiphonal singing, the swaying of bodies, and especially lines and stanzas which appealed to his imagination. These he wove into his own

---

[31] Massebeau, *op. cit.*, pp. 19-20.

peculiar musical forms and to them gave a unique quality all his own.

Many Negroes in the Carolina coast country, as in other sections of the South before the Civil War, belonged to the white churches. The tendency for Negroes to join the white churches was accelerated as the abolition movement gained in influence in the North. Southern slaveholders, especially those on the large plantations in the Deep South, became very solicitous about the spiritual condition of their slaves. The churches were soon aroused, influential men espoused the cause of slave conversion, and a concerted effort was made to evangelize the slaves of the Southern plantations. In so far as the churches were concerned this movement reached its highest efficiency in the Methodist missions to the slaves instituted by William Capers, of Charleston, later a bishop in the Methodist Church. In the enthusiasm to evangelize the slaves, missionaries were sent direct to the plantations, where the Gospel was preached in a manner understandable to unlettered Negroes. The children were carefully catechised in the fundamental doctrines of the church. Long before this they had been admitted to the churches, where they sat in the galleries, but now they were admitted in great numbers. The Missionary Society of the South Carolina Conference in 1835 reported 2,603 colored members and 1,330 children under catechetical instruction.[32] C. C. Jones declared: "Dr. Dalcho mentions that in 1822 there were 316 colored communicants in the Episcopal churches of Charleston and 200 children in their colored Sunday-schools."[33] C. E. Leveret, writing from Edisto Island in 1845, claimed that of the four thousand Negroes on the island, "100 are communicants of the Episcopal Church, and about 200 attend our services; 157 are communicants of the Presbyterian Church; 100 of the Baptist Church. The Methodist minister visits 11 plantations; there are 345 church members and 180 children catechised."[34] John Rivers wrote from James Island the same year:

[32] Jones, *Religious Instruction of the Negroes*, p. 80, quoted in Harrison, *op. cit.*, p. 81.
[33] Jones, *Religious Instruction of the Negroes*, p. 73.
[34] *Proceedings of the Meeting in Charleston, S. C., on the Religious Instruction of the Negroes* (Charleston, S. C., 1845), p. 45.

BACKGROUND OF THE SPIRITUALS 163

There are 1,500 negroes in James Island; 18 belong to the Episcopal Church . . . ; 300 to the Presbyterian. . . . The negroes attend public worship all the year, and after the morning services, on the Sabbath, there is a special service adapted to, and intended for their use. They are then instructed in the Catechism, the Lord's Prayer, the Creed, and Commandments, all of which is explained. . . . Dr. Capers' and Mr. Clarkson's Catechism are used, and Dr. Watts' hymns. My most orderly negroes are those connected with the church. Religious instruction promotes the discipline and subordination on plantations. My conclusions are the result of experience on my own plantation.[35]

Thomas Fuller, representing the Beaufort District, reported that in 1845, 2,132 Negroes belonged to the white Baptist Church in Beaufort and 900 to the church on St. Helena Island, while 314 belonged to the Methodist Mission, whose minister numbered 20 plantations in his charge. Fifty-one Negroes belonged to the Episcopal Church in Beaufort.[36] The area round Georgetown was strongly Episcopal, for John H. Tucker noted in 1845 that there were 1,100 colored baptized members of the Protestant Episcopal Church, of whom 150 were communicants.[37]

The statistical reports of the churches of this period indicate a great influx of slaves into the churches. At the time of the division of the Methodist Episcopal Church (1844) there were in the Southern area 125,000 colored members,[38] "a larger number of practically heathen converts than all the missionary societies of America had gathered upon all the fields of the heathen world."[39]

It is not generally known how influential the white churches were with the Negroes and to what lengths many earnest white men went to furnish religious instruction to them. The city of Charleston was very active through its many churches, and one is amazed at the earnestness of the whites in giving religious advantages to the Negro. F. R. Shackelford, Superintendent of one of the Sunday schools in Charleston, writing in May, 1845, to those in charge of a meeting which was to consider the

[35] *Ibid.*, pp. 46-47.
[36] *Ibid.*, p. 48. [37] *Ibid.*, p. 35.
[38] Elmer Talmadge Clark, *The Negro and His Religion* (Nashville, Tenn., 1924), p. 33. [39] *Ibid.*

religious instruction of the slaves, reported a belief that all the churches of Charleston had Sabbath schools for Negroes, and he illustrated by a specific example:

> The coloured Sabbath school in *Trinity Church,—Methodist Episcopal,* has been organized 12 months. Beginning with 30 scholars, we have steadily advanced to 170. We have twenty teachers, male and female, and have every encouragement to persevere. This school has been constituted a *missionary society*. Its anniversary was celebrated on the first Sabbath of the year; at which time, some of the parents of the children, men of piety and intelligence, were called upon to address the school, which they did in a forcible, impressive and Christian manner.[40]

On June 14, 1819, a committee of the Board of Managers of the Bible Society of Charleston, referring to the number of colored church members in the city, reported that "upward of one-fourth of the communicants are slaves or free persons of color. . . . In every Church they are freely admitted to attend on divine service. In most of the churches distinct accommodations are provided for them, and the clergy in general make it a part of their pastoral care to devote frequent and stated seasons for the religious instruction of catechumens from amongst the black population."[41]

Thus the Negroes of the Carolina rice community had frequent and rather intimate contact with the white churches, their public worship, their theology, and, especially through the Sunday schools, their Bible. So it was not only in the camp meeting that the coastal Negro found material for his religious songs, but also in the churches, generally not the poor little log buildings of the pinelands but the better equipped churches of the well-to-do planters, among them the sedate Episcopalian lately sprung from the Church of England. Indeed, it would appear as though the camp meeting was a secondary influence in the religious life of the sea-island Negroes as distinguished from the Negroes of the back-lying rice plantations. The camp meeting was distinctly a pineland and upcountry institution, and I have found no records of its presence on any of the islands. There were, as indicated above, a few in the rice country, the

---

[40] *Proceedings of the Meeting in Charleston, S. C., on the Religious Instruction of the Negroes,* pp. 38-39.

[41] Harrison, *op. cit.,* p. 67.

BACKGROUND OF THE SPIRITUALS 165

hinterland of the islands. Many slaves of the coast country heard, Sunday after Sunday, the stately liturgy of the Anglican Church, and had an opportunity to hear the dignified ritual and intercessions of the Prayer Book. But doubtless most of them were moved by the more homely appeals of the Methodist and Baptist preachers and to a somewhat lesser degree by those of the Presbyterians. At any rate, they must have been attentive listeners as they sat in the galleries of the white churches, dressed up in their Sunday best and enjoying a day of cessation from toil and a few hours of relief from the watchful eye of the overseer. No doubt many of them went to sleep in the cozy surroundings of the church; but many of them must have heard what the preachers said, for their spirituals are replete with Biblical references, especially the dramatic episodes of the Old Testament and the brilliant imagery of the apocalyptic writings. The latent mysticism of the African found the rich symbolism of The Revelation very congenial to his imagination, and he seized upon its dramatic elements and colorful settings and wove them into his own songs as they arose spontaneously in cabin or in church. It is significant that much of the symbolism of the Old Testament apocalyptic writings was borrowed from Babylonia and Northern Africa, especially Egypt. Perhaps, after all, the unlettered slave saw something in the Oriental imagery of the apocalypse that the white man of the West could not see. Certainly he was captivated by its beauty and lost no opportunity to use it as a medium for his own religious expression. The slave's social and economic status made it easy for him to appreciate the hopeful view of the Old Testament seer. The apocalyptic note is always sounded during periods of distress; all such literature of the Bible had its origin in periods of persecution and dejection. Ezekiel's brilliant imagery grew out of the desolation of the Babylonian exile, and the colorful pictures of hope in The Revelation had their genesis in the fiery persecution by the Roman government under Domitian.

Psychologically, apocalyptic writing is an effort in the direction of compensation; it is a form of release, a flight from reality. The present moment is so dark that the prophet in imagination leaps over all barriers of reality and projects himself into a glorious future—a future that promises a rectification of all injustice and poignantly predicts a time when "God shall wipe away all tears from their eyes." I do not know whether or not the Negro fully appreciated the effectiveness of apocalyptic forms. It is a sharp weapon, a message in code—incendiary. The strange imagery is understood only by the initiated; to the enemy the images are meaningless. It is a clever device, always used by people under oppression. Perhaps the Negroes sensed this, and embraced it because they, too, felt the hand of oppression.

The apocalyptic elements of the Bible appealed to the Negro also because of their magnificence. The Negro has always liked high-sounding phrases and eloquent speech, and his innate artistic sense responded doubly to the grandeur of the apocalyptic style. Indeed, The Revelation is suggestive of a great symphony, in which brass instruments and thundering drums play the dominant role, with flashing lightning, earthquakes, and mighty winds accompanying. There are in the Apocalypse strange living creatures which shine like burnished brass: wild beasts, flying eagles, the four horsemen; harps, trumpets; the River of Life, the Tree of Life, fountains of water; kings, captains, mighty men, angels, voices from heaven, and the throne of God itself. The brilliance of such imagery caught the imagination of the Negro and brought from him the naïvely beautiful prayer songs, so uniquely his own.

The following parallel columns of Biblical materials and passages from Negro spirituals show how deeply the slaves of the Carolina coast drew upon the dramatic episodes of the Old and New Testaments and particularly the apocalyptic passages. I have with considerable care gone through the three most conspicuous collections of spirituals of this section,[42] and for part of them, at least, have traced their Biblical lineage. So "Biblical" are the prayer songs of these Negroes that scarcely a fourth of them would fall without the range of the Old and New Testament canons.

Selections from Bible	*Selections from the Spirituals*
Rev. 7:16. They shall hunger no more, neither thirst any more.	I'm gwine eat an' nebbuh git hongry Some o' des days, Hallelujah!

[42] Allen, *op. cit.*; Ballanta, *St. Helena Island Spirituals*; Society for the Preservation of Spirituals, *op. cit.*

BACKGROUND OF THE SPIRITUALS

Isa. 50:10. They shall not hunger nor thirst, neither shall the heat nor sun smite them.

Rev. 6:15-17. And the kings of the earth . . . hid themselves in the dens and in the rocks of the mountains; and said to the mountains and rocks, Fall on us, and hide us from the face of him that sitteth on the throne, and from the wrath of the Lamb.

Isa. 2:10. Enter into the rock, and hide thee in the dust, for fear of the Lord, and for the glory of his majesty.

Rev. 22:8. I John saw these things and heard them; and when I heard and seen, I fell down to worship before the feet of the angel. . . .

Rev. 7:16-17. Neither shall the sun light on them, nor any heat. For the Lamb, which is in the midst of the throne, shall feed them, and shall lead them unto living fountains of waters: and God shall wipe away all tears from their eyes.

Rev. 7:4. And there were sealed an hundred and forty and four thousand of all the tribes of the children of Israel.

I'm gwine to drink an' nebbuh git thirsty
Some o' des days, Hallelujah![43]
1. Cyan' hide sinner, cyan' hide
2. Cyan hide liar, cyan hide
3. Cyan hide gambler, cyan hide

I run to de rocks to hide my face
O Lawd I run, O Lawd I run.[44]

Walk in Jerusalem my dear bruddah
Walk in Jerusalem jis like John.[45]
Tell John don' call de roll, till I git dere.[46]

Gwine to rest from all my labuh, W'en I dead,
Een duh mawnin', eh Lawd
My soul so happy now

Eh, Lawd, w'en I dead.
Gwine to walk and talk wid Jedus
W'en I dead, etc.[47]

John saw de number no man could number
Comin' up on high.
John saw de hundred and forty-four thousand,

---

[43] Society for the Preservation of Spirituals, *op. cit.*, p. 298. Reprinted by permission of the Macmillan Company.
[44] Ballanta, *St. Helena Island Spirituals*, p. 35.
[45] *Ibid.*, p. 47.
[46] Society for the Preservation of Spirituals, *op. cit.*, p. 300. Reprinted by permission of the Macmillan Company.
[47] *Ibid.*, p. 244.

Rev. 20:15. And whosoever was not found written in the book of life was cast into the lake of fire.

Dan. 12:1. And at that time shall Michael stand up, the great prince which standeth for the children of thy people.

Rev. 8:10. . . . and there fell a great star from heaven . . . and it fell upon the third part of the rivers, and upon the fountains of waters. 9:1. And I saw a star fall from heaven unto the earth.

Rev. 6:12. . . . and the moon became as blood: and the stars of heaven fell unto the earth, even as a fig tree casteth her untimely figs, when she is shaken of a mighty wind.

Rev. 1:5. Unto him that loved us and washed us from our sins in his own blood.

Rev. 5:9. . . . for thou wast slain, and hast redeemed us to God by thy blood, out of every kindred, and tongue, and people.

Rev. 13:16. And he causeth all . . . to receive a mark in their right hands or in their foreheads.

9. . . . and receive a mark in his forehead, or in his hand.

Comin' up on high.
Tell John not to call de roll till I git dere,
Sinner man you better believe.[48]
Write muh name on de book of life
De angel in de heben gwine to write my name.[49]
Michael row de boat ashore,
    Hallelujah!
Michael boat a gospel boat,
    Hallelujah![50]

Oh what a mournin' (sister),
Oh what a mournin' (brudder),
Oh what a mournin',
When de stars begin to fall.[51]

1. And de moon will turn to blood in dat day.
2. And you'll see de stars a-fallin'.
3. And de world will be on fire.
4. And you'll hear de saints a-singin.[52]

1. Een duh wilduhness, een duh wilduhness,
En duh blood pit 'e maa'k on me.
2. Een duh fo'head, een duh fo'head,
En duh blood pit 'e maa'k on me.

5. En duh blood, en duh blood,
En duh blood done sign my name,

---

[48] Ballanta, *St. Helena Island Spirituals*, p. 46.
[49] *Ibid.*, p. 37.
[50] Allen, *op. cit.*, p. 23.
[51] *Ibid.*, p. 25.
[52] *Ibid.*, p. 53.

BACKGROUND OF THE SPIRITUALS

11. ... and whosoever receiveth the mark of his name.

Ezek. 10:9, 10. And when I looked, the four wheels by the cherubim, one wheel by one cherub: and the appearance of the wheels was as the color of a beryl stone. And as for their appearances, they four had one likeness, as if a wheel had been within a wheel.

Rev. 6:2. And I saw, and beheld a white horse: and he that sat on him had a bow: and a crown was given unto him, and he went forth conquering, and to conquer.

Rev. 19:11. And I saw heaven opened, and behold, a white horse: and he that sat upon him was called Faithful and True.

Ezek. 37:1-10. And the hand of the Lord was upon me ... and set me down in the midst of the valley which was full of bones ... they were very dry ... and as I prophesied there was a noise, and behold a shaking, and the bones came together, bone to his bone ... and the breath came into them, and they lived, and stood up upon their feet, an exceeding great army.

Gen. 32:24. And Jacob was left alone: and there wrestled a man with him until the breaking of the day.

Oh Lawd, duh blood done sign my name.[53]

Wheel, wheel, wheel, O wheel my Lawd,
Ezekial said 'twas a wheel in a wheel,
Wheel in a wheel.[54]
Dere's a lil w'eel a turnin' in my heart.

O Jedus rides dat milk white hawss
. . . .
All glory praise his name.
All my sins done taken away,
Done taken away.[55]

King Jesus a-ridin' on a milk-white pony
An' I so glad, an' I so glad.[56]

O Lawd dese bones ob mine
. . . .
Comin' togeder in de mornin'.
I look at me hand, me hand look new
   Comin' togeder in de mornin'.
I look at me foot it look so too,
   Comin' togeder in de mornin'.[57]

And I had a mighty battle
   Like-a Jacob and de angel,
   Jacob, time of old;
I didn't 'tend to lef' 'em go

---

[53] Society for the Preservation of Spirituals, *op. cit.*, p. 266. Reprinted by permission of the Macmillan Company.
[54] Ballanta, *St. Helena Island Spirituals*, p. 2.
[55] *Ibid.*, p. 11.
[56] Heard by the writer when a boy; not in the above-mentioned collections.
[57] Ballanta, *St. Helena Island Spirituals*, p. 71.

26. And he said, Let me go, for the day breaketh. And he said, I will not let thee go, except thou bless me.

Till Jesus bless my soul.[58]

Exodus 5:1 ff. And Moses and Aaron went in, and told Pharaoh, Thus saith the Lord God of Israel, Let my people go. . . .

Moses down in Egupt lan'
Yuh gottuh tek duh chillun outuh Pharaoh han'.[59]
Go down Moses, Let my people go.

Lev. 25:10, 13. It shall be a jubilee unto you: and ye shall return every man unto his possession, and ye shall return every man unto his family.

My Lawd call me, I mus' go
I gwine to shout Jubilee.[60]
Rock o' Jubilee.[61]

Dan. 5:5. In the same hour came forth fingers of a man's hand and write over against the candlestick upon the plaister of the wall. . . .

Dere's a handwritin on de Wall.
1. Oh Daniel.
2. Who write de letter?
3. John write de letter, etc.[62]

Gen. 6:13, 14. And God saith unto Noah . . . make thee an ark of gopher wood . . . and of every living thing of all flesh, two of every sort shalt thou bring into the ark. . . .

Who buil' de Aa'k? Norah, . . .
'Twas Norah buil' de Aa'k.
En forty day, en forty night
Rain fall on Norah Aa'k.
Who tu'n loose de bud?
    Norah, . . .
'Twas Norah tu'n um loose.[63]

Exodus 3:8. And I am come down to deliver them out of the hand of the Egyptian . . . unto a land flowing with milk and honey.

I'm goin' to feast off milk and honey,
    O yes,
I'm goin' to feast off milk and honey,
Some o' dese days, hallelujah![64]

---

[58] Allen, *op. cit.*, p. 17.
[59] Society for the Preservation of Spirituals, *op. cit.*, p. 290. Reprinted by permission of the Macmillan Company.
[60] *Ibid.*, p. 306.   [61] Allen, *op. cit.*, p. 25.
[62] Ballanta, *St. Helena Island Spirituals*, p. 29.
[63] Society for the Preservation of Spirituals, *op. cit.*, p. 242. Reprinted by permission of the Macmillan Company.
[64] Ballanta, *St. Helena Island Spirituals*, p. 82.

BACKGROUND OF THE SPIRITUALS

Gal. 6:2. Bear ye one another's burdens, and so fulfil the law of Christ.
5. For every man shall bear his own burden.

Bear yo' burden, bear yo' burden,
Bear yo' burden in de heat ob de day.[65]

Matt. 7:3. And why beholdest thou the mote that is in thy brother's eye, but considerest not the beam that is in thine own eye?

I saw de beam in my sister's eye
Can't saw de beam in mine.[66]

Matt. 28:2. . . . and the angel of the Lord descended from heaven, and came and rolled back the stone from the door, and sat upon it.

De angel roll de stone away
De angel roll de stone away
Twas on a bright and shiny mornin'
De angel roll de stone away.[67]

II Cor. 5:1. . . . we have a building of God, an house not made with hands, eternal in the heavens.

Oh, uh got a mansion up on high.
Well, 'e ain' mek wid han'.
No—'e ain' mek wid han', . . .[68]

John 3:7. Marvel not that I said unto thee, ye must be born again.

Rebawn again, rebawn again,
Ef you want tuh git to Heben got to rebawn again.

Nearly all the great names of the Bible are reflected in the Carolina spirituals, from the picturesque characters of Genesis to the spectacular prophet of The Revelation. The river Jordan, modest stream of Palestine, is the subject of many lines and stanzas. The journey from life to death is often pictured as a crossing over "Jerdan," and one would think, from the Negro's description, that the river was a mighty torrent comparable to Niagara or the Mississippi at flood stage. The most famous of the Jordan songs is "Roll, Jordan, Roll."

"Det' [Death] ain't you got no shame" is a spiritual which casts an interesting light on the Negro's poetic insight. It was evidently sung at funerals. One verse begins, "Tek my chile en gone, gone," and another, "Tek my ma en gone, gone," etc.[69]

[65] *Ibid.*, p. 16.   [66] Allen, *op. cit.*, p. 17.
[67] Ballanta, *St. Helena Island Spirituals*, p. 80.
[68] Society for the Preservation of Spirituals, *op. cit.*, p. 322. Reprinted by permission of the Macmillan Company.
[69] *Ibid.*, p. 248.

The song, "Down in the Walley [Valley] on my prayin' knees,"[70] presents an interesting figure, as does the line, "I gwine to rally wid de angel Gabriel."[71] Gabriel is a luminous figure in all Negro hymnology, and his name is often introduced, abruptly, in any line or stanza of a hymn. Being the most picturesque figure of first-century angelology, he easily captured the imagination of the early slaves.

The beautiful spiritual, "Face duh risin' sun," is evidently suggested by the concept of the resurrection morning. In most graveyards in the South the headstones face the East, "duh risin' sun." This is an old practice, and, I think, is generally kept up. The Negroes in the Port Royal section sing the spiritual this way:

> We will all sing tuhgedduh [together] on dat day,
> We will all sing tuhgedduh on dat day,
> En I fall upon muh knees
> En face duh risin' sun,
> Oh Lawd hab mussy on me.[72]

The catechism, which influenced the devotional songs and religious concepts of the slaves, was the textbook par excellence in the religious instruction of the Negroes. Since they could not read, the instruction was oral but thorough. The catechetical instruction of children, as well as of adults, laid the foundation for the elementary theological concepts which the Negroes readily acquired and vividly reflected in their songs. Catechetical instruction involved a crude educational technique which made the fixing of religious ideas more effective than the general preaching. The lines from the catechism were learned verbatim and, as a result, fixed the Negro's religious terminology.[73]

---

[70] *Ibid.*, p. 318.   [71] *Ibid.*, p. 298.
[72] *Ibid.*, p. 270.
[73] A fuller account of the activities of the missionaries as well as a more detailed description of the catechism and its use in the oral instruction of the slaves will be given in another chapter.

CHAPTER IX

RELIGIOUS INSTRUCTION OF THE SLAVES

> O, must I be like de foolish man?
> O, yes Lord;
> He build his house upon de sand,
> O, yes Lord.

"WILLIAM THE THIRD, by the Grace of God, of England, Scotland, France, and Ireland, King, Defender of the Faith, etc. To all Christian people to whom these Presents shall come, Greeting. . . ." Thus in the year 1701 the Society for the Propagation of the Gospel in Foreign Parts came into being with the solemn sanction of the King through a royal charter.[1] The Society purposed to send ministers of the Church of England to the American Colonies, not only to serve planters of the Anglican faith, but also to carry the Gospel to the Indians and Negroes.[2] The Royal Charter continued: "And our further will and pleasure is, that the first President of the said Society, shall be *Thomas*, by Divine Providence, Lord Arch-bishop of *Canterbury*, Primate and *Metropolitan* of all England. . . ."[3] "Accordingly in June 1702, the Reverend Mr. *Samuel Thomas* was sent thither . . . ," and after some period of service in the Goose Creek community reported to London "that he had taken much pains also in instructing the *negroes*, and learned twenty of them to read."[4]

Apparently little was accomplished in evangelizing the Carolina slaves during the first half of the eighteenth century; I think it is erroneous, however, to claim, as some do, that the Anglican missionaries were lacking in zeal. Certainly they faced the hardships which were inevitable in the settlement of a new colony and shared equally in the hazards and dangers which

---

[1] The charter is printed in David Humphreys, *Historical Account of the Incorporated Society for the Propagation of the Gospel in Foreign Parts* (London, 1730).

[2] See an excellent summary in Charles Colcock Jones, *The Religious Instruction of the Negroes in the United States*, pp. 1-46.

[3] The Royal Charter, Article X.   [4] Humphreys, *op. cit.*, pp. 81-82.

were a part of the experience of every man and woman who dared to live his life within striking distance of the inhospitable Yemassees. These missionaries must have been prompted by high motives to leave their peaceful cures in England in order to enter a field of service so arduous as that presented by the early colonies. Most of the time and energy of these early ministers was perforce spent upon the planters and their families, introducing them to the refinements of the Anglican liturgy and to the Christian graces that were likely to be neglected amid the raw beginnings of a plantation regime. Furthermore, they were faced with the embarrassing possibility of unwittingly creating a situation which might result in the manumission of slaves because it was not then certain that a slave could accept Christianity and at the same time be held in bondage by a Christian. This point was finally cleared up by the church dignitaries in the mother country (when pressure was applied by the Liverpool slave traders), who made it plain to the planters in America and in the Sugar Islands that freedom in Christ, as applied to slaves, did not extend to civil rights but that a slave's freedom was a spiritual matter and that his full freedom would be consummated in the next world. Thus the rationalization of the institution of slavery in America furnished its perennial thorn in the flesh even from the beginning, and because of considerations such as these, slave conversion in the early days made little progress.

The ministry of the Reverend Samuel Thomas on Goose Creek was of short duration—only four years—for he died in 1706. The same year Dr. Le Jeau succeeded to the Goose Creek cure, and on occasion preached in "Charles-Town" and visited the French settlements in Orange Quarter.[5] He found "parents and masters indued with much good will and a ready disposition to have their children and servants taught the Christian religion."[6] The Society reported that "he instructed and baptized many negroes and Indian slaves,"[7] and that "the communicants increased, and in 1714, they arose to 70 English, and 8 negroes."[8]

Another of the early Anglican ministers with whose name is associated slave conversion was the Reverend Mr. Ludlam, who

---

[5] *Ibid.*, pp. 83-84.
[7] *Ibid.*
[6] *Ibid.*, p. 84.
[8] *Ibid.*, p. 86.

arrived in "Charles-Town" in 1724. It was reported that "there were in his parish a number of negroes, natives of the place, who understood English well; he took good pains to instruct several of these in the principles of the Christian religion, and afterwards admitted them to baptism. He said if the masters of them would heartily concur to forward so good a work, all those who have been born in the country might without difficulty be instructed and received into the church. Mr. Ludlam continued his labors among the negroes and every year taught and baptized several of them; in one year, eleven, besides some mulattoes."[9]

The Indian War of 1715 greatly hindered the English missions to the Colonies. Immediately preceding the war, Anglican clergymen were sent to the parishes of St. Paul's (1705), St. John's (1707), St. Andrew's and St. Bartholomew's (1713), and St. Helen's (1712). A Mr. Hasell, who was commissioned to St. Helen's Parish, found in the settlement 565 whites, 950 Negroes, 60 Indian slaves, and 20 free Negroes.[10]

The Reverend Gilbert Jones, who was appointed to Christ Church Parish in 1711, reported difficulties with the masters and mistresses in his efforts to convert their slaves.[11] He was succeeded by the Reverend Mr. Pownal, who wrote that there were in his parish 470 free born and "about 700 slaves, some of which understand the English tongue; but very few know anything of God or religion."[12] To St. George's Parish, with its church at the old town of Dorchester, on the Ashley River, near Summerville, Peter Tustian was sent as missionary in 1719.[13] All that remains of this village is the ruins of the old church; the whole area is overrun by the jungle growth of the rich river land. Tustian's successor in 1723, a Mr. Varnod, reported that in his church 17 of the 50 communicants were Negroes and that he had baptized several grown persons, besides children and Negroes, the latter belonging to Alexander Skeen, Esquire.[14]

To St. Andrew's Parish, near the beautiful Magnolia Gardens, was sent a missionary named Taylor, who reported to the

[9] *Ibid.*, pp. 86-87.
[10] Jones, *Religious Instruction of the Negroes*, pp. 10-11.
[11] *Ibid.*, p. 11. [12] *Ibid.*
[13] *Ibid.* [14] *Ibid.*

Society "the great interest taken in the religious instruction of their negroes by Mrs. Haige and Mrs. Edwards, and their remarkable success; 14 of whom on examination we baptized."[15] The clergy of South Carolina in a joint letter informed the Society that "Mr. Skeen, his lady, and Mrs. Haige, his sister, did use great care to have their negroes instructed and baptized."[16]

Thus briefly told are a few facts relating to the early ministry on the Carolina coast as projected by the Society for the Propagation of the Gospel in a new and undeveloped country; the leaven was at work, and a small but persistent minority among the Anglican clergy kept prodding the English conscience in behalf of colonial slaves. As early as 1673 a strong plea was made to colonial plantation owners to take thought for the spiritual condition of their slaves. *Baxter's Christian Directory*, which was rather widely distributed in its day, contained a chapter entitled "Directions to those Masters in Foreign Plantations who have negroes and other Slaves, etc." Its first direction to masters was to "understand well how far your power over your slaves extendeth and what limits God hath set thereto," and continued:

Remember that they have immortal souls, and are equally capable of salvation with yourselves; and therefore you have no power to do anything which shall hinder their salvation. Remember that God is their absolute owner, and you have none but a derived and limited property in them; that they and you are equally under the government and laws of God; that God is their reconciled, tender father, and if they be as good doth love them as well as you, and that they are the redeemed ones of Christ. Therefore so use them as to preserve Christ's right and interest in them.

The second direction reads thus:

Remember that you are Christ's trustees, or the guardians of their souls; and that the greater your power is over them the greater your charge is of them and your duty for them. So must you exercise both your power and love to bring them to the knowledge and the faith of Christ, and to the just obedience of God's commands.

So serve your necessities by your slaves as to prefer God's interest and their spiritual and everlasting happiness. Teach them the way to heaven, and do all for their souls which I have before directed

[15] *Ibid.* [16] *Ibid.*

UNDERSTANDING HEARTS

you to do for all your other servants. Though you may make some difference in their labor and diet and clothing, yet none as to the furthering of their salvation. If they be infidels, use them so as tendeth to win them to Christ and the love of religion, by showing them that Christians are less worldly, less cruel and passionate, and more wise and charitable and holy and meek than any other persons are. Woe to them that by their cruelty and covetousness do scandalize even slaves and hinder their conversion and salvation!

Make it your chief end in buying and using slaves to win them to Christ and save their souls. Do not only endeavor it on the by [sic] when you have first consulted your own commodity itself; and let their salvation be far more valued by you than their service; and carry yourself to them as those that are sensible that they are redeemed with them by Christ from the slavery of Satan, and may live with them in the liberty of the saints in glory.[17]

Clergymen of high station in the Church of England delivered sermons upon the duty of instructing the Negro slaves in the Christian religion. An exhortation of the Bishop of St. Asaph was esteemed of such value that two printings were distributed among the British plantations in the West.[18] The Bishop of London, Dr. Gibson, to whom the religious oversight of the plantations was committed in 1727, addressed a letter to the "Masters and Mistresses of Families in the English Plantations abroad; exhorting them to encourage and Promote the Instruction of their Negroes in the Christian Faith." Feeling that a missive from so important a source as the See of London would move the lethargic planters to action, the Church of England distributed ten thousand copies of the letter among all the Colonies on the continent and all the British islands in the West Indies.[19] This letter, a long and very interesting document, answered the various objections to slave conversion usually offered by the planters. The Bishop pleaded for action: "I find the numbers [slaves] are prodigiously great; and am not a little troubled to observe how small a progress has been made in a Christian country toward the delivering those poor creatures from the pagan darkness and superstition in which they were bred, and the making them partakers of the light of the Gospel. . . . I find there has not only been very little progress made in the work, but that all attempts toward it have been too

[17] *Ibid.*, pp. 6-7.
[18] *Ibid.*, p. 15.
[19] *Ibid.*, p. 16.

industriously discouraged and hindered etc."[20] The same year another strong message was sent out from the See of London under the caption, "The Bishop of London's Letter to the Missionaries in the English Plantations: exhorting them to give their assistance towards the Instruction of the Negroes of their several Parishes in the Christian Faith."[21]

Dean Stanhope, of Canterbury, asserted in 1714 that the Society had met with success in its efforts to Christianize the slaves, and spoke of "children, servants and slaves catechised."[22] The work of the Society for the Propagation of the Gospel in Foreign Parts was continued in Carolina until the Colonies broke away from the mother country. In 1785 an affectionate valedictory was delivered to the missionaries remaining in America.[23] Jones concluded: "Thus terminated the connection of this noble society with our country, which from the foregoing notices of its efforts, must have accomplished a great deal for the religious instruction of the negro population."[24]

It is thus clear that the Church of England not only urged the conversion of slaves in the Colonies, but also attempted to bridge the moral gap which threatened the work of Christianization, namely, the delicate question, referred to earlier in the chapter, as to the effect of baptism upon the slave's civil status. This was adroitly circumvented by both Church and State, and their action furnished a striking example of the power of economic forces over the appeal of Christian idealism. The slave trade was not to be intimidated by mere Christian ideals, because slavery was rapidly becoming a lucrative business, not only in England, but also in New England and the Southern Colonies. Commerce was on the march; ideals had to wait. Consequently, the Bishop of London, in his letter to "Masters and Mistresses," assured all slaveowners:

Christianity and the embracing of the Gospel does not make the least alteration in civil property, or in any of the Duties which belong to Civil Relations, but in all these Respects it continues Persons just in the same State it found them. The freedom which Christianity gives is a Freedom from the bondage of Sin and Satan and from the Dominion of Men's Lusts and Passions and inordinate

[20] *Ibid.*
[21] *Ibid.*
[23] *Ibid.*, pp. 29-30.
[22] *Ibid.*, p. 27.
[24] *Ibid.*, p. 30.

Desires; but as to their outward condition, whatever that was before, whether bond or free, their being baptized and becoming Christians makes no manner of change in it. As St. Paul has expressly told us (I Corinthians, vii, 20), where he is speaking directly to this very point: "Let every man abide in the same calling wherein he was called;" and at the 24th verse; "Let every Man, wherein he is called therein abide with God."[25]

Not only did the Church allay the fear that baptism might affect the civil status of the slaves, but the State also added the weight of its influence in behalf of the institution of slavery. The utterance of the Bishop of London was based upon the decisions of two high law officers of the Crown, who had declared the fears to be groundless. The Slave Act of 1712 (South Carolina) also clinched the matter so definitely that no baptized slave could possibly infer that his acceptance of the Christian life could in any sense alter his status as property. Indeed, the statute set out in pious tones an adroit reconciliation of the Christian religion with the practice of slavery and welded the shackles more securely upon the black man:

xxxiv. Since charity and the Christian religion which we profess obliges us to wish well to the souls of all men, and that religion may not be made a pretense to alter any man's property and right, and that no person may neglect to baptize their negroes or slaves, or suffer them to be baptized for fear that thereby they shoud be manumitted and set free: *Be it therefore enacted* by the authority aforesaid, That it shall be, and is hereby, declared lawful for any negro or Indian slave, or any other slave or slaves whatsoever, to receive and profess the Christian faith and be thereinto baptized; but that, notwithstanding such slave or slaves shall receive and profess the Christian religion and be baptized, he or they shall not thereby be manumitted or set free, or his or their owner, master, or mistress lose his or their civil right, property, and authority over such slave or slaves, but that the said slave or slaves with respect to his servitude shall remain and continue in the same state and condition that he or they was in before the making of this act.[26]

Neither the Church nor the Society for the Propagation of the Gospel in Foreign Parts held scruples against the system of slavery. At least, these agencies participated in the handling

[25] *Ibid.*, p. 21.
[26] Edward McCrady, "Slavery in the Province of South Carolina, 1670-1770," *American Historical Association, Annual Report, 1895*, pp. 652-653.

of slaves, though with some reluctance and twinge of conscience, no doubt.

Anticipating that the Society would endow, in part, the parishes with slaves, the Church by the act of 1740 provided that such Negroes were to be a part of the glebe. In 1710 the Society accepted from General Codrington, of Barbados, two valuable plantations upon the condition that they be kept entire with at least three hundred Negro slaves upon them; the returns from the crops were to maintain a "convenient number of professors and scholars, under the vows of chastity and obedience, who were required to practice and study physic and surgery as well as divinity, that they might endear themselves to the people and have the opportunity of doing good to men's souls while they were taking care of their bodies."[27]

The Society, however, soon found that it was laboring under the embarrassment of supporting the system of slavery and of finding it necessary to purchase additional Negroes "to keep up the stock."[28] In Carolina the organization took a further step: not only did it accept as endowment plantations manned with slaves whose labor was to support its missionaries, but it even purchased slaves to be teachers and religious leaders of other slaves. These purchased slaves were to be taught to read so that they might pass on to others the rudiments of education and religion.[29]

It is only fair to say that, even though the Church vacillated between its Christian principles and the constant economic pressure to fortify the institution of slavery, it made serious efforts to do something good for the increasing number of Negroes being imported for the plantations of the South. The most distinctive step in this direction was the founding of a school for Negroes in Charleston in connection with St. Philip's Church.[30] An advertisement by the Reverend Alexander Garden, commissary of the Bishop of London, in the *South Carolina Gazette* of March 11, 1743, stated that the Society for the Propagation of the Gospel had much at heart the sending of the Gospel to both the Negro and Indian slaves in His Majesty's

---

[27] *Ibid.*, p. 662.
[28] *Ibid.*, p. 663.   [29] *Ibid.*
[30] Jones, *Religious Instruction of the Negroes*, p. 38.

RELIGIOUS INSTRUCTION

Colonies in America and that they would purchase certain country-born young Negroes and instruct them in reading and the rudiments of the Christian religion so that they might in turn instruct all Negro and Indian children who might be born in the Colonies.

For the furtherance of this purpose the Society, about fifteen months previously, had purchased two Negroes who were in training and would devote themselves to this work. One of them, when sufficiently qualified, was to be stationed in Charleston so that all Negro and Indian children might receive instruction without cost to their masters and queries.[31] Such was the naïve conception of education and instruction in religion. The following year, the *Gazette* published an announcement that Dr. Garden had received contributions to the amount of £226 for the missionary venture. Among the contributors were the Honorable Charles Pinckney, Joseph Wragg, Robert Pringle, Jacob Motte, Colonel Otheneil Beale, Benjamin Smith, and Sara Trott.[32]

In 1744 upward of 60 children were instructed in it [the school] daily, 18 of whom read in the Testament, 20 in the Psalter, and the rest in the spelling book. In 1746 there were 55 children under tuition and 15 adults were instructed in the evening. In 1755 there were 70 children in the school, and books were given for their use. In 1757 Mr. Clarke informed the society that the negro school in Charlestown was flourishing and full of children, and, basing his judgment upon the success of the institution, he lamented "the want of civil establishment" in the province for the Christian instruction of 50,000 negroes. Reverend Mr. Smith examined the proficiency of the children twice a week, and the school was deemed to be in a flourishing condition. But Andrew, one of the teachers, died, and the other, Harry, "turned out profligate"; and as the society had not invested to any greater extent in slaves "to keep up the stock" for the purpose of education, they had no other black or colored persons to take charge of the school, and it was discontinued. Although it is not so mentioned, the education of these negro children must have been restricted to reading, as they were prohibited by law from being taught to write.[33]

[31] McCrady, *op. cit.*, p. 663.   [32] *Ibid.*
[33] Frederick Dalcho, *Historical Account of the Protestant Episcopal Church in South Carolina* (Charleston, 1820), quoted in McCrady, *op. cit.*, p. 664.

One of the factors that spurred the conscience of the slaveholder and made him solicitous of the spiritual welfare of his slaves was the disturbing suspicion that, after all, slavery was wrong; there was always some voice to condemn it. As early as 1688 the Quakers protested against the system, and they, with the Moravians, showed considerable interest in the welfare of the Negroes.[34] The churches, generally, while they did not dare condemn the institution, busied themselves in offering the Christian religion to the slaves.

The decades preceding and following the Revolution constituted a period which did little to stimulate enthusiasm for slavery. These were the days when *liberty* was the chief word in Colonial speech, and to conscientious patriots there occurred doubts as to the genuineness of a *liberty* which enslaved a part of its population. Henry Laurens, of Charleston, a devoted patriot, a diplomat, and a man of affairs, wrote in 1776 a letter to his son regarding his views of slavery:

> You know, my dear son, I abhor slavery. I was born in a country where slavery had been established by British kings and parliaments, as well as by the laws of that country ages before my existence. I found the Christian religion and slavery growing under the same authority and cultivation. I nevertheless disliked it. In former days there was no combating the prejudices of men supported by interest; the day I hope is approaching when, from principles of gratitude as well as justice, every man will strive to be foremost in showing his readiness to comply with the golden rule. Not less than twenty thousand sterling would all my negroes produce if sold at public auction to-morrow. I am not the man who enslaved them; they are endebted to Englishmen for that favour; nevertheless I am devising means for manumitting many of them, and for cutting off the entail of slavery. Great powers oppose me—the laws and customs of my country, my own and the avarice of my countrymen. What will my children say if I deprive them of so much estate? These are difficulties, but not insuperable. I will do as much as I can in my time, and leave the rest to a better hand.
>
> I am not one of those who arrogate the peculiar care of Providence in each fortunate event, nor one of those who dare trust in Providence for defence and security of their own liberty while they

---

[34] Clarence Vernon Bruner, *An Abstract of the Religious Instruction of the Slaves in the Antebellum South*, quoted in George Peabody College for Teachers, "Contributions to Education," No. 112 (Nashville, Tenn., 1933), p. 32.

RELIGIOUS INSTRUCTION 183

enslave and wish to continue in slavery thousands who are as well entitled to freedom as themselves. I perceive the work before me is great. I shall appear to many as a promoter not only of strange, but of dangerous doctrines; it will therefore be necessary to proceed with caution. You are apparently deeply interested in this affair, but as I have no doubts concerning your concurrence and approbation, I most sincerely wish for your advice and assistance, and hope to receive both in good time.[35]

The spirit of freedom of the times produced in George Washington similar sentiments, which he expressed in a letter to General Alexander Spotswood, dated November 23, 1794. After discussing Spotswood's suggestion of selling Virginia land in preparation for a projected move to the West, Washington concluded:

With respect to the other species of property concerning which you ask my opinion, I shall frankly declare to you that I do not like even to think, much less talk, of it. However, as you have put the question, I shall in a few words give you my ideas of it.

Were it not then that I am principled against selling negroes, as you would do cattle at a market, I would not in twelve months, hence, be possessed of a single one as a slave. I shall be happily mistaken if they are not found to be a very troublesome species of property ere many years have passed over our heads (but this by the bye)—For this reason, and because there is but little sale for what is raised in the Western country, it remains for you to consider whether their value would not be more productive in lands, reserving enough for necessary purposes, than to carry many of them there.[36]

With the approach of the American Revolution, the influence of the Church of England naturally waned in the Colonies. In South Carolina the most active work in behalf of the slaves was done by the Methodists, Baptists, Presbyterians, and Episcopalians. Jones, writing in 1842, declared that "the Methodist is the only denomination which has preserved returns of the number of colored members in its connection."[37] There is, however, sufficient information available to show that

---
[35] Laurens, *op. cit.*, pp. 20-21.
[36] Phillips (ed.), *Plantation and Frontier*, II, 56-57.
[37] Jones, *Religious Instruction of the Negroes*, p. 42. This fact makes it possible to give a more accurate picture of just what this denomination did.

all the denominations were interested in slave conversion. The two organizations which worked most effectively with the Negroes were the Methodists and Baptists. The Presbyterians of the Carolina coast region were less actively engaged in rural problems, and the Episcopalians for the most part closed their churches during the malarial months of the summer.[38] The Methodists and Baptists generally stayed by the plantations, along with the white overseers, throughout the long summer months and continued their preaching and catechising of the slaves. These latter denominations appear to have possessed a peculiar genius for rural evangelization; they were predominantly the churches of the common people. The Methodist missionaries made themselves agreeable to the "po' buckra" and the overseer. The latter occupied a unique place in the social scale. He did not move with the masters of the plantations and he was not quite in the class of the landless poor whites from which he generally sprung, but occupied an uncertain position somewhere between these extremes. He was, as Bassett says, a sort of proconsul moving in a narrow province among his subjects, the African slaves, the plantation mules, and the cattle.[39] The Reverend M. L. Banks, of the South Carolina Conference (Methodist), gives an interesting glimpse of the plantation overseer and his family and the relationship which existed between them and the plantation missionary. Banks was appointed to the Cumbahee mission, made up of the great rice plantations which bordered the placid tidal river of that name, and their thousands of slaves. He stated that a comfortable home for the missionary was provided by the planters and that there was no change of preachers for five years, something unusual for Methodist itinerants. "Indeed," he wrote, "I stayed on the work as long the Yankee gunboats would allow me to stay."[40] Concerning his relationships with the overseers and their families, Banks added:

   I must speak here of the overseers on this work. They and their families were, in the aggregate, respectable members of society, and connected with the Methodist Church. They lived in comfort, and

---

[38] Charles Wilson, *Twenty-two Years in the Mission Fields of South Carolina*, quoted in Harrison, *op. cit.*, pp. 219-220.

[39] John Spencer Bassett, *The Southern Plantation Overseer, as Revealed in His Letters* (Northampton, Mass., 1925), p. 7.

[40] Banks, *op. cit.*, quoted in Harrison, *op. cit.*, pp. 268-270.

their tables were spread with tempting viands. The missionary felt at home among them. I had a very warm attachment for many of them, and parted from them with a pang of regret.

Abram Thomas stood at the head of his class as an overseer. He was independent, having a fine plantation of his own in Southwestern Georgia. His salary was $3,000 a year, and besides this his table was furnished, free of charge, with everything the plantation afforded. It took a consideration of this sort to induce him to leave his comfortable home in George. I esteemed Stephen Boineau as a Christian gentleman. He was courteous, refined, intelligent, and pious. His wife was his equal in every respect. The children were orderly and obedient. A better-regulated household I have seldom, if ever, visited. Sib Jones, Boineau's brother-in-law, was the wag of Combahee. He was pleasant, playful, and witty. If the missionary was ever troubled with the blues, let him visit Sib and they were sure to vanish.[41]

The early part of the nineteenth century witnessed a quickening of interest in the spiritual well-being of the slaves in the Carolina coast country. The Honorable Charles Cotesworth Pinckney, of the Episcopal Church, Charleston, delivered an address before the Agricultural Society of South Carolina (1829) in which he pleaded for the religious instruction of Negroes. The appeal met with such favor that it went through two or more editions and was widely read.[42]

About the year 1834 the noted cotton and rice planter, Whitemarsh B. Seabrook, addressed the Agricultural Society of St. John's, Colleton, South Carolina, on the same subject. His address, published in the Liberty County Association publication (Georgia), was entitled "An Essay on the Management of Slaves, and especially on their religious instruction."[43]

The committee of the Presbyterian Synod of South Carolina and Georgia on religious instruction of the Negroes reported strongly in favor of increased attention to the spiritual state of the slaves, being very careful, however, to make plain that their work would in no way infringe upon the civil statutes, which at this time were growing increasingly strict. Indeed, not only did the statute of 1834 forbid the teaching of a slave to read or write and prohibit all meetings of Negroes except when some

[41] Banks, *op. cit.*, quoted in Harrison, *op. cit.*, pp. 269-270.
[42] Jones, *Religious Instruction of the Negroes*, pp. 70-71.
[43] *Ibid.*, p. 79.

white person was present, but the violation of the law also carried a penalty not to exceed $100, and six months' imprisonment for a white person and fifty lashes and $50 for a free person of color.[44] Thus it is clearly seen why the Presbyterians delivered themselves so circumspectly when they touched upon the delicate subject of offering any kind of instruction to the slaves. The stringency of the law, of course, was an outgrowth of abolition propaganda from the North. The resultant dangers of Negro insurrection were met by the South with ironclad legislation.

But in spite of the delicacy of the situation, enthusiasm for the religious instruction of Negroes continued apace, increasing in momentum until it reached its height at the beginning of the Civil War. The instruction, of necessity, had to be oral, a circumstance which was a severe limitation upon effective teaching, and the churches adapted themselves to the law and did what they could to introduce Negroes to the principles of the Christian religion. This, as will be shown later, resulted in a one-sided presentation. None dared to turn loose upon the slaves all the implication of Christian idealism.

The Presbyterian Committee, reporting in 1833, subjoined a series of resolutions to their report, as follows:

1. That to impart the gospel to the negroes of our country is a duty which God in his providence and in his word imposes on us.
2. That in the discharge of this duty we separate entirely the civil and religious condition of the people; and while we devote ourselves to the improvement of the latter, we disclaim all interference with the former.
3. That the plan which we shall pursue for their religious instruction shall be that permitted by the laws of the state, constituting the bond of this Synod.
4. That we deem religious instruction to master and servant every way conducive to our interests for this world and for that which is to come.
5. That every member of this Synod, while he endeavors to awaken others, shall set the example and begin the religious

[44] John Belton O'Neall, *The Negro Law of South Carolina* (Columbia, S. C., 1848), p. 23, quoted in Susan Markey Fickling, *Slave Conversion in South Carolina* ("Bulletin of the University of South Carolina," No. 146, Sept. 1, 1824), p. 18.

RELIGIOUS INSTRUCTION

instruction of the servants of his own household, systematically and perseveringly, as God shall enable him.

6. That we cannot longer continue to neglect this duty without incurring the charge of inconsistency in our Christian character; of unfaithfulness in the discharge of our ministerial duty; and at the same time meeting the disapprobation of God and our consciences.[45]

In the early 1830's the Reverend William Capers (later Bishop), of the South Carolina Conference, made extensive plans for sending missionaries directly to the large plantations of the coast region, where the Negroes had little opportunity because of their great numbers to attend the white churches.

In 1823 the Reverend Dr. Dalcho, of the Episcopal Church, Charleston, wrote a pamphlet entitled *Practical Considerations, Founded on the Scriptures, Relative to the Slave Population of South Carolina*. Dalcho, like most of his contemporaries, had the embarrassing task of trying to adjust the institution of slavery to the Christian religion. He boldly stated, however, in his introductory paragraph the aim of the pamphlet: "To show from the scriptures of the Old and New Testament, that slavery is not forbidden by the divine law; and at the same time to prove the necessity of giving religious instruction to our negroes." Referring to the relation of Negroes to the Episcopal churches in Charleston in 1822, he reported 316 colored communicants in the white churches and 200 Negro children in their Sunday schools.[46]

Jones asserted that there were forty thousand Negroes connected with the Baptist denomination in 1813 in the states of Pennsylvania, Delaware, Virginia, North Carolina, South Carolina, and Georgia, and quoted an anonymous authority[47] as stating that "among the African Baptists in the Southern states there are a multitude of preachers and exhorters whose names do not appear on the minutes of the associations. They preach principally on the plantations to those of their own color, and their preaching, though broken and illiterate, is in many cases

---

[45] Jones, *Religious Instruction of the Negroes*, pp. 73-74.
[46] *Ibid.*, p. 69.
[47] Probably David Benedict, *A General History of the Baptist Denomination* (Boston, 1813).

highly useful."[48] The Baptist denomination must have been particularly active in the Carolina sea islands, especially toward the south near Beaufort and Savannah. Today the great majority of Negroes around Port Royal and St. Helena are Baptists. Another factor, doubtless, which made for the great numbers of Baptists was the dramatic aspects of baptism as practiced by that group. The "baptizings" in the rivers and creeks were always impressive occasions, accompanied as they were by much singing, candidates in white, great throngs flocking to the river's edge, and a simple ritual understandable to the Negro. This ritual made a powerful appeal to all Negroes. Their deep earnestness and the picturesque setting united to make one of the most beautiful of religious observances.

The Bible Society of Charleston reported in 1819 that one fourth of the communicants in the city were slaves or free persons of color, that in every church they were freely admitted to divine service, that in most of the churches distinct accommodations were provided for them, and that the "clergy in general made it a part of their pastoral care to devote frequent and stated seasons for the religious instruction of catechumens from amongst the black population."[49] Furthermore, "from the beginning, with scarcely an exception, the negroes applying for admission into the churches have been under the instruction of white ministers or members; have been baptized and have partaken of the Lord's Supper at the same time with white candidates and members, and have been subject to the same care and discipline; no distinctions being made between the two classes of members in respect to the privileges and discipline of the churches."[50]

By the year 1834 the Methodists were exerting themselves greatly in behalf of the Negroes in the city of Charleston. The extent of their work and the fine relationships existing between whites and Negroes in the churches were recorded by the Reverend William Martin in his reminiscences of work among the slaves:

And when I was stationed in Charleston, with Revs. William M. Kennedy and George F. Pierce, in 1834, we had under our

---

[48] Jones, *Religious Instruction of the Negroes*, p. 58.
[49] *Ibid.*, pp. 60-61. [50] *Ibid.*, p. 61.

RELIGIOUS INSTRUCTION

pastoral care 3,249 colored members. All the Methodist churches, as previously estimated, were built with reference to the accommodation of the colored people. They sat under the same roof and enjoyed the same preaching with the white people; they communed at the same altars; they were served by the same hands, and drank in remembrance of the crucified One from the same cup. They shared in the same class meetings and love feasts; they were married and baptized by the same ministers, and thousands upon thousands of them were brought to a saving knowledge of the truth, and were made happy partakers of the gospel hope of salvation.

Sunday was welcomed by the slaves. It meant a break in the routine, a cessation from labor, and the enjoyment of many diversions not permissible during the week. Sunday with the slaves was strikingly like the old Hebrew Sabbath. It was a day of relaxation and rest—rest for man and beast from the arduous toil of agricultural life. The Negro always enjoys the Sabbath more than the white man. And it means more to him. His church attendance he takes more leisurely and more happily. Lowery, a former slave, wrote as follows:

> The older and more serious ones went to "meetin," or visited the sick, or made social calls, while the youngsters met other youngsters from the adjoining plantations and spent the day in wrestling, jumping, boxing, running foot races and sometimes fighting. In the summer season they would sometimes roam through the fields from plantation to plantation in search of watermelons and fruits. They would plunge into the dark and dense swamp in search of wild muscadine grapes, or through the fields for blackberries, or the pine woods for huckleberries.[51]

On some of the plantations the colored boys were required to do light work, such as keeping crows and rice birds from the fields where they threatened to damage the young crops. But Frierson, reported one of his former slaves, never required these duties: "He was a God-fearing man, and held that the Sabbath was a day of rest for man and beast. He kept the day as sacred, and required all his slaves, as nearly as possible, to do the same."[52]

The white Methodist preacher, Lowery wrote, came to Shiloah Church once a month for preaching service. This church

---

[51] Lowery, *op. cit.*, pp. 69 ff. The Frierson plantation was in Sumter County, near the town of Lynchburg, S. C.
[52] *Ibid.*, p. 69.

was near the Frierson plantation, and the white people were accustomed to worship there. On these particular Sundays, in order to provide some religious worship for the slaves, Frierson set aside a place in his front yard for the religious services of his slaves. This meeting became noteworthy throughout the whole neighborhood, and Negroes and whites attended in large numbers. Seats, accommodating about three hundred people, were arranged under the great water oaks in the front yard of the "big house." On the long front piazza the white people sat.

The services were always conducted by colored preachers. They were invited from the various plantations, and were listened to with great respect by all. Of course they had to get the consent of their masters to come and were always required to bring a ticket which testified to the legitimacy of their mission. If the preacher lived some distance away, the master usually furnished him a mule to ride, and on occasion the saddle horse or buggy horse was used.

The pulpit consisted of a table on which was spread a clean white cloth, and on this were placed a pitcher of water, a Bible, and a hymn book. "No white preacher was ever allowed to stand behind that table, though some of them very much desired to do so. That long piazza was usually filled with devout worshippers and the seats below with zealous colored Christians. . . . Sometimes when the old preacher would warm up to his subject and grow loud, if not eloquent, the audience would break forth in shouts of joy and praise. While some colored sister would be jumping out in the audience some of the white ladies were known to act in a similar manner in the piazza."[53]

The planter's solicitude for the spiritual advancement of his slaves was a queer mixture of affection for the slave and regard for his own interests. The Southerner defended slavery because his whole economic life was tied up with the institution; in his higher moments he knew the system was wrong in principle. The result was some strange mental gymnastics in which he undertook to reconcile opposing points of view.

A Southerner of discernment who was reared on a sea-island plantation declared:

The spiritual betterment of the slave was ever uppermost in the minds of the planters. As a matter of "good business" alone, it paid,

[53] *Ibid.*, pp. 70-71.

to say nothing of the real, true desire on the part of the owner to lift them up into a higher moral and Christian atmosphere by granting them all the church privileges they might desire—an effort to which they readily responded. Being of a mercurial and emotional nature the Church was to them a kind of safety valve for pent-up feelings, and the spiritual exaltation to which they were so easily worked up was an antidote to discontent and insurrectionary tendencies. Hence their education along religious lines was never neglected. It was altogether of an oral nature, as it was forbidden that they should be taught to read and write.[54]

By the year 1840 the slave question was becoming exceedingly acute in the churches. Until this period there were no actual sectional divisions, but for a long time the controversial slavery issue had been producing a definite cleavage in most of the Protestant churches. The North was rapidly becoming unalterably opposed to slavery, while the South found itself caught in the meshes of a complicated economic system and knew not how to escape. The break within the churches themselves was inevitable. The following summary by Elmer T. Clark gives in the briefest possible form the predicament of only one of the churches, the Methodist:

In 1844 came the lamentable division of American Methodism over the question of slavery. The issue did not concern the nature of slavery, for both the North and the South agreed that it was an evil; the question was how best to meet the practical situation. Slavery was an accepted institution in the South, and the laws of many states forbade the freeing of slaves. The radical abolition wing of the Church insisted that nonslaveholding be made a condition of membership. This would, of course, have wrecked the Church in the South by depriving it of members and outlawing it in public sentiment. The South contended not for slavery, but for the privilege of preaching the gospel to slaves and whites alike.

Bishop James O. Andrew had by death and marriage become a slaveholder. Under the law he could not free his slaves, but he had declared his willingness to do so when possible or allow them to go to free States, and he had by deed secured to his wife the slaves owned by her previous to their marriage. No personal blame for slaveholding attached to them, nor could he extricate himself under the law from his unpleasant predicament. His character was without a flaw, and few men have been more diligent in evangelizing the slaves. It was irony that one of the slaves' best friends should

[54] Mikell, *op. cit.*, p. 238.

have been the immediate cause of a division in the Church over the question of slavery.

The General Conference of 1844 deposed Bishop Andrew by a simple vote without a trial and without preferring charges, by a resolution providing that he desist from exercising the functions of a bishop while connected with slavery. The very life of the Church in the South was involved, and this was freely recognized on both sides. If the Southern delegates submitted to the deposition of a bishop, a preacher, or a member merely for being a slaveholder when the laws of the State would not permit emancipation, such submission would have sounded the death knell of the Church in the South.

They could not and would not submit, and the result was a division of the Church under an instrument known as the Plan of Separation. This instrument the Northern branch repudiated in 1848, but it was later upheld in every point by the unanimous opinion of the United States Supreme Court. The Southern delegates met in Louisville in May, 1845, and set up the Methodist Episcopal Church, South, and its first General Conference assembled in Petersburg, Va., one year later.

The real attitude of Southern Methodism to the Negro at the time of the division is indicated by the fact that it then had in its fold 125,000 colored members, "a larger number of practically heathen converts than all the missionary societies of America had gathered upon all the fields of the heathen world." At the first General Conference plans were laid for the prosecution of the work of evangelism among the slaves, to which the Church felt providentially called. Bishop Andrew, the innocent cause of the division, declared, "Whatever becomes of the other mission work, we will never abandon our Negro missions," and his words became the general sentiment of the newly organized Church.

The division removed the last vestige of suspicion from the minds of the planters, who were convinced that these Methodists had no intention of interfering in civil affairs. The missionaries were more eagerly welcomed, they secured a readier access to the slaves, and money for support came pouring in. Soon the whole South was alive with missionary activity. Not only the plantation missionaries, but the regular pastors, the masters and mistresses of the slaves, even the boys and girls, became evangels and teachers. In one instance the governor of his State went from cabin to cabin on a plague-infested island ministering to the stricken colored people.[55]

[55] Elmer T. Clark, *Healing Ourselves* (Nashville, Tenn., 1924), pp. 96-98. Reprinted by permission of Cokesbury Press, Publishers.

RELIGIOUS INSTRUCTION

The extent of the interest in slave conversion about this time was evidenced by a significant meeting in Charleston, in May, 1845. A committee of prominent laymen and clergymen issued a call, and as a preliminary step sent a circular letter to prominent planters, asking for information regarding the number of Negroes on their plantations, the numbers of ministers or teachers among them, the type of instruction given, and the results. The reports, published in pamphlet form, and the proceedings of the meeting constitute one of the most valuable records of this work. The reports themselves are so vivid and contain so much of local color that, instead of attempting anything like a summary, I have selected four which are representative and will let them tell their own colorful story of the interest in religious instruction in the Carolina coast country. It is significant that although Episcopal planters were solicitous about the spiritual welfare of the slaves, the Methodist and Baptist Churches attracted by far the greater number of Negro members.

R. F. W. Alston, of the Georgetown District, declared:

The parish of Prince George, Winyah, numbers about 13,000 slaves. The number attached to the Episcopal Church, to which I belong, about 300: the number worshipping with the Methodists, 3,200. The Baptists would claim full half this number—say 1,500. The rector of All-Saints, Waccamaw, visits 2 plantations in the parish, each once a fortnight. The rector of Georgetown also labours in this field. The Methodists allow class-leaders, and the Baptists admit preachers of colour. I have a place of worship for my negroes, open to all denominations of Christians. The Methodist missionary preaches to my people every alternate Sabbath, after catechising the children, about 50. By the rules of my plantation the Methodists and Baptists have prayer-meeting at given houses, each twice in the week, besides Sunday, when they meet, and pray and sing together. These meetings are exclusively for the negroes on my own plantation. I have had this custom for 15 years, and it works well. The number of negro children catechised by the Methodist preachers is, at least, 1,000, and by the other denominations, 300. Of my own negroes, and those in my immediate neighborhood, I may speak with confidence; they are attentive to religious instruction, and greatly improved in intelligence and morals, in domestic relations, etc. Those who have grown up under religious training are more intelligent, and generally, though not always, more improved than those who have received instruction as adults. Indeed the degree of intelligence which, as a class, they are acquiring, is worthy of deep consideration.[56]

In the Charleston District, James H. Ladson, who on alternate Sundays led the services for the slaves, the Methodist missionary preaching every two weeks, reported that on his Sundays he read from the Episcopal Prayer Book. As stated above, the preponderant numbers won by the Methodists and Baptists testify to the effectiveness of their simple sermons, prayers, and singing. The stately passages of the Anglican liturgy as expressed in the Prayer Book, the product of generations of English religious culture, were a far less effective medium in appealing to the slaves than the homely language of the evangelical ministers. Ladson's report, in part, was as follows:

On my plantation, religious service is held every alternate Sunday throughout the year, by the missionary and by myself, when present, once every Sunday; having, therefore, on such alternate Sundays, a double service, morning and afternoon. The plan under which instruction is given is that of the Methodist Episcopal Church, prayer, singing and a plain sermon by the missionary; and, as adopted by myself, the service of the Episcopal Prayer-book, omitting the portion of the Psalter, followed by a familiar and affectionate appeal of my own, with such assistance as I am able to procure from books of sermons. And here I take pleasure in commending the *"sermons for negroes,"* lately published by the Reverend Mr. Glennie. The missionary frequently catechises the children on weekdays, after the form published by the Rev. Dr. Capers. . . . My chapel has now been built about 9 years. It can accommodate 100 or 110 when filled. The bell from the steeple summons the negroes about a half hour before service, and is loud enough to be heard by the negroes of adjoining plantations, some of whom are permitted to come and hear the word of God read and preached. I am satisfied that the influence of the instruction upon the discipline of my plantation, and on the spirit and subordination of the negroes has been most beneficial. Their spirits are cheerful, as I judge from their gaity of heart, and the respect for the overseer, and drivers, is evinced by, generally, a ready obedience to orders. We have had no runaway for years, and an offer to such as exhibit dissatisfaction to exchange them for others, by a sale, is usually met with aversion.

[56] *Proceedings of the Meeting in Charleston, S. C., on the Religious Instruction of the Negroes,* pp. 34-35.

My neighbors concur with me in the remark that I have a well-ordered people.[57]

From the parish of St. Andrew, within whose bounds were two plantations destined for garden fame, the present Middleton and Magnolia Gardens, came a report from N. R. Middleton, in which he supplied interesting information in regard to religious instruction on his own plantation and the part his family took in teaching the slaves:

The number of people on my place is 116, of which number 13 are communicants of the Episcopal Church with one or two exceptions. There are 13 baptized infants and one candidate for adult baptism. Rev. J. S. Hanckel is the only minister, and my wife and myself the only teachers employed among the people. I read the service and teach the catechism to all the people, every Sabbath afternoon. After family prayers on Wednesday night, I teach those who come voluntarily to be instructed. The children are taught constantly during the week by Mrs. M. and our sons, and know the catechism and several hymns. The children learn more readily than the adults: but many of the latter are very consistent and worthy professors. My experience is decidedly favorable to religious instruction. Among my people vicious habits have certainly been weakened, and a moral sense awakened. In every respect I feel encouraged to go on. Negroes are not what some would make them out to be: they are capable of good feelings, and being influenced by good principles, and I do not hesitate to give it as my opinion, that where every good motive may be wanting, a regard to *self-interest* should lead every planter to give his people religious instruction.[58]

From Beaufort came a statement from Thomas Fuller, who disapproved of the Negroes' attending town churches, believing they should be instructed on the plantations. Reference has already been made to the predominant number of Negroes of Baptist persuasion in the Beaufort and St. Helena area. This Baptist majority was won as early as 1845, a fact which Fuller's report revealed:

In St. Helena Parish, there are 6,740 Negroes—of which 51 belong to the Episcopal Church in Beaufort in which I worship: 1 to the E. Church in St. Helena Island: 2132 to the Baptist Church in Beaufort: 900 to the B. Church on St. Helena and 314 to the Methodist mission in the Parish. One Methodist missionary devotes

[57] *Ibid.*, pp. 53-55.   [58] *Ibid.*, p. 42.

the whole of his time to the negroes: he teaches the people and catechises the children on 20 plantations: number of children catechised 300. No coloured teacher employed. There is great difficulty in conveying religious knowledge to the minds of adult negroes who have grown up in ignorance. The children and youth receive and understand the instructions of their teachers with comparatively great readiness and ease: and their intelligence and docility are decidedly improved. I am sorry to say, that while in general, our negroes have manifestly improved in their manners and appearance, the benefit they have derived from religious instruction as it regards their morals, their various relations, their virtue, regard to truth, and observance of the Lord's day, is by no means so apparent and satisfactory as we desire. Their improved manner and appearance result, very much, from their habit of coming every Sunday, into town to worship. This habit exerts, I think, a decidedly bad influence on their morals. Removed as so large a number are, every Sunday from the control and discipline of the plantations, and impossible as it is for the Church to know and control their conduct, they use their liberty in ways and for purposes adverse to their morals. Nothing seems to me more essential in order to their becoming a religious people, than that they receive their religious instruction at home, and that they be subjected to the supervision on the plantation, of the minister of a Church, that will investigate and correct their wrong views and bad habits, and will help their infirmities. It is owing, I think, to the want of religious instruction and discipline on the plantations, that the influence of religious instruction on the discipline of plantations and the spirit of subordination among the negroes is so little seen and felt.[59]

It may be surprising to learn that a group of Carolina slaves took up a collection for missions in Africa, and this actually occurred on the plantation of J. Grimke Drayton, near Charleston. Drayton wrote: "Of their own accord, my people planted and tended, year before the last, in their own time, a *missionary crop*. They made $16, which was appropriated to the extension of the gospel. The Rev. Mr. Hazelhurst, one of our missionaries to Africa, visited and addressed them. They were much affected by his statement of the spiritual condition of their brethren, and they immediately made up a contribution for the furtherance of his mission."[60]

The Methodist Church furnished the most accurate statistics regarding details of missionary activity among the slaves. Har-

[59] *Ibid.,* pp. 48-49. [60] *Ibid.,* pp. 50-51.

RELIGIOUS INSTRUCTION

rison stated that at the close of the Civil War over three hundred missionaries were engaged in the work of the slave missions and that they were capable men "adapted by nature and by grace, as well as by education" to do the work assigned.[61] The conferences of the Methodist Episcopal Church, South, had, by the year 1864, appropriated for plantation missions a total of $1,873,466.27.[62] The following table by Harrison[63] shows graphically the appropriations by conferences for the two periods, 1829-1844 and 1844-1864. In 1844 the Methodist Episcopal Church was divided. After the war, missionary activity in behalf of the Negroes ceased, and the South used its waning energy in an effort to set its house in order.

AMOUNTS APPROPRIATED FOR PLANTATION MISSIONS FROM 1829 TO 1864

Conference	1829-1844	1844-1864	Total
South Carolina	$ 58,879.81	$ 315,197.18	$ 374,076.99
Georgia	41,980.80	255,050.72	297,030.52
Tennessee	14,524.56	83,094.14	97,618.70
Mississippi	19,302.79	130,773.06	150,075.85
Memphis	8,683.45	120,751.00	129,434.45
Alabama	17,366.36	340,166.67	357,533.03
Virginia	2,400.00	109,825.00	112,225.00
North Carolina	2,110.70	66,316.53	68,427.23
Arkansas	1,104.50	27,804.22	28,908.72
Florida	905.90	46,416.42	47,322.32
East Texas		26,133.86	26,133.86
Louisiana		70,769.06	70,769.06
St. Louis		3,900.00	3,900.00
Louisville		6,700.00	6,700.00
Texas		68,066.88	68,066.88
Holston		9,891.48	9,891.48
Wachita		25,351.48	25,351.48
Total	$167,258.87	$1,706,207.70	$1,873,466.27

[61] Harrison, *op. cit.*, p. 298.
[62] *Ibid.*, p. 326.
[63] *Ibid.*

CHAPTER X

THE PLANTATION MISSIONS

> The preacher reads the hymn divine,
> And we remember not a line,
> But sing right on;
> And with the text we start to shout,
> Forgetting shame, or pride or doubt,
> To heaven most gone.

THE SUBJECT of the plantation missions, with missionaries sent directly to the slaves, is so large that only the high lights of that movement will be noticed here. The enterprise gained momentum with such rapidity that at the time of the Civil War it was easily the most significant missionary effort in the world. All of the churches were interested and all contributed to the movement, but the Methodist, because of its peculiar polity, especially the itinerant system, made what appears to be the most significant contribution. In 1829 the Missionary Society of the South Carolina Conference began its work with two missionaries and 417 members. Within fifteen years the work had spread to other conferences and 71 missionaries had attached themselves to 68 missions with a colored membership of 21,063. In 1844 the Southern Conferences had expended for this work $22,379.25, the South Carolina Conference leading the list with $7,356.20.[1] Commenting on the work accomplished between 1845 and 1860, William Martin, of the Congaree Mission, wrote:

> At the end of the Conference year 1845, at which time I was sent to the work, Georgia and Florida having been organized into a separate Conference, there was [sic] in the South Carolina Conference 25 ministers devoted to the colored missions alone, supported by collections taken up within the Conference bounds, and the colored membership had increased to 41,074. In 1860 we had in the South Carolina Conference alone a colored membership of 49,774. This year there were 30 ministers employed in this great work, and the South Carolina Conference raised for domestic colored missions

[1] *Ibid.*, p. 196.

$24,463.54. For several years previous to the war the South Carolina Conference raised and expended annually for the religious advancement of the negroes sums varying from $20,000 to $32,000, and employed from 25 to 35 of her ministers in preaching to them the glorious gospel of the blessed God.[2]

These figures did not represent the actual financial outlay, for many individual gifts were made to the preachers, and innumerable perquisites in the way of parsonages, gifts of supplies, and the like, none of which were included in the above figures. By the year 1864 the Southern Conferences had appropriated in actual cash nearly two million dollars.[3]

The following record is taken, for the most part, from the accounts of Methodist preachers, who wrote vividly of their experiences with the Negroes and of the hardships and joys which came to the men appointed to stations along the Black Border. In addition to the vicissitudes of the work itself, these men braved the hazards of disease—chills and fever, dysentery, and the dreaded cholera.

Besides newspaper accounts and the preachers' quarterly reports to their church papers, there is at least one valuable collection of reminiscences of the missionaries themselves, made by H. A. C. Walker, of the South Carolina Conference, who proposed at one time to write a History of Missions to the Blacks.[4] Walker never published his work, but the excellent "Notes from the Pioneers," in W. P. Harrison's *The Gospel among the Slaves*, is a useful substitute for Walker's projected work.

As indicated above, the motives that actuated the churches in their feverish efforts to Christianize the slaves were many and varied. There was always in the subconscious mind of the best of the Southern people the thought that slavery was wrong. Many of them apparently realized that the stars in their courses fought against slavery. They knew that the cards of the universe were stacked against them. Henry Laurens, of Charleston, had written to his son out of the depths of his heart when he declared, "I abhor slavery." But "great powers oppose me, the laws and customs of my country, my own and the avarice of my countrymen," he wrote. "What will my children say if I deprive them of so much estate?"[5] Fredrika Bremer, a Swedish

[2] *Ibid.*, p. 262.
[4] *Ibid.*, p. 215.
[3] *Ibid.*, p. 326.
[5] Laurens, *op. cit.*, pp. 20-21.

traveler, visiting Joel R. Poinsett on his Pee Dee River plantation, commented: "He [Poinsett] earnestly desires that his native land should free itself from this moral obliquity, and he has faith in its doing so; but he sees the whole at present involved in so many ways, and the difficulties attending any change so great, that he leaves the question to be solved by the future."[6] In her comment on the missionary work then in progress at Poinsett's plantation she was, however, a little critical: "Yesterday—Sunday—there was, in the forenoon, divine service for the negroes in a wagon-shed, which had been emptied for that purpose. It was clean and airy, and the slaves assembled there, well dressed and well behaved. The sermon and the preacher (a white missionary) were unusually wooden. But I was astonished at the people's quick and glad reception of every single expression of beauty or of feeling."[7]

Joseph Le Conte, the noted geologist and a professor in the University of South Carolina (then South Carolina College), recorded in his autobiography the keen sense of relief that he experienced when the slaves were set free. Although he was left poor, he felt that a great burden of responsibility had rolled from his shoulders. And so did many Southern people feel. The oversight of slaves and the thousand and one duties attendant upon plantation life were a great burden. Many devoutly wished that they might cut through the tangled skein of civil, economic, and social forces that then enmeshed the South. The biting sarcasm of the abolitionists, their well-planned and effective propaganda, with the constant dread of Negro insurrection as a result, made the South take a position on slavery which it did not, in its heart of hearts, wish to maintain. But the evils of embittered propaganda were abroad on both sides. The great cleavage became more and more distinct and the final break inevitable. Well-poised men on each side soon lost their reason and were caught in the maelstrom which hurled them undreamed distances from their ideals. Le Conte wrote:

> At first I was extremely reluctant to join in, and was even opposed to the secession movement; I doubted its necessity and dreaded the impending conflict and its result. A large number of the best and most thoughtful men all over the South felt as I did;

[6] Fredrika Bremer, *The Homes of the New World; Impressions of America* (New York, 1854), I, 287-288. [7] *Ibid.*, p. 289.

PLANTATION MISSIONS

but gradually a change came about—how, who can say? It was in the atmosphere; we breathed it in the air; it reverberated from heart to heart; it was like a spiritual contagion—good or bad, who could say? But the final result was enthusiastic unanimity of sentiment throughout the South. Those who were latest and most reluctant, because they saw the seriousness of the result, were also the most earnest and most reliable.[8]

There is little doubt that the desire to evangelize the slaves was prompted not only by the normal enthusiasm of the Christian church to uplift a lowly people, but by a deep, though unexpressed, sense that there was something inherently wrong about slavery. The enthusiasm, then, for slave conversion was at least a form of compensation for a felt wrong. Many good men and women found themselves hopelessly involved in a situation from which they could not extricate themselves. Christianization of the slaves became in part a form of release. Then, there were callous and conscienceless slaveholders whose only regard was profit. They realized the value of religion as a factor in keeping the Negro docile. At this period Southern churchmen issued numerous tracts and sermons defending slavery and upholding it by scriptural authority. Both of these groups were quite willing to convert the slaves. There were many who not only believed the evangelization of the slaves was a solemn duty, but who also proved the genuineness of their profession by living their lives among them, amid the dangers and hazards of a malarial region in summer and the uninspiring association of hordes of underprivileged human beings who were not even permitted to read and write. With the accomplishments of these missionaries to the plantations this chapter will deal.

But how is the work of the plantation missions to be appraised? To what extent has the Negro race profited by their labors? At this distance from the scene an impartial judgment of their work is possible. Certainly, the excellent records of their activities, in newspaper accounts, church statistics, and reports from the field, provide the student of this generation with an adequate basis for judgment.

Bassett well pointed out the striking incongruity in the teaching of the slaves. Since the Negro was forbidden by law to

[8] Le Conte, *op. cit.*, p. 179.

learn to read, he was denied access to all religious literature, including the Bible itself. His instruction had to be oral, with all the limitations that entailed. Texts and sermons must be carefully chosen to fit the scheme of bondage: "There must be no argument based on such texts as 'The truth will make you free,' and 'The laborer is worthy of his hire.' Doctrines that would make a man wish to raise himself to something better and higher were impossible; for they were sure to create dissatisfaction with slavery. The religious instructors of these people so unhappily placed had to recognize these facts and to preach a doctrine of contentment and humility. In an instinctive reaction against the hard lot of this world they dwelt at large upon the joys and beauties of the world to come."[9]

A Negro named Lunsford Lane left an interesting account of the narrow range of preaching used among the slaves. Lane, born in North Carolina, purchased his freedom, and became an abolitionist lecturer in the North before the Civil War. He wrote:

> I often heard select portions of the Scriptures read in our social meetings and comments made upon them. On Sunday we always had one sermon prepared expressly for the colored pepole, which it was generally my privilege to hear. So great was the similarity of the texts that they were always fresh in memory: "Servants, be obedient to your masters"—"not with eye-service, as men-pleasers." "He that knoweth his master's will and doeth it not, shall be beaten with many stripes"; and some others of this class. Similar passages with but few exceptions, formed the basis of most of these public instructions. . . . I will not do them the injustice to say that connected with these instructions there was not mingled much that was excellent. There was one very kindhearted clergyman whom I used often to hear; he was very popular with the colored people. But after he had preached a sermon from the Bible that it was the will of Heaven from all eternity that we should be slaves, and our masters be our owners, many of us left him, considering, like the doubting disciple of old, "This is a hard saying, who can hear it?"[10]

It was generally understood that the men who were sent as preachers among the Negroes had to be "true and tried." There

---

[9] Bassett, *op. cit.*, pp. 1-3.
[10] William George Hawkins, *Lunsford Lane* (Boston, 1863), p. 65, quoted in Bassett, *op. cit.*, pp. 14-15.

could be no equivocation on the issue of slavery: no word was to be said that would encourage the hope of freedom. The abolitionists were doing enough of this, and the South had already had its taste of Negro insurrection. The planters were very suspicious of propagandists. A preacher must watch his step lest he touch off a spark which would blaze into a mighty fire, bringing down upon his head the condemnation of the community and perhaps dismissal from his chosen work. He was hedged in by the law which threatened to throw him into prison should he be caught teaching slaves to read and write. Said one missionary: "We have no schools, teachers, nor scholars; for in this state there is a law prohibiting the teaching of letters to the slaves, selling or giving them books of any description whatever; therefore we can only tender to them oral instruction. This is done by catechising the little negroes, etc."[11] Surely the plantation missionary had a hard road to travel as he contemplated the full import of the Christian message and the numerous limitations which prevented its complete expression.

William Capers, the first superintendent and chief exponent of plantation missions, in the *Southern Christian Advocate* for June 3, 1843, described the missionaries' work:

> There sounds the bell in the belfry of the Negro mission. . . . But let us enter; the congregation has assembled, all in clean, though coarse apparel; here are the children, too, on the front benches. We pass over the straw-carpeted floor, and enter a new pulpit, formed from the drapery of the oak and pine—the moss is twisted and wound round upright posts, enclosing a space large enough for the minister to stand in, and festoons of moss hung in front with cord and tassel attached, the latter formed by the burr of the pine. . . . The missionary rises, the negroes follow his example, and repeat after him the Apostles' Creed. Explanatory questions are then asked and readily answered, the Commandments are then repeated, a portion of the Scripture read and explained, a hymn sung and prayer offered, after which the sermon is delivered.

The textbook of the missionaries was especially prepared for the oral instruction of the slaves, and was usually called a *catechism*. A dozen or more such texts were in use in the low country. Perhaps the two most widely used among the Gullah Negroes were the *Catechism* by Capers and another compiled by

[11] *Christian Advocate and Journal* (New York), VIII, 94 (Feb. 7, 1834).

C. C. Jones, both of which reflect a curious aspect of the life and times of ante-bellum days and the peculiar circumstance of interpreting the Christian religion to an enslaved people. Each had an introductory section made up of hymns, prayers, Commandments, the Creed, portions of Scripture, the latter relating to duties of husbands and wives, parents and children, and masters and servants. Under the heading, "Duty of Masters," Jones cited appropriate scripture from both the Old and the New Testaments.[12] First among the half-dozen quotations was "Masters give unto your servants that which is just and equal: knowing that ye also have a Master in heaven."[13] Under the caption, "Duty of Servants," the citations were principally drawn from the letters of Paul. "Servants be obedient to them that are your masters according to the flesh with fear and trembling, in singleness of your heart, as unto Christ. Not with eye-service as men-pleasers; but as the servants of Christ doing the will of God from the heart."[14] Again: "Exhort servants to be obedient unto their own masters, and to please them well in all things; not answering again; not purloining, but showing all good fidelity; that they may adorn the doctrine of God our Savior in all things."[15] Following the citations of scripture on the subject of the duty of servants, was the heading, "Our Savior's Rule": "Therefore, all things whatsoever ye would that men should do to you, do ye even so to them: for this is the Law and the Prophets."[16] One wonders whether the clerics of that trying and difficult period were not aware of the incongruity of the Golden Rule with their "scriptural defense" of slavery.

The *Catechism* stated further that

It is the duty of Masters to *provide* for their Servants, both old and young, good houses, comfortable clothing, wholesome and abundant food; to take care of them when old, and infirm and crippled and useless; nurse them carefully in their sickness, and in nothing let them suffer, as far as their means will bear them out; and *keep their families together*. It is their duty to protect their

---

[12] Charles Colcock Jones, *A Catechism of Scripture Doctrine and Practice, for Families and Sabbath Schools, Designed also for the Oral Instruction of Colored Persons* (Savannah, 1844), p. 17.

[13] Col. 1:4.

[14] Col. 3:22 ff. Not accurately quoted.

[15] Titus 2:9-10.   [16] Matt. 7:12.

PLANTATION MISSIONS

Servants, from abuse or ill-treatment, and have justice done them when they are wronged. They are their Fathers and Guardians; Servants are members of their households, etc.

As for the servants, the *Catechism* enjoined them

to count their Masters "worthy of all honour," as those whom God has placed over them in this world; *"with all fear,"* they are to be *"subject to them,"* and obey them in all *things*, possible and lawful, with good will, and endeavour to *please them well*, . . . and let Servants serve their masters as faithfully behind their backs as before their faces. God is present to see, if their masters are not.

Should they fall into the hands of hard and unjust and unequal masters, and *suffer wrongfully*, their course according to divine command is to *take it patiently*, referring their case to God; looking to him for support in their trials, and for rewards for their patience. And the Lord will surely remember them.

Servants were further admonished to tell the truth and not to steal from their masters, for "he requires truth, and honesty, in all persons and under all circumstances." Servants were not to run away or to harbour a runaway: *"Christian Servants should be examples to all others of obedience and honesty,* otherwise they will bring a reproach upon Religion, and brand themselves in the eye of all as hypocrites." And then: "Are you a servant? Care not for it. If you are a Christian you are the Lord's Freeman. And if you are faithful in your station, you shall, as well as other men, higher and greater than yourself, obtain the Crown of Life. God places one man in one station and one in another, according to his will. What he requires is, that *every man in his particular station*, serve him, and all will be well for time and eternity."

It is obvious that the position of the slaveholder was fraught with fatalism; that it offered no hope of progress and was based upon the assumption that what is, is right; that man is born to a station in life (at least the slave was) and that his highest duty was to conform to the *status quo*. The Church truly had a difficult job whenever it undertook to defend slavery and at the same time teach the Christian religion.

The questions and answers of Capers's *Catechism*[17] were

[17] William Capers, *Catechism for the Use of the Methodist Missions, etc.* (Nashville, Tenn., 1876). This appears to be an abridgement of the antebellum edition, and was used in Methodist Sunday Schools for some years

somewhat simpler than those of Charles C. Jones. It should be said that the catechetical sections in some of these little texts covered practically the whole of the Bible, beginning usually with profound theological and philosophic questions, briefly answered, and running the whole gamut of theological disputation. From the *Catechism* of William Capers:

    Ques. Who made you?
    Ans. God.
    Q. What did he make you for?
    A. For his glory.
    Q. Who is God?
    A. The Almighty, maker of heaven and earth.
    Q. What do you know of him?
    A. God is holy, just and true.
    Q. What else do you know of him?
    A. God is merciful, good, and gracious.
    Q. How old is he?
    A. God does not grow old; he always was, and always will be.

Then followed questions and answers on the creation of man, the fall of man, the promise of a Savior, Christ's incarnation, the child Jesus, the ministry of Christ, the death and resurrection of Christ, the judgment, etc.

The Jones text contained this significant conclusion:

You have now finished this Catechism. You have learned something of the great God, Father, Son and Holy Ghost, who made us, and takes care of us, and all things. You have learned something of the Angels, both good and evil:—of man also: of ourselves, how we came into the world, how happy our first Father was: how he sinned and brought upon us all, sin, death, and hell. You have learned something of God's great mercy towards us: how he sent Jesus Christ, His well-beloved Son, into the world to suffer and die for our salvation. . . .

You have learned something of the Ten Commandments. . . .

You have learned something of the Church of God upon earth. . . .

May God bless to you this instruction . . . and take you to be with him in Heaven forever.[18]

---

after the war. The slave edition is very rare. The only copy known to the present writer is found in the library of the University of South Carolina, and contains the material especially designed for slaves.

[18] Jones, *A Catechism, etc.*, p. 154.

PLANTATION MISSIONS

Taking up again the story of the plantation missions as told by the missionaries themselves, we begin with a report in 1835 from J. C. Coggeshall to his church paper in New York City. This being prior to the division in the Methodist Episcopal Church, the South Carolina preachers were reporting at that time to the secretary of the Board of Missions, Nathan Bangs, who was publishing their reports in the *Christian Advocate and Journal*. A missionary wrote from the rice fields as follows:

The Black River and Pee Dee mission, to which I was appointed by the bishop, at the last session of the South Carolina conference, was formerly a part of the Black River circuit. Within its limits there were two societies containing, as by the class papers, 40 white members and 1,043 blacks; and in the neighborhood of these churches an entire population of slaves exceeding 6,000 in number. . . .

I entered upon my labors on the first Sabbath after the rise of the conference, after which I was absent a short time in removing my family within the bounds of the mission. Finding it necessary to build a pole house in the pine land to locate them as far distant from the river as practicable regarding their health, my time has been fully occupied in forming my plans, attending to my studies, meeting my appointments, and locating my family. . . .

I have 24 appointments at the plantations, and have declined adding to them, lest I spread my work beyond my ability to attend to it. These appointments I fill in the following manner. On Sunday at nine o'clock A. M., I meet all the black members who attend at my appointments at the church—I preach to them, or give catechetical instruction until twelve. This being the hour for public preaching, I preach to the entire congregation in attendance at the church; and at the close of this service examine the white classes. Our services are concluded by half past two or three o'clock, P. M. I then ride to my appointment at a plantation, so to meet the class belonging to the plantation visited at four o'clock, P. M., when I preach to this class, and at the conclusion of preaching examine them in class meeting, after which I ride yet to another plantation, meet the class here at seven o'clock, P. M., and conclude my labors for the Sabbath in preaching to and examining this class.

Four of the nights during the week I visit other plantations, commence preaching at seven o'clock, and examine the class.

At the respective appointments on the plantations I do not permit any present but to the plantation that I attend, of the blacks, and under this regulation necessarily observed, having due regard to the police of the plantation, my congregations are as large as may be profitable, numbering from 50 to 150 members, and the classes containing from 10 to 90 members. By this arrangement I am enabled to attend fully to the class examinations.

I have stated evenings monthly for Church trials and class business, at which periods the evenings are exclusively devoted to it. This is necessary as well to attend to the administration of our Discipline as to instruct them in it.

I have put a stop to all preaching by our black brethren, which I found them engaging in, contrary to the law of the state, and the police of the country, and have encouraged them to hold prayer meetings twice a week, their leaders being present to direct the same, and to attend to their class meetings, according to the Discipline, obtaining the owners sanction of the measure, which is readily granted.

I have not yet been enabled to attend to the catechetical instruction of the children. Such whose ages justify it have been occupied on the plantations during the planting season. Had it been otherwise, my health having failed me somewhat, I could not have found time and strength of body to give it the attention it demands. The time is at hand when the night appointments must necessarily be stopped until after the sickly season, when they will be resumed. I shall, as soon as I can get through my second round of appointments, stop them, when in the day, during the week. I hope to do something of my duty in catechizing the little negroes.[19]

The extent of the missionaries' labors is indicated by the large number of plantations assigned to each. On the Pon Pon and Combahee Mission, R. J. Boyd wrote: "We now attend 19 [plantations] in number, on which we have 10 regular preaching places, at several of which there are houses of worship erected for the purpose."[20] Thomas D. Turpin, of John's Island and Wadmalaw, wrote: "I now have 12 plantations at which I preach and catechize."[21] From the islands below Savannah, Thomas C. Benning reported: "I have 10 preaching places, one or more on each island, at which I attend once a fortnight, having to depend somewhat on the state of the tides."[22] The missionary stationed at the May and New River Mission, Theo Huggins, asserted: "I attend once in two weeks at 13 planta-

---

[19] *Christian Advocate and Journal*, IX, 174 (June 26, 1835).
[20] *Ibid.*, VIII, 166 (June 13, 1834).
[21] *Ibid.*, VIII, 170 (June 20, 1834).
[22] *Ibid.*, VIII, 138 (April 25, 1834).

PLANTATION MISSIONS

tions, where there are about 460 souls. Here I catechize 168 children who are improving. A few young ladies are taking interest in the instruction of these children, and if this could be general, it would be much in favor of a speedy reform."[23] Near Savannah, two ministers, Samuel J. Bryan and J. B. Barton, wrote that their parish included "18 plantations, and about 2000 souls. We visit and catechize on every plantation once in two weeks, and preach at 15 places every other Sabbath. . . . We have not been engaged twelve months on this mission, and yet many sing with interest all the songs and verses, and answer all the questions on 40 pages of the catechism for colored children. Many of these children have improved in their manners and morals. They are lively, clean, and affectionate. We are looking, laboring, and praying for a general reformation."[24]

Not only were these preachers looking forward to a "general reformation" among the slaves, but also, like one from Waccamaw Neck, Theo Huggins, they were declaring that if those engaged upon this work "shall be prudent and faithful, this shall become as the garden of God."[25] The extent of the labors of Huggins would dwarf the work of a typical city pastor:

> The missionary has access to 21 plantations, on which there are upward of 2,000 adults, who are served every other Sabbath; and they appear to be very willing to be instructed in the things of religion. We have received this year 482 members, dropped 8, and 2 have died.
>
> There are 390 children receiving oral catechetical instruction, as we believe, to great advantage.[26]

Reference should be made to the attitude of the preachers sent to this work. So far as the records show, none complained and none exhibited attitudes of condescension as though they were doing a menial task. On the contrary, the appointees to the plantation work rejoiced in the opportunity offered them and felt that they were doing the most truly Christian service possible for a minister. One declared, "I must confess I was

[23] *Ibid.*, VIII, 182 (July 11, 1834).
[24] *Ibid.*, VIII, 138 (April 25, 1834).
[25] *Ibid.*, XI, 74 (Dec. 30, 1836).
[26] *Ibid.*

pleased with the idea of preaching the gospel to the poor."[27] Another, William Martin, wrote as follows:

I was appointed a missionary to the plantations of the Congaree River. . . .

Yes, my heart was enlisted in this work of giving the gospel to our servants in the South, and I began with health renewed, and, thank God, I gave to this work six years of the prime of my life and ministry. It was no sinecure. I knew it was hard work and poor pay—in fact, so poor that all our own resources and the income of a school my wife opened were found necessary for our support. But the work paid in many ways besides money: it was a great work, a momentous work, a special one for the South. If we did not do it, no one would or could. No one should think himself too good for it. I for one did not.[28]

That the life of a plantation missionary was not an easy one is attested to by the words of George W. Moore, serving the Combahee Mission: "In going to and fro on my work on the mission, I have ridden horseback, in a gig, and often on a negro's back. Sometimes it would be in a boat pushed through the mud. Often I have had to be pushed some distance through the mud to get to water to baptize the negroes."[29] Again: "I recollect on one occasion preaching with a negro holding a lightwood torch at my back to throw light on my Bible and hymn book."[30]

Chief among the hazards which beset the missionaries and their families was that of poor health. The cause of malaria was unknown; there were no screens, knowledge of infectious diseases was very inadequate, and doctors were few. Old records and letters reveal a pathetic story of the ravages of disease in the low country. The health problem was made more difficult by the great preponderance of Negroes over whites. It is true that many of the slaves, because of their adaptability to the tropics, were not susceptible to malaria, the dreaded chills and fevers, but this disease was a scourge among the whites during the late summer and autumn. Maladies which struck terror to the hearts of every one were dysentery and cholera. The old

---

[27] *Ibid.*, VIII, 30. (Oct. 18, 1833).

[28] From reminiscences of the Reverend William Martin, written for the press, and incorporated in Harrison, *op. cit.*, p. 256.

[29] *Ibid.*, p. 208. [30] *Ibid.*, p. 204.

PLANTATION MISSIONS

graveyards on St. Helena Island and in other wealthy sections, where tombstones have remained intact, testify to the great number of infants and children who died. A Doctor Auld of Edisto Island, writing about the year 1800, asserted: "The climate of Edisto may be considered as sickly. In the course of fifteen years, a number greater than three-fourths of the inhabitants have died. Some families in that period are extinct, and in all of them death has been once or twice, and in some three or four times an unwelcome visitor. Two funerals have occurred in a day, but the instances are rare. And two instances can be adduced of two funerals in a family in one day. From the commencement of the sickly season of 1798 to the corresponding period of the succeeding year, 37 persons died."[31] Dr. Auld further recorded that "the year 1802 will long be remembered on this Island for the ravages produced by dysentery."[32] Some of the whites were stricken, but the disease took its greatest toll among the Negroes: "In the year 1798 the deaths from fever amounted to twenty-four, very nearly an eighth of the whole number of inhabitants. Of those who died, seventeen were children under five years of age, and seven were adults. The year 1803 was equally sickly, yet the deaths from fever amounted to no more than seven: of these, three were children."[33] The doctor's explanations of the causes of sickness, and the remedies recommended, contain an element of humor which one can hardly resist relating. He believed that "heat and moisture combined in access are agents of dissolution; that the dissolution of vegetable and animal substances generates putrescent effluvia, and that these effluvia, acting upon the system, induce diseases which often destroy life."[34] As to remedies for autumnal fevers, he advised "early, large, and repeated bleedings, assisted by active mercurial purges, and emetic and nauseating medicines. . . ."[35] Vegetable acids and sugar were condemned, since "in their decomposition in the stomach, they evolve much gaseous and acid matter, which not only debilitate this viscus, but by the painful distentions and eructations which they excite, exhaust the patient without producing a corresponding effect upon his disease."[36] Doubtless, in spite of this treat-

[31] Ramsay, *op. cit.*, II, 281.
[33] *Ibid.*, II, 281.
[35] *Ibid.*, II, 281.
[32] *Ibid.*, II, 282.
[34] *Ibid.*, II, 282.
[36] *Ibid.*, II, 282.

ment, some of the patients recovered. At any rate, the big words and high-sounding phrases produced an illusion behind which the medical profession protected its austere dignity. Those inclined to make fun of the preachers of the early part of the nineteenth century and their religion might take thought of the doctors. David Ramsay, the historian who recorded these statements of Dr. Auld, was himself a medical doctor and practiced "physic" in Charleston for years.

From the Savannah and Black River Mission:

The circumstances under which we make this report calls for unfeigned gratitude to the author of all good, that we should live in the midst of cholera, sickness, suffering and death, etc. . . . Since the appearance of cholera on this mission, over 500 have fallen victims to it, and the disease continues to prevail; when and where it may stop our heavenly Father only knows.

The planters have generally moved their slaves from the rice fields to the up or pine lands, where they remain in camps, or tents, and the cases that occur in those camps are generally more mild, and if medical aid is timely afforded, the disease generally yields to medicine. We continue to visit the camps, hospitals, and barns into which the sick and dying are placed, and frequently when trying to talk and pray with them, we are made to rejoice together in God our Savior. Yesterday, while preaching in the road under some oaks between the camps, 30 or 40 desired our prayers.[37]

Thomas Benning wrote from the vicinity of Savannah: "The dreadful cholera has been raging in the neighborhoods."[38] Charles Wilson, in "a manuscript found in the collection of the Reverend H. A. C. Walker,"[39] commented:

From the beginning of our labors on Jehossee Island to the commencement of 1844 our course was generally onward and prosperous. But at that time that terror and destroyer of humanity, cholera, made its appearance for the first time on the island. Gov. Aiken, then in Washington, was duly notified when the disease became epidemic, and, like a man true to his responsibilities, hastened away from his family and business in Congress to afford whatever comfort and assistance might be in his power to his suffering and dying people, and for near or quite three weeks, regardless of danger, passed his time in visiting from hospital to hospital both day and night.

[37] *Christian Advocate and Journal*, IX, 38 (Oct. 31, 1834).
[38] *Ibid.*, IX, 42 (Nov. 7, 1834).   [39] Harrison, *op. cit.*, p. 215 n.

The first case occurred while Brother Bass, who was with me, and I were at Conference. But as soon as we returned and heard of the situation of our charge at that place we went among them, desirous of rendering any assistance in our power, though not without serious apprehension of danger. The first hospital I went into had a corpse lying in the front room in preparation for the grave— a young man, whose mother was sitting by his side and in deep sorrow. I offered what comfort I could, prayed with her, and left. In that day's round of visits I saw four corpses. From the disease's first appearance there were two physicians on the place in constant attendance night and day. About three hundred of the negroes were removed to camp, which was composed of temporary buildings in the woods. Dr. Kinloch was called from Charleston. Brother Bass or I was there every day almost, rendering whatever assistance we could by offering the comforts of religion to the sick and dead. The disease continued about six weeks, in which time I think over seventy died.[40]

The missionaries to the slaves not only performed duties related to preaching and catechising, but also entered sympathetically into the lives and fortunes of the colored people. Not only did they baptize their infants, according to the rites of their respective churches, and visit the sick, but they also buried their dead and participated in the gruesome night funerals so common among the Negroes in the Deep South. The ministers tried always to utilize such occasions for the propagation of the good life and better conduct among the Negroes. A. M. Chreitzberg, stationed on the Beaufort Mission, vividly described his participation in a funeral:

It was not uncommon often to be sent for to go to see dying negroes. I thank my Master that I never once turned a deaf ear to any of these calls. Once I performed the burial rite over one of these humble slaves at night. The memory lingers vividly to this day.

I left home about sunset, on a calm and pleasant evening, and took my way along the high bluff of the river. The distance was four or five miles, so that it was dark ere I arrived at the plantation. Just before the dead man's door was the corpse, already in its narrow house. Beside it sat the widow, and to her I addressed myself, bidding her trust in God, the Husband of the widow and the Father of the fatherless. His fellow-servants were seated around, the deep-drawn sigh showing their sorrow for the departed, their sympathy

[40] *Ibid.*, pp. 227-228.

with the bereaved. I addressed them on the uncertainty of life, the necessity of making preparation for death—in a word, I preached Jesus and the resurrection, and by the glimmering of the lightwood fire was the burial service read, and the body committed to the dust.

It was after 9 o'clock, as I took my way homeward, and passed through the dark avenue of oaks, trusting to the instinct of my horse to find the way, illumined momentarily by the fitful flash of the firefly. It was a time for serious thought, for a communion with the heart and with God. I asked myself if I had tried in every way to fulfill my duty since I had come to these perishing souls to teach them the way, the truth, and the life. . . .[41]

A missionary of the South Carolina Conference assigned to the islands near Beaufort incorporated in his report a description of some experiences with torchlight burials:

On one occasion of burial, I have reason to believe much good was done. A woman, who was a member of the Church, and who had died in full hope of immortal life, was to be buried at night, it being the most convenient time for the people to be together. Accordingly I met the people at the time appointed. The plantation being large, many were present. The corpse was conveyed about a quarter of a mile to the burial ground, the procession moving slowly and silently along, with lighted torches interspersed through the ranks. This presented a solemn scene; but after we arrived at the burying place it was still more solemn. A grove standing in the midst of a large clearing, which had been sacredly kept for years as belonging to the dead, undisturbed by even the footsteps of man, except when another was to be laid in the earth, and under the shade of the cedars. Here we all met in the midst of the grove, around the grave. It was a dark night, but in the midst of the grove it was still more dark. All was silent, except the thrilling note of the whippoor-will, who had made this lonely retreat its home; all around us lay the graves of the dead of all sizes. The reflection from the many torches presented them full to view in every direction, as though they had but just been closed; so thick was the shade above that no grass grew on that spot. I have attended many of my fellow beings to the grave; but never did I witness a more solemn time, and yet I felt it a blessed time. I felt it a duty to try and improve the occasion of our being together; and indeed it was a time of weeping —some of the most stubborn were melted into tears. The husband of the deceased and her infant child were near the grave; he, before a careless man, now wept aloud—and since that period has shown

[41] *Ibid.*, pp. 254-255.

his grief was not of a worldly kind; he has offered himself to the Church, and his child he has had baptized. Many others on the plantation have become serious, and are now on trial.[42]

One is interested to know just how these "knights of the saddle-bags" spent their time. Again the routine reports of the Methodist circuit rider furnish humble and eloquent accounts of the manner of their lives day by day. John Bunch, of the North and South Santee Mission, near Georgetown, reported that he and his co-laborer, Massey, each preached four times a Sunday on the various plantations and that the fourth Sabbath they spent at home in rest with their families. Of the other days of the week he asserted: "They are spent in catechising the negro children by a regular form of catechism, composed by Dr. Capers for the benefit of small children, and especially the negro children of our charge on the missions of our state. The children's part consists of four lessons; and I may say with safety that there are but very few exceptions out of three hundred, or perhaps even four hundred, but that can repeat the answer to each question throughout the four lessons, as soon as the question is asked them. I do assure you, that the work of catechising both the little negroes, and the members on trial in our Church, by a regular form, is an excellent work."[43]

Thomas D. Turpin, of John's Island and Wadmalaw Mission, who served twelve plantations, reported that with his regular church members there were "200 [Negro] children to whom I tender catechetical instruction."[44]

Writing from the Pon Pon and Combahee Mission, R. J. Boyd declared:

We have arranged the mission so as to be able once a fortnight to preach at each place, on the Sabbath (this requires hard labor, for beside preaching two or three times, we have to ride several miles between each appointment) and during the week, visit the sick, catechize the children, and hold class meetings. The latter, however, we will dispense with during the sickly season, as we are compelled when we hold them, to do it at night; and exposure to the night air of these swamps is very injurious to health. And in view of this, I would advise all who are in like situations with myself to keep

[42] *Christian Advocate and Journal*, XI, 206 (Aug. 18, 1837).
[43] *Ibid.*, VIII, 30 (Oct. 18, 1833).
[44] *Ibid.*, VIII, 170 (June 20, 1834).

closely shut up at night, during the sickly months, and make a free use of the chloride of lime in their chambers. This has a great tendency to correct the deleterious quality of the atmosphere; and thus, by the blessing of God, and making use of those precautionary measures, we may escape the fever which has such a tendency to dampen the spirits of the missionary at the reception of his appointment. But to return, we also have requested the members to meet at the place appointed for worship on the Sabbath that we are absent, and hold a prayer meeting, subject to the inspection of the master or overseer, and allow them to hold no meetings on the week nights, except those appointed or attended by us, for this reason that they frequently run into a great many extravagancies, and often continue their meeting all night.[45]

George W. Moore, who had within his charge the Negroes on Governor Aiken's plantation on Jehossee Island, preached generally in an old cooper shop "opposite the Bluff Place." He wrote: "Here we usually held a sunrise prayer meeting and catechised the children from the estate place. I have often been interested in seeing the little fellows running on the rice bank toward the cooper shop, and entering almost out of breath. The first thing they would do would be to clasp my hand and tell me 'how-dy,' and while upon my knees in prayer they would get as near as possible, some of them leaning against my feet with their heads."[46]

A. M. Chreitzberg, writing in later years of his services as a missionary on the Beaufort Mission, declared that the two or three hundred Negro children whom he catechized "were kept together under the care of an elderly female," and orders were given to have them all assembled whenever the preacher came on his catechizing rounds. The plantation authorities co-operated with the ministers by freeing all children of duties on the days the estates were visited. They came, he wrote, "generally smiling and clean for their instruction." One can imagine the many disciplinary problems, and humorous situations that must have been experienced by the old "mauma" who was charged with the responsibility of handling so large a brood of slave children:

On Sundays we would preach twice, thrice, and even four times a day, to old and young alike. It was no holiday time, this work of

[45] *Ibid.*, VIII, 166 (June 13, 1834).
[46] Harrison, *op. cit.*, pp. 199-200.

a plantation missionary, but one that required the utmost concentration of effort, the most unflagging spirit of zeal, and, in some instances, a self-sacrifice that was heroic. Especially was this true of those whose labors lay among the slaves of the rice plantations. Here their lives were constantly in jeopardy from the deadly miasmatic exhalations of the rice fields; but thanks to the watchful care of a beneficent Providence, and to the retreats afforded by the pine lands, but few of them died. As to the slaves themselves they seemed to thrive better in these localities, owing to their similarity in temperature and topographical features to their own country.[47]

It is evident that the slave was more impressed by the sincerity of the missionaries' motive through his visitation of the sick and burial of the dead than by his preaching. Through such human contacts the Christian gospel was most effectively portrayed. Catechetical questions and church doctrines made little appeal as compared with the handshake and the prayer of the minister as he knelt by the bed of a sick slave. Chreitzberg described one of the duties of the missionary:

Another duty of the missionary, in addition to catechising the children and preaching to the adults, was to visit the sick and aged at their cabins. In this way he reached a surer and firmer spot in the negro heart than in almost any other; for by these visits he made it plain to the occupant of the humble cabin that he was not ashamed to enter it, or to grasp him by his rough and toil-worn hand as a friend and brother; or, kneeling upon the floor beside the rude bed, to offer fervent petition to God in his behalf. In very few instances did it fail to take the simple, rugged heart and bind it firmly to the Cross.[48]

There was an element of sternness in the religion taught to the slave. Membership in the church meant more than signing one's name on a roll or shaking hands with the preacher. Nineteenth-century fundamentalism made up its mind on most things. Its religious tenets were simple and straightforward. For it, most questions had been settled—even such behavior as Sabbath-breaking or liquor-drinking. Methodists and Baptists might quarrel among themselves as to the biblical mode of baptism, but they were of one mind on liquor, Sabbath observance, sex matters, and the like. Negroes were admitted to the church on trial or probation, and some were expelled because

[47] *Ibid.*, pp. 247-248.   [48] *Ibid.*, pp. 250-251.

they did not live up to the requirements of church membership. The "class meeting," an institution peculiarly Methodist, lent itself admirably to the problems of slave conversion. It was in the "class" that instruction was given to adults, questions asked, doctrines explained, and a general check-up made upon the individual. Here each member could speak and, if he desired, give his religious experience. The result was that it quickened interest in what the ministers were trying to do, gave opportunities for personal service, and provided a kind of clearing house for the details of church membership. One minister reported that he had organized twelve classes on his mission.[49] Another wrote: "I am not able to hold class with them, according to [the Methodist] discipline on other causes; but have such an examination among them as to ascertain their state."[50] In another instance there were 247 Negro members in regular standing, while 57 were still on probation.[51]

Expulsions were common items in the reports. The Pon Pon and Combahee Mission reported: "We have received between 55 and 60 on probation; dropped and expelled between 75 and 80, leaving about 800 in the Church. Having got clear of so many dead weights, we now have a fair prospect of success before us."[52] The fiery John Bunch wrote from Santee:

I have expelled 10 or 12 for Sabbath-breaking and other sins; and I must say it has had a good effect upon the Sabbath-breakers in general; and I now hope the Church will be able to put it down among them, by close attention to Discipline. When my next round of appointments among them came, they asked my pardon with tears in their eyes, saying they would never do the like any more if I would again take them into the Church. I received them back again, assuring them I would turn any man out of the Church for working on Sunday. I have received on trial about as many as I have expelled this quarter, one half being those that were expelled, which makes our loss about 6, and our increase about 12. But I think we are gaining ground much faster now than when we were taking in great numbers. Our members begin to understand the nature of the foundation on which their faith and hope are fixed, I mean the cross of Christ and the mediatorial throne of grace.[53]

[49] *Christian Advocate and Journal*, VIII, 94 (Feb. 7, 1834).
[50] *Ibid.*, IX, 30 (Oct. 17, 1834).
[51] *Ibid.*, VIII, 94 (Feb. 7, 1834).
[52] *Ibid.*, VIII, 166 (June 13, 1834).
[53] *Ibid.*, IX, 14 (Sept. 19, 1834).

PLANTATION MISSIONS

One can hardly realize how ignorant and pagan were the masses of slaves on the larger rice plantations and what great obstacles the missionary met in his endeavor to teach the Christian religion among them. Their numbers as compared to the whites constituted a weight of inertia which made effective work almost impossible. Thomas C. Benning wrote somewhat discouragingly of his "charge" of five small sea islands, southeast of the city of Savannah, on which he found eighty whites and twelve hundred blacks.[54] In the low country the slaves saw little of their masters or other whites from whom they might have learned some of the civilities of life. Only the house servants on these great estates knew their masters' families. As a result, the large plantations of the rice section had the greatest number of unenlightened Negroes, among whom every kind of superstition flourished. The hordes of field hands under the domination of the overseer and his Negro drivers constituted the greatest problem for the missionaries. Mission work in Africa could hardly have been more difficult.

Because of their superstitious tendencies and their proneness to religious excesses the white ministers looked with disfavor upon Negro preachers and Negro religious gatherings, especially when whites were not present. In the coastal region very few Negroes were permitted to preach. Despite these objections there was considerable leadership in religion among the Negroes, especially where they were permitted to organize religious societies. The presence of these societies was very disturbing to Thomas D. Turpin, stationed on the May and New River Mission. He reported that many Negroes in this section had no contact with the minister to whose church they belonged and that they therefore organized themselves into religious societies and were indulging in practices quite out of harmony with Christian principles. They were, he found, doing a crude kind of penance in expiation of sins, upon indictment by their leaders. There were three degrees of punishment for three degrees of offenses. The leaders arranged the punishment to fit the crime. Turpin explained: "If the crime was of the first magnitude, the perpetrator had to pick up a quart of benne[55]

[54] *Ibid.*, VIII, 138 (April 25, 1834).
[55] Benne is a small seed, slightly resembling flaxseed, though of a straw-yellow color, and grown in the low country. Charleston is noted for its

seed ... poured on the ground by the priest; and if of the second, a quart of rice; and if of the third, a quart of corn; and that they also had high seats and low seats, but incorrect views relative to those who ought to be punished; and that it was also a rule among them never to divulge the secret of stealing; and if it should be divulged by any one member, that one had to go on the low seat, or pick up the benne seed."[56]

Generally the planters favored the enterprise and gave it their financial and moral support. Once they were convinced that preachers could be trusted, that is, that they would do nothing to incite rebellion and would accept the *status quo* of the slave and preach a simple gospel suited to his existing condition of servitude, they gave their support and good will. At this time the lines of opinion were tightly drawn. Antislavery sentiment in the North was like an ominous cloud. The South had not only its economic system at stake; its whole social and political structure was endangered. The abolitionists were not at this time moved by sentiments of sympathy toward the Southern white people. Their views were fanatical. Under the stress of propaganda and a sense of righteous indignation their fiery solicitude for the slave caused them to hate his owner. In return the people of the South stood by the old order. Many, like Poinsett and Pettigrew, clung to the hope that the tangled threads might in time be unraveled and that slavery might pass without cataclysm and bloodshed. But that could not be. The hotheads on both sides poured oil on the raging fire.

Charles Wilson, writing of his service on Ashepoo River and of the support the mission received from R. B. Rhett, a prominent planter, explained the planters' attitude:

During this year, 1835, Hon. R. B. Rhett put up at his own expense a comfortable church building on his plantation on the Ashepoo. Here we preached regularly to his own negroes and to those of his brother, Mr. Thomas Rhett, never failing to have large and interesting congregations. Through the lavish kindness of Hon. Mr. Rhett, I and my family occupied his residence during his stay in Washington. This put me in the center of my work, and enabled me to leave home after eight o'clock in the morning, reach the most distant place in my charge, catechise the children, visit the sick, and

---

benne candy, made in quaint, old-fashioned kitchens. The benne seed are mixed in the candy as peanuts are used in peanut candy.

[56] *Christian Advocate and Journal*, VIII, 90 (Jan. 31, 1834).

PLANTATION MISSIONS

return before two in the afternoon. On Sabbath mornings I was also enabled to hold sunrise prayer meetings on the neighboring plantations and to return home in time to set out for my regular day's preaching. This kind hospitality on the part of Mr. Rhett not only rendered my work doubly pleasant and satisfactory, but also of increased profit to those among whom I labored. I could give them far more time and attention and devise many ways for their instruction and entertainment. I now began to spend an hour of each night of the week with those on the place in teaching them the various hymns used by the Church. Having a natural ear for music, they soon made rapid progress. But these delightful meetings were brought to a close by a severe illness that now attacked me, and laid me low with hemorrhage of the lungs. The devotion of these negroes to me at this period was one of the brightest chapters of my missionary life. I cannot speak of it too highly. As soon as they had finished their daily labors they were at my bedside ready to do any act of kindness in their power. Though weak from suffering, I nevertheless endeavored to talk to all who came, and many scenes that I think God must have loved to witness occurred in my sick room. When at last, having recovered, though with my health seriously impaired, I came away, I believe it was as a much better Christian and a more useful minister.

The Hon. Mr. Rhett was, I think, a truly pious man. He seemed deeply interested in the spiritual welfare of the black population of his country, and contributed most liberally every year to the support of the mission.[57]

M. L. Banks, who in former years had served as a missionary among the plantations along the Combahee River, recorded his interesting contacts with three prominent planters of that vicinity, Charles Lowndes, James B. Heyward, and Daniel Blake:

Of the Combahee planters I have very pleasant recollections. They valued the missionary not only as the pastor of their slaves, but as a companion of themselves and families. They welcomed him to their houses, and were not afraid of their families coming in contact with him. It was not so everywhere. They lived in princely style. The dishes on their tables were of the best quality and in great variety. I declined nothing but the wines and liquors, and it was a trial to do that. To hold to my temperance principles under a perfect battery of both masculine and feminine hospitality was not the easiest thing in the world to do.

[57] Harrison, *op. cit.*, pp. 220-221.

Charles Lowndes, James B. Heyward, and Daniel Blake had very neat chapels on their plantations, where not only their negroes but themselves and their families worshiped. Charles Lowndes lived the lowest down on the mission. His house was the home of the missionary whenever he chose to make it so. He was a noble, upright, conscientious man, extremely courteous to those in an inferior situation. James B. Heyward lived near the center of the mission. His was an attractive home. He had a large estate, but was a plain man, simple in manner, courteous in deportment, fine-looking, and of a dignified bearing. He gave liberally to the support of the mission.

Daniel Blake's plantation lay in the extreme upper end of our mission. He, as I remember, was an Englishman by birth. He was a noble specimen of humanity. He despised affectation and looked with perfect contempt upon all snobbery. There was no man more in sympathy with the work of the South Carolina Conference among the rice fields and cotton plantations of the country than he. Though a member of the Episcopal Church, I think he was about half Methodist. At the handsome church building in sight of his residence, where I preached to the negroes of his place, he was a regular attendant and a close listener. When he had company on preaching day at the church, he proposed to the company that they all go out to the preaching, and they did it. He once said to me that he wanted the missionary on Combahee not only to preach to his people, but to visit his family. He lived up to that sentiment. His house was the missionary's home.

Mr. Blake was a most humane master, and his negroes were devoted to him. I think they would have fought for him to the death had the occasion for it arisen. I remember preaching to his people on the atonement and used an illustration which they interpreted to mean that their master had sold them to a neighbor. The excitement was tremendous. They ran to him from all parts of the quarter to know if such was the case. He explained, and they were content. There was, in their eye, no other master like the one they had. I think there was not a great deal of clear money made on Mr. Blake's plantation. He fed and clothed his negroes too well and worked them too moderately to admit of that. Among the devout masters who will be saved in heaven with their pious slaves I feel safe in counting Daniel Blake, the missionaries' friend and the negroes' benefactor.[58]

Charles Wilson, who put a fine touch of local color into his narrative, displayed a high degree of enthusiasm for the work,

[58] *Ibid.*, pp. 270-272.

and his gratification was unbounded at the spectacle of a planter's being so moved that he did a little preaching on his own account at one of the Negro meetings:

> We preached in barns, cooper shops, hospitals, and other plantation buildings, which were generally fitted up in comfortable style. So far as we could judge we had the entire confidence of the planters, which they evidenced by their kindness and liberal hospitality. As to the negroes themselves, their artless expressions of gratitude, their rapt attention bestowed upon our sermons touched us deeply and made us all the more resolved to be faithful. In the early part of this year we added another plantation to the mission. This was that of Mr. Mason Smith, one mile above the ferry. A touching incident is connected with the establishment of this mission. Going to keep the appointment, Mr. Smith met me, telling me how glad he was to see me, and how gratified at the prospect of having regular religious service among his blacks. He accompanied me to the house where the meeting was to be held. We found it well filled with a neatly dressed congregation, with countenances giving ample proof of their own joy and gratification in the prospect before them. I read a chapter in the Bible, gave out and sung a hymn, the negroes all joining in. I then prayed and preached a sermon, which I endeavored to make as plain as possible to them.
>
> At the close of the sermon Mr. Smith arose and addressed himself with deep emotion to his people. He said: "Now, my people, you have heard preached to you this day from that blessed book (pointing to my Bible) the very truths I have always been trying to impress upon your mind; and now I feel perfectly willing to commit your religious instruction and spiritual to these men of God. May God be with you." By this time his feelings got so completely the mastery of him that he burst into tears and rushed from the room, praying God's mercy upon them and upon himself. The emotion displayed by their master had an electrifying effect upon the negroes, and scarcely have I witnessed such a scene as now took place. The results were many converts to the Church. And never have I known a more submissive and orderly plantation in my life as a missionary, nor a Church that gave less trouble in the administration of the discipline. It was touching to see the love and gratitude bestowed upon their minister, and they were always desirous of making him some little gift.[59]

George W. Moore, of the South Carolina Conference, described a flourishing church on Big Island and the sympa-

[59] *Ibid.*, pp. 217-218.

thetic co-operation received from Thomas Cuthbert, a resident planter: "[Cuthbert] built a comfortable Church, and allowed his people to attend week days as well as Sundays. On preaching days he would not permit any of his people to do anything to interfere with the hour of service. Every time we visited his place he gave up the labor of sixty hands for half the day. On this place I baptized thirty at one time, twenty-nine by immersion and one, the driver, by pouring. Mr. Cuthbert and his little daughter, he being a widower, were generally present at the church. He would always commune with his people."[60]

All the preachers liked to work on Jehossee Island because it was one of the most efficiently operated rice plantations in the South and especially because of its magnanimous owner, Governor Aiken. References to Aiken's generosity, his well-ordered plantation, and the state of contentment of his slaves appeared in Moore's report:

Here we preached in a room next to the hospital, so that the sick might hear as well as those who were not sick. Gov. Aiken was exceeding kind to us; so was his overseer, Mr. Bagwell. The first letter I received from Gov. Aiken, inclosing his donation of $100.00, impressed me sensibly. It had the same effect upon Bishop Andrew, who asked me to let him keep it.

The overseers would generally send up to the estate place for us a large boat rowed by six or eight hands. I remember a conversation that took place between Dr. Capers and one of the hands on the boat. The Dr. asked him, among other things, how he liked the overseer, which is the test question among the negroes. In reply he said: "Massa he good man; he nebber promise nuffin he no gib you. If he promise you whippin', you's as sho' to git 'em as if you had 'em on you' back.[61]

One of the most significant aspects of the slave conversion movement was the ardor with which the Carolina low country planters espoused the cause. Reading the records, one is impressed with the crusading spirit which possessed the most important people of the section. Perhaps it was, in part, an unconscious atonement for their defense of slavery. They became very zealous in the work, and many of them personally instructed the slaves. Fathers and daughters joined in the

---

[60] *Ibid.*, pp. 207-208.   [61] *Ibid.*, p. 201.

undertaking, the latter instructing groups of Negro children. George W. Moore wrote: "One pleasing part of the Beaufort work was that the young ladies took quite an active part in the instruction of the colored children, both in Beaufort and on the plantations of their fathers. Frequently I found them under the shade of the spreading oak, with a group of little negroes around them, instructing them in the catechism. The planters too, were active in the work. Some of the wealthiest and most distinguished gentlemen would spend every Sabbath afternoon in imparting religious instruction to the negroes, young and old."[62]

One instance of opposition is found in the report of R. J. Boyd, who resided in Walterboro and served plantations on the big rivers below the village. The slaveowner in this case was a widow who spent most of her time in the North and left the details of plantation management to her son. The mother, stirred by abolition sentiment and afraid that her slaves might receive insurrectionary notions, ordered her overseer to permit the missionaries to come on her plantation only on Sundays and to keep a watchful eye upon them. The only other opponents of the work mentioned by this minister were a few overseers, whose attitude was disregarded.[63]

On the Back River Mission the preacher in charge reported that "the owners of every plantation on the mission are kind, and many of them were very liberal in their subscriptions to the missionary society . . . the best they have is always spread before the missionary."[64] Near Savannah the owner of a large plantation was credited with "building a good church for his people" and contributing $100 to the work.[65] The Cooper River Mission prospered and enjoyed the good will and cooperation of the proprietors there. A Mrs. Simons gave a comfortable church to the Negroes on her estate, and a very good church building was found on the place of Colonel James Gadsden. At Dr. Prileau's the minister reported that he preached "sometimes in a negro house and sometimes under a spreading oak. I also preach under a brick shed where the negroes from several of the plantations on the eastern branch

[62] *Ibid.*, pp. 203-204. [63] *Ibid.*
[64] *Christian Advocate and Journal*, X, 70 (Dec. 25, 1835).
[65] *Ibid.*, VIII, 138 (April 25, 1834).

of the Cooper attend. We hope soon to have a Church here."[66] From the islands below Savannah came this word of optimism:

> Success has crowned the efforts of the missionary on these islands, the blacks evincing such evident marks of spiritual and moral improvement as to secure the confidence of their owners and managers. As a proof of the confidence in the missionary and his good work, a neat house of worship has been erected on Skidway island, 35 feet by 25. Ten plantations are regularly visited, on all of which the owners and manager show kindness to the missionary, and encourage him in his work, while the blacks themselves evince a desire to learn the ways of God more perfectly. One hundred and ten children are under a course of instruction, and about the same number of adults are in the church.[67]

After reading many reports and reminiscences of plantation missionaries, one is undeniably impressed with the peculiar interest and pride these ministers took in their work on Edisto Island. If Edisto had a rival in their minds it was the delightful section stretched along the Combahee River. But Edisto Island seems early to have established itself as an important community and to have built up a sentiment and pride almost unique in the Carolina coast region. Its life perhaps approached more nearly a feudal aristocracy than did that in any other section of America. Its rich alluvial lands, unsuited to rice culture, produced a more valued crop, the silky sea-island cotton. In Colonial days its planters shipped quantities of indigo to many British ports. During the trying months preceding secession, when South Carolina was pondering her hazardous step of withdrawing from the Union, a citizen from this region arose and declared that Edisto Island would secede if South Carolina did not. A reckless assertion, to be sure, and indicative of the kind of sentiment which hastened the war; but a prouder, more independent people never lived, and upon slavery and sea-island cotton they produced a culture unique in Southern plantation life. The isolation of the island contributed to its distinctive character. It could be approached from the mainland only by water. Even today its atmosphere is wholly exotic. It would appear that its cultural tone is the result of the impact of Africa upon English colonial culture. One who

---

[66] Harrison, *op. cit.*, pp. 209-210.
[67] *Christian Advocate and Journal*, X, 70 (Dec. 25, 1835).

walks its solitary moss-draped roads at dusk or watches the blue line of the sea across the wide expanse of odorous marsh receives impressions totally different from those induced by the common American scene. There is something foreign and delightfully strange about this region. The land seems to be haunted by a culture that has vanished and by a once-proud people, whose ideals and ambitions were thwarted. The rapid staccato speech of the Gullah Negro, the wild, unfamiliar sounds typical of solitary places, the smoky-blue haze hovering above the level landscape, and the melancholy droning of the surf—all contribute to create the impression of other-worldliness. There is a stretch of beach facing the Atlantic, site of the old ante-bellum summer colony, Edingsville, long abandoned, where one may sit for a month and never see a human face and rarely, if ever, a sail. Here, unspoiled by man, nature reigns in all her native wildness and charm.

Of this island the missionaries wrote enthusiastically as they recorded their reminiscences of the days spent among the slaves. One of these missionaries, M. L. Banks, wrote:

My first experience as a missionary to the slaves was on the Edisto, Jehossee and Fenwick Mission. It was in 1849. Rev. Charles Wilson was my senior and, as I remember, the founder of the mission. He was the negro's friend. He sacrificed much to show him the way of life, and he succeeded. About twenty years of his ministerial life was spent on this mission. It must have been a severe trial to himself and family to be isolated from congenial companionship during these long years. What but devotion to the negro's spiritual wellbeing could have reconciled him to this? He was there for near two decades, and likely would have ended his life there but for the war and its results. In those days we had a number of preachers who could adapt themselves to the comprehension of the negro in preaching. Of these Charles Wilson was in the lead. But he never talked nonsense. He never let himself down to the negro's way of talking, but strove to lift him up to his own. I once asked Brother Wilson to give me some lessons in the art of Preaching to the negroes. His reply was characteristic. "In preaching to negroes," said he, "I always preach the best I can." He thought that any sort of talk was not good enough for them.

Our work that year covered three islands. Fenwick was difficult of access, with a wide river or sound lying between it and the Edisto. Crossing over and back in a small boat was not without its perils. On Fenwick we were furnished with a pony to ride to our appointments. This sturdy little fellow was so used to mosquitoes that he showed little discomfort, though his neck was covered with them as a network.

Jehossee was separated from Edisto by a small creek spanned by a bridge. That, to me, was the most interesting part of the work. Ex-Governor Aiken lived there, and was the sole owner of the island. He owned hundreds of negroes and few slaves ever had a kinder master. His negro quarters looked like a little village, and much whiter and cleaner than many villages I have seen. The large building he had erected for his people to worship in was generally crowded at the hour of preaching. The worshipers appeared in decent apparel, and not a few were dressed like ladies and gentlemen. What a privilege it was to hear them sing! I have sat in the pulpit and listened until I would weep for joy.

Mr. Mikel, another planter, also had a nice church erected for his negroes in a pretty spot. He and his family were in the habit of worshiping with them. They would kneel at the chancel where their slaves did, and receive the holy communion at the hands of the same minister.[68]

Charles Wilson, another missionary, declared:

I received my first appointment to the mission field at the Conference held in Charleston, S. C., in 1834, to the Combahee, Ashepoo, and Pon Pon Mission. I was sent as a co-laborer with Dr. Boyd, who had labored there a part of the previous year with Brother Coburn.

This mission was in the midst of the rice fields, then looked upon as "the graveyard of South Carolina." But despite this, I knowingly slept in their midst two or three nights of every week the year round. During such times, in the sickly season of the year, I have known as many as two corpses to be carried to the graveyard within hearing of my room. Whether this exposure of myself was a piece of recklessness on my part or not I do not now pretend to say, but this much I can assert; I have never enjoyed better health.

In the early part of the year I learned that Mr. Thomas Hutcheson owned a small island on the west side of the Ashepoo, on which he had about two hundred negroes entirely destitute of all religious instruction; and though I had never seen him, nor had he ever heard my name, yet I became anxious to pay his island a visit, and wrote him a letter informing him that I had heard that he owned a large number of negroes remote from all religious privileges, and that I would be happy to visit his island in the character of a Methodist missionary to the blacks, and referred him to Col. Morris, Gov-

[68] Harrison, *op. cit.*, pp. 265-266.

PLANTATION MISSIONS

ernor Aiken, and other gentlemen with whom he was acquainted for particulars respecting my object, and immediately received an answer that he would be happy to see me; and accordingly, arrangements were made, and on the appointed day, sometime in May, a boat was sent for me. Upon reaching the shore I found a horse and servant waiting to take me up to his dwelling. I found him polite and glad to see me, particularly on the business on which I had come; desirous that his negroes should have the gospel preached to them. I told him that we would preach to them regularly once a fortnight if he would send a boat for us, with which he seemed delighted.

After preaching to a large congregation in a barn, himself and overseer and family in the number, we parted, all gratified with the prospect, but none more so than the negroes, who seemed to look as if a sort of jubilee was beginning to dawn on Hutcheson's Island.

I asked an intelligent-looking old black man how long he had lived on that island and what they had done in that time for religious instruction. He replied that he had been living there for forty years, and that nearly all the people I saw had been born and raised there; that no minister of any denomination had ever been on the island to his knowledge before; that nearly all the people that had been in the meeting-house that day had never heard a white man preach before; and that they had been wholly dependent upon each other for all the religious instruction they had ever gotten. This statement I believed to be altogether true from my knowledge of the surrounding country and the locality of the island. My heart was filled with gratitude and thankfulness to God for the great privilege of being an honored instrument in his hand of carrying the gospel to those who had never heard it before, although they were in my own native land.

After a year's preaching, at the first opportunity given them, one hundred and eleven came forward, a larger number, I am disposed to think, than ever has been on an ordinary occasion received into the Church at one time within the South Carolina Conference. They all, with but few exceptions, proved true to their vows. . . .[69]

I spent four years on the Pon Pon Mission. At the end of that time, my health being sadly impaired through repeated attacks of fever, I was given an assistant, Brother Nathan Bird. Having now more leisure, I was again pressed with the old desire to add new fields to my work. Through the invitation of Col. Morris, who had his summer house at Edingsville, I now began preaching on Edisto Island. I found the fields white to the harvest and the planters almost unanimous in their desire to have the work of evangelization pushed among their people. One of them, Mr. J. J. Mikell, had

[69] *Ibid.*, pp. 215-232.

already gone so far as to erect a comfortable chapel on one of his plantations, not knowing whom he might get to serve his people. My first preaching appointment on this island, the second Sunday in October, 1840, was a memorable one to me. Mrs. Townsend, a zealous and pious member of the Baptist Church, and its most active member on the island, invited me, there being no pastor in charge, to preach at her church. At the hour appointed I reached the building in company with Col. Morris, at whose home I was staying, and found a large collection of blacks and a considerable number of the planters. I next had an invitation from Mr. Lee, the Presbyterian minister to preach in his church. I again had a crowded house and spoke with much freedom. Mr. Lee, who was a faithful and zealous minister, had already done much efficient work among the blacks on the island. The day following I returned home with the deep conviction that here was a promising door for mission work waiting to be opened. The mission was subsequently established, and I was sent to serve it. Six hundred dollars a year for the support of the missionary was readily subscribed by Messrs. J. J. Mikell, William Seabrook, Maj. Murray, and the Messrs. M. A. and S. Seabrook.

I had on the Edisto Mission, to begin with, six preaching places and eleven plantations to serve. One of these was Gov. Aiken's place on Jehossee Island, which for convenience sake was taken from the Pon Pon Mission and attached to the Edisto. Unlike Edisto, which is a cotton-growing island, Jehossee is mostly a rice plantation and owned entirely by Gov. Aiken. It is naturally a part of Edisto but has been made into a separate island by the opening of a creek by a canal connecting the two rivers.

The mission on Jehossee had from the first been one of the most promising in the bounds of the Conference. I became acquainted with it in 1834, my first year in the mission fields; and from then to the present time, a period of twenty-two years, I have preached regularly on the place, with the exception of 1837 and 38, when it was in charge of Dr. Boyd.

There is quite a commodious chapel on this island, which has been erected by Gov. Aiken as a place of worship for his blacks. At first it stood in a grove of live oaks on the lawn in front of his dwelling; but his plantation enlarging, it was subsequently removed to a more central spot. Here an addition of twenty feet was made to the building, which had become too small to accommodate the crowds. A portico has also been attached to the front. This chapel has a bell, and a regular sexton is in attendance. The occasion is rare when it is not filled to the door with the blacks, with the exception of a small space reserved for the whites. In this church alone, sixty-two couples of blacks have been united by the sacred ties of

Christian marriage. I recollect to have married here at one time, five couples.[70]

One of my most important fields on the Edisto Island Mission was the plantation of Mr. J. J. Mikell, already referred to. He had a new and commodious chapel which was largely attended. I soon gathered into the Church at this place a number of orderly and highly interesting people. Our efforts among them were greatly facilitated by a well-ordered system of plantation discipline. Though a firm and decided Presbyterian, Mr. Mikell nevertheless gave his hearty and unswerving support to the Methodist mission. Always, when at home, he and his family attended the preaching at the negro chapel. He was an exceedingly liberal man. Unaided he built a mission house at a cost of $300.00 in the village, besides providing a winter residence for me nearly all the time of my stay.[71]

Thus ends the story of the Southern white man's effort to instruct the slave in religion. Every man must be his own judge of the worthwhileness of the undertaking. I have tried to give only the facts and to let the participants themselves speak. When in 1861 the overpowering fleet of Union gunboats ploughed into Port Royal Harbor with its heavy contingent of infantrymen, taking possession of the whole island territory, the white people perforce withdrew to the interior, leaving the slaves in the hands of their new friends and liberators. The story of the Port Royal Experiment in education and citizenship constitutes a little-known chapter in South Carolina history. The freedmen were enfranchised, put into public office and into places of responsibility, which they were in no sense prepared to occupy. The dark years of Reconstruction ensued. The hopes and promises of the Northern liberators turned out as dust and ashes, and whether for good or ill, white political supremacy won. With the excitement of war over, emancipation zeal sated, and only the drab and tedious business of human rehabilitation ahead, the friends from the North went back home. The Southern white people had already withdrawn. For the following seventy-five years the Negro of the South fought his battle singlehanded and alone, and with doubtful success.

[70] *Ibid.*, pp. 225-227.   [71] *Ibid.*, pp. 228-229.

CHAPTER XI

NEGRO LIFE IN THE RICE COMMUNITY

> I am a trouble in de mind,
> O, I am a trouble in de mind;
> I ask my Lord what shall I do,
> I am a trouble in de mind.

THE WORD *plantation* as originally used in the Southern Colonies was synonymous with the term *settlement*, or *colony*. The old records tell much of planting *colonies*, later known as *plantations*. Alexander Hewatt, writing in 1779 of the Charleston, South Carolina, settlement, declared, "No colony that ever was planted can boast of greater advantages."[1] In 1584 Hakluyt wrote a treatise on the American colonization entitled *Discourse of Western Planting*. The late Ulrich B. Phillips explained Hakluyt's use of the word: "This usage of the word in the sense of a colony ended only upon the rise of a new institution to which the name was applied. The colonies at large came then to be known as *provinces or dominions*, while the sub-colonies, the privately owned village estates which prevailed in the South, were alone called plantations."[2]

The Gullah Negro's social and economic life was set in the scheme of the rice and cotton plantation. All that he knew, all that he saw and felt grew out of his experiences in this unique situation. The plantation was a complete world in itself. Its social experiences ran the whole gamut of life from the informal trial of a slave for murder to the christening of infants by the visiting plantation missionary. Economically, it furnished everything, from the large boats for transport purposes to the thread spun by the women and used in plantation sewing rooms. Governor Aiken's plantation on Jehossee Island had its own hospital, with slave nurses and midwives. In his *Autobiography* Professor Joseph Le Conte described his boyhood experiences on the Georgia coast:

[1] *An Historical Account of the Rise and Progress of the Colonies of South Carolina and Georgia*, II, 302.
[2] *Life and Labor in the Old South*, p. 309.

In these early days, everything was done on the plantation. There were tanneries in which the hides of slaughtered cattle were made into leather. There was a shoemaker's shop, where, from the leather made on the place, the shoes for all the negroes were made by negro shoemakers. There were blacksmith and carpenter shops, where all the work needed on the plantation was done by negro blacksmiths and carpenters. All the rice raised on the plantation was thrashed, winnowed, and beaten by machinery made on the spot, driven by horse-power, and the horses by negro boys. All the cotton was ginned and cleaned and packed on the place. As the cotton was Sea Island, or long-staple, Whitney's invention was of no use, and only roller gins could be used, at first, foot-gins, and later horse-gins. For the same reason—viz., the fineness of the staple—the cotton was all packed by hand and foot, the packer standing in the suspended bag. All these operations of tanning, shoemaking, blacksmithing, carpentering, the thrashing, winnowing, the beating of rice, and the ginning, cleaning, and the packing of cotton, were watched with intensest interest by us boys, and often we gave a helping hand ourselves. There was always especial interest in the ginning of cotton by foot and the thrashing of rice by flail, because these were carried on by great numbers working together, the one by women, and the other by men, and always with singing and shouting and keeping time with the work. The negroes themselves enjoyed it hugely.[3]

Jenkins Mikell, of Peters Point plantation, Edisto Island, in an accurate account of the process of ginning sea-island cotton on his father's place, incidentally revealed the types of work assigned to the slaves and the many and varied tasks they performed on a cotton plantation: "The operation was long, tedious and fatiguing. It was done on gins operated by foot, a crude plantation, or domestic, device for getting out the seed from the lint—one man to a gin. He would stand on his left leg and work a crank-like arrangement, somewhat on the principle of the crank that drives a sewing machine, first with his right foot, and when he got tired working that leg, he would hop on his right foot and work his gin with his left foot—never stopping his gin as he changed, only when he needed rest. To see thirty or forty men, all in a row, ginning at the same time is an interesting and amusing sight to the looker-on. As each man has

[3] Le Conte, *op. cit.*, pp. 22 ff.

thirty pounds of lint cotton to gin out for his day's work, he had no time to loaf."[4]

It was the duty of the women to examine carefully each pound of the lint as it came from the gin, and free it from all flecks and foreign matter. With such methods the ginning of a crop of cotton from a plantation was a long and tedious process, accomplished only with an abundant supply of labor.

A South Carolina Negro, formerly a slave, relating his experiences on the Frierson plantation, described its varied tasks:

> On rainy days, when it was too wet to do outdoor work, the men and boys got out corn, as they said in plantation language, for the mill, while the women and girls carded and spun cotton and wool. A task of so many hanks of yarn was given them for a day's work, which was a reasonable task, and when it was finished they carded and spun for themselves. They more or less completed their tasks before night, and by working after night they were enabled to do almost as much for themselves as they did for the white folks during the day. The weaving was almost invariably done by the young white ladies, or by some one of the servant girls who was taught especially to do it. Thus everybody on the place was kept well clothed, both the white folks and the slaves. That which the slave women carded and spun at night was their own, and they usually hired their young white missus, or some other white woman of the neighborhood, to weave it into cloth for them, and thus they always had good, clean clothing for Sunday wear, so that they could go to "meetin" without embarrassment.[5]

One of the New Englanders participating in the Federal occupation of the Port Royal area described incidents on St. Helena Island in connection with the rationing of corn to the Negroes:

> The prettiest thing is the corn-shelling on Mondays, when the week's allowance, a peck a hand, is given out at the cornhouse by the driver. They all assemble with their baskets, which are shallow and without handles, made by themselves of the palmetto and holding from half a peck to a bushel. The corn is given out in the ear, and they sit about or kneel on the ground, shelling it with cleared corn-cobs. Here there are four enormous logs hollowed at one end, which serve as mortars, at which two can stand with their rude pestles, which they strike up and down alternately. It is very hard

[4] Mikell, *op. cit.*, pp. 19 f.
[5] Lowery, *op. cit.*, p. 31.

THE RICE COMMUNITY 235

work, but quicker than the hand process. After it is all shelled, the driver puts a large hide on the ground and measures each one's portion into his basket, and men, women, girls, and boys go off with the weight on their heads. The corn-house is in a very pretty place, with trees about it, and it is always a picturesque sight—especially when the sand-flies are about, and the children light corncobs to keep them off. The corn is ground by hand by each negro in turn for themselves; it is hard work and there are only three hand-mills on the place, but it makes very sweet meal and grits.[6]

The general aspect of the Southern plantation has often been described. Too often the glamour and romance thrown about it have presented a distorted picture of the average plantation scene. The following sources give briefly a realistic picture untouched by the glow of fiction of the actual appearance of several coastal plantations. It should be said that all the "big houses" in the tidewater section were built high off the ground, many supported by arched masonry of brick or tapia ("tabby") artistically done. These semibasements were frequently used as dining rooms and served as cool retreats during hot weather. The *Charleston City Gazette*, in 1825, printed the following plantation advertisement:

For Sale: That valuable plantation called the Point Plantation upon the Wondoo River, about 16 miles only from the city with a good landing at the House. This tract contains by a late survey 1120 acres, all well-wooded—about 300 acres clear, and some of it under fence, of excellent cotton and provision land. This land would be to an industrious purchaser very valuable. Upon the premises there is a good dwelling house of six rooms, a good kitchen, Overseer's house, cotton house, corn house, and fodder house, a new carriage house and stable, also a mule stable, an ox house, and dairy all in good order, also an excellent well of water in the yard, a good garden with a number of choice fruit trees—the terms will be accommodating to an approved purchaser, and possession given immediately.

Apply to Ogier & Carter, Broad Street.

N. B. There are negro houses to accommodate 50 or 60 negroes.[7]

---

[6] Pearson, *op. cit.*, pp. 52 f.
[7] *A Documentary History of American Industrial Society*, ed. John R. Commons, Ulrich B. Phillips, Eugene A. Gilmore, Helen L. Sumner, and John B. Andrews . . . (Cleveland, Ohio, 1911), Vol. I; Phillips, *Plantation and Frontier*, I, 252.

The Northerners who lived among the coastal Negroes during the Civil War did not have such a romantic idea of the Negro quarters as had some writers of fiction. It should be kept in mind that they observed the quarters during a period of disruption after the owners had fled the country and when the plantations were run down and the premises and buildings were unkempt. This condition was quite consistent with the nature of the Negro, who, because of his overlord's strictness, always followed, when left to himself, the line of least resistance.

The Negro quarters of the Smith plantation on St. Helena Island were described by one New Englander as follows: "We drove through the negro quarters, or 'nigger-house,' as they themselves call the whole settlement, and they flocked to the doors to look at us, bowing and smiling as they went by. There were eight or ten separate houses just raised from the ground so that the air could pass underneath, and, as we looked in at the doors apparently with very little furniture, though in some we saw chairs which were evidently Massa's. Dirty and ragged they all were. . . ."[8] The quarters on the Fripp plantation, Pine Grove, St. Helena Island, were also described by a Northern resident: "These houses are all built of hard pine, which is handsome on the floors, but the rest of the woodwork is painted, in this house, an ugly green, which is not pretty or cheerful. The walls are always left white. Clapboards are unknown, but hard-pine boards, a foot or more broad, are put on in the same way, and everything outside is whitewashed. The place is very attractive-looking, grapevines and honeysuckles and pine woods near."[9]

Lowery, writing of his master's plantation in Sumter County, observed: "At some distance in the rear of the white folks' house stood the barns and other outhouses, and a little to the east of these was the large horse and cow lot and the stables. In front was a beautiful avenue skirted on each side with lovely oaks of different varieties. And, strange to say, about three hundred yards in front of the white folks' house, and to the east of this beautiful avenue, was located the 'negro quarters.' On most plantations in those days the 'negro quarters' was located in the rear, or at least some distance from the white folks' house. But

---

[8] Pearson, *op. cit.*, p. 18.
[9] *Ibid.*, p. 21.

THE RICE COMMUNITY 237

not so in this case, for these were located in front, but a little distance from the house and from the avenue."[10]

An understanding of the coastal Negro and his life on the cotton and rice plantation is impossible without some knowledge of his owner, from whom he received much of his culture and general outlook upon life. A large part of the Negro's good manners and grace is attributable to his upbringing among cultured white people. The Carolina planters, many of them at least, were men of intelligence and ingenuity. They were alert to what was going on about them and were conversant with national and international affairs. Their leadership in Colonial government and their prominence in affairs of state until the time of the Civil War attest their ability and their influence in national affairs. In Colonial times they sent their sons abroad to be educated and in the early nineteenth century were patrons of the better colleges in New England. They traveled in Europe and, through trade and commerce, kept in touch with the chief cotton, rice, and indigo markets of the world. Between 1760 and 1775 there were few gentlemen in Charleston who had not been to Europe.[11] Their contacts with the West Indies and with England were far more intimate than are those of the most prominent South Carolina agriculturist today. The plantation society of the eighteenth century was vibrant with life and enthusiasm. Its commercial and social center was Charleston, where many of the planters had elaborate town houses. Wallace declares that Charleston of the eighteenth century had "a society not only of great energy, force, and progress, but it possessed in a marked degree what such societies wait much longer for—culture, refinement, and a delicately organized social life."[12]

It should be remembered that the South Carolina coastal population contained a large element of energetic English planters, who were moved by the spirit of adventure and who were looking ever for new commercial worlds to conquer. When, in their opinion, the Sugar Islands became crowded, many of these merchant princes and planters came with their slaves to more spacious lands along the Carolina coast. Englishmen of

[10] Lowery, *op. cit.*, p. 32.
[11] Wallace, *op. cit.*, pp. 33 ff.
[12] *Ibid.*, p. 34.

238   GULLAH

this type came from Barbados, Antigua, the Leeward Islands, Jamaica, Bermuda, and the Bahamas to settle along the tidal rivers of the Carolina coast. The following list, compiled by McCrady with the assistance of Langdon Cheves, reveals the names of many prominent families in South Carolina then and now:

> The colony was continually receiving new additions from Barbadoes and the other West India Islands, bringing with them their negro slaves. These were all Church of England people, and formed a great part of the church party in the colony. They settled principally upon the Cooper River; some of them were of the Goose Creek men of whom the Proprietors warned Ludwell to beware.
>
> Sir John Colleton, one of the Proprietors, was from Barbadoes, and so were his two brothers, James the Governor, and Major Charles Colleton. From that island came Sir John Yeamans, the Landgrave and Governor; Captain John Godfrey, Deputy; Christopher Portman, John Maverick, and Thomas Grey, among the first members-elect of the Grand Council; Captain Gyles Hall, one of the first settlers, and an owner of a lot in Old Town; Robert Daniel, Landgrave and Governor; Arthur and Edward Middleton, Benjamin and Robert Gibbes, Barnard Schinkingh, Charles Buttal, Richard Dearsley, and Alexander Sheene. Among others from Barbadoes were those of the following names: Leland, Drayton, Elliot, Fenwicke, Foster, Fox, Gibbon, Hare, Lake, Ladson, Moore, Strode, Thompson, Walter, and Woodward. Sayle, the first Governor, was from Bermuda. From Jamaica came Amory, Parker, Parris, Pinckney, and Whaley; from Antigua, Lucas, Motte, and Percy; from St. Christopher, Rawlins and Lowndes; from the Leeward Islands, Sir Nathaniel Johnson, the Governor; and from the Bahamas, Nicholas Trott, the Chief Justice. Some of these were probably but temporarily on the islands; some had been long-established residents.[18]

Of the best-known Charleston merchants of the Colonial period, many of whom were planters as well, Wallace mentions Isaac Mazyck, Gabriel Manigualt, Henry and James Laurens, Christopher Gadsden, Benjamin Smith, Miles Brewton, Andrew Rutledge, Robert Pringle, William Wragg, Joseph Kershaw, and Daniel De Saussure.

Prior to 1860 it was not uncommon to find in the homes of planters amazingly complete libraries and even scientific instru-

[18] Edward McCrady, *The History of South Carolina under the Proprietary Government, 1670-1719* (New York and London, 1897), pp. 327 f.

ments, with which they carried on their individual research. Before the day of highly specialized interests, such men developed a broad outlook upon life and a kind of wisdom which is in striking contrast to the limited outlook of many modern experts. The practice of cultivating varied interests also developed a type of personality all too rare in contemporary society. The agricultural journals of that day reveal an originality of thought and a program of experimentation which indeed is surprising. They introduced new crops, some of which became staple commodities like rice and cotton, and for years grew indigo on a commercial scale, winning an international reputation as producers of this dye. Olives were grown on the Chisholm plantation near Beaufort. Citrus fruits were grown for some time, but the cultivation was finally abandoned. Many other plants and seeds imported from foreign countries were cultivated.

An outstanding example of scientific interest exhibited by a South Carolina planter is given by Professor Joseph Le Conte in his *Autobiography:*

I take this opportunity to do justice to the brilliancy and originality of Langdon Cheves, a planter on the coast of South Carolina, near the Savannah River, by recording some views of his expressed to me in a conversation at Flat Rock on the origin of the species. We had both read that remarkable book *Vestiges of the Natural History of Creation,* published in 1844, and he had cordially embraced the idea of origin of species by transmutation of previous species, while I contrarily held to Agassiz' views of creation according to a pre-ordained plan. We had it hot and heavy. When I brought forward the apparently unanswerable objection drawn from the geographical distribution of the species and the manner in which contiguous fauna pass into one another, i.e., by substitution instead of transmutation, his answer was exactly what an evolutionist would give today—viz., that intermediate links would be killed off in the struggle for life as less suited to the environment; in other words that only the fittest would survive. It must be remembered that this was before the publication of Darwin's book, and the answer was wholly new to me and struck me very forcibly.

Why did he not publish his idea? No one well acquainted with the Southern people, and especially with the Southern planters, would ask such a question. Nothing could be more remarkable than the wide reading, the deep reflection, the refined culture, and the originality of thought and observation characteristic of them; and yet the idea of publication never entered their minds. What right had anyone to publish anything unless it was something of the greatest importance, something that would revolutionize thought? My father was an extreme instance of such indifference to publication, and I myself for the same reason was slow to publish. Many important observations that I made on the geological processes going on about me everywhere in the South, especially on the formation of soil by the rotting down of rocks *in situ* and on mountain sculpture in Tennessee, I gave every year in my class lectures, but did not dream of publishing. Soon after the war Hall and Hunt visited the South and brought out these facts, and very rightly received due credit therefor.[14]

Since I desire to give a true picture of the social history of the coastal Negro and realize that this can be done best by offering pertinent source material, I present the following items. One can imagine a sea-island planter opening his Charleston paper, the *City Gazette* of March 10, 1796, and reading the following advertisement:

FIFTY PRIME NEGROES FOR SALE. To be Sold, on Tuesday the 15th instant, by the Subscribers, before their office near the Exchange.

About fifty prime orderly Negroes; consisting of Fellows, Wenches, Boys and Girls. This gang taken together, is perhaps as prime, complete and valuable for the number as were ever offered for sale; they are generally country born, young and able, very likely; two of them capable of acting as drivers, and one of them a good jobbing carpenter. The wenches are young and improving; the boys, girls and children are remarkably smart, active and sensible: several of the wenches are fitted either for the house or plantation work; the boys and girls for trades or waiting servants. The age, descriptions and qualifications of these negroes, may be seen at the office of the Subscribers, and of Brian Cape and Son, or of Teasdale or Kiddell, merchants, in Queen-street, who can give directions to those who desire it where the negroes may be seen.

These negroes are sold free from all incumbrances, with warranted titles, and are sold on account of their present Owner's declining the Planting Business, and not for any other reason; they are not Negroes selected out of a large gang for the purpose of sale, but are prime, their present Owner, with great trouble and expence, selected them out of many for several years past. They were purchased for stock and breeding Negroes, and to any Planter who particularly wanted them for that purpose, they are a very choice and

[14] Le Conte, *op. cit.*, pp. 174-176.

NEGRO CABIN NEAR PORT ROYAL

A TIDAL RIVER, DAWHOO

THE RICE COMMUNITY

desirable gang. Any Person desirous of purchasing the whole gang by private contract, may apply to Brian Cape and Son; the Terms if sold together will be made convenient to the Purchasers, and the conditions of public sale (if not contracted for in the mean time, of which due notice will be given) will be very easy and accomodating, and which will be declared on the Day of Sale.
March 3.   COLCOCK & PATERSON[15]

In 1825 the *Gazette* printed this notice:

A Wench, complete cook, washer and ironer, and her 4 children—a Boy 12, another 9, a Girl 5, that sews; and a Girl about 4 years old.

Another family—a Wench, complete washer and ironer, and her Daughter, 14 years old, accustomed to the house.

A Wench, a house servant, and two male children; one three years old and the other 4 months.

A complete Seamstress and House Servant, with her male Child, 7 years old.

Three Young Wenches, 18, 19, 21, all accustomed to house work.

A Mulatto Girl, about 17, a complete Seamstress and Waiting Maid, with her Grandmother.

Two Men, one a complete Coachman, and the other a Waiter. Apply at this Office, or at No. 19 Hassell-street.[16]

Advertisements of slaves for sale in the Charleston newspapers were commonplace. The arrival of a slave ship in the harbor was always heralded abroad. Notices like the following, which appeared in the *Evening Gazette* for July 11, 1785, were frequently read:

Just arrived in the Danish ship Gen Keith, Captain Kopperholt, and to be sold, on Friday, the 15th instant, on board the vessel at Prioleau's wharf, a choice cargo of windward and gold coast negroes, who have been accustomed to the planting of rice. The appearance of the negroes will sufficiently quiet a report which has been circulated of their being infected with scurvy.

The sale to be continued from day to day until the whole is disposed of.

The conditions will be moderate as possible, and will be known on the day of sale by applying on board to
                                    A. PLEYM.[17]

---

[15] Phillips, *Plantation and Frontier*, II, 57 f.
[16] *Ibid.*, II, 58.   [17] *Ibid.*, II, 52 f.

Even the simple names of the slaves suggest the situations they experienced and in a way make more vivid a conception of the ways of bondage. Old plantation record books with their casual entries throw light upon the hardships of Negro slavery and have new meaning for the student of human affairs. Louis Manigault was a prominent rice planter whose slaves were many and whose acres spread over a number of plantations. The following list of Negroes and the entries concerning some of them are taken from his plantation record of 1860 and represent the slaves on his Gowrie plantation at that time:

John	Jack, Savage (Chief Carpenter)	Nancy Hunt
Nancy Hunt	Amey	George (Carpenter—Run away 26th Oct'r, 1860; returned 25th Jan'y, 1861
George—Driver	John Izard (Carpenter, Brick layer)	
Betty		
Minda	Clary	
Nat	Primus	Simon (Run away 2d Jan. 1861; returned 25th January, 1861.)
Martha	Lucy (With Overseer)	
Julia	Billy (Carpenter)	
Charles (Trunk Minder)	Jenny	Polly & Moses
Juna	Dolly	Lydia
Jack (Short)	Scotland	Captain (Drowned in river June, 1860)
Louisa	Fortune (Ran away again April, 1860. Sold in Savannah, May 1860 for $1200, as he was always running off).	In House.
Mendoza		
Tommy		Dolly
Catherine		Nancy (Gowrie)
Hector (Post Boy)		Martha (Age 22 yrs., a fine Mulatto Woman given me by my Father, to act as Nurse and c. for our Child. —Ran away in Charleston, May, 1861, caught four months after, no longer with me).
Joaney (Plantation Cook)		
Tyrah	Abel	
Betsey (Old, Carpenter's Cook)	Binah Currie	

We purchased in July, 1860 for $500. of Mr. James R. Pringle of Charleston, So. Ca. a driver Named "John" who is at present the only Driver on the Plantation, both George and Ralph, our former Drivers, being broken. Driver John is 44 years of age. Mr. Capers, our Overseer, tells me that he has had much trouble with the Negroes the past Summer and several Runaways. Two are now out since October 25th, 1860, and not a word has been heard of them —December, 1860. . . . N.B. I gave blankets to every Man, Woman and Child on the plantation, Dec'r, 1860.

THE RICE COMMUNITY 243

On 25th January, 1861 all our Runaways (5 in number) were brought in through fear of the dogs. Our Children were poisoned at the Camp by Old Betsey.[18]

A Carolina rice or cotton plantation was a well-organized business unit. However bad slavery may have been, it was not an unmixed evil. Regrettable as an institution and devoid of justification morally, there were nevertheless many valuable lessons and discipline learned under slavery by the Negroes fresh from savagery and barbarism in Africa. And for thousands of them their lot in life was less severe under benign masters in the slave states than was their portion in their native land, where slavery also existed and where their owners practiced every barbarous and cruel device from capture to sale to foreign traders.

A most interesting document revealing the intricate organization of a rice plantation is *The Overseer's Contract* prepared by Plowden C. J. Weston for use on his several plantations along the South Carolina coast.[19] The official set-up of Weston's plantations may be displayed graphically as follows:

Proprietor
Overseer
Drivers   Watchmen   Trunk   Nurses   Yard   Public   Child's
                       Minders   Watchmen   Cook   Cook

The various duties and stations listed above did not apply to household duties in the "big house." The house servants constituted a distinct class in the slave group, with many and varied functions. House servants were jealous of their status and always considered themselves above field hands. It was in the household group that the more cultured and intelligent slaves were found, and after freedom it was from that group that most of the refining influences and good manners were transmitted to the free Negroes. No doubt the gentle bearing and amiability of many of the sea-island Negroes today is a social inheritance from the household servants of the slave era.

The overseer has been the most neglected of all persons connected with the Southern plantation. John Spencer Bassett's

[18] *Ibid.*, I, 139.
[19] Printed in pamphlet form by A. J. Burke, 40 Broad St., Charleston, S. C.; also published in *De Bow's Review*, XXII, 38-44 (Jan., 1857). Quoted by Bassett, Phillips, and others.

book, *The Southern Plantation Overseer,* is a distinct contribution to our knowledge of plantation life. According to Bassett, the overseer of ante-bellum days stood midway between the planter on the one hand and the mass of slaves on the other. He is now the forgotten man of the Southern plantation. The proprietor left records of himself in many ways, and his name has been recorded in local history because he came to be a part of a kind of plantation dynasty. He has been portrayed in history, in fiction, in modern advertising, and in numerous motion pictures. The Negro has always been a popular subject, appearing in all forms of literature. His romantic career from savagery to civilization, through American slavery and the Reconstruction period to his present position in the world, has always formed the basis of a vibrant human-interest story. But the plantation overseer has been lost to students of Negro life. The overseer wrote nothing but occasional letters to his proprietor, had no family backing to perpetuate his name, and as a result passed into oblivion. His social status was an inferior one. As Bassett pointed out, he may have belonged to the church of the planter, but he and his family on Sunday mornings sat apart from the planter's family. And while in time of sickness and trouble the mistress of the house may have ministered to the overseer's family, taking her best jam, cordial, and mustard plasters, all were aware that it was not a visit to social equals.

Overseers as a rule came from the small farmer or landless class. In South Carolina they generally lived in the pinelands, not the rich coastal section. These pineland farmers owned few, if any, slaves. They worked their own fields and generally were illiterate and crude. They were as distinctly classified socially as the slaves. The Negroes knew them as "poor whites," or "po' buckra." The overseer was a kind of shock-absorber for the proprietor. He took his orders from the planter and acted as intermediary between the slave and his master. He administered punishment and kept a watchful eye upon the slaves' behavior throughout the day. In him the administration of the rules and regulations handed down from the planter was vested. In the words of Bassett, the overseer in the eyes of the slave was the very symbol of slavery.

James H. Hammond, a prominent South Carolina planter, writing of the overseer's duties, declared: "The overseer must never be absent a single night, nor an entire day, without permission previously obtained. Whenever absent at church or elsewhere he must be on the plantation by sundown without fail. He must attend every night and morning at the stables and see that the mules are watered, cleaned and fed, and the barn locked. He must keep the stable keys at night, and all the keys in a safe place, and never allow anyone to unlock the barn, smoke-house, or other depository of plantation stores but himself. He must endeavor, also, to be with the plough-hands always at noon."[20]

This constant surveillance made the overseer in the eyes of the slaves the feared personage of the plantation. He made their lot hard by exacting the task and enforcing all regulations. The planter's situation was entirely different: he was set apart, and often acted as a benevolent judge in matters of discipline; consequently, the planter was often beloved and respected by the slave, while the overseer was the incarnation of slavery at its worst.

If there was any personage on the plantation more feared and despised by the Negroes than the overseer, it was the driver. His status was the more despicable in the eyes of the slaves because he himself was a Negro. His power was great; his job was to get the work done; he was the taskmaster. The drivers were often chosen either because of their moral effect upon the slaves or their ability to intimidate because of physical prowess. Indeed, "Their power was supposed to be limited and negligible, when, in fact, it was absolute and intolerable."[21]

Mikell intimated that this supremacy of the driver emboldened him to invade the sanctity of the slave's home and satisfy his lusts without regard to marital relationships: "In a word, he was the serpent in the domestic Eden of many a young family. One had to submit and appear not to see, kill the offender, or run away from the scene of one's disgrace. The latter was generally the alternative accepted, which made matters worse."[22] Weston, in *The Overseer's Contract*, wrote as follows: "Drivers are, under the overseer, to maintain discipline and order on the place. They are to be responsible for the quiet

---

[20] Bassett, *The Southern Plantation Overseer*, p. 5.
[21] Mikell, *op. cit.*, pp. 134 f.
[22] *Ibid.*, p. 134.

of the negro-houses, for the proper performance of tasks, for bringing out the people early in the morning, and generally for the immediate inspection of such things as the overseer only generally superintends."

Watchmen were responsible for the safety of buildings, boats, flats, and fences. They kept the hogs and cattle from damaging the growing crops, and reported to the overseer any signs of stealing or trespass. In addition, they helped to kill the hogs and beeves at butchering time.

Trunk-minders undertook the whole care of "trunks," including the elaborate system of ditches and floodgates which covered the rice fields. The rice fields were flooded or drained at will, and the care of the machinery which made this possible was the duty of trunk-minders.

"Nurses," asserted Weston, "are to take care of the sick, and to be responsible for the fulfilment of the orders of the overseer or doctor, (if he is in attendance). The food of the sick will be under their charge. They are expected to keep the hospital floors, bedding, blankets, utensils, etc. in perfect cleanliness. Wood should be allowed them. Their assistants should be entirely under their control. When the proprietor and overseer are absent, and a serious case occurs, the nurse is to send for the Doctor.

"Yard Watchman is responsible for the crop in the yard and for the barns.

"Cooks take every day the provisions for all the people, the sick only excepted. The overseer is particularly requested to see that they cook cleanly and well. One cook cooks on the Island, the other on the main, for the carpenters, millers, highland hands, etc."[23]

On the Weston plantations there was no cooking in the cabins; all meals were prepared by the public cook in large kettles and pots at a kind of community kitchen. The practice on many of the larger plantations where the fields were at long distance from the quarters was to take food out into the fields. Even breakfast was served in the fields at times in order to get the hands off to work early.

Weston had a special cook for the children, known as the "Child's Cook." "The child's cook," he explained, "cooks for

[23] *Ibid.*

THE RICE COMMUNITY

the children at the negro-houses; she ought to be particularly looked after, so that the children should not eat anything unwholesome."

Weston laid down very explicit rules for his overseers, and in common with all planters, emphasized the importance of taking good care of the Negroes. This care was of course good business as well as benevolence. On this subject he remarked that "The Proprietor, in the first place, wishes the Overseer MOST DISTINCTLY to understand that his first object is to be, under all circumstances, the care and well-being of the negroes. The proprietor is always ready to excuse such errors as may proceed from want of judgment; but he never can or will excuse any cruelty, severity, or want of care towards the negroes. For the well-being, however, of the negroes, it is absolutely necessary to maintain obedience, order, and discipline, to see that the tasks are punctually and carefully performed, and to conduct the business steadily and firmly, without weakness on the one hand, or harshness on the other."

It was the custom among all the planters to give their overseers the power to grant passes, known as "tickets," to slaves who wished to visit other plantations or to go anywhere. Any slave caught abroad without a "ticket" was punished. Weston required that "The names of all the men are to be called over every Sunday morning and evening, from which none are to be absent but those who are sick, or have tickets. When there is evening Church, those who attend are to be excused from answering. At evening list every negro must be clean and well washed. No one is to be absent from the place without a ticket, which is always to be given to such as ask it, and have behaved well. All persons coming from the Proprietor's other places should shew their tickets to the Overseer, who should sign his name on the back; those going off the plantation should bring back their tickets signed. The Overseer is every now and then to go around at night and call at the houses, so as to ascertain whether inmates are at home."

Holidays were respected on the rice plantations. No Negroes were required to work on Sundays, Good Friday, or Christmas Day unless it was to go for a doctor or to nurse the sick. Additional holidays allowed by Weston were the two days following Christmas Day and harvest. On these days the people could work for themselves. Only half tasks were to be done on Saturdays, except during planting and harvest seasons. Weston wrote, "A task is as much as the meanest full hand can do in nine hours, working industriously"; and he added: "No negro is to be put into a task which he cannot finish with tolerable ease. It is a bad plan to punish for not finishing a task; it is subversive of discipline to have tasks unfinished, and contrary to justice to punish for what cannot be done. In nothing does a good manager so much excell a bad, as in being able to discern what a hand is capable of doing and in never attempting to make him do more."

The more successful planters were careful to see that their slaves received their full allowance of food and clothing so that they might be in good physical condition and maintain a profitable degree of contentment. Weston urged his overseers when they dealt out rations not to "strike" the measures but rather to heap them up. No damaged supplies were to be rationed. The corn was to be carefully winnowed, and the small rice, subject to souring, was to be discarded when it became inedible.

The schedule of allowances provided daily, Sundays excepted, was as follows:

During Potato-time
To each person doing any work........................4 qts.
To each child at the negro-house........................2 qts.

During Grits-time
To the cook for public-pot, for every person doing any work...1 qt.
To the child's cook, for each child at the negro-houses.......1 pt.
Salt to the cook for public pot........................... pt.
Salt to child's cook.................................... pt.

On every Tuesday and Friday throughout the year.
To cook for public-pot, for whole gang of workers, trades
 drivers, &c, Meat................................... lbs.
To child's cook for all the children, Meat................ lbs.

On every Tuesday and Friday from April 1st to October 1st.
To the plantation cook for each person doing any work,
 instead of the pint of grits, Small Rice................ lbs.
To the child's cook for each child instead of the ½ pt. of
 grits, Small Rice.................................... lbs.
To plantation cook for the whole gang of workers,
 tradesmen, drivers, &c., Peas........................ qts.

THE RICE COMMUNITY

Every Thursday throughout the year.
To the child's cook, for all the children, Molasses.......... qts.

Weekly allowance throughout the year—to be given out every Saturday Afternoon.
To each person doing any work, Flour................. 3 qts.
To each child at the negro-house...................... 3 pts.
To each person who has behaved well, and has not been sick during the week, 2 Fish or 1 pt. Molasses
To each nurse....................................... 4 Fish
    or 1-½ pt. Molasses.
To head-carpenter; to head-miller; 3 Fish or 1-½ pt. Molasses each.
To head-cooper; to head-ploughman " " " " " " each.
To watchman; to trunk-minder " " " " " " each.
To drivers; to mule-minder " " " " " " each.
To hog-minder; to cattle-minder " " " " " " each. and to every superannuated person.

Monthly Allowance—On the 1st of every Month.
To each person doing any work, and each superannuated person, Salt .... 1 qt.
Do..Tobacco 1 hand.

Christmas Allowance.
To each person doing any work, and each superannuated person.—

    Fresh Meat— 3 lbs.
    Salt do. — 3 lbs.
    Molasses — 1 qt.
    Small Rice — 4 qts.
    Salt —½ bushel

To each child at the negro-houses.—

    Fresh Meat—1 ½ lbs.
    Salt Meat —1 ½ lbs.
    Molasses — 1 pt.
    Small Rice — 2 qts.

Additional Allowance.
Every day when rice is sown or harvested, to the cook, for the whole gang of workers in the field.......... Meat. lbs.

No allowance or presents, besides the above, are on any
   consideration to be made—except for sick people,
   as specified further on.

The Reverend Dr. McLeod, writing from Edisto Island about the year 1800, explained how the slaves were provisioned in that quarter:

> Exclusive of hats, shoes, salt, tobacco, pipes, and other occasional considerations, every grown negro is annually furnished with two suits of clothes, or 12 yards, partly plains and partly osnaburgs, or some adequate substitute, for their summer and winter wear. The boatmen are generally provided with surtouts of the fear-nought description, and greater attention than formerly begins of late to be paid to their accomodation and comfort, in a more enlarged and improved construction of their dwellings. Some of the planters have it in contemplation to furnish them with regular rations of beef or some other animal food, particularly during those stages of the year in which they are most exposed to greater and more constant exertions of labor. If this laudable design were carried into general execution, it would render them more able and more willing to encounter the fatigue of the field, at those periods when laboring under the relaxing and exhausting influence of an almost vertical sun. Exclusive of considerations of humanity, it would be a pledge and assurance that their daily tasks would be not only completed but more effectually done and in a style of better execution. A circumstance that would amply compensate even in point of interest, any expenses consequent on such an indulgence.[24]

McLeod thought that slaves on the sea islands enjoyed some advantages denied their brothers on the mainland: "Their proximity to and frequent intercourse by water with Charlestown, afford them an opportunity of carrying to market their poultry, corn, ground provisions, and whatever else they may have to dispose of. And being settled on it in the vicinity of creeks and rivers, they can supply themselves with fish and oysters in quantities proportionate to their exertions."[25]

Many and varied were the instructions given to the overseer by the planter. Weston closed his *Overseer's Contract* with what he called "Miscellaneous Observations," prefacing them with the remark that "The proprietor wishes to impress on the over-

---
[24] Ramsay, *op. cit.*, II, 280.
[25] *Ibid.*

seer the criterions by which he will judge of his usefulness and capacity," and then proceeding to particularize as follows:

First—by the general well being of the negroes; their cleanly appearance, respectful manners, active and vigorous obedience; their completion of their tasks well and early; the small amount of punishment; the excess of births over deaths; the small number of persons in the hospitals, and the health of the children.

Secondly—the condition and fatness of the cattle and mules; the good repair of all the fences and buildings, harness, boats, flats, and ploughs; more particularly the good order of the trunks and banks, and the freedom of the fields from grass and volunteer.

Thirdly—the amount and quality of the rice and provision crops. The Overseer will fill up the printed forms sent to him every week, from which the Proprietor will obtain most of the facts he desires, to form the estimate mentioned above.

The Overseer is expressly prohibited from three things, viz: bleeding, giving spirits to any negro without a Doctor's order, and letting any negro on the place have or keep any gun, powder, or shot.

When carpenters' work is wanted, the Overseer must apply in writing to Mr. . . . Miller.

When the Overseer wishes to leave the plantation for more than a few hours, he must inform the Proprietor, (if he is in the Parish).

Whenever a negro is taken seriously ill, or any epidemic makes its appearance, or any death or serious accident occurs, the Proprietor (if in the Parish) must be immediately informed, as well as of any serious insubordination or breach of discipline.

No gardens, fowl-houses, or hog-pens are allowed near the house; a space will be fenced out for these purposes, and they will be under the charge of the watchman.

No trees are to be cut down within 200 yards on each side of the houses.

Women with six children alive at any one time, are allowed all Saturday to themselves.

Fighting, particularly amongst the women, and obscene or abusive language, is to be always rigorously punished.

During the summer, fresh spring water must be carried every day on the Island. Anybody found drinking ditch or river water must be punished.

Finally—The Proprietor hopes the Overseer will remember that a system of strict justice is essential to good management. No person should ever be allowed to break a law without being punished, or any person punished who has not broken a well-known law. Every person should be made perfectly to understand what they are punished for, and should be made to perceive that they are not punished in anger, or through caprice. All abusive language or violence of demeanor should be avoided: they reduce the man who uses them to the level with the negro, and are hardly ever forgotten by those to whom they are addressed.

Reference has already been made to the great amount of sickness which periodically harassed the plantation communities. There were frequent scourges of smallpox, dysentery, and cholera. Unexpected hurricanes swept up from the Caribbean and caused great loss of life and property to the island residents. As early as 1760 the ingenious Eliza Lucas, writing from her plantation near Charleston, lamented, "A great cloud seems at present to hang over this province."[26] She also added that "a violent kind of smallpox rages in Ch. Town that almost puts a stop to all business. . . ."[27]

In 1907 David Doar, of Harrietta plantation, near McClellandville, speaking before the Agricultural Society of St. James, Santee, declared: "In 1822 the fiercest gale ever known on the coast, swept over them, carrying wholesale destruction to the crops, houses and everything else, even human lives were sacrificed to its fury. A great many white people were drowned, and scores of negroes on the rice fields and Islands, were lost. Not 20 years after came the Asiatic cholera, in 1836, and almost decimated whole plantations of its negroes, though not many of the white people succumbed to its ravages. The negroes had to be moved into the pine lands and put into camps, before the disease could be checked. I have heard my father say what a dreadful time it was, he himself had to be amongst the negroes in their time of trouble."[28] He further related: "In 1848 smallpox broke out in upper part of Parish amongst the whites, and Mr. Lincoln wrote to the Commissioners: 'I had to close my school on account of the dreadful disease, which has broken out in the neighborhood.' In 1867 we again had a visitation of

---

[26] Eliza (Lucas) Pinckney, *Journal and Letters of Eliza Lucas* (Wormsloe, Ga., 1850). Extract from a letter of March 15, 1760. Also printed in Phillips, *Plantation and Frontier*, I, 309.

[27] *Ibid.*, I, 309.   [28] Doar, *op. cit.*, p. 25.

THE RICE COMMUNITY 253

smallpox, but it was chiefly amongst the negroes, a great many of them died."[29]

Louis Manigault, of Charleston, wrote in his plantation records of the vicissitudes of plantation life along the Savannah River:

> Considering the immense losses We have experienced during the past three years, the Cholera having swept off in 1852 and 1854 many of our *very best* hands, a destructive freshet visiting us in August, 1852, just in the midst of harvest, (Damaging to a great degree not only the standing Crop, by rendering the grain soft, of a dingy Colour, & almost unfit for market, but causing also a vast quantity of Volunteer & light rice in the Crop of 1853). In thinking also of the ever memorable Hurricane of 8th September, 1854, full moon, & wind N.E., the salt water direct from the Ocean submerged the plantations on the Savannah River, such a thing not having happened for fifty years, the consequence being that We, on Savannah River, made only ¼ of a crop, most of the Crop Cut, and in small stacks, swept away, and the entire plantation strewed with loose rice, a vast injury to the Crop of 1855. Considering all this; I do not complain of our present Crop. Rice this year, caused as is supposed by the now pending Crimean War, has been very high, & our entire crop has sold well. I lost my Overseer, Mr. S. F. Clark, of Consumption in Dec'r, 1855, but since the last Cholera (Dec'r, 1854) we have lost no one of any Consequence, and perfect health has prevailed on the plantation.[30]

The cost of medical service for the slaves was indicated by Manigault in an entry of April 15, 1845: "Allen Smith informed me that he pays Dr. Wragg, settled in Savannah $1.50 per head for to attend to all his Negroes by which the Doctor engages to go up, say eight miles by water, whenever he is wanted there, merely by a boat being sent for him—so that if there are 100 Negroes he gets for all his Service $150, without any charge for Mileage or anything else. Dr. Pritchard asked me I think $1.25 per head for his medical services during the year, but I preferred going by the visits."[31]

A clipping in the Charleston *Courier*, with date line of Savannah, September 9, 1834, gave distressing intelligence of the ravages of cholera:

[29] *Ibid.*
[30] Phillips, *Plantation and Frontier*, I, 141.
[31] *Ibid.*, I, 166.

The Cholera has spread in every direction. Of the sufferers, Mr. Merchant is in proportion to the number of hands, the greatest. On Mr. J. P. Williamson's Swamp plantation, three were taken on Sunday, and all died. He has abandoned his crops at Clifton, and moved his pine lands, leaving six at Clifton too ill to be removed. It is now at Barclay's, Gordon's, Potter's, Young's, and in fact on almost every plantation on the River as low down as Mr. Petigru's. A letter says, the state of things at Mr. Merchant's is awful indeed. The person in charge is complaining that he cannot attend to all the sick. In nearly every case that has proved fatal, the people become cold and pulseless in one or two hours. At Brampton, eight cases, since Monday, two extremely ill. God only knows what is best to be done. I have just received a letter from Mr. Sharpe, stating three deaths today, with many severe cases. He has commenced moving Mr. Potter's people.[32]

Pregnant women received special attention from the nurses, and overseers were given minute instructions regarding their tasks. Weston wrote:

Lying-in women are to be attended by the midwife as long as is necessary, and by a woman put to nurse them for a fortnight; they will remain at the negro-house for four 4 weeks, and will then work two weeks on the highland. In some cases, however, it is necessary to allow them to lie up longer. The health of many women has been entirely ruined by want of care in this particular. Women are sometimes in such a state as to render it unfit for them to work in water; the Overseer should take care of them at these times. The pregnant women are always to do some work up to the time of their confinement, if it is only walking to the fields and staying there. If they are sick, they are to go to the hospital and stay there until it is pretty certain their time is near.

Henry Laurens, of Charleston, cautioned one of his overseers: "Two of the women with child and near their time be very careful of them and employ a proper woman if any in the neighborhood or agree with Dolly Hayes to take care of them until they can go about. Mrs. Laurens has given baby clothes to one and will send some for the other next week. All these people even the boys are fit to go to work therefore improve their time as Mr. Ball may direct. . . ."[33]

[32] *Ibid.*, V, 316 f.
[33] Wallace, *op. cit.*, p. 65.

THE RICE COMMUNITY

Another letter reveals Laurens's kindly solicitude for his sick slaves on a Georgia plantation. To the overseer he wrote:

Let Sam have everything that he shall stand in need of; he is a good hand, but sickly, and note what rum and sugar he uses, and give all the workmen a dram of grog when you see occasion. . . .

The women are to make their own clothes, and you will remember that some are to be clad in striped flannel, which you may also give for the children. Give blankets where they are really needed.

Be kind to Berom in his affliction.[34]

Any picture of the overseer's life and station in the plantation regime would be incomplete without some notice of the rambling, ungrammatical letters he wrote to his proprietor. Ulrich B. Phillips and John Spencer Bassett collected and printed a goodly number of letters which make a considerable contribution to a better understanding of the plantation overseer. The letters reveal the illiteracy, the crudeness, and often the unhappy lot of the men who at once were underlings and tyrants. The only reason for the preservation of their letters was that for business purposes they were filed away in the planter's desk. Other than that they were little esteemed by their authors or recipients. The letters deal with the condition of the crops and plantation affairs. They fairly bristle with hard luck stories, of incorrigible Negroes, of runaways, of punishment, death, and disease.

The following letter was written to Charles Manigault, of Charleston, June 13, 1860, by his overseer on Gowrie and East Hermitage plantations, in Chatham County, Georgia:

All things found going on quite well excepting the death of London who was drowned on Monday morning about 9 ocl. The cause of this sad calamity is this, viz., George brought London & Nat to Ralph, saying they deserved punishment, they were taken to the Barn, when Ralph went for the key to put them in George allowed London to leave him, and when spoken to by Ralph about not making an exertion to stop London his answer was he would not dust his feet to stop him. London went on to Racoon sqr then took the River at the mouth of the canal, in the presence of some of Mr. Barclay's negroes and Ralph who told him to return, George should not whip him until my return, his ans[wer] was he would

[34] *Ibid.*, p. 66.

drown himself before he would and he sank soon after, the remains of him is now quite near no. 15 Trunk, Gowrie. My orders have been no one is to touch the corpse and will there remain if not taken off by the next tide, this I have done to let the negroes see when a negro takes his own life they will be treated in this manner. My advice to you about George is to ship him, he is of no use to you as a driver and is a bad negro, he would command a good price in Savannah where he can be sold in a quiet manner.[35]

The following excerpts from a letter written by the overseer on Retreat plantation, Jefferson County, Georgia, and addressed to Miss Telfair, one of the owners, living in Savannah are dated November 20, 1836:

I have received your letter of the 15th inst. I have received the Negroe shoes and given them out also I have gave them their winter clothing that is the woolin Home spun as far as it was wove and will soon have the Ballance wove all the children have had cloth the winter shirts will then be spin & weave. . . . The sickness was very prevalent in this Neighborhood more so than I ever saw though it is jinerly helthy. At Presant I expect to send three Hundred Bales of Cotton from this Plantation this year all though it has Roted ver much in Places that is if I can save what is yet in the fields. . . .

Charlotte & Venus & Mary & Little Sary have all had children and have not received their baby clothes also Hetty & Sary & Coteler will want baby clothes. I see a Blanket for the old fellow Sampson he is dead. I thought I wrote you that he was dead. Little Peggy Sarys daughter has not ever drawn any Blanket at all, and when they come I think it would be right to give her the Blanket that was sent to Sampson.[36]

In another letter, 1840, Miss Telfair's overseer wrote:

You mention in your letter that you do not wish your negroes treated with severity. I have ever thought my fault on the side of lenity; if they were treated severe as many are I should not be their overseer on any consideration.

The meat held out this year to give eleven allowances commencing in Jany. it held out to Novr. which is one month longer than usual; it requires 1050 lbs. to give your negroes here one allowance, the bacon Mr. Habersham sent up, though good was not dry, it lost considerable in drying, that which I killed was small and lost more in drying than it otherwise would have done.

[35] Phillips, *Plantation and Frontier*, II, 94.
[36] *Ibid.*, I, 332-334.

THE RICE COMMUNITY

I wrote you about the 3rd Inst. giving you an account of the plantation stock &c which letter I hope you have recd. before this. I then wrote that three of your negroes were sick, to wit Lydia, & two of Charlot's children, since then the two children are dead, namely Maria & Edna. . . .[37]

This chapter on the plantation experiences of the Negro should not close without giving some of the brighter aspects of his life as a slave. There was little recreation provided for the slaves. It was a day when play even among many white people was looked upon with suspicion. What recreation the Negro had he usually got as a by-product of his labor. The gangs of laborers in the fields provided a social situation upon which the Negro, with his innate love of fun and banter, capitalized to a large extent. And, besides, such levity was encouraged by the planters, for they realized that contented field hands did more work than unhappy ones. Plantation owners in the interior of the state gave particular attention to cornshucking time and to log rolling, making them semisocial occasions. At such times great pots of savory meats and quantities of sweets were prepared in the plantation kitchen and placed on long picnic tables to be consumed at the conclusion of the tasks. Lowery, a slave, claimed that the Negroes had to work during the day and therefore sought much of their recreation at night. Fish were plentiful in Pudden Swamp, but there was little time for the slaves to fish. There was, however, time at night for hunting coon and 'possum. 'Possums usually inhabit the woodland, while coons are found in the swamp. Nothing was better for a Sunday morning's breakfast than 'possum; according to Lowery, "They first parboiled it and then roasted it or baked it brown. Sweet potatoes were also boiled and skinned and roasted around it. The slaves were very fond of such dishes."[38]

Records show that Christmas time was a bright spot in the year's routine although few of the slaves were acquainted with the historical significance of the holiday. Since they were not permitted by law to learn to read or to write, their only avenue to learning was through the spoken word. They were usually given three days at Christmas, Christmas Eve, Christmas Day, and the day after Christmas, as they were usually designated.

[37] *Ibid.*, I, 336.   [38] Lowery, *op. cit.*, pp. 53 ff.

It was the custom to kill the fattened hogs just before Christmas so that the white folks and the slaves might have plenty of fresh meat for their holidays. The expression "a hog-killing time" arose from this custom. Favorite dishes at this season were backbones, spareribs, and rice. On some of the plantations the custom of having all the slaves gather in the front yard of the "big house" for a dram on Christmas morning was observed. A lively time followed and all seemed very merry.

But this was not the case on every plantation, a fact to which Lowery bears witness: "Mr. Frierson was a Christian man and therefore believed in and practiced the principles of temperance. He, nor a single member of his family, were ever known to indulge in strong drink. Such a thing as whiskey was unknown on that plantation. . . . But Christmas was observed on Mr. Frierson's place in a way that was highly enjoyable to all. It was the custom on all the plantations around to give at the beginning of each winter to each male among the slaves a new outfit, consisting of shoes, pants, coat and cap. The women and girls got shoes and dresses. Mr. Frierson made it a point to give these out on Christmas morning."[39] In anticipation of this distribution about a month before Christmas the right foot of each slave was measured. Frierson would then get into his buggy and drive to the county seat, about twenty miles away, to buy shoes for everyone. Sam, the trusted foreman, would go for the shoes in a two-horse wagon as there were about fifty slaves on this plantation. There were shoes for little feet, baby feet, feet of courting adolescents, crooked feet of old men and women—and, I doubt not, more elegant shoes for the ladies of the "big house."

In describing further the festivities on Christmas morning this exslave wrote: "Breakfast is over and all hands repair to the 'house.' Presently the yard is full of darkies with smiling faces and joyous hearts. And there are as many piles on that long front piazza of the white folks house as there are hands on the place. In each pile there are shoes, a suit, or dress, and a cap. On each pile there is a tag with the name of the person written on it for whom it is designed. Now imagine, if you can, the exquisite joy that thrilled each heart as his or her name was called."[40]

[39] *Ibid.*, pp. 64 ff.   [40] *Ibid.*, p. 67.

A corn crop in the South is harvested in a somewhat different manner from that used in other parts of our country. "Pulling fodder," or stripping the leaves from the corn in August, after it is "laid by," has from time immemorial been practiced in the South but not with the sanction of the agricultural experts. A field of Southern corn in September is a denuded field, each stalk having been stripped of its leaves and left standing with its two or three ears bare and exposed to the hot sun. "Before frost" is ordinarily the time to "break corn." The Negroes, sent into the field, take half a dozen rows at a time, break the ears from the stalks, and toss them into piles down the length of the center row. A two-horse wagon is driven down the rows, and the piles of corn are gathered until the wagon body is level full. It is then taken to the barns or corn cribs, which, on Southern farms, are usually to be found in an inclosure called the "horse lot." Generally the corn is not shucked all at once, but is stored away in the dry shucks.

Under the slave regime, when each family was rationed weekly with corn and other provisions, it was more satisfactory to have all the corn shucked at one time. From this practice the term *cornshucking* arose. Planters were wise enough to make the occasion a great social event so that purposes of utility were nicely blended with those of fun and hilarity. The result was that an arduous task was completed with the least sense of physical effort. On the plantation where Lowery was reared the corn was brought from the fields and placed in two high piles preparatory for the shucking. "Then the night is set for the corn shucking: for it was usually had at night, so that the slaves from the adjacent plantations could come and enjoy the sport. Invitations were sent far and near, and they were readily accepted. Great preparations were made in food and drink. The only drink allowed at the corn shucking was coffee, but it was customary on some of the plantations to have whiskey at corn-shuckings, but Mr. Frierson never allowed it."[41] From fifty to seventy-five men, besides the women, came to the cornshucking. One of the chief attractions was the food served. Great pots of meat and rice, bread, and coffee were served when the huge piles had been shucked.

To add zest to the work, the element of rivalry was always

[41] *Ibid.*, pp. 59 ff.

introduced. Captains for the two groups were chosen, who pitted their skill in shucking against each other. To be a captain was a much coveted honor. When one was thus designated, his cap was decorated with the inner shucks of an ear of corn, and all looked upon him with smiles and some with envy as he mounted the pile of corn preparatory to the starting signal. At a given sign the shucking began, and excitement ruled as all were eager to see who would win! Songs which always accompanied the shucking, were led by the captains.

They shucked, they sang, and they shouted. Then they knew that a bountiful supper awaited them just as soon as the work was done. . . . In the midst of it all they could sniff the aroma of hot coffee, and the delicious odor of roasted meats and other nice dishes. . . . Fully two score colored women are there to wait on the table. And they eat, and eat, and drink, to their satisfaction. The supper being over, with the moon shining brightly (moonlight nights were invariably selected for the corn-shuckings) the boys spend some time in wrestling, foot racing and jumping before going home. . . . This is kept up until a late hour of the night, and then they retire to the various plantations whither they belong.[42]

Another of the co-operative schemes adopted by the planters was the "log rolling." There was always land to be cleared, a task which was laborious and fatiguing, requiring many hands. Land was plentiful, but most of it was in wood, as it is today in the Deep South. The underbrush had to be cut and cleared. This was placed in piles, and after it had dried out sufficiently, was burned. "Clearing up new grounds" was a familiar task for slaves. Then the trees had to be cut down, and sometimes the stumps dug. The hardest part of the job, and that which required the greatest number of strong men, was getting the logs out of the fields. Some of the best were used for saw logs, but most of them were put on huge piles, and when they had dried out, were burned.

On an appointed day, planters from the various plantations in a community would send their best hands, the strongest, most vigorous men, to a designated place for the "log rolling." The captain of a squad would then match his men, that is, divide them up into pairs of equal size and weight. Each pair had a "hand stick." These sticks, six of them, were placed under a

[42] *Ibid.*, pp. 97 f.

THE RICE COMMUNITY 261

huge log. At a given word, the twelve men, each with one hand grasping the stick and the other steadying the log, would rise with a grunt and a groan and bodily lift the timber, carry it off, and dump it onto the pile. The men chosen for these feats of strength took much pride in their fine muscles and liked to draw up their arms, showing off their powerful sinews. Wives and sweethearts took equal pride in their prowess, so that, when a weakling was found among them, one who could not or would not lift his share of the burden, he was ridiculed and laughed to scorn.

At twelve o'clock the horn was blown for dinner. The big meal, prepared in advance, was one of the best incentives for work. Probably the expression, "eating like a log-roller," had its origin in such activities. After a rest of about two hours, the work was resumed for the remainder of the day. At a later time the children and women gathered up the bark, chips, and small brush and threw them on the heaps for burning. At night, when fifty or seventy-five of the heaps were ablaze, a spectacle was presented which deeply impressed the Negroes as beautiful to behold.[43]

Lowery, upon whom I have drawn freely for intimate glimpses of his experiences as a slave on the Frierson plantation, has given a valuable picture of his place as "waitin' boy" in the Frierson household. Modestly he refers to himself as the "little boy Jimmie," and tells his story thus:

> Just as soon as he became old enough, his old master took him from his mother to be his waiting-boy. This necessitated his eating at the yard and sleeping in the white folks' house. Family prayers were invariably had, evening and morning, and Jimmie was always called in. The family sat in a semi-circle around the fire-side, and Jimmie's little chair formed part of that semi-circle. . . .
>
> Jimmie was something of a privileged character on Mr. Frierson's plantation. It is true he had to work in the field along with the other hands. Sometimes he dropped corn and peas; sometimes he thinned corn and cotton; and sometimes he hoed or plowed. But when Mr. Frierson would go off on business in his buggy, Jimmie had to go along and drive him. When his daughters went to church or to make social calls, he went to drive them, and to care for the horses. So Jimmie had the privilege of attending all the big meetings, the weddings, and the parties of the white folks. All this

[43] *Ibid.*, pp. 89 ff.

proved to be of considerable advantage to him in gaining knowledge and information. Frequently on his return from some of these trips, the slaves would gather round him—old and young—to hear him tell what he saw and heard.[44]

As regards the education of the slave children, especially the boys, Mikell declared: "Their order of education, along the working line—they got no 'book learnin', as they styled going to school—was commenced when they had learned to run about and play as assistant 'minders' of young children committed to the care of very old Maumas to watch over while the parents were at work. Later, they brought wood and water for the house. Still later they would ride the mules and drive the cattle to water, then pen the cattle at night, keep the five-acre lot around the 'big house' clear of trash and do other chores, suited to their ages, too numerous to mention...."[45]

There were many sad experiences that came to the Negro on Southern plantations, but they were not all sad. The Negro has always had a resilient character and has adapted himself admirably to his situation. His chief form of release from the exactions of bondage was song and rhythm. Whether in the church, with its solemn religious service, or in the quarters, where levity and social pleasures were most likely to prevail, he lifted his spirit in song, and for a fleeting moment, at least, forgot the shackles that bound him. Indeed, it may be the result of this innate quality of his nature and his love of fun that he survived slavery and was enabled after emancipation to rise rapidly from his low estate. The Indians, who were the first American slaves, chafed under the rigors of the system, pined away, and died. The white indentured servants and redemptioners, who became virtual slaves for a period of years in order to pay their passage from Europe, had ever before them the glimmering hope that one day the debt would be paid and they would be free and privileged to sit each man under his own vine and fig tree. This promise the Negro did not have; consequently, true to his nature, he made peace with his conquerors on their own terms, adjusted himself as happily as he could, and awaited emancipation. It appears to me that in many respects the Negro race, historically, has been strangely in har-

[44] *Ibid.*, pp. 99 ff.   [45] Mikell, *op. cit.*, p. 133.

mony with the Sermon on the Mount. Surely something good must be in store for the Southern Negro. Contemporary aggressive Negro organizations which are demanding rights and fostering campaigns of self-pity may do good; only time can tell; but they are peculiarly out of harmony with the historical position of the Negro, who through his native strategy has gone far up the heights. It would appear that the meek really inherit the earth and that the aggressor stirs a thousand foes.

Examples of the Negro's ability to forget himself in the surge of hilarious social life are numerous. Fiction writers who know little of the Negro's nature have given cheap imitations of his jovial moments, and the minstrel stage and movies have so grossly misrepresented him that it must be painful for wholesome Southern Negroes to witness the performances so often given. Mrs. Harriette Kershaw Leiding, of Charleston, recorded the words of Maum Katie, who related to her some of the jingles and antics of the plantation dances in which she participated. The account was transmitted to Professor Henry C. Davis, of the University of South Carolina, who published it in the *Journal of American Folklore*. The words of Maum Katie are as follows:

I tol' you about de ole days when I could dance, an' sing, an' pick cotton wid de best of dem, 'cause you know I done been raise' roun' de white folks eber since I been leetle mite,—wen I ain't but so leetle dat I can hide underneat' old Miss' rocking chair. Den wen I gets bigger, I cum out an' hide underneat' her apern; den I get so big an' fat dat I gets to be a regular wheeligo gal: dat's our name for a big, bustin' gal.

Ole Miss she laff, an' say to Marster, "let them have it, let them have it; they work all the better for it." O Lordee! dem were happy days: I always had my stomach full of vittles den. An' atter de fiel'-work, I teks my "fly-away" (dat's my hat), an' I teks de calico dress Miss done gib, an' I go to de nigger-yard; an' glory, how I done dance! . . .

Here's de way we start. All de cullud folks crowd into de leetle room an' begin for sing:—

> Hurrah, ladies, two on de floor,
> Here we go to Baltimore.
> Swing e lady roun' de town,
> Sling 'em roun' de floor.

Then the gals begin to sing,—
> A hack a back, ladies!
> Wanter go to Aiken;
> So, Mr. Jones, you can take me dere.

An, den dat gal go off wid e partner. Den another gal she holler out,—
> A hack a back, ladies!
> Wanter go to Augusta;
> So Mr. Brown can take me dere . . .

An' by an' by all of dem get paired off dat-away. Den atter a while, somebody say, "Le's play Mr. Cooler."

Den somebody else holler out, "I holler for Mr. Cooler! [I call for Mr. Cooler!]"

Den some buck nigger who can cut up, he pint heself to be Mr. Cooler; an' he mok about, an' he mok about (look around), and atter a little he choose a lady. Den all wat lef' out begin to call on him fer helf 'em play, an' dey sing t'ree times,—
> Ole Mr. Cooler, wat is de matter
> Stay away so long?

Den Mr. Cooler he say,—
> At your call.

Lordee! he been polite: he ac' jes' like a king. An' atter dat, all ring up, an' go roun' an' begin to sing, wid Mr. Cooler in de middle,—
> Mr. Cooler he lub sugar an' tea,
> Mr. Cooler he lub candy,
> Mr. Cooler he can wheel an' turn,
> An' receive de one dats handy.

Den Mr. Cooler he shuffle, an' do monkey-tricks in de ring. He act like a mule, an' he paw, an' he snort, an' he back. Den all sing again,—
> There's a mule in the middle, an' you can't get him out.
> There's a mule in de middle, an' you can't get him out.
> He wants some one to help him out, Miss Susie or Miss Julia.

Den Miss Julia she says,—
> Spread your carpet on de floor,
> Meet your true love at de door,
> You mus' say yes, an' den we'll go
> Ober de hills an' far away.

Den all we-uns begin fer hum, an' do like de bee,—
   Um-hum, um-hum,
   You black-eyed bee,
   Where will de weddin'-supper be?
   Way ober yander in, de holler tree,
   Um-hum, um-hum.
Den dat couple dey git out an' leab de gal in de ring.

I do declare he mak' you laff fitten to bus' yourself, 'cause ebery nigger wat gets in, he got to be a animal ob some kind. De men mak' de fun, caze dey go like de mule, or dey hops roun' like de bullfrog, or dey bellows like de ox, an' dey do whatsoever de name of the animal dey takes. When de gal gets in de ring, dey is flowers, an' dey jes' caper' 'bout a little mite, an' prance, An' show he foot. Den here's de way we all sing wid de gal in de middle:
   My true love's gone, won't you help me to sing.
   My darlin' is a rose in de middle, an' I can't get her
      out.
   She wants someone to help her out, I think it's Mr.
      Benjy . . .
Den, Miss, atter we done play dis till we been tired, we sing a funny little song about rice-cake:
   Rice-cake, rice-cake,
   Sweet me so,
   Rice-cake sweet me to my heart.
Den dey do some kissin'.

An' sometimes dey play in de ya'd, an' play "Roxanna, go, gal, go" . . .
   All dat de buckra gib, you wear in de buckra fiel'
   All dat your sweetheart gib you. . . .

At this point, Maum Katie's memory failed, and she never came past this point in her version of these plantation dances.[46]

[46] Henry C. Davis, "Negro Folk-Lore in South Carolina," *Journal of American Folklore*, XXVII, 252-254 (July-Sept., 1914).

CHAPTER XII

HARDSHIPS OF SLAVERY

*Oh sometimes it makes me tremble, tremble, tremble;
When I think 'bout my troubles bein' so hard.*

THE HARSHER aspects of slavery are readily discernible in the regulations for the punishment of refractory Negroes—lashes, imprisonment, or branding on the cheek. "Riding patrol" was a necessary outgrowth of the system, but instead of being a wholesome disciplinary device, it often degenerated into sporting expeditions at the expense of runaway slaves. Similarly, records of slave trials betray the evils of slavery; and the pathetic petitions of free Negroes who, because of their intolerable status, sought to sell themselves into slavery, make it certain that the institution was doomed through its own inherent wickedness. There were also slaves who with hard work had purchased their freedom, and others who when they discovered they had to be sold, tried to make arrangements with buyers whom they knew to be kind and considerate.

One of the most remarkable letters ever written by a slave is that of Billy Proctor to John B. Lamar, of Macon, Georgia. The original letter is written in a clear, strong hand, presumably Proctor's own. Although the practice was illegal, a good many house servants were taught to read and write, and Proctor may have been one of those favored few. The letter is as follows:

MR. JOHN B. LAMAR, MACON, GA.

SIR, As my owner, Mr. Chapman has determined to dispose of all his Painters, I would prefer to have you buy me to any other man. And I am anxious to get you to do so if you will. You know me very well yourself, but as I wish you to be fully satisfied, I beg leave to refer you to Mr Nathan C. Munroe D. Strohecker and Mr Bogg. I am in distress at this time, and will be until I hear from you what you will do. I can be bought for $1000— and I think that you might get me for 50 Dolls less if you try, though that is Mr Chapman's price. Now Mas Jon, I want to be plain and honest with you. If you will buy me I will pay you $600— per year untill this money is paid, or at any rate will pay for myself in

HARDSHIPS OF SLAVERY 267

two years. I knew nothing of this matter last night when at your house, or I would have mentioned it while there. I am fearfull that if you do not buy me, there is no telling where I may have to go, and Mr. C. wants me to go where I would be satisfied —I promise you to serve faithfully and I know that I am as sound and healthy as anyone you can find. You will confer a great favour sir, by Granting my request, and I would be very glad to hear from you in regard to the matter at your earliest convenience. I would rather not say anything to Mr. C about this matter untill I can hear from you, for I assure you I am in great distress and trouble at this time, but if you will grant my request you will please write me a few lines, and I will come immediately to Macon to see you.

Your obedient & Humble Svt

AMERICUS, GA. December 1, 1854   BILLY PROCTOR[1]

I. E. Lowery, a slave on the Frierson plantation, was the son of a free Negro, Uncle Tom. The latter was born a slave, but purchased his freedom and that of his mother long before the Civil War. Lowery and his mother, Namie, were slaves, for the child followed the status of the mother.[2] Free Negroes were not uncommon in the community, as Lowery explained: "There were some free colored people in the neighborhood. Some of these were freeborn, but others bought their freedom. But all of them according to the then existing laws, had to have some white man to be their guardian. That is, some white man to look after their interest to see that they got their rights, and to protect them, if necessary. And Mr. Frierson was chosen by some of these free colored people as their guardian."[3]

There were not a few individuals in the South who at times desired to set free certain of their slaves. To do so became increasingly difficult as the tragic 1860's approached. The laws became more and more stringent as abolition propaganda from the North became more widespread. A public notice of a desire to emancipate a slave is found in the Baton Rouge (Louisiana) *Gazette* for November 11, 1826:

PUBLIC NOTICE. The Heirs of Isaac Le Blanc, inhabitant of the parish of Iberville, having intention to emancipate their slave, a negro man named Jacob, upwards of thirty years of age, every person, who may have any legal opposition to the said emancipation,

---
[1] Phillips, *Plantation and Frontier*, II, 41.
[2] Lowery, *op. cit.*, p. 99.
[3] *Ibid.*, pp. 42 f.

are required to file the said opposition, in the office of the Parish Judge of the said parish, within forty days from the date of the present notice.

D. B. DUPUY, Sheriff[4]

Iberville, 8th November, 1826.[5]

Slaves were sometimes manumitted by the will of a deceased owner. A significant instance of this is recorded in the New Orleans *Commercial Times* for July 10, 1846:

> MANUMITTED SLAVES. Three hundred and eighty-five manumitted slaves, freed by the will of the late John Randolph, of Roanoke, passed through Cincinnati, on the 1st. instance, on their way to Mercer county, Ohio, where a large tract of land is provided for their future homes. The *Times* of that city, understands that the law of that State, known as the Black Law, requiring every colored person coming into the country to give security not to become a public charge, will be rigidly put in force, in this instance. Judging from the proceedings of a late public meeting in Mercer county, we imagine this to be true.[5]

The student of the social history of the Negro must consider the money value placed upon slaves. Like that of all commodities, the price of Negroes varied with the economic law of supply and demand. In the Colonial period the price of slaves was directly related to the prices of indigo and rice. In 1775, because of the great demand for labor among the indigo planters, slaves sold for as much as £40 sterling, and a few at £290 currency, while £24 sterling on the average was received "for the most mangy creatures that were ever seen."[6]

About the year 1800 the Reverend Donald McLeod, of Edisto Island, wrote that in his neighborhood "An active young fellow sold detached from his family, readily commands from $700 to $800; and young wenches in proportion."[7] As the middle of the nineteenth century approached, the price of slaves was noticeably higher. A table of slave prices current at Richmond, Virginia, in December, 1853, bears out this fact:

Best Men, 18 to 25 years old............1200 to 1300 dollars.
Fair   do.   do. .... 950 to 1050   "

[4] Phillips, *Plantation and Frontier*, II, 142.
[5] *Ibid.*, II, 143.
[6] Wallace, *op. cit.*, pp. 77 f.
[7] Ramsay, *op. cit.*, II, 280.

HARDSHIPS OF SLAVERY

Boys, 5 ft.	850 to	950 dollars.
Boys, 4 feet 8 inches	700 to	800 "
" " " 5 "	500 to	600. "
" " "	375 to	450 "
Young Women	800 to	1000 "
Girls, 5 feet	750 to	850 "
" 4 " 9 inches	700 to	750 "
" " "	350 to	452 "

Pulliam and Davis, Richmond, Va.[8]

The amazing prices paid for slaves at Macon, Georgia, in 1860 are recorded in the following news item in the Macon *Telegraph:*

We learn that the average price of negroes in Crawford [County] at the sales last Tuesday, was $1,113; and there was an undue proportion of old negroes and children. The best field hand, a boy 21-years old. sold for $1900.00. One woman seventeen years old and a baby nine months old, brought $2,150. None of the above were purchased by heirs. Among those that were so purchased, a woman (18) and a child (3) brought upwards of $2,500.—One woman (30) and 3 children, the oldest 6-yrs, sold at $4,525. A child eleven years old, sold for $1,525.

Lands sold for about $18 an acre; a little above for Oak and Hicory lying on Echeeconee and fifteen dollars and a fraction for pine land. None of the lands were purchased by heirs.[9]

One of the great problems of overseers was that of runaway slaves. The letters of overseers have much to say on this subject, and advertisements in the papers bear testimony to the frequency of such escapes. As late as November 14, 1861, exactly one week after the Federal fleet had entered Port Royal, an overseer named William Capers wrote to his proprietor, Charles Manigault, telling of the capture of three runaway slaves. The plantation was East Hermitage, on the Savannah River, as yet untouched by the invading foe. It appears that even so close to Port Royal the plantation managers took very lightly the Yankee invasion, unaware of the long struggle ahead and the utter collapse that awaited them. This letter, with

---

[8] William Chambers, *Things as They Are in America* (Philadelphia, 1854), p. 277. Also printed in Phillips, *Plantation and Frontier*, II, 71 (quoted from 2d ed., London, 1857).

[9] Phillips, *Plantation and Frontier*, II, 72 f.

many other interesting ones, is in the possession of Mrs. H. Jenkins, of Pinopolis, South Carolina. Capers's letter follows:

DEAR SIR: At 9 3/4 Ocl., reached here all Negroes doing well, the three are safe, Big George, Dov. Jack, Little George. Ishomail begged to remain; he betrayed his brother and little George. Jack caught in Back River by Driver John, in the small canoe; he resisted the Driver. George (big) attempted to run off in the presents of the entire force and in my presents. He was caught by Driver John between Conveyor House and No. 1 door. I gave him 60 straps in the presents of those he ran off in presents of. Everything else is as quiet as possible. Gentlemen be assured that I will act in a calm and determined manner: I will stand by your interests until there is no more of me. I apprehend but little trouble after a week or so. The three men should be sent away, and if you can obtain $1000, for big George "to be sent to Cuba" let him go or you will loose him; he should not be among a gang of Negroes. I have not time or space to write all.[10]

An entry in the diary of Henry Ravenel, of St. John's Parish, South Carolina, relates incidents of a search for runaway Negroes in a near-by swamp.

1819. July 12. A party of Gent^m from Pineville commanded by Major S. Porcher went into the swamps to attack a party of runaway negroes supposed to be armed. The squadron consisted of the following gentlemen, John and Jos. Palmer, Thos. Porcher, P. Porcher, I. Porcher & c. During our researches through the swamps an unfortunate accident occurred, by one of our party firing through mistake, supposing him a negro, at another, Thomas L. Gourdin, shot Jas. Haillard in the foot a slight wound. We proceeded from Milford down to Richmond and then came out.

N. B. The above party did not see or hear of any runaway negro in the swamp. Two captains companies turned out on the other side of the river, but were equally unsuccessful. Some time previous to our excursion a party from Williamsburg patrolled the swamp and shot a couple of negroes, a fellow . . . belonging to C. Lenud, the other owner unknown, both negroes died. A few days after our hunt another party from Williamsburg on a similar hunt shot a fellow of T. Gaillard and took some others armed, amongst them a ringleader named Billy from Southward. He gives intelligence of a party of 30 negroes most of whom are armed, some in Hell Hole Swamp the rest in Santee Swamp, and a regular chain extending toward Georgetown.[11]

[10] *Ibid.*, I, 320 f.   [11] *Ibid.*, II, 91.

HARDSHIPS OF SLAVERY

A queer advertisement appeared in a New Bern (North Carolina) newspaper, the *Carolina Sentinel*, in which the owner, Francis Gooding, offered a reward of twenty-five dollars for the return of his runaway slave, John, or, as the notice implied, he would sell him for a consideration if anyone wanted to buy him "on the run." The advertisement stated in part that "Should any person be disposed to purchase him as he runs, I will take six hundred dollars, and give a good title."[12]

The *Virginia Gazette*, Williamsburg, on March 26, 1767, published this harsh notice concerning the escape of a Negro woman:

Run away about the 15th of December last, a small yellow Negro wench named Hannah, about 35 years of age; had on when she went away a green plains petticoat, and sundry other clothes, but what sort I do not know, as she stole many from the other Negroes. She has remarkable long hair, or wool, is much scarified under the throat from ear to the other, and has many scars on her back, occasioned by whipping. She pretends much to the religion the Negroes of late have practised, and may probably endeavour to pass for a free woman, as I understand she intended when she went away, by the Negroes in the neighborhood. She is supposed to have made for Carolina. Whoever takes up the said slave, and secures her so that I get her again, shall be rewarded according to their trouble, by

STEPHEN DENCE[13]

Doubtless Stephen Dence would have paused in his writing had he realized that this advertisement with its cruel connotation would have reflected on his good name down through the years.

Elisha Cain, overseer on Retreat plantation, Jefferson County, Georgia, was very much perplexed over the conduct of an incorrigible slave woman named Darkey, and wrote to his employer, Alexander Telfair, of Savannah, November 4, 1833:

I get on Pretty well with all the negroes Except Darkey she is the most troublesome one on the place Making disturbances amongst the Rest of the negroes and there is hardly any of them will Even go near the yard, she is of such a cruel disposition, not Even her sisters family. She could not stay in the yard with the girls you sent up without making an interruption with them. at length she go so high I went there and give her a moderate correction and that had a Bad affect she then threatened their lives and said she

[12] *Ibid.*, II, 92.   [13] *Ibid.*, II, 93.

would poison them they became alarmed and ask me permission to move to the Quarter about one weeke. as I have commenced the subject I will give you a full history of my Belief of Darkey. to wit I believe her disposition as to temper is as Bad as any in the whole world I believe she is as unfaithful as any I have Ever Been acquainted with in every respect I believe she has Been more injury to you in the place where she is than two such negroes would sell for. I do not believe there is any negro on the place But would do Better than she has Ever done since I have been acquainted with her. I have tryed and done all I could to get on with her hoping that she would mend. but I have Been disappointed in Every instant. I can not hope for the better any longer.[14]

The subject of the punishment and disciplining of slaves on the Southern plantation has been much exploited in literature. It is true that too often the handling of slaves was ruthless and unnecessarily harsh. Especially was this the case on the large plantations, where hundreds of Negroes were under the direct control of overseers and drivers far removed from the influence of the planter, who was himself generally careful of the welfare and good treatment of the slaves. Too often the punishment of recalcitrant slaves was subject to the temper and caprice of the overseer. In a moment of anger and frustration he was likely to let his feelings dictate the degree of punishment, and too often the spirit of revenge entered into what purported to be the administration of justice. Weston, in his *Overseer's Contract*, wisely stipulated that "It is wise to allow 24 hours to elapse between the discovery of the offense and the punishment"; and that "No punishment is to exceed 15 lashes; in cases where the Overseer supposes a severer punishment necessary, he must apply to the Proprietor etc."[15] He further suggested that confinement (not in stocks) was to be preferred to whipping and recommended the denial of Saturday's allowance and the doing of whole tasks on that day as sufficient for ordinary offenses. Drivers or other Negroes were not to punish any person in any way except by order of the overseer and in his presence.[16]

[14] *Ibid.*, II, 39.
[15] Plowden C. J. Weston, a South Carolina rice planter, in *The Overseer's Contract*, in pamphlet form, Charleston. Also published as "Management of a Southern Plantation. Rules Enforced on the Rice Estate of P. C. Weston, Esq., of South Carolina," *De Bow's Review*, XXII, 40 (Jan., 1857).
[16] *Ibid.*, XXII, 40.

HARDSHIPS OF SLAVERY

It appears that Charles Manigault, of Charleston, devoted much time to correspondence with his overseers. The following extracts from his letters have been recorded in that significant book of source material, *Plantation and Frontier*, edited by U. B. Phillips. Like much of the rare manuscript material dealing with South Carolina, these letters, too, are in the possession of Mrs. H. Jenkins, of Pinopolis, South Carolina. Writing from Paris, France, March 1, 1847, to his overseer, a Mr. Haynes, on Savannah River, Manigault advised:

With regard to Jacob (whom you say is the only disorderly one) you had best think carefully respecting him, and always keep in mind the important old plantation maxim—viz. "never to *threaten* a negro" or he will do as you & I would when at school *he will run*. But with such a one whenever things get too bad, you should take a certain opportunity, when for instance he is with the Driver in the provision room, and you at the door, with a string in your pocket—then pull it out and order him tied—for if in such a case a negro succeeds in dodging & running from you, the annoyance is great—but having got him, if you wish to make an example of him take him down to the Savannah Jail, & give him prison discipline & by all means solitary confinement for 3 weeks, when he will be glad to get home again—but previous to his coming out let them jog his memory again, mind then and tell him that you and he are quits—that you will never dwell on old quarrels with him—that he has now a clear track before him, & all depends on himself, for he now sees how easy it is to fix "a bad disposed nigger." Then give him my compliments & tell him that you wrote me of his conduct, & say if he don't change for the better I'll sell him to a slave trader who will send him to New Orleans, where I have already sent several of the gang for their misconduct, or their running away for no cause. . . .[17]

His overseer, William Capers, of Gowrie plantations, wrote on September 18, 1863: "Jack Savage . . . has been quite impertinent to Mr. Tapper who was fixing the Engine &c . . . & said to old Charles he had not come home to be killed up with work, his general deportment since Sunday morning indicates a disposition to run away. I have him securely confined & I advise you to sell him."[18] A few days later Capers wrote further on the same subject:

[17] Phillips, *Plantation and Frontier*, II, 31 f.
[18] *Ibid.*, II, 32.

Yours of the 18th just to hand . . . I have described Jack Savage to a man who does not sell negroes only in the market but buys and sells away from this place. From my description of Jack he offers $1800. I will bring Jack to Savannah by Friday & put him in jail where he can be seen. Mr. Saddler, the person making the offer can decide of the price offered & your approval of offer, the negro to be sent away, far from us. I have been making inquiry respecting negroe sales. They are selling here at a high price. Jack, if 30 years old would bring $2500. Please inform me how to act for you at an early day.[19]

Court records throughout the slave states throw considerable light upon the social history of the Negro in the South. Apparently the field has not been much exploited by students of Negro history. The following is an abstract of the court record of the trials of slaves for crimes in Baldwin County, Georgia, from 1812 to 1832:

November 12, 1812: The State v. Major, a slave, the property of John Neeves, on the charge of rape. Verdict of Guilty. Sentence of hanging.

January 11, 1815: The State v. Fannie Meiklejohn, a slave, the property of the heirs of William Meiklejohn. Charged with murdering an infant. Verdict of not guilty.

April 18, 1815: The State v. Tom, a slave, the property of Joseph Andrews. Charged with murdering a slave and adjudged guilty. Sentenced to be branded on each cheek with the letter M, to have 39 lashes laid on his bare back forthwith in the market place and be remanded to jail, to receive 39 lashes on April 19 and be remanded to jail until April 20; then to receive 39 lashes more and be discharged.

November 21, 1816: The State v. John, a slave, the property of William McGehee, charged with stealing a $100 bill. Verdict of guilty. Sentenced to receive 39 lashes on the bare back three days in succession. . . .

April 28, 1821: The State v. Peter, a slave, the property of Eden Taylor, charged with the murder of a slave. Was found guilty of manslaughter and sentenced to be branded on the right cheek with the letter M, and to receive 39 lashes on three successive days. . . .

No date: The State v. John, a slave, the property of William Robertson, charged with burglary. Found guilty but recommended

[19] *Ibid.*, II, 33.

to mercy. Sentenced to be branded on the right cheek with the letter T, and to be given 39 lashes on three successive days. . . .

On the same day this same slave, John, was sentenced to be hanged for assaulting a white man with intent to kill. . . .

July 12, 1828: The State v. George, a slave, the property of Mrs. Elizabeth Smith, charged with larceny from the house. Verdict of not guilty.

July 8, 1829: The State v. Caroline, a slave, the property of Robert B. Washington, charged with maiming a free white person. Verdict of not guilty.[20]

The presence of large numbers of slaves in a community and their predilection to leave home at night in order to visit friends on other plantations brought into being in the slave states a kind of rural police system, or "patrol," as it was generally called. The details of patrol varied with different communities. In some sections it appears to have been purely voluntary; no compensation was given for the work. The chief business of the patrol was to see that no Negroes were away from their plantations without passes after certain stipulated hours of the night. In Milledgeville, Georgia, the hours of patrol were from 9 P.M. to 3 A.M.[21]

I. J. Mikell explains the practice on Edisto Island, where all slaves leaving the plantation at night were required to wear a copper badge properly numbered or a pass written by some member of the family. He implies that "riding patrol" was sometimes abused by young bloods who looked upon the duty as a sport and engaged in the needless chasing of Negroes for the fun of it. A Negro boy going-a-courting on a neighboring plantation might forget the formality of securing his pass or "ticket," and, when accosted by a member of the patrol, make a break for freedom rather than suffer the inevitable consequence, a lashing. "Then would come," says Mikell, "the joy of pursuit, which in most cases would prove futile, as a man on horseback found it difficult to negotiate cow-paths and by-paths by night."[22] The evils to which such practices led are obvious. It

---

[20] *American Historical Association, Annual Report* (1903), I, 462-464; Phillips, *Plantation and Frontier*, II, 123-125.

[21] From the minutes of the Town Council of Milledgeville, Ga. Item of Jan. 31, 1831. *American Historical Association, Annual Report* (1903), I, 467-470; Phillips, *Plantation and Frontier*, II, 147 f.

[22] Mikell, *op. cit.*, pp. 41 f.

would appear that any arrangement of the social order which is wrong and unfair to one race of people inevitably requires equally sinister devices for its perpetuation.

The Milledgeville ordinances, referred to above, underwent a gradual evolution from 1823 to 1831. In 1823 the law provided that a marshal divide the whole list of citizens, subject to patrol duty, into thirty squads. Each squad was required to do patrol duty one night each month. A citizen who did not want to serve could secure exemption for six dollars a year. In 1831 an ordinance was passed providing that not only the marshal, but also each of three sergeants receive a salary of a hundred dollars a year. They were to command the patrol in succession, and each night five citizens were to perform duty under the officer in charge. Persons who failed to serve were fined from one dollar to five dollars. An item of the minutes of 1825 required the apprehension of all slaves between ten and sixty years of age found off their masters' plantations without a pass after the ringing of the market bell. Slaves apprehended were required to be kept in the town guardhouse until morning, when their owners were notified. Before his release the slave received twenty-five lashes on the bare back, and the owner was required to pay a dollar. Not many months later the ordinance was amended to exempt the slave from whipping for the first offense.[23]

The late David Doar, master of Harrietta plantation, St. James Parish, preserved a patrol summons, issued to his father and signed by Captain John Butler, which he used in 1907 in explaining to a Santee audience the working of the patrol system in his native parish during the slave regime:

MR. S. D. DOAR,
    SIR:

You are hereby required to take under your command all persons, liable to patrol Duty, Bellevue to D. Horry's Wambaw plantation and from Wm. Lucas's Wambaw place, to Islington, the last included, and perform patrol duty according to law, and return this Warrant with a list of Defaulters, on oath, to Commanding Officer of Company at next Muster day.

                        (Signed) JOHN BUTLER, CAPT.[24]

[23] Minutes of the Town Council of Milledgeville, Ga., in *American Historical Association, Annual Report* (1903), I, 467-470.

[24] Doar, *op. cit.*, p. 23.

HARDSHIPS OF SLAVERY 277

Another factor which made the Negroes' lot a hard one, especially in sections where the slave population outnumbered the whites, was the constant fear of insurrection which haunted the white man. The planters of the Carolina low country had abundant reason for these fears. They had heard lurid accounts of a band of slaves, who, in 1740, had assembled at Stono, near Charleston, surprised and killed two young white men in a warehouse, and, equipping themselves with guns and ammunition which they seized, had marched off in the direction of Jacksonborough, burning houses and murdering as they went. They forcibly entered the house of a Mr. Godfrey, murdered his wife and children, took all the firearms he had, and set fire to the house. For a distance of about fifteen miles they pillaged every plantation, taking all slaves who would follow them until their company was a formidable one. In a moment of exultation and intoxication (they had got possession of some rum on their march), they paused in an open field to rejoice over their victory. Word of the insurrection, spread rapidly and quickly, reached the Presbyterian Church in Wiltown, where many planters were in attendance, all armed, according to the requirements of the law. They hurriedly assembled under the command of Captain Bee, and, upon approaching, opened fire on the Negroes, killing a few; many of the Negroes fled to the woods. The greater number was captured and tried. Those who had been compelled to join the band were pardoned, but the leaders and original insurgents suffered death.[25]

Just four years later the Charleston community was shocked by the intelligence of the murder of several whites by slaves in the Parish of St. Andrew. A Savannah newspaper printed the following item:

From St. Andrew's Parish we have the following melancholy account viz. That on Tuesday morning the 29th ult. six new Negro fellows and four wenches, belonging to Captain Morris, killed the Overseer in the field, after which they went to the house, murdered his wife, and dangerously wounded a carpenter named Wright, also a boy who died next day; they then proceeded to the house of Angus McIntosh, whom they likewise dangerously wounded; and being there joined by a sensible fellow, the property of said McIntosh, they went to the house of Roderick M'Leod, wounded him very much, and killed his son, who had fired upon them on their

[25] Ramsay, *op. cit.*, I, 62 f.

coming up and broke the arm of the fellow who had joined them. Their leader and McIntosh's negro have been taken and burnt, and two of the wenches have returned to the plantation.[26]

Freshest of all in the minds of coastal planters was the threat of the Vesey plot in Charleston in 1822. A horrifying insurrection planned and almost executed included the murder of the whites and a general freeing of the Negroes. The leaders of the plot were apprehended and hanged.

To the planters the presence of free Negroes among the slaves presented a constant threat to the peace of the community. Insurrection schemes could be more easily planned by the manumitted slaves since they could move in and out among their fellows without hindrance. The status of the free Negro was peculiar. He had no civil rights, yet he was absolutely free of the restrictions that kept his brother in slavery. Manumission usually arose out of the nobler impulses of slaveowners; yet these acts of benevolence bred a spawn of problems and difficulties to slaveholders which in some communities threatened the whole system. Thus it was that the evils inherent in slavery tended to generate forces leading toward its own dissolution and death. The defenders of slavery were constantly trying to check these forces and to keep the machine running. Indeed, it began to look as though the white people of the South might perish by their own invention. They were caught in a trap. The only possible alternatives were general emancipation, which was humanly impossible, or stricter and harsher laws which would keep the Negroes in subjection. They chose the latter and drank the cup of bitterness to the very dregs.

For fifty years before the Civil War there was constant talk of colonizing the free Negroes in some foreign land, usually Africa, so as to remove the problem of the manumitted slave. An editorial in a Milledgeville, Georgia, newspaper in 1817, after strongly urging some sort of colonization of free Negroes, affirmed: "Nor will the policy of such a measure be questioned by anyone who duly estimates the danger to which our tranquillity is constantly exposed by having among us a race of people, possessing neither the rights of citizens nor the protection of slaves. With the example of St. Domingo before our

[26] News item from the (Savannah) *Georgia Gazette*, Dec. 7, 1774, in Phillips, *Plantation and Frontier*, II, 118 f.

HARDSHIPS OF SLAVERY 279

eyes, it is strange we would have permitted partial freedom to exist so long, especially when it is known to have the effect of making slaves discontented with their situation, and exciting them to insurrection."²⁷ This editor further proposed: "But we ought not to stop at this. A gradual reduction of slavery should be immediately attempted. . . . If the government will find means of conveying out of the country such slaves as may be emancipated, and would likewise purchase annually a certain number, particularly females, for transportation, it is believed our black population would soon become harmless if not extinct."²⁸ Similar sentiments were expressed in the editorial column of the Atlanta *Daily Intelligencer* in 1860. After strongly advocating the right of the city recorder to sell into slavery free Negroes convicted of violating the city laws, which right it was contended was "conferred upon him by the last General Assembly," the editor continued: "We are opposed to giving free negroes a residence in any and every Slaveholding state, believing as we do, that their presence in slave communities is hurtful to the good order of society and fraught with great danger to our 'peculiar institution'; and we speak of this matter now, as the question has been raised, for the purpose of awakening the sentiment of the community to the dangerous element which manumission has placed among us."²⁹ Perhaps no historical document so vividly reflects the anxiety of the white people regarding Negro insurrection as the *Memorial of the Citizens of Charleston to the Senate and House of Representatives of the State of South Carolina*. Its formulation came quickly upon the heels of the discovery of the Vesey plot. The memorial, as stated in the preamble, was written under the pressure of deep anxiety and solicitude "resulting from the recent discovery of a projected insurrection among our colored people."³⁰ The harshness and the apparently unreasonable position taken in the petition can be explained only upon the grounds of fear and hysteria induced by the intended insurrection. Its first petition was that the legislature "send out of the state, never again to return, all free persons of color."³¹ It was maintained that "The hopes of the free negroes will increase

[27] Editorial from the (Milledgeville) *Georgia Journal*, Jan. 1, 1817, in Phillips, *Plantation and Frontier*, II, 158.
[28] *Ibid.*, II, 158.   [29] *Ibid.*, II, 159 f.
[30] *Ibid.*, II, 103.   [31] *Ibid.*, II, 105.

with their numbers, and when they shall have equalled the whites, which it can easily be shown will happen before many years are passed, they will expect and claim all the privileges, rights, and immunities of citizens, which if denied them, as they must be, they will be driven by despair to obtain by force what cannot be effected in any other way. . . ."[32] The petitioners were alarmed at the rapid increase of free Negroes in the Charleston area, and, to substantiate their contention, showed the disproportionate increase of free persons of color as compared with the whites, over a ten-year period. The memorial continued:

> In eighteen hundred and ten, there were one thousand six hundred and eighty (1680) free persons of color in the Parishes of St. Michaels and St. Philips; in eighteen hundred and twenty, but ten years afterwards, they had increased to three thousand and sixty-two (3062); in the same period, the whites had only increased about 85 per cent, or in other words, the whites in ten years have increased about (1/7) one seventh, and the free people of color have nearly doubled—Should the free people of color increase for the next thirty years as they have done for the last ten, in the year one thousand eight hundred and fifty, they will amount to 18,402, whilst the whites will only have amounted to 21,824; so that in thirty years, the whites in the Parishes of St. Philip and St. Michaels will exceed the free persons of color only by 3,422, whilst at this moment they exceed them by 11,896.[33]

It was further contended that the free Negroes would not emigrate; they would remain in the place of their nativity and offer serious competition to the poorer whites who worked in the trades and the mechanical arts. Free Negroes did not work on plantations, but became carpenters and craftsmen in the various trades. Because of the competition the poor whites would be forced to seek employment in other sections, thereby making insignificant the white population as compared to the free blacks. Another point made by the petitioners was thus expressed:

> The superior condition of the free persons of color, excites discontent among our slaves, who continually have before their eyes, persons of the same color, many of whom they have known in slavery, and with all of whom they associate on terms of equality—freed from the control of masters, working where they please—going

[32] *Ibid.*, II, 106.   [33] *Ibid.*, II, 107.

HARDSHIPS OF SLAVERY

whither they please—and expending their money how they please—the slave seeing this, finds his labor irksome; he becomes dissatisfied with his state, he pants after liberty! A liberty he can never hope to acquire by purchase or faithful services, for the Legislature has deemed it expedient to close the door against emancipation, his only chance for freedom is to combine with others and endeavor to incite an insurrection.[34]

Then in words of desperation and with an apparent awareness of their inhumanity, the memorialists declared: "It becomes us, however painful it may prove, to sacrifice feeling to reason, and mistaken compassion to a stern policy, and expel from our territory every free person of color, that we may extinguish from our territory at once every gleam of hope which the slaves may indulge of ever being free—and that we may proceed to govern them on the only principle that can maintain slavery, the principle of fear."[35] It was also desired that a law be passed preventing persons of color from holding real property, and the statement was made that many free Negroes were becoming rich and that some were already owners of plantations. It was hoped that Negroes would be prevented from residing upon premises where no white person lived. Finally, the memorialist prayed for stricter laws relating to white persons concerned in insurrections of the slaves, especially inciting to insurrection. They asked that present laws be amended so as to "subject to the punishment of death all white persons who shall be principals, advisors or abettors in any actual or projected insurrection of the slaves."[36] They recommended that "a law be passed, prohibiting under severe penalties, all persons from teaching Negroes to read and write."[37]

[34] *Ibid.*, II, 108 f.
[35] *Ibid.*, II, 110 f.
[36] *Ibid.*, II, 115.
[37] *Ibid.*

CHAPTER XIII

THUNDER OVER PORT ROYAL

> Oh what a mournin' (sister),
> When de stars begin to fall.

THE THUNDER that boomed over Port Royal came from the guns of the Federal fleet that steamed into the harbor on the eventful day of November 7, 1861. Eventful because it marked the passing of a social and economic order which lent color and importance to the Southern scene and initiated a new system involving one of the most interesting experiments in human rehabilitation ever undertaken on the American continent, a scheme no less ambitious than the emancipation and education of eighteen thousand[1] Negroes whose only training and background had been that of the slave plantation.

Charleston was well fortified, and the Federals contented themselves with blockading this important port. The Confederacy, however, gave relatively little attention to the back door of the Carolina coast, the rich agricultural islands lying to the south of Charleston. Small forces guarded the entrances along the coast, and at Port Royal only two minor fortresses watched the door to one of the most magnificent harbors in the country.

The Union vessels, about fifty in number, recently from Hampton Roads and under command of Commodore S. F. Du Pont, had been assembling themselves in battle array for some days. They came into the harbor, moving slowly in a great ellipse, firing as they moved. Immediately the batteries from Hilton Head and Bay Point challenged the invaders, but the resistance of the Confederates was negligible. Their feeble earthen breastworks were quickly leveled and their small guns silenced. The forts were soon evacuated, and General Thomas F. Drayton, commanding the Confederate forces, withdrew his men to the mainland. Josiah Tattnall, who commanded an

[1] Educational Commission for Freedmen, *First Annual Report (May, 1863)* (Boston, 1863), pp. 7 f.

insignificant Confederate fleet, retreated hurriedly, setting fire to his ships and leaving the whole Port Royal area, including the beautiful village of Beaufort and the rich alluvial islands thereabout, with their baronial homes, plantations, and slaves to the mercy of the Union forces. Du Pont's ships carried twelve thousand soldiers under command of General T. W. Sherman, who immediately landed and took charge.[2] The town of Beaufort was sacked. Between the soldiers and a minority of the Negroes, intoxicated with the idea of freedom, the lovely little village was plundered and left in partial ruin. "These ignorant and benighted creatures flocked into Beaufort," wrote General Stevens, "and held high carnival in the deserted mansions, smashing doors, mirrors, and furniture, and appropriating all that took their fancy. After this loot, a common sight was a black wench dressed in silks, or white lace curtains, or a stalwart black field hand resplendent in a complete suit of gaudy carpeting just torn from the floor. After this sack, they remained at home upon the plantations, and reveled in unwonted idleness and luxury, feasting upon the corn, cattle, and turkeys of their fugitive masters."[3]

To the Negroes the invasion of the Federals was known as "gun-shoot," and for years after they reckoned events as before "gun-shoot" or after "gun-shoot." It was difficult to realize that the peaceful islands had been invaded. Even though the planters had been warned of the possibility of invasion, they could hardly take seriously the attack upon so unpromising a station as Port Royal, for it offered no rich stores and could hardly be considered a strategic military post. But they misunderstood their foes, who were attracted by the broad acres of sea-island cotton just being harvested and the peaceful homes of the planters and who desired most of all to break into the slavery problem, press into the interior, and satisfy their keen

[2] *Rebellion Record*, ed. Frank Moore, III (Diary), 107; (Documents), 105-117; *War of the Rebellion: A Compilation of the Official Records of the Union and Confederate Armies*, Ser. I, Vol. VI, contains scores of official reports concerning the Battle of Port Royal and naval and military activities along the South Carolina coast. *War Letters of William Thompson Lusk* (1911). (Copy in the Beaufort Township Library.) Captain Lusk was present during the Battle of Port Royal and was for some time thereafter stationed in Beaufort, where he wrote many of these letters. They are of interest, chiefly from a military point of view.

[3] Stevens, *op. cit.*, II, 353.

hunger for freeing the colored man. They were the more eager because this was South Carolina, the most rebellious of the rebel states, for the chastisement of this particular state added a touch of sanctity to the cause much publicized in the North.

One can imagine the consternation which spread to the plantations as the ponderous sounds of the cannonading reverberated throughout the quiet country, rolled up tidal creeks and across wide expanses of marsh—sounds unnatural and before unheard except for the strange and mellow thunder of the guns in Charleston Harbor at the opening of the war. But now the Yankees had come to the plantations. Doubtless many of the wiser Negroes sensed the meaning of it all and realized that their day of Jubilee had come. There was a tingle of excitement and the long hope was realized. Some were afraid and others simply bewildered. All slaves were hurriedly called together and advised to leave the islands for the mainland. Many of them naturally refused to go and defied all orders. All plantation boats and river craft were quickly commandeered and supplies packed upon them for the flight to the mainland. The whites all left, taking what they could and going where they knew not. The planters waited to the last possible moment to leave the islands. The Confederate Government had fixed a final date for the evacuation; the Federal troops were at the gates. Mikell, of Edisto Island, declared:

> The limit of time allowed by the Confederate Government for leaving had expired when my father had finished getting ready his cotton for market, and no extension of time was granted. Our slaves were hurried across the river to the mainland and were finally settled in the middle of the State, away from the coast. . . . Our work animals and implements we likewise got off. All our cattle, sheep and the bulk of our provisions were left behind. All of the luxuries of our own production attending a well-appointed plantation in a semi-tropical climate shared the same fate. The household effects of "master and man" we could not remove—some old pieces of mahogany, old family relics and priceless—were left behind.[4]

Overnight the islands were bereft of all white people except the Northern invaders. The planters placed their wives and children in the fastest boats and turned them over to trusted slaves, who with their strong black arms propelled the heavy

---

[4] Mikell, *op. cit.*, pp. 20 f.

craft up the tidal rivers, with the tide and against the tide whichever came, until they reached the mainland and the hospitable homes of friends, who helped them in their flight. Many lived in box cars along railroad sidings and were glad to get them, using what scanty clothing and household effects they could bring with them. Women were frightened, children cried. Some fled to Charleston, arriving there just in time to be greeted by the dreadful fire of December, 1861. Worried and harassed, they left Charleston. By May, 1862, nearly all of the city's population had taken flight to the upcountry.[5] Towns became overcrowded and provisions were scarce. Confederate money was often refused. Want and the pinch of poverty were immediately felt amid the disorder. The men who had directed affairs and governed the intricacies of plantation life were now in the army. Only old men and boys were left to manage the farms. Many ignorant upcountry farmers looked upon the coastal refugees with suspicion, claiming that they were responsible for the war. Women who had known only surroundings of culture had to barter their clothing for food. One woman in a moment of desperation swapped her pretty jacket for two turkeys.[6]

Describing the flight of the residents of Beaufort, Nancy De Saussure wrote: "When the tidings of the invasions of their town was brought to them, the people, thinking the town would be shelled, fled in their carriages, many of them not waiting to dress themselves, so great was their fright. This long procession of carriages and wagons passed through our village about dusk, the occupants not knowing what to do or where to go. Every house was thrown open to them and these refugees remained in the neighborhood during the war. They were taken care of, until in turn we had to flee before Sherman's army."[7] The Mikell family made a dramatic flight from Edisto Island in a twelve-oared boat pulled by as many lusty slaves, with the dependable "old Andrew" as stroke oar. The family yacht, as it was called, was quickly commissioned, and as much baggage was taken on as would be allowed. It was necessary for the refugees to reach the only back waterway to Charleston, Wappo

[5] *News and Courier*, Charleston, Jan. 5, 1892. Article signed "M. B. W."
[6] *Ibid.*, Jan. 5, 1895.
[7] Nancy (Bostwick) De Saussure, *Old Plantation Days* (New York, 1909), p. 67.

Cut, by sundown. The Confederates permitted no boat of any description to cross the deadline after the sunset gun had been fired. The city of Charleston was under blockade of the Federal navy, and these waterways to the rear, although too small for large craft, were zealously guarded by the Southerners. Mikell wrote:

It was to reach this dead line in time that we were racing with twenty miles still to go and three hours to make it in. The responsibility and nerve racking strain on my old father was terrible, with no one to help him bear it, with an invalid wife, young daughters and small children under his protection, the burden was crushing. At four o'clock of a winter's afternoon, with the sun an hour high, we were still seven miles or more from the line, fortunately the tide had begun to favor us, which helped somewhat. My father would call out to his stroke oar, "A little more speed, Andrew, more speed!" "Yes, sir, Maussa!" he replied. Then the call for the reserve power of his men was made. Raising his mighty voice, Andrew began to sing that great boat song, "Roll, Jordan, Roll," which, when sung by twelve oarsmen, keeping time with their oars, was inspiring. One could feel the great canoe quiver and spring forward under the spiritual exaltation of the men. Then, as the tune died away into a distant echo, the boat would glide back into its old stride. But time was too precious for this. A short period to allow of their catching their breath, and again the old command from the anxious helmsman:—"More speed, Andrew, faster!" "Yes, sir, Maussa!" was again the reply and again his rough but earnest voice would sing out their old camp meeting song: "The Jews cast Daniel in the Lion's Den," to be taken up in short order by his willing crew when the boat would again quiver and respond to the increased power.[8]

Mikell continued:

The men were expending their last ounce of reserve power, their faces were ashen, eyes protruding, breath coming through their open mouths like steam escaping, and yet they kept on, their loyalty to the family goading them to action. The sun had dropped below the tops of the trees. Before us was the last straight stretch of water. Near half a mile ahead we saw the guard preparing to fire the evening gun. My father, standing bare-headed, with his white locks lifted by the evening breeze, with eyes closed, was praying that we might be seen before it was too late. And we were seen. Sensing something out of the ordinary, the soldiers took in the situation

[8] Mikell, *op. cit.*, pp. 28-36.

and gave us three cheers, which acted like wine on our exhausted crew. We were just in time. As the prow of the good old boat crossed the imaginary line there was a flash, a roar. The sunset gun had been fired. We were safe. The men rested on their oars, the boat slowed down. Some of the oarsmen fell from their seats, others were unable to stand. My sisters wept hysterically, the children cried in sympathy, and my invalid mother swooned. Reaction from the mental strain had set in, but we were safe. Anything else did not matter. A forty-mile row against time, with less than an hour's rest, the men being urged to the last extremity of endurance at every dip of the oar, was without parallel in these waters,—perhaps in any others. And this was their second day of a forty mile row....

We hobbled across the Ashley River with our exhausted crew, and landed at one of the rice mills, where our carriage awaited us. Then—*home*. And night with all its tragedies settled down over land and sea.[9]

Commodore Du Pont wrote: "The inhabitants have fled, and the town is abandoned to the negroes, who are reported to me to be in a lawless condition.... They were wild with joy and revenge.... They have been shot down, they say, like dogs, because they would not go off with their masters.... The Confederates were in an utter panic; they deserted everything."[10]

A Captain Rogers, of the army of occupation, describing the situation in Beaufort, as he saw it, reported: "Beaufort has been taken by the gunboats, the town having been abandoned by the whites. The negroes were pillaging the town. They said the whites were shooting them right and left, in order to drive them back into the interior."[11]

A contemporary correspondent related the events which occurred upon the landing of the troops:

When our troops took Hilton Head Island the fields were white with cotton ready to be picked. It was a beautiful sight, and novel to most of our men. You must read the reports of the capture of Fort Walker and Fort Beauregard. Some parts read like a romance.

Fort Walker was on Hilton Head, and Fort Beauregard was on Bay Point. The extreme points of these two islands form the entrance to Port Royal Sound, which is about three miles wide.

[9] *Ibid.* [10] Botume, *op. cit.*, p. 34.
[11] *Rebellion Record*, ed. Frank Moore, III (Documents), 113.

This sound is a wonderful harbor, where many of our gunboats are now lying.

You will not be South long before you will hear about the advantages of Port Royal Harbor, for the officers and soldiers are very much impressed by it. They say it will take in the navies of the world. It is in the heart of South Carolina, and is only twenty miles from Savannah, and thirty from Charleston.

When our men landed on Hilton Head, the negroes guided them to the Rebel officers' headquarters, which was on the Pope Plantation. Here they found a very fine library. There were, besides the books, complete files of old papers, some dating as far back as 1812. Hard, wasn't it, to have all these things destroyed?[12]

Miss Botume came early among the freedmen as a teacher. Her description of the scene upon landing at Beaufort is so realistic that it might well be included here:

A curious crowd of white men and negroes stood around waiting for our boat to come up. Here we were welcomed by General Saxton and his staff; and in spite of the turmoil and confusion around us, and the insignia of war, we ceased to feel like strangers in a strange land. There were soldiers everywhere, "saluting" the general as we passed. Not a white woman was to be seen, excepting some officers' wives and a few teachers expecting friends, and who only appeared in public under a good escort.

Negroes, negroes, negroes. They hovered around like bees in a swarm. Sitting, standing, or lying at full-length, with their faces turned to the sky. Every doorstep, box, or barrel was covered with them for the arrival of a boat was a time of great excitement. They were dressed—no, not dressed, nor clothed, but partly covered with every conceivable thing which could be put on the back of a biped. Some of the women had on old, cast-off soldiers' coats, with "crocus bags," fastened together with their own ravelings, for skirts, and bits of sail cloth for head-handkerchiefs. Many of the men had strips of gay carpeting, or old bags, or pieces of blanket, in which they cut arm-holes and wore as jackets. Their pants were tied below and above the knees and around the waist with pieces of rope to keep them on. Words fail to describe their grotesque appearance. Fortunately they were oblivious to all this incongruity— . . . they were only parts of a whole; once "massa's niggers," now refugees and contrabands. So all looked up with a smile, and put their hands to their foreheads in military fashion, with a "How d'ye gineral? How d'ye missis?," as we passed along.[13]

[12] Botume, *op. cit.*, p. 29.   [13] *Ibid.*, pp. 31 f.

I have already remarked upon the keen powers of observation of the Northern invaders. In spite of their lack of love for the "rebels," they were constantly moved by the beauty and serenity of the Carolina low country. No one has surpassed Colonel Higginson in his descriptions of the beauties of the coastal region. In contrast to the dilapidation just described, I insert a passage from Higginson revealing a brighter scene:

> How can I ever describe the charm and picturesqueness of that summer life? Our house possessed four spacious rooms and a piazza; around it were grouped sheds and tents; the camp was a little way off on one side, the negro-quarters of the plantation on the other; all was immersed in a dense mass of waving and murmuring locust-blossoms. The spring days were always lovely, while the evenings were always conveniently damp; so that we never shut the windows by day nor omitted our cheerful fire by night.[14]

The young Massachusetts Colonel continued: "From this early spring-time onward, there seemed no great difference in atmospheric sensations, and only a succession of bloom. After two months one's notions of the seasons grew bewildered, just as very early rising bewilders the day. . . . So when we had lived in summer so long as hardly to remember winter, it suddenly occurred to us that it was not yet June."[15] As though he feared that he might praise the woodland of the South too much, Higginson made this comment: "It seemed to me, also, that the woods had not those pure, clean, *innocent* odors which so abound in the New England forest in early spring; but there was something luscious, voluptuous, almost oppressively fragrant about the magnolias, as if they belonged not to Hebe, but to Magdalen." He added, "Such immense and lustrous butterflies I have never seen but in dreams."[16] Heavy, voluptuous odors emanated from the masses of gardenias which grew in such profusion in the low country, so named by Linnaeus for Dr. Alexander Garden, who practiced "physic" in Prince William Parish and in Charleston. Higginson did not mention the flaming poinsettias that graced the gardens of Charleston all winter long. This flower was named for Joel R. Poinsett, Minister to Mexico, who brought it from that country to the United States and introduced it to South Carolina gardens.

[14] Higginson, *op. cit.*, p. 136.
[15] *Ibid.*, p. 146.   [16] *Ibid.*

But turning again to the uglier picture of war and invasion, it is difficult to imagine the feelings that surged through the souls of the Negroes as they found themselves in possession of the plantations—no master, no overseer, no driver, no work—just heaven for a moment. I doubt not that many faithful slaves for a while guarded the property of their former masters. But the temptation was too great for them to be able to withhold their hands. Finally, they yielded, entered the big houses and made themselves at home. Surely some big black field hand took his place on the front piazza in the master's rocking chair, and, placing his big bare feet on the banister, as he had often seen the master do, sat and surveyed the plantation scene. Who would not have done so under the conditions? They took the furniture from the big house and hid it away for future use. Nothing was safe or secure. Between the innocent Negroes, whose momentary plight was fascinating, and the invaders, including the "missionaries" and teachers, whose curiosity knew no bounds, pandemonium and confusion reigned in the whole plantation area. The Northerners took possession of the homes of the planters, lolled in their spacious parlors, slept in their high, four-poster beds, ate from their silver plate, and read their private letters, hidden away in trunks and old bookcases. The following excerpt from a letter reveals the way in which the missionaries and teachers made themselves at home in the residences of the planters. The particular party was given on a great plantation on St. Helena Island, Coffin's Point: "Thanksgiving Day, Nov. 26. We sat down to dinner—sixteen Massachusetts people, six minister's sons. . . . We wondered what was the last [dinner party] as large that had dined in this old house, but Robert [a former slave] says he never saw such a large party here—Mr. Coffin used to give his dinners in Charleston."[17] Speaking of the pillage of houses by the Negroes, E. S. Philbrick, a Northern plantation superintendent, who himself occupied one of the houses, writing about Pine Grove plantation on St. Helena, declared: "The people broke in on Christmas and took what we left there, appropriating it to their private uses. I found Frank had the side-board in his new house (the old carriage house). I told him to give it up and asked where the rest was. Mily had taken the desk, for safe-keeping, and

[17] Pearson, *op. cit.*, p. 232.

offered to deliver it when wanted, but the bedsteads are not reported. Ranty had locked up the large dining-table in the peas-house."[18]

Upon the landing of the soldiers at Port Royal the military authorities were faced with a very serious problem, the task of caring for the thousands of slaves who swarmed about the docks and walked the countryside, dazed by the rapid succession of events which had recently befallen them. There was great confusion everywhere. General T. W. Sherman, commanding the area, issued a proclamation urging all the freedmen to occupy the plantations and to take up the duties of planting as of old but under their new authority, the United States Government. The General lamented in an order from Hilton Head issued in February, 1862, just three months after the soldiers landed, that in few instances were the suggestions heeded by the former slaves. Not only had they been disregarded, "but hordes of totally uneducated, ignorant and improvident blacks have been abandoned by their constitutional guardians, not only to all the future chances of anarchy and starvation, but in a state of such abject ignorance and mental stolidity, as to preclude all possibility of self-government and self-maintenance in their present condition."[19]

General Sherman fully realized by now the gravity of the situation in which he was suddenly placed. The planters who had disciplined these slaves and looked after their every want, in so far as their wants were heeded, had left the islands perforce and with their families had taken refuge in the interior. These thousands of Negroes, in their confusion and want, presented a problem in social adjustment which the military authorities were quick to sense. The General's order stressed the importance of farming the land and thereby providing food for the Negroes. They were to be put to work under the direction of farm agents designated by the government. These agents were to operate the plantations for the government. The territory was to be divided into districts, and "For each of these districts a suitable agent will be appointed to superintend the management of the plantation by the blacks; to enroll and organize the willing blacks into working parties; to see that they are well fed, clad, and paid a proper remuneration for their

[18] *Ibid.*, p. 136.   [19] Botume, *op. cit.*, pp. 16 f.

labor; to take charge of all property on the plantations, whether found there, provided by the government, or raised from the soil, and to perform all other administrative duties connected with the plantations that may be required by the government."[20] Furthermore, teachers were to be provided for each district, "whose duties will consist in teaching them, both young and old, the rudiments of civilization and Christianity. . . ." The order closed with the following appeal: "Never was there a nobler or more fitting opportunity for the operation of that considerate and practical benevolence for which the Northern people have ever been distinguished."[21]

The news spread quickly to all parts of the North. Great enthusiasm was aroused, particularly in New England. Many men and women of benevolent tendencies offered themselves for the missionary enterprise. The ardor of abolition sentiment was fanned into a new flame. Elizabeth Botume, inspired by the words, "Never was there a nobler or more fitting opportunity," was led to enter the cause. "This seemed like a divine call," she added.[22] Societies for the education of the freedmen sprang up over night: the Freedmen's Aid Society of Boston, the National Freedmen's Relief Commission of New York, and the Pennsylvania Freedmen's Relief Association were among the pioneer organizations. Societies were formed in churches of all denominations, and members of families and neighbors formed independent clubs—all with the desire to help the Negroes of the South.[23]

The Treasury Department in Washington, desiring to see that the plantations were properly run and anxious that the Negroes should be more adequately cared for, undertook a more systematic and careful management of the lands temporarily abandoned by the planters. To do this most effectively, the responsibility was placed in the hands of one man, Edward L. Pierce, of Massachusetts. Pierce had just previously done commendable work at Fortress Monroe among the contrabands.[24]

[20] *Ibid.*, p. 17.   [21] *Ibid.*, pp. 17 f.
[22] *Ibid.*, p. 19.   [23] *Ibid.*, pp. 18 f.
[24] After the beginning of the war, slaves came to be known as "contraband" in the following manner: "Three fugitives, the property of Colonel Mallory, commander of the Rebel forces near Hampton, were brought into Fortress Monroe by the picket guard. They represented that they were about to be sent South, and hence sought protection. Major Cary came in with a flag of truce, and claimed their rendition under the 'Fugitive Slave Law,' but

The call was sent out for men and women who would go South to teach the Negroes and manage the plantations. Their undertaking was a very ambitious one, as indicated in the constitution of the Boston society, namely: "the industrial, social, intellectual, moral, and religious improvement of persons released from slavery in the course of the war for the Union."[25]

The sea-island cotton crop of 1861 was unusually good, but much of it was still in the fields when the Federals arrived in November. Some of it had been gathered and stored away preparatory to ginning. Of course no little part of it had been burned before the residents left their homes. The crop was of sufficient importance to fire the imagination of Northerners and to make the prospect of conducting one of those plantations a bright one for New England philanthropists. Anyone reared in the Cotton Belt and acquainted with the arduous details of producing the crop and with knowledge of the leisurely labor of Negroes can but be amused at the naïve enthusiasm of those who rushed in where angels feared to tread. Upon his arrival at Port Royal, E. S. Philbrick, capable engineer of Boston, wrote to friends that his ship was anchored in the harbor and that he would soon disembark, but in the meantime he was reading a book on cotton culture preparatory to taking over the management of several cotton plantations.

On March 3, 1862, Pierce and his co-laborers, sixty-four in number, set sail from New York. In the party were fifteen women. Their departure was proclaimed as "The first missionary expedition to propagate industry, religion, and education among the contrabands at Hilton Head, as well as to encourage agriculture and like useful measures."[26] The government gave the "missionaries" an allowance for transportation, subsistence and quarters, while the benevolent societies paid their salaries from twenty-five to fifty dollars a month.[27] There was a great rush of applicants who offered themselves for service in the Port Royal area. "Indeed," Elizabeth Botume remarked, "it seemed sometimes, if 'transportation' and 'subsistence' could be

---

was informed by General Butler that, under the peculiar circumstances he considered the fugitives, 'contraband' of war."—Text of an order sent to Union Army Headquarters. Quoted in Botume, *op. cit.*, p. 10.

[25] Educational Commission for Freedmen, *First Annual Report* (1863), p. 4. [26] Botume, *op. cit.*, p. 19.

[27] Pearson, *op. cit.*, p. vi.

secured for so many there might be a special superintendent and teacher for each colored family emancipated."[28] Philbrick, evidently a very practical fellow, did not like the looks of the party with which he was traveling. He described them as ". . . a rather motley-looking set. A good many look like broken-down schoolmasters or ministers who have excellent dispositions but not much talent."[29]

The party was sworn in by Collector Barney, of the Port of New York, six at a time. It was a cold, drizzling March morning, the rain freezing as it fell. The steamer *Atlantic's* staterooms for the most part were taken out to make room for troops and cargo. What rooms were left were assigned to ladies and old gentlemen. There was a general mixture of cabin passengers, recruits, sutlers' and quarter-masters' agents, and crew, the latter not being dressed in uniform but in old garments that might be procured anywhere.

Missionaries on a great crusade! They were headed for the land of the Secessionists, to make straight the crooked paths of the South Carolina planters, to plant cotton with free labor, to live in the plantation homes recently left by their owners. They were to begin a new day, to whisper into the ears of the black folk of the South the glad tidings that they were now free. They were to bring into full fruition, overnight, the ideals and dreams of the New England abolitionists. Their righteous heel was to be placed upon the neck of the benighted "Secesh," and their hungry zeal to be sated in the ripe fields of the sea-island country.

A small group of New England women taught on Edisto Island during the war. Among them was Mary Ames, whose diary throws an interesting light upon the times and conditions of this period. Mary Ames and her friend, Emily Bliss, listened to interesting stories told by teachers who had returned to their New England homes for brief visits, and they became very eager to follow the example of their friends. "We went to Boston," she wrote, "saw the chief of the Freedmen's Bureau, were examined, and enrolled as teachers. We were ordered to leave at once for Hilton Head. . . . Our families ridiculed our going, and tried to stop us, prophesying our return in less than a month. We made our preparations which were not elaborate,

[28] Botume, *op. cit.*, p. 20.   [29] Pearson, *op. cit.*, p. 2.

a chair, a plate, knife, fork and spoon; cup and saucer, blanket, sheets and pillow-cases, and sacking for a bed of hay . . . and we added some crackers, tea and a teapot."[30] They sailed from New York on May 1, 1865, landing at Hilton Head four days later. There they reported to the authorities, were received coldly, and advised to proceed to Charleston. This they did as soon as possible, taking one of the small steamers plying between these ports, were huddled amid a horde of soldiers, sat all night upon a bench without a back, arrived in the city next morning, weary and disheartened. In Charleston they were cordially greeted by New England officials. One from Massachusetts was especially kind and considerate to the novitiates. "Emily, weary, discouraged, and homesick," wrote Mary Ames, "threw herself sobbing into his arms, saying, 'Oh, sir, have you a wife?' At once he took in the situation, called an ambulance and put us in charge of a sergeant with a note to his wife."[31]

They were taken to the home of a Mrs. Pillsbury, where they found very pleasant surroundings: "They [the Pillsburys] were living in one of the most elegant mansions in Charleston; the furniture, pictures and ornaments were all as their owner had left them. The garden was a delight; I never saw finer roses." The young teachers were offered places in the Negro schools of Charleston, but they felt unprepared for regular teaching and declined. They did accept the offer to go to Edisto Island, where several thousand Negroes had been sent after Sherman's march. Leaving Charleston, they sailed along the shore and into the mouth of the Edisto River, landing just at sunset. Miss Ames wrote, "It seemed like a fairy-land—everything so fresh and green—the air so soft."[32] On the boat were a hundred and fifty Negroes, who upon landing immediately built fires to cook their supper. The live oaks with their hanging moss and the singing Negroes with their lighted fires made a beautiful and impressive picture at that time of day, "fust dark." This spot is still known as "Steamboat Landing." The visitor there today is impressed by the changed scene. Everything is quiet and desolate except the stately live oaks with their hanging moss and the majestic river, as beautiful today as ever. Social and economic change have not affected the landscape.

[30] Ames, *op. cit.*, pp. 1 f.
[31] *Ibid.*, p. 4.
[32] *Ibid.*, pp. 6 f.

The river is as placid and beautiful in these days of decadence as when sea-island cotton bloomed in yellow and red along its shores and thousands of slaves sang from bateaus that drifted with the tide. The teachers spent the night on the little boat, occupying the Captain's cabin. Next morning they went ashore and were invited to breakfast at army headquarters on the William Seabrook plantation. The house, still standing, is a picture of quiet dignity and grace; sleepy, sorrowful Spanish moss everywhere; luxurious magnolias with immaculate blossoms, heavy with the scent of bay and laurel; cassena modestly standing in the lesser places, with sweet myrtle nearby, and the humbler partridge-berry growing underneath.

The diary relates that the young women were given an army wagon and sent to the Whaley plantation to set up school: "The drive was delightful, the road shaded and cool, winding under immense live-oak trees covered with moss; the wild grape was in bloom, and the air filled with its perfume." After a while they reached what appeared to have been once a pretty avenue with Negro cabins on each side and a large house at the end. The Negroes came flocking out to see the newcomers. Dr. Whaley had owned a hundred slaves and had abandoned the place four years before when the islands were occupied by the Northern army. "The house had a desolate appearance," wrote Miss Ames, "the windows gone, and shutters hanging by one hinge. Our trunks, box, and chairs were placed on the piazza and the army wagon was driven away. We looked at each other; our hearts were full, and if we could have seen any honorable way to escape and go home we certainly should have gone."[33] The front door was opened by a black man and woman, the latter having half a dozen children hanging to her skirt. The rooms were littered with sticks, broken plaster, and dirt. The Negroes had occupied the place since the owner left. The teachers selected two rooms and asked Uncle Jack and Aunt Phoebe if they would clean them up. There were no brooms, mops, or any conveniences for housecleaning. They gathered gray moss and wiped up the floors; then they threw buckets of cold water about, while the Negroes with their bare feet shuffled about over the moss, making the floors fairly clean. There were no beds; so the "Missionaries" slept on the floor.

[33] *Ibid.*, pp. 8-10.

An old Negro woman protested they were intruders and had no right in the house. The teachers explained that they were sent there by the United States Government and must stay. The old woman in her anger threw stones and bits of crockery into the windows and gave promise of starting an insurrection. A heavy rain and thunder storm brought temporary peace to the place, but the poor teachers found it impossible to sleep. Miss Ames bravely got out her hammer, which she held in her hand all night, determined to brain the first intruder. Next day, bright and early, they hung a large American flag out in front of the big house. This seemed to please the Negroes; they became more friendly. Jim and Sarah, with their six children, were living in the back part of the house.[34]

The Washington government obviously had no definite policy in the conduct of affairs at Port Royal. The situation was a very novel one, and the authorities were merely feeling their own way in the solution of problems as they arose. In time of war a conquered territory is usually handled in a routine military manner, but here were nearly twenty thousand slaves, round whom there had gathered much sentiment, dumped suddenly into the lap of the army, Treasury Department, or some other governmental agency, nobody knew what. As previously stated, General T. W. Sherman, who was first upon the field, planned to conduct the plantations by placing "agents" in charge who would gather the matured crop for the government. The next step was the appointment by the Treasury Department of Edward L. Pierce, who gathered about him a hundred or more teachers and plantation superintendents with a very ambitious program of rehabilitation and teaching. The three groups constantly stepping upon each other's toes were the military authorities, the Treasury Department's appointee, and the numerous assistants, commissioned by the various Freedmen's Aid Societies. Pierce with his collaborators had been in the South less than two months when the conduct of affairs in the islands was taken from the Treasury Department and placed in the hands of the War Department. On April 29, 1862, Brigadier General Rufus Saxton was placed in charge with authority "to take possession of all the plantations heretofore occupied by the

[34] *Ibid.*, pp. 12 ff.

rebels. . . ."[85] Pierce then resigned his position as special agent. General Saxton's appointment was pleasing to all the teachers and superintendents, who found in him a sympathy and understanding which was a great asset in the prosecution of their tasks. Nearly all the correspondence of the period refers to General Saxton in favorable terms. He visited their schools, spoke at their celebrations, and joined heartily in the jubilations which marked the early days of occupation.

In the *First Annual Report* of the Educational Commission we find the situation described thus:

> General Saxton was so well satisfied with the teachers and superintendents appointed by the Commission, and by the Societies of New York and Philadelphia, that he made a special request for more from the same sources, and declined to accept any who were not accredited to him by these associations. At his request, the additional superintendents were sent out in July, and others have since been chosen, making in all a total of seventy-two sent to Port Royal by this Committee.[86]
>
> The teachers were settled as soon as possible occupying the deserted mansions of their former owners, and began the work of reorganization of labor under new auspices, the establishment of schools, and the introduction of a new and better way of life for those under their charge.[87]

The teachers very soon learned that education administered in the usual way would be of little help to the Negroes. They continued, however, to "hold school." The Commission also made the amazing statement that "Each superintendent had the charge of from one to five plantations, according to their location, and the number of blacks upon them." And there was assigned to each superintendent the equally impossible task of caring for "from two to five hundred negroes, who looked to him for instruction and direction, at all times, and in every department of their duties."[88] Such confidence in their ability could be possessed only by theorists whose dreams outran the facts, especially when one considers these men had absolutely no knowledge of plantation management in a semitropical climate, of cotton culture, or of Negroes. But the adventure was

---

[85] Pearson, *op. cit.*, p. 48.
[86] Educational Commission for Freedmen, *First Annual Report* (1863), p. 14.
[87] *Ibid.*, p. 11. [88] *Ibid.*, p. 12.

great although it turned out to be but the abortive culmination of an otherwise worthy antislavery movement.

The sporting element in the adventure is evidenced in much of the contemporary correspondence. A young Harvard graduate wrote from the Coffin's Point plantation, whose big house still looks serenely out over St. Helena Sound:

> It is the largest plantation on the islands, numbering in its full days over 250 hands, or head as the negroes call themselves.
>
> A large amount of cotton is still in store here, for which the boat I hope will call this week; meanwhile the cotton-agent and a guard occupy the house, with us. The former has been on the place three or four months in charge of a large district with several plantations; he is a smart young fellow, very dashing and jockey-like. We were received by the guard with shouldered arms and by this agent, who did their best to induce or rather bluff us into leaving the premises and taking possession of another house; for we have two plantations besides this, estates belonging to William Fripp's sons.[39]

A young superintendent wrote, "Several men have been acting badly too; I actually knocked a man down the other day,—and I think I did right,—for the first time in my life."[40] Another young graduate of Harvard, acting as superintendent on the Oliver Fripp plantation, declared: "On the whole, affairs conduct themselves pretty quietly and regularly. The cases of discipline are the most vexing and amusing. It is a peculiar experience to be detective, policeman, judge, jury, and jailer,—all at once,—sometimes in cases of assault and battery, and general plantation squows [sic],—then in a divorce case,—last Sunday in a whiskey-selling affair; a calf murder is still on the docket."[41] Philbrick related a semihumorous experience with a grievance committee of Negro women who were dissatisfied with their pay. The spokesman for the committee was an old woman named Grace:

> I'se come to you, sir,—pause,—I'se been working fer owner three years, and made with my chillun two bales cotton last year, two more this year. I'se a flatfooted pusson and don't know much, but I knows those two bales cotton fetch 'nough money, and I don't see what I'se got fer 'em. When I take my leetle bit money and go to store, buy cloth, find it so dear, dear Jesus!—the money all gone and leave chillun naked. Some people go out yonder and plant

[39] Pearson, *op. cit.*, pp. 11 f.
[40] *Ibid.*, p. 138.   [41] *Ibid.*, p. 70.

cotton for theyself. Now they get big pile of money for they cotton, and leave we people 'way back. That's what I'se lookin on, Marsa. Then when I come here for buy 'lasses, when Massa Charlie sell he sell good 'lasses, then when Mister W. sell he stick *water* in 'em, *water enough*. Molasses turn thin, but he charge big price for 'em. Now I'se done working for such 'greement. I'se done, sir. Where upon chorus of women join in like a flock of blackbirds all talking at once.[42]

The Port Royal correspondence reveals a gradual decrease of enthusiasm after a few years on the part of the superintendents and an admission of their inability to cope with the difficulties. They often attributed their failures to the lack of character of the Negroes. One superintendent wrote in 1864:

The untrustworthiness of these people is more apparent and troublesome than ever. I feel as if it would not be safe to allow them to gin the cotton—it seems certain that a great deal of it would be stolen. Their skill in lying, their great reticence, their habit of shielding one another (generally by silence), their invariable habit of taking a rod when you, after much persuasion, have been induced to grant an inch, their assumed innocence and ignorance of the simplest rules of *meum* and *tuum*, joined with amazing impudence in making claims,—these are the traits which try us continually in our dealings with them, and sometimes almost make us despair of their improvement—at least in the present generation. It is certain that their freedom has been too easy for them,—they have not had a hard enough time of it. In many cases they have been "fair spoiled."[43]

The Negroes were a constant puzzle to the Northerners and often tried their patience. Indeed, it appears that the Southern planter was far more patient, because he understood the Negro, than were the friends from the North. A frustrated superintendent wrote in 1863 as follows:

Although the statement seems absurd, I must nevertheless affirm, that it is more bother to take care of a plantation of one hundred and twenty working hands than it is to exercise that number in the "School of the Company," and that the satisfaction derived from the faithfulness of honesty of perhaps thirty is hardly sufficient to atone for the anxiety and distrust with which one regards the remaining ninety, who lie by habit and steal on the least provocation, who take infinite pain to be lazy and shirk, who tell tales of others, of which themselves are the true subjects, and from whom all the artifices of

[42] *Ibid.*, p. 303.   [43] *Ibid.*, p. 287.

THUNDER OVER PORT ROYAL 301

the lawyer cannot draw fair statement of fact, even when it is obviously for their own interest to tell the whole truth. "Wherefore he is called the everlasting Niggah."[44]

The troubles of the military authorities and those assigned to Negro relief were many times multiplied by the influx of Negroes who flocked to the Port Royal area that they might be within Federal lines. Doubtless many came out of sheer curiosity, having heard of the invasion and of their liberators. A large number was "rescued" from outside plantations by soldiers. In May and June, 1863, General Montgomery made several raids upon plantations up the Combahee and Ashepoo rivers for Negroes who apparently wanted to come within the Federal lines.[45] Northern writers imply that these were rescue parties. This is hardly a fair statement of the case, for in many instances the Negroes were quite content to stay on the plantations where they had been born and reared. Their masters were fighting in the Confederate armies, and they had a rather free hand on the plantations. Their sympathy for the Southern white people in this time of stress is a lasting tribute to their generous nature and forgiving spirit. Doubtless a considerable number of Negroes who loved adventure and who were stimulated with promises of free land and political preferment by the invaders, grasped the opportunity to follow their liberators. It must be remembered also that these "rescue parties" had an eye to recruiting Negroes for the Union Army, and their zeal was fired with the happy prospect of Negro regiments. This, above all else, the freedman deplored. He was not a soldier but a good-natured lover of peace. The military authorities undertook to house and feed the hordes which had flocked into the district. They constructed "quarters" for many; others slept in barns and even in the open where shelter could not be provided. The houses, as described by a Northerner, were like huge wooden boxes. These square structures contained four rooms or compartments, and in each room was a large fireplace, windows with board shutters and bunks built along the wall. A rude bench or two and a pine table constituted the furniture. Characteristic of the utensils found in these houses were homemade piggins, or buckets from native cedar. Gourds and tin dippers were used as drinking cups.[46] As the war con-

[44] *Ibid.*, p. 237.   [45] Botume, *op. cit.*, p. 51.   [46] *Ibid.*, pp. 51 ff.

tinued, the difficulties of many increased, and when, near its close, William Tecumseh Sherman came with his devastating army through Georgia and South Carolina, gathering scores of idolizing Negroes at every mile, uncounted numbers were dumped in and round Port Royal to be cared for by the authorities. The suffering among the Negroes must have been great and the task before the authorities an impossible one. The Negroes who joined Sherman on the march, Brigadier A. S. Williams described in an official report:

Negroes of all ages and every variety of physical condition, from the infant in its mother's arms to the decrepit old man, joined the column,—from plantation and from cross-roads, singly and in large groups, on foot, on horseback, and in every description of vehicle. The vehicles were discarded as obstructing the progress of our very long column. Beyond this no effort was made to drive away the fugitives. The decrepit, the aged, and the feeble were told of the long journey before them and advised to remain behind.

I estimated that from six to eight thousand slaves, at different points in the campaign, joined the march of this corps, of whom something over two thousand five hundred reached our camp before Savannah.[47]

Of the numbers of Negroes who drifted southward with Sherman, General H. W. Slocum, commanding the left wing of the army of Georgia, reported:

Negro men, women and children joined the columns at every mile of our march, many of them bringing horses and mules, which they cheerfully turned over to the quartermaster's department. I think at least fourteen thousand of these people joined the two columns at different points on the march; but many of them were too old and infirm, and others too young, to endure the fatigue of the march, and were left in the rear. More than one-half of this number, however, reached the coast with us. Many of the able-bodied men were transferred to the officers and the subsistence department, and others were employed in the corps, as teamsters, cooks, and servants.[48]

A letter from Port Royal reveals the extent of suffering among the Negroes and the great task the invaders faced in caring for them:

[47] *Ibid.*, pp. 79 f.   [48] *Ibid.*, p. 79.

But now hundreds and thousands are coming in, shivering, hungry, so lean and bony and sickly that one wonders to what race they belong. Old men of seventy and children of seven years have kept pace with Sherman's advance, some of them for two months and over, from the interior of Georgia; of course little or nothing could be brought but the clothing on their backs and the young children in arms. Since their arrival in comparatively comfortable quarters, great sickness has prevailed, and numbers and numbers have died. The Government gives them rations, and has tried to give them clothing.[49]

Laura M. Towne, an outstanding teacher and one of the founders of the Penn School on St. Helena Island, lived amid the sufferings of the Negro refugees. In another letter written from Port Royal, we read as follows:

Miss Towne gave us quite an interesting account of the Georgia refugees that have been sent to the Village. The hardships they underwent to march with the army are fearful, and the children often gave out and were left by their mothers exhausted and dying by the roadside and in the fields. Some even put their children to death, they were such a drag upon them, till our soldiers, becoming furious at their barbarous cruelty, hung two women on the spot. In contrast to such selfishness, she told us of one woman who had twelve small children—she carried one and her husband another, and for fear she should lose the others she tied them all together by the hands and brought them all off safely, a march of hundreds of miles. The men have all been put to work in the quartermaster's department or have gone into the army, and the families are being distributed where they can find places for them.[50]

Another factor which added to the confusion and hindered the work of rehabilitation as planned by the Freedmen's Aid Societies was the series of false hopes held out to the Negroes. There was much wild talk about citizenship and elevation to power and influence as though these things could be given rather than achieved. Many false dreams were whispered into the ears of the Negroes, such as free land, proprietorship, and even a large Negro territory. The *Freedmen's Record*, of Boston, carried in its columns of May, 1866, the information that "It was the intention of General Sherman to give the island [Edisto] entirely to the blacks, that they might fairly work

[49] Pearson, *op. cit.*, pp. 307 f.
[50] *Ibid.*, pp. 293 f.

out their destiny. But in the course of reconstruction, the former owners have claimed their lands; and the colored population have for months been in a constant state of anxiety as to the final disposition of their little homesteads."[51] On May 9, 1862, only six months after the occupation of Port Royal, Major General Hunter, commanding the Department of the South, declared all slaves in South Carolina, Georgia, and Florida to be free. This brought added difficulties to the superintendents, who were already beset with the difficulties of plantation management and the problems presented by Negroes, who were bent on a great holiday. The order was nullified by President Lincoln on May 19. It was easy enough to make ambitious and attractive plans in Boston and Philadelphia under the stimulus of idealistic oratory and the fever of abolition enthusiasm, but to put these plans into effect among thousands of semibarbarians, who hardly knew their right hand from their left, was a realistic task, the magnitude of which they did not comprehend. Furthermore, the superintendents were living in a hostile country and spoke the language of enmity with the words "rebel" and "secesh" often on their tongues. They came to chastise and to put righteousness in the place of wickedness, but they came with a sword. Confusion among themselves and resentment on the part of the Southerners were inevitable results, and the Negro, as usual, paid the price. It was further evidence of the truth that war never settles anything. Emancipation was achieved, but suspicion and race antagonism followed in its train. There surely was a better way out. Slavery was doomed and would have passed anyway; and had it passed without resort to arms, many of the amiable relationships which had hitherto existed between white and black would have remained today.

The harsh aspect of the war is seen in the pitiable plight of the planters as they straggled back to view their homes now possessed by others. A correspondent of the New York *Nation*, writing in 1865, described Dr. Clarence Fripp, of St. Helena Island, as he talked to a group of Northern soldiers and traders in a little hotel at Hilton Head: ". . . a person who had the easily distinguishable appearance and manners of a South Carolinian. This gentleman, a person of some fifty odd years old, dressed tolerably well in a suit of grey clothes, with a large

---

[51] *The Freedmen's Record* (Boston, May 1866), p. 90. A pamphlet.

NEGRO CHURCH, EDISTO ISLAND

I LOOK DOWN DE ROAD AND DE ROAD SO LONESOME

display of crumpled linen at the collar and cuffs of his coat, sat before the stove smoking, and talking very freely about his present poverty and his plans for the future. . . ." After explaining that he had left St. Helena when Du Pont forced an entrance, leaving his plate and furniture behind, and that his plantation had been sold, Dr. Fripp set forth the situation in which he now found himself: ". . . some Massachusetts man bought it, and he didn't know when he'd get it back. Up in Greenville he soon spent all his money to support his family, but if he'd had money he couldn't have saved his property. How was he to come back inside the Yankee lines and pay the tax? The Commissioners knew very well it couldn't be done; the sale was a perfectly unfair thing. . . ." In coming back to Beaufort, he said: "He hoped to be able to pick up a little medical practice; but if his profession failed him, he supposed his son and himself could put up a cabin somewhere in the vicinity and get fish and oysters enough to live on. . . ." He even talked of circulating a handbill at Greenville asking for money for his needs, and the correspondent added: "This gentleman, it is currently reported, has made several visits to the plantation which he formerly owned, and the negroes living there have collected for his use nearly a hundred dollars."[52] Another case in point is that of Dr. Cowan Hazel. After his plantation had been sold to Negroes by the United States Government, he returned to St. Helena Island to resume his practice among the Negroes and the few white people who had returned.

Getting a small stock of drugs on credit to use in conjunction with his practice, he started life anew. . . . The whites had no money to employ a physician, so that his principal business was among the colored people, a people who have the science of credit and nonpayment of bills reduced to a fine point. He would be called out on a cold night to ride a mule ten miles or more to find his colored patient sick with a slight attack of colic;—his fee a promise to pay in a month—and the month never came,—as his reward. As a boy growing up with slaves on his plantation he was ever trustful and indulgent, and he never refused them the credit they asked. They reciprocated the fondness, but never paid the bill.[53]

As planters returned to their former estates, they were variously described: "Secesh are coming back quite freely nowadays and

[52] "The South as It Is," *Nation*, I, 682 (Nov. 30, 1865).
[53] Mikell, *op. cit.*, p. 251.

looking about as much as they please. Old Ben and young Ben Chaplin, several of the Pritchards and Captain Williams, that owned a plantation on Ladies Island."[54] From another letter:

> Julian Coffin has visited Mr. Soule, etc., asking leave to go into his old room, to take some of his father's old books, and left after a few hours, since which none of us have heard any thing further of them.[55] Nearly all the Secesh are back in Beaufort, confidently expecting that they will get their land back in season to plant next year.[56]

From Edisto Island, Mary Ames wrote: "During the winter and spring, planters were coming and going to arrange with the government representative for their repossession. Many of them were gentlemen, who came into our school and whom we entertained at our table, but when they were in possession and were joined by their families, it was different. The women ignored us."[57]

The late James Henry Rice, of Chee-ha plantation, expressed the Southern viewpoint: "Former slaves were organized and armed and for a time they left the plantations. There was an orgy of stealing and thousands of acres of land are still held by descendants of white scalawags, for which not a dollar was ever paid."[58]

Thus the thunder over Port Royal in November, 1861, was ominous and pregnant with meaning. It not only marked the beginning of a significant social experiment which was to last for four years, but it proclaimed the passing of a colorful society and the breakup of an economic order that vanished overnight. As one stands on the silent docks of Port Royal today and looks out upon its placid harbor, upon which no sail can be seen, it is difficult to realize that here men's hearts were once deeply stirred to hatred and antagonism. In contrast to such stirring memories is the gentle peace which has settled over the land. Quiet prevails everywhere. Wisps of blue smoke curl from Negro cabins scattered here and there over the flat fields. Picturesque black people of all ages walk the white shell roads

---

[54] Pearson, *op. cit.*, p. 311.
[55] *Ibid.*, p. 326.
[56] *Ibid.*, p. 314.
[57] Ames, *op. cit.*, pp. 122 f.
[58] Rice, *op. cit.*, p. 12.

leisurely, laughing. The peace of the ancient live oaks, bearded in moss, lends dignity and grace to the landscape. White sea gulls preen themselves upon the solitary docks or bask lazily along the sunny sand beaches—even the winds are gentle and sweet scented with the mellow odor of the marsh.

CHAPTER XIV

THE PORT ROYAL EXPERIMENT

> No mo' peck o' corn for me
> No mo', no more;
> No mo' peck o' corn for me
> Many t'ousand go.

THE IDEALS and purposes of the movement which came to be known in the North as the Port Royal Experiment were fostered mainly by the various Freedmen's Aid Societies, then growing rapidly among the abolition faction. The activities of these societies were generally viewed with favor by the Washington government. Military authorities at Port Royal, while less enthusiastic about abolitionist aims than the societies, gave their co-operation in a surprisingly generous way. The *First Annual Report* of the Educational Commission for Freedmen declared enthusiastically that "at the outset it was supposed that the most we should be called upon or allowed to do, would be to send a few missionaries and teachers to teach the rudiments of education, and while we then saw the great importance of organizing industry and bringing order out of the chaos at Port Royal, we little thought that means could be obtained, or authority granted by the Government to assume the entire charge of the agriculture, education, and to a certain extent, the religious teaching of the freedmen of Port Royal; but such has been the result. . . ."[1] Their work fell roughly into two main divisions, namely, the establishment of schools for the Negroes and the rehabilitation of the freedmen upon the plantations of their former masters. We shall look first at the educational picture. The report of *The American Freedman*, general organ for all the societies, stated in its issue for May, 1866, that the societies had sent into the South six hundred and thirteen teachers. Of all the states, South Carolina received the greatest number, one hundred and twenty-nine. Of these, Charleston received thirty-six and its neighboring islands, eight or ten. The

[1] Educational Commission for Freedmen, *First Annual Report* (1863), p. 3.

THE PORT ROYAL EXPERIMENT

remainder were scattered among the islands between Charleston and Port Royal.[2] The following table shows the location of schools by states and what societies sustained them:

	District Columbia	Maryland	Virginia	North Carolina	South Carolina	Georgia	Florida	Alabama	Mississippi	Louisiana	Tennessee	Kentucky	Missouri	Arkansas	Kansas	Illinois	Ohio	Totals by each Association
N. E. Branch	10	29	36	26	56	25	...	...	...	...	...	...	...	...	...	...	...	18
N. Y. Branch	14	6	48	52	61	5	27	...	...	2	...	...	...	...	...	...	...	21
Pa. Branch	16	...	17	...	9	...	...	3	...	...	...	14	...	...	...	...	...	5
Baltimore Branch	...	26	...	...	...	...	...	...	...	...	...	...	...	...	...	...	...	2
Cleveland Branch	...	...	...	...	1	...	3	...	...	...	...	...	...	...	...	...	...	4
Michigan Branch	...	...	...	...	1	...	...	...	...	...	...	...	...	1	2	...	...	4
N. W. Fr. Aid Comm	...	...	...	...	...	...	...	11	14	4	2	2	8	6	2	3	...	52
Indiana Fr. Aid Comm	...	...	...	...	...	...	...	...	...	9	...	...	...	...	...	...	...	9
Western Fr. Aid Comm	...	...	...	...	...	...	...	4	6	...	35	3	...	3	...	...	1	52
W. Pa. Fr. Aid Comm	...	...	...	...	...	...	...	7	...	...	5	...	...	...	...	...	...	12
Portland Fr. Aid Assoc	1	...	3	2	...	...	2	...	...	...	...	...	...	...	...	...	...	8
Total in each state	41	61	104	80	129	31	29	28	20	6	65	5	8	10	4	3	1	613

The one hundred and twenty-nine teachers sent to South Carolina were distributed as indicated below, with the sustaining society appearing opposite the location of the school and the number of teachers sent out. For example, St. Helena Island had five teachers supported by the Pennsylvania Branch, Beaufort had nine, seven of whom came from the New York Branch and two from the New England Branch.

SOUTH CAROLINA—129[3]

Ashdale	1	New York Branch	1
Beaufort	9	New York Branch	7
		New England Branch	2
Camden	2	New England Branch	2
Combahee	1	New York Branch	1
Charleston	36	New York Branch	13
		New England Branch	23
Columbia	10	New York Branch	10
Darlington	2	New England Branch	2
Edgerly	1	New York Branch	1

[2] *The American Freedman* (New York) I, 25 f. (May, 1866). This journal was the organ of the American Freedmen's and Union Commission.
[3] *Ibid.*

Edisto Island	7	New England Branch	7
Greenville	6	New York Branch	6
Georgetown	4	New York Branch	1
		New England Branch	3
Gadsden	2	New York Branch	2
Hilton Head	6	New England Branch	6
Hopkins	1	New York Branch	1
James Island	5	New York Branch	5
Jehossee's Island	2	New England Branch	2
John's Island	1	New England Branch	1
Mitchelville	2	New York Branch	2
Marion	2	New England Branch	2
Lexington	2	New York Branch	2
Orangeburg	3	New England Branch	3
Pineville	1	New York Branch	1
Perryclear	1	New York Branch	1
Pleasant Retreat	2	New York Branch	2
Port Royal Island	2	Pennsylvania Branch	2
Rockville (Wadmelaw)	2	Pennsylvania Branch	2
Red House	1	New York Branch	1
Rhett Place	2	New York Branch	2
River View	1	New York Branch	1
St. Helena Island	5	Pennsylvania Branch	5
Summerville	3	New England Branch	3
Woodlawn	1	New York Branch	1
Woodlawn	1	Michigan Branch	1
Woodlawn	1	Portland F. A. Com.	2

But what of the character of these six hundred teachers who swarmed southward? In spite of the slighting remark of Philbrick, quoted above, of the first contingent of which he was a member, that "a good many looked like broken-down schoolmasters or ministers who have excellent dispositions but not much talent," many of these men and women were well trained, young, and capable of doing excellent work. Among those who came to St. Helena Island to serve as teachers and plantation superintendents were graduates of Harvard, Yale, and Brown universities. Some were divinity students, some medical students, and others practicing physicians. Their salaries were, on the average, about forty dollars a month with subsistence.[4] They lived in the deserted homes of the planters and were rationed by the government, with the addition of what they produced on the plantations. Doubtless to many of them the mission south was something in the nature of a sporting adventure, and their letters give considerable evidence of this; but certainly they braved the hazards of an inhospitable summer

[4] G. G. Johnson, *A Social History of the Sea Islands*, p. 167.

climate and lived in a country and among a people almost totally strange to them. Some of them, like fair-weather friends, returned to their beloved New England and New York almost immediately. Others remained until after the war, and a few, like Laura M. Towne and Ellen Murray, of Pennsylvania, devoted their lives to the cause and lived and died among the Negroes. And today Penn School, which they founded, stands as a monument to their devotion and is perhaps the only thing of worth which came out of the Port Royal Experiment. On Edisto Island there are three graves bearing testimony to the sacrifices endured by the teachers of the freedmen. Ellen Kempton, a Miss Stanton, and J. B. Blake, who lived on the Mikell plantation, lost their lives in St. Pierre Creek when their boat capsized. Their own people in the North sent down stones to mark their graves.[5] The work of these teachers has been highly praised, and one would be base indeed who undertook to dim the glory of the high motives which actuated many of those who came south. But a candid appraisal of their success educationally as adduced from their own letters forces the conclusion that relatively little good was done by them. I shall in the main, however, let them speak for themselves, especially those who labored in the vicinity of Port Royal, St. Helena Island, and Edisto Island. Miss Elizabeth Botume, who came to the islands as late as 1864, found that the authorities had provided her with a schoolhouse built designedly for teaching "contraband" children. As a rule, the schools were conducted in churches, cotton barns, or kitchens. The house just mentioned was built of palmetto logs, with a side porch. There were a few rude wooden benches, and some of the windows were glazed. It was erected with funds sent to General Saxton from the ladies Freedmen's Aid Society of England. Its single room was equipped with a blackboard, which leaned against a post, a tall pine desk for the teacher, and a high office stool. There was a huge box stove provided, with the stovepipe projecting from the window. When the new teacher approached the school on the first day, she found the side porch full of chattering children. When they spied her, they all gave a whoop and a bound and disappeared from sight. She rang a small cracked bell that she found on the desk, and soon bright

[5] Ames, *op. cit.*, pp. 20, 106 f.

eyes began to peep in at the door. But when the children were approached, they went scampering under the house and elsewhere.

"Again I rang the bell," wrote Miss Botume, "with the same result, until I began to despair of getting my scholars together. When I turned my back they all came out. When I faced about, they all darted off. . . . Going toward half a dozen little fellows huddled together on one bench, they simultaneously darted down under the seat, and scampered off on their hands and feet to a corner of the room, looking very much like a family of frightened kittens. . . . All of these children were black as ink and shy as wild animals. . . . I had seen some of them before . . . but they all looked alike to me now."[6]

A comical incident occurred when the doctor came to school to vaccinate the children against smallpox. One girl was induced to come to the front and bare her arm, but when the doctor raised his lancet, it was too much for her. She ran screaming from the room, with the whole school following her. Such a reaction was quite normal, for the children were afraid of white people, especially strangers. Referring to a teacher of whom they were somewhat skeptical, one was heard to remark, "Us ain't know she." The doctor wisely decided to come back another day. By this time the children had overcome their worst fears and permitted the doctor to vaccinate them. In fact, after they were accustomed to it, some of the more ambitious boys, unaware of the pain that would follow, asked if they might have some of that "leetle stuff" put on their other arm, so proud were they of the bit of court plaster which each wore over his scar. Miss Botume had great difficulty in making up a roll of her pupils. They had but one name, but when they discovered the distinction of having a surname, each undertook on the spur of the moment to invent for himself a "title." One little girl upon cross-examination confessed her name to be "Nothing but Phyllis, ma'am." An older girl rebuked her thus: "Pshaw, gal! What's you'm title?" Whereupon she gave the name of her old master. Some of the combinations were very amusing: one little boy gave his name as Middleton Heywood (evidently Heyward); whereupon another boy yelled, "Not so, boy; you ain't Massa Middie's boy." "I is." In their search for names

[6] Botume, *op. cit.*, pp. 42 ff.

the boys gave many ridiculous ones, such as "Squash," "Pumpkin," and "Cornhouse." The girls were "Honey," "Baby," "Missy," and "Tay." To these they attached the old family names of the planters, Rhett, Barnwell, Elliott, Middleton, *et al.* Next morning, when the New England teacher called the roll, no one answered; they had forgotten their names of the day before. So the teacher had to make out a new roll. She remarked: "I could not distinguish one from another. They looked like so many peas in a pod. The wooly heads of the girls and boys looked just alike." Referring to further names, she added, "Amongst these were most of the months of the year and days of the week, besides a number of Pompeys, Cudjos, Sambos, and Rhinas, and Rosas and Floras. I wrote down forty new names and began to despair of ever getting regulated."[7] This teacher interestingly commented on her attempts to organize a school in the Negro refugee quarters. Sitting down on a hen-coop, she proceeded to take down the names of the children. The old colored woman, accompanying her, admonished the children to "scrape de foot and hab manners." These were the names given: Sambo, Silver, March, April, Cornhouse, Quash, Juno, another April, Phebe, Flora, Rose, Missy, Girly, Tant, June, November, Friday, Monday, Gumbo, and Jack.[8]

The Negro's ambition took many directions under the influence of the new education. They particularly desired the term "Mr." prefixed to their names. A New England teacher related that she "heard Joe tell Flora, 'Don't call me Joe again; my name is Mr. Jenkins.'"[9] The Port Royal teachers were daily surprised and perplexed by the attitudes of their pupils. Time meant nothing to them, and a schedule of any sort was beyond their comprehension:

Whilst the zeal of these people for learning never flagged they had no possible conception of time, or the fitness of things. Men, women, and children hurried to the schoolhouse at all hours and at most unseasonable times expecting to "catch a lesson." Reproof was unheeded, or not understood; "Us had something particular to do" was the invariable excuse. Finally I told the children to start for school as soon as they had eaten their breakfast. This had no effect.

[7] *Ibid.*, pp. 45 ff.   [8] *Ibid.*, p. 60.
[9] Pearson, *op. cit.*, p. 52.

I learned in time that breakfast, as we understand it, was to them an unknown term. They ate when they were hungry. Then I said, "Come as soon as you are up." The next morning I heard a low chattering and suppressed laughter and looking out of my window I saw the piazza was filled with black heads. An eager crowd was waiting for me. Every morning after that the whole "gang" came to escort me to school. Usually one bolder than the rest would come to the door and announce, "Us waiting on you, Ma'am." I soon began to feel that it was I who was under supervision and kept up to my duty, and not my poor neighbors.[10]

In this school they brought the babies along, even the tiniest creatures; but brought up under the law of the survival of the fittest, they required little care. When hungry, they ate a little cold hominy and went to sleep. "I have seen eight and ten of these little black creatures asleep on the piazza at a time," wrote Miss Botume. Then she added: "Our greatest trial was dogs. No colored man considered himself safe or even respectable, without one or more miserable looking curs. These always ran around after the children, and darted into the schoolroom whenever the door was open; then someone of the older people would call out, 'Drive out dat dog.'"[11] The Negroes old and young hungered for "larning." In late autumn, after the cotton had been picked and the potatoes banked and the "pinders" gathered, old as well as young people flocked to school. "Us wants book-larning, *too*, bad," they said again and again. "Us ain't know nothing, an' you is to larn we."[12] A man hurried to Miss Botume's school with the hope "to catch one or two lessons, for he was jes crazy for larn."[13]

"When we drove past the negro houses," wrote Miss Botume, "the men and women often came out with their books and begged us to give them lessons in reading, which we did, sitting in the wagon. They had a profound respect for education, and felt that if they could read they would come nearer to the white race, and could better compete with them; all of which was true."[14] "The copy-books were handed around for inspection," continued Miss Botume. "One woman having her child's book given her, showed it with great pride to those sitting near, declaring she was 'proud for mad' and 'glad for

---

[10] Botume, *op. cit.*, p. 68.
[11] *Ibid.*, pp. 94 f.
[12] *Ibid.*, p. 63.
[13] *Ibid.*
[14] *Ibid.*, p. 221.

mad,' that her child 'could larn for write like that.' Looking over her shoulder I saw she was showing the book 'bottom side up.' I turned it for her, when she said apologetically, 'Dem chillen know a heap more na me. When they come home, they talk so smart, I ain't know what they say, but I is proud all the same.' "[15]

The Northern teachers were constantly impressed with the politeness of the Negroes. When given anything, they invariably responded with the "curtsy," a lovely sort of acknowledgment characteristic of the Negro—not a bow, but a kind of bending of the knees, a slight dip of the body, together with an amiable expression of countenance. The children rarely spoke since they were exceedingly shy before strangers; but their exquisite good manners were exhibited in the "curtsy." A teacher from Pine Grove plantation, St. Helena, wrote: " 'Learning' with these people I find means a knowledge of medicine. And a person is valued accordingly. Flora wanted to know how much learning Miss Helen [Mrs. Philbrick] had, and it was a long time before I could make out what she meant."[16] Great curiosity in regard to the schools was shown by the Northerners residing in the Port Royal area: "Most of these were interested, but all were full of curiosity. I must confess, the ignorance of some of these visitors in regard to the condition of the contrabands was positively astounding. The questions asked of teachers and scholars were amusing and exasperating."[17] Even the generals came with their staffs, in full regalia, to visit the Port Royal schools. What must the children have thought of all this grandeur, and of their humble parents, all suddenly magnified. It must have been like a glorious dream, one brief ecstatic moment, all too soon to vanish. Miss Botume, speaking of General Saxton's visit, remarked that

> Promptly at three o'clock the general and his party came in sight. There were General Saxton and his staff officers, and General O. O. Howard and his staff. Brave men on horseback, and fair ladies in carriages, and I stood alone to greet them, with no school for them to see.

[15] *Ibid.*, p. 224.
[16] Pearson, *op. cit.*, p. 25.
[17] Botume, *op. cit.*, p. 107.

I begged the general to drive on to Old Fort, which was one of the points of interest, whilst one of the party went back to order forward the children. He met the whole gang hurrying alone. They had seen the general's party drive by, and concluded it was time for them to start. Something was to be done, and they must be on hand. Their nonchalance as they marched into the schoolroom was exasperating after all the time I had spent in anxious waiting. In less than ten minutes the room was full of scholars seated in order, with clean and shining faces and well-combed heads. Each child wore the wooden comb stuck on the top of the head like a top-knot, for ornament, and they evidently felt fine.

The variety and grotesqueness of their clothing defies description. No doubt each had assumed the best thing he could find, no matter to whom it belonged. Girls had on men's coats, some of which were so big they reached to the ground. Boys had entire suits made of bedticking and old horse blankets.[18]

Among the teachers on Edisto Island were Mary Ames and Emily Bliss, two attractive young women from Massachusetts. Mary Ames kept a diary while in the South, and in it we find many interesting side lights on her experiences as a teacher of "contrabands." These young ladies were sent to the Whaley plantation, on Edisto Island, and lived in the big house, which they shared with a Negro family. The Negroes had no bedding of any kind, but at night father and mother and six children stretched themselves on the floor before the fire to sleep. They ate their meals sitting on the floor of the front piazza. Possessing only one bowl, one plate, and one spoon, they took turns eating hominy or beans with a tiny bit of salt pork.[19] School was opened with fifteen "scholars," some "filthy and nearly naked. One or two knew their letters, but none could read." These gentlewomen, mere girls, unaccustomed to the rigors of a war-torn country, "dismissed early, as the children seemed tired, and we were decidedly weary."[20] At a later time their spirits rose, and they recorded enthusiastically that they had a hundred and forty "scholars" enrolled, with sixty or seventy in daily attendance. All were respectful and eager to learn. It was noticed that all the children and adults held their books sidewise. When asked why, a man answered, "We

---

[18] *Ibid.*, pp. 110 f.
[19] Ames, *op. cit.*, p. 27.
[20] *Ibid.*, p. 23.

THE PORT ROYAL EXPERIMENT 317

wish to learn to read on all sides."²¹ Another entry relates that "Nearly the whole school escorted us home today. We sat on the piazza, and dealt out needles, thread, combs and dresses from Mrs. Pillsbury's store."²² The young teachers were bothered with "intolerably hot days" and bad children. A hundred and one students were too many for the keeping of proper order. "I am well worn out before the afternoon," wrote Miss Ames, "with shouting and stamping, and I am obliged to help Emily when she gets into difficulty."²³ "The big boys are unruly," she added, "[but] Emily is a good singer, and when the school is too much for us, we start singing, and that calms them down."²⁴ One day a woman came to school with a prayer book, asking to be taught to read it. When the teachers explained that they would willingly teach her but that it would be a long time before she could learn to read such a book, she was satisfied, and upon leaving, "put her hand under her apron and brought out two eggs—one she put in Emily's lap, the other in mine."²⁵ In January smallpox broke out among the soldiers on Edisto Island. Many of the school children contracted the disease, and the school was closed for five weeks. In their desire to secure gifts of clothing from the teachers the infected children would ignorantly force themselves into their bedrooms.²⁶ The discouraged young women wrote:

A very warm morning. We find our half-mile walk to school tiresome. A large school, sixty-six scholars, and rather unruly. Poor Emily is not adapted to deal with rough boys. I am obliged to go to her aid and, stamping my feet and shouting my commands, bring them to order. We are teaching the children the days of the week, the months, and also to count.

When we feel tired we sing, which they all enjoy. They particularly delight in singing "Hang Jeff Davis to a Sour Apple Tree."²⁷

And homesick, she wrote, "Rain for two days. No children came, and we enjoyed the holiday. Heard a boat whistle, but the rain will prevent our sending the boys to camp for letters."²⁸ On another day, we find this entry:

²¹ Ibid., p. 25.
²² Ibid., p. 37.
²³ Ibid., pp. 57 f.
²⁴ Ibid., p. 39.
²⁵ Ibid., p. 31.
²⁶ Ibid., p. 12.
²⁷ Ibid., p. 29.
²⁸ Ibid., pp. 62 ff.

Eighty children and not enough room for them. We heard the alphabet classes and turned them out in the yard to play.[29]

When we made out the school report to send to Boston, we were surprised that out of the hundred, only three children knew their age, nor had they the slightest idea of it; one large boy told me he was "Three months old." The next day many of them brought pieces of wood or bits of paper with straight marks made on them to show how many years they had lived. One boy brought a family record written in a small book.[30]

In September, 1866, these inexperienced, romantic young women left the island and turned their faces toward their native Massachusetts. "The houses all about us," they wrote, "were occupied by Edisto families, who had taken possession of their own . . . we said goodby to Edisto and our negro friends."[31]

The quality of education on St. Helena Island seems to have been no better than that on Edisto and Port Royal. A young Harvard graduate wrote that they had five schools on Pine Grove plantation, teaching about one hundred and forty scholars.[32] From the same plantation another teacher explained that the school was held on the piazza as it saved a walk in the hot sun to the praise house; besides, the praise house was full of fleas.[33] After assembling the children at the praise house for school, an operation which was always attended with difficulty, one teacher complained that "Like as not, they have half of them to be sent back to wash their faces and hands. Asked the little children questions, such as, 'What are your eyes for?' 'For see long.' 'Teeth?' 'For chaw long,' etc."[34] On some of the St. Helena plantations a trusted Negro was sometimes allowed to assist in teaching. On the Smith plantation "The children were all assembled by Cuffy, and he was teaching them when we went in. Mr. G— read the Bible, substituting words that they could understand, made a very simple prayer, all kneeling, and then heard their words and letters for an hour, with a great deal of tact and ability."[35] A teacher on Coffin's Point plantation, owned by T. A. Coffin, tells of a Negro named Bacchus who helped with the schoolwork. Bacchus, a cripple, whose hands

[29] *Ibid.*, p. 69.
[30] *Ibid.*, p. 110.
[32] Pearson, *op. cit.*, p. 60.
[34] *Ibid.*, p. 36.
[31] *Ibid.*, p. 125.
[33] *Ibid.*, p. 35.
[35] *Ibid.*, p. 20.

THE PORT ROYAL EXPERIMENT

were turned backwards, had little control of his arms, but he was much respected by the children. "Mr. G. has made him a sort of school master," wrote Bacchus's teacher, "and he had always kept school when Mr. G. was away." Bacchus, when he became hungry, left his pupils, to go out and eat hominy; it was a custom, it seems, when anyone became hungry to go out and eat hominy. Having often seen the Union soldiers at drill and in military regalia, Bacchus decided that a little militarism would help the school; "so he marched up the thirty-five children, six or seven in a row, holding hands to keep them straight, and with two of the oldest boys for captains on each side to administer the raps with their sticks if they did not keep in line, walking backwards himself to oversee the whole company, with a soldier's cap on his head, and shouting out his orders for them to sing their different tunes all the way—the funniest spectacle himself imaginable."[36] This teacher upon returning from a vacation in New England, visited Bacchus's school. All complimented her, saying she looked "more hearty" than when she went away. Her visit was a success, for she "returned with two dozen eggs and the morning school at my heels."[37] Limus, a man of about fifty and a shrewd driver on one of the plantations, came to school almost every day to be taught. "He has a wife here and grown children," wrote his teacher, "and another on the other plantation, the rascal. He is very smart and learns well."[38]

The whole plan of education and rehabilitation in the Port Royal area was confused and distorted because of the constantly conflicting elements entering into the situation. To the Negroes were made vague promises, which their white friends could not keep, especially the promise of free land. Then there was the thought that they were the wards of a benevolent government, which was to set them on their feet. And, upon all those high hopes, occasioned by their release from the restraints of bondage and the prospect of ownership of the soil, fell military conscription like a bursting shell. The Negroes were scared out of their wits, and the plantation managers and teachers rose in arms against the military authorities because the draft was completely upsetting their well-ordered plans. The Negroes were kept in

[36] *Ibid.*, pp. 64 f.
[37] *Ibid.*, p. 121.
[38] *Ibid.*, p. 37.

constant dread of the conscription squad, and the appearance of a soldier on the plantation was the signal for the timid Negroes to take to the woods and marshes. Here they hid themselves until it appeared safe for them to return. Mention has already been made of the Negro regiment recruited by the dashing young Colonel Thomas Wentworth Higginson, of Massachusetts. This unit, known as the *First Regiment of South Carolina Volunteers*, was made up principally of Port Royal and Beaufort Negroes. The severity of measures used in the draft can hardly be disputed. Letters from the plantations bear certain testimony to the harshness of the soldiers as they rounded up Negro recruits. I doubt not that many a Port Royal Negro on more than one occasion prayed that he might be delivered from his friends. One Northerner wrote: "They are carrying out the draft with excessive severity, not to say horrible cruelty. Last night three men were shot,—one killed, one fatally wounded, it is thought, and the other disappeared over the boat side and has not been seen since. . . ."[39] Young Negro men were afraid to go to church, and they even refrained from attending services on the much-beloved baptism day. A little group was found with one of their number reading to them the New Testament. They were staying away from the church because they had heard that "soldiers had come to catch we."[40] At Fripp Point the soldiers "caught old Simon and Mike, a boy of about fifteen. . . . They got sixty men in all, most of them old, a waste of Uncle Sam's money. Of course our people here are warned and all off again."[41] A plantation manager on St. Helena lamented that "The holidays and the hunt for deserters have so broken up the labor that nothing of any consequence can be done now till after New Year's, when I hope the work will move on smoothly again."[42] A captain and a lieutenant with about fifty Negro soldiers came to Coffin's plantation to hunt for Negroes. The superintendent wrote: "They met no young men except Sancho and Josh, whom they chased into the marsh opposite Coffin nigger-house, and then shot Josh. He was taken with a bullet in his leg and a buckshot in his head. . . ."[43] From another letter we read: "There came a

---

[39] *Ibid.*, p. 253.
[40] *Ibid.*, p. 249.
[42] *Ibid.*, p. 240.
[41] *Ibid.*, p. 185.
[43] *Ibid.*, p. 188.

posse of men from the First South Carolina Regiment, without a white officer, to hunt after deserters on [t]his plantation. They met the men they wanted and shot them all three in broad daylight; one is badly wounded and may not recover, but the others probably will. After shooting one man they were going away to leave him, and Mr. Wells went and took care of him and sent him to the hospital."[44] After Negroes were conscripted and taken into the army, there was no certainty that they would stay. Many of them deserted and hid away about the plantations. A Port Royal letter reveals: "Primus has come home. He deserted about a week ago and has been all that time getting here.... One day they [soldiers] brought in fourteen, and the next day twelve of them had gone [deserted], and the next day the other two."[45] Of course, many of the freedmen made good soldiers and were loyal to the Union Army from the beginning to end.[46]

The greatest excitement during the Port Royal occupation grew out of the land sales. There were thousands of acres of abandoned lands in the area made vacant by the flight of the planters when the Federals came into Port Royal. In a little while practically all of this land was jeopardized because of the nonpayment of the Federal direct tax, recently imposed by the Washington government. Even if the planters in the Confederate Army had had the money to pay the taxes, they could hardly have made their way through the Union lines to do so; consequently, thousands of acres of land were sold for taxes. Some of the land was bought by individuals, but the greater part by the government. The disposition of these government lands became the bone of contention, over which the opposing forces wrangled. It was the desire of the government and the friends of the Negro in the North that these lands should go to the freedmen. Indeed, so sanguine were their hopes that some such goal might be attained that General W. T. Sherman, in his memorable march to the sea, upon reaching Savannah, was moved to issue his famous Field Order No. 15, in which he declared: "The islands from Charleston, south, the abandoned rice fields along the rivers for thirty miles back from the sea, and the country bordering the St. John's river, Florida, are

[44] *Ibid.*, p. 236.
[45] *Ibid.*, pp. 189 f.
[46] See Higginson, *op. cit.*, p. 273.

reserved and set apart for the settlement of the negroes...."[47] The history of the land sales in and about Beaufort is an interesting but intricate story. Indeed, its full presentation would require a treatise of considerable length; here I shall give but a brief outline of the principal events concerning those sales and then show from contemporary letters some of the more intimate and human aspects of the situation, especially how the proceedings affected the Negroes themselves. Laura J. Webster, in her monograph, *The Operation of the Freedmen's Bureau in South Carolina*, has written what is perhaps the best documentary account of the government's land transactions in this area. She has summarized the various acts of Congress by which the government took over the land as follows: first, the seizure and sale of lands on which the direct tax had not been paid; second, the seizure of property of all persons engaged in aiding "the rebellion"; third, the collection and sale by the treasury agents of abandoned property in the insurrectionary districts.[48] After the launching of the Freedmen's Bureau the lands seized by the government were disposed of as follows: "first, land sold or leased to Northerners and negroes by the United States tax commissioners; second, land held by the negroes in forty acre tracts for which they had possessory titles granted in accordance with Sherman's special field order; third, land occupied without authority by the negroes; fourth, land set aside by the tax commissioners, or 'school farms,' and fifth, unoccupied lands."[49] Interesting side lights on the government's action in regard to the abandoned lands about Port Royal, their confiscation and sale for taxes, are given in an address by Congressman William Elliott, of Beaufort, before the House of Representatives in Washington, in 1888.[50] In August, 1861, Congress passed an

[47] *Executive Documents*, 1st Session, 39th Congress, 1865-1866, No. 11, p. 10. This document, which is the *Report of the Commissioner of the Bureau of Refugees, Freedmen, and Abandoned Lands*, contains many valuable facts related to the final disposition of lands held by the Negroes, and the many difficulties the government experienced in making adjustments between the Negroes and the original owners.

[48] Laura Josephine Webster, *The Operation of the Freedmen's Bureau in South Carolina* (Northampton, Mass., 1916), p. 93.

[49] *Ibid.*, p. 9.

[50] *Congressional Record*, 50th Congress, 2d Session, Vol. XX, Part 3, Appendix 239. Other sources are, U. S. *Statutes at Large*, XIV, 507; 38th Congress, *An Act to Establish a Bureau for the Relief of Freedmen and Refugees, March 3, 1865*; U. S. *Statutes at Large*, XV, 173; 39th Congress

THE PORT ROYAL EXPERIMENT 323

act providing for the collection of a tax amounting to $20,000,-000, the amount to be apportioned among the several states, including those in insurrection. The money, of course, was to be used chiefly in the prosecution of the war. The amount apportioned to South Carolina was $363,570.67. The seceding states were naturally averse to paying out money that would be used for their own defeat and destruction. Besides, they had financial troubles of their own in supporting the Confederacy, which was in dire need of all the resources it could command. Consequently, no tax was paid by the Southern States for nearly a year. On June 7, 1862, Congress put teeth into its former law through a supplementary act designed to force the collection of these taxes in the insurrecting districts by demanding the tax direct from the land. Most of the Northern States paid it out of their state treasuries. Elliott wrote: "After the capture of Port Royal in 1861, and after the passage of the supplementary act for the collection of this tax in the insurrecting districts, some time in the year 1862, commissioners were appointed and sent into that section of the State, and as the result of their operations 110,000 acres of land in those parishes [St. Helena and St. Luke] and the entire town of Beaufort, consisting of some 500 lots containing valuable improvements, were sold."[51]

The commissioners sold land for taxes in five Southern states, viz., Virginia, Florida, Arkansas, Tennessee, and South Carolina, but only in South Carolina was it sold to individual purchasers.[52] In all other cases it was bought by the government.

A matter that concerned the Federal Government during the military occupation of Port Royal and vicinity was the securing of suitable lands for war, naval, military, revenue, charitable, educational, and police purposes. To this end a board of "selection" was appointed, consisting of two generals and the three direct-tax commissioners who were to select lands for the Government. The exact acreage and prices paid are a matter

---

1865-1867; an act to continue in force and to amend *"An Act to Establish a Bureau for the Relief of Freedmen and Refugees,"* and for other purposes; De Treville v. Smalls, 98 U. S. 513 and others.

[51] *Congressional Record,* 50th Congress, 2d Session, Vol. XX, Part 3, Appendix, p. 240.

[52] G. G. Johnson, *A Social History of the Sea Islands,* p. 183. For an excellent summary of the land sales see pp. 183-190.

of record in the published reports of the commissioners. Suffice it to give here the summary of Elliott:

> So the entire town [Beaufort] with the exceptions I have named, passed into the hands of the United States Government at a most insignificant cost, the entire property valued at over a half million dollars having been purchased for $17,512, or about one-thirtieth of its assessed valuation for taxation. They also selected for Government purposes over 39,000 acres of land, bidding it in at a nominal figure, the average price being 34 cents an acre; and also 19,000 other acres of land which they bid in at an average price of 56 cents an acre, all of this land having been worth in 1861 from $20.00 to $40.00 an acre.[53]

The inconsistencies and the tangled skein of affairs of the Beaufort land sales were further detailed by Elliott, who pointed out the striking features of the enforcement of this law in South Carolina:

> Harsh as they were, there may have been some compensation to the sufferers if the sacrifice of their property had brought relief to the rest of the State, but it was not so to be. This ancient town and these 110,000 acres, worth, at a reasonable valuation $2,500,000—these homes of an entire community—were all sacrificed to raise the pitiful sum of $11,855.
>
> Subsequently many plans for disposing of the Government property were carried out. In the year 1864, the Government, under the same act—the thirtieth section—resold much of the property, and thus gave to the soldiers and the sailors of the United States, many of whom were then in and around the town of Beaufort, special terms of purchase, to wit, one-fourth cash and the balance in three years. . . .
>
> By the amendment of 1866 to the Freedmen's Bureau Act, Congress further legislated relative to this matter, and directed that a large amount of the lands which were held by the government should be cut up into small parcels and sold to freedmen, who were not allowed to pay more than $1.50 per acre, and no person of any other race was allowed to purchase at any price. . . .[54]

Now looking at the picture from the viewpoint of a group who had, above all else, the well-being of the Negro at heart, namely, the New England Freedmen's Aid Society, one finds the following statement appearing in the second annual report

---

[53] *Congressional Record*, 50th Congress, 2d Session, Vol. XX, Part 3, Appendix, p. 241. [54] *Ibid.*

of the society (April 21, 1864). This particular section of the report dealt with the condition of the freedmen in the coastal area, and is, in part, as follows:

In March, 1863, the United States sold at auction 16,479 acres of land out of 76,775 acres subject to sale for non-payment for taxes. The lands, with the buildings, brought but 93⅓ cents per acre. About 3,500 acres were taken by the blacks. The number of acres now owned by the Freedmen is said to be not far from 7,350. More recently, at the sale of the town of Beaufort, from seventy-five to eighty houses and house lots were bought by the blacks, at prices ranging from $40 to $1,800. The aggregate paid for 64 of these was $32,927, and at this rate the lots purchased must have cost about $40,000.

On the 16th of September, 1863, instructions were issued to the United States Direct Tax Commissioners for the sale by auction of the 60,000 acres reserved at the sale in the spring. Of these remaining lands, 6,081 acres were to be reserved for school purposes, and 13,370 for "war, military, naval, revenue, and police purposes," leaving 40,845 acres to be sold; of which 24,316 acres were to be put up in lots not exceeding 320 acres, and 16,529 acres to be disposed of at private sale, to heads of families of the African race, in lots not exceeding 20 acres.

The announcement of the intended sale of 24,000 acres in large lots was received with great dissatisfaction by the friends of the Freedmen. Many thought the blacks had an exclusive claim to those lands which had so long been drenched with their sweat and blood, and nearly all saw with alarm the threatened revival of the old system of large proporietorships.[55]

Now let us take a brief glance at a few of the dispossessed planters in order to understand something of the attitudes being engendered toward the Negro. Can one imagine a situation which would breed more contempt and bitterness than to find aliens inhabiting one's property, even one's own house and home? And it must be remembered that, regardless of whose fault it was, the Negro, in the long run, had to pay the price exacted by the antagonism between the North and South. To this day racial antipathy in any section of the South is directly proportional to the degree of harshness of the Reconstruction devices imposed by the Northern conquerors. The white people

[55] New England Freedmen's Aid Society, *Second Annual Report* (April, 1864) (Boston, 1864), p. 15.

of the South have been much stricter with the Negro because of the near collapse of white culture and civilization, and especially is this true of the Deep South, where the Negroes far outnumber the whites. Many of the planters never returned, and did not wish to return, to their plantation houses. Many of them were too far advanced in life to adjust themselves adequately to the new social and economic status. A few, under the redemption act, regained part of their estates and returned sadly to rebuild the broken country. Dr. Clarence Fripp, of St. Helena, shortly after the close of the war secured from General Saxton a surgeon's contract to practice medicine on his native island. He took up his residence adjacent to his former home, which was at that time occupied by Miss Towne, ot Pennsylvania.[56] A part of the Corner Farm was redeemed by the heirs of Captain John Fripp, and five acres of the 400-acre estate of Mrs. Eliza H. Chaplin were repossessed by the former owner. Edgar W. Fripp redeemed only 732 acres of his 1,284-acre estate.[57] We read in a Port Royal letter written to New England: "Mr. Eustis and a Mr. Pritchard, living on Pritchard's Island, near Land's End, paid taxes before the sale."[58] In the case of Dr. Cowan W. Hazel, "His landed estate on St. Helena Island was sold to negroes by the United States Government the third year of the War Between States and never recovered by him, so that with the emancipation of the slaves, at the close of the War, he was left penniless, with none to whom he could turn to help to support his widowed sister and his superannuated father."[59]

A Mr. Philbrick, of Boston, a young plantation superintendent, a "missionary," and a land speculator, who bought eleven plantations at the forced sales, expressed the opposing viewpoint:

I have had a letter from Charleston written by a lawyer on behalf of Captain John Fripp and his three daughters! The writer says but little about his legal rights, but appeals to my "sense of justice and generosity," to see if some compromise can't be made. He doesn't say exactly what he wants, but intimates that both parties

---

[56] G. G. Johnson, *A Social History of the Sea Islands*, p. 194.

[57] *Ibid.*, p. 195. (Direct Tax Case, No. 17, 498 filed in Court of Claims March 25, 1892: No. 17, 366 filed Feb. 6, 1892.)

[58] Pearson, *op. cit.*, p. 171.   [59] Mikell, *op. cit.*, pp. 250 f.

could profit by such an arrangement and save the vexations of a law suit. I don't see exactly what he has got to give, except his old title, which he probably values a good deal higher than I do. I wrote him telling him I was hampered in acts of "generosity" by the fact that the present title was not in me alone, but that about a dozen other gentlemen were interested and asked him to make us a definite proposition.[60]

The opprobrious terms *carpetbagger* and *scalawag* did not spring from the overactive imagination of a distraught people. These persons actually existed in the flesh. Elizabeth Botume, commented: "I must confess 'carpet-baggers' sprang up in this vicinity like caterpillars over the growing cotton-fields. The poor contrabands might well exclaim, 'Save me from my friends, and I will take care of the enemy!'" And again, "A great many speculators were flocking into the department, to buy and lease the old plantations." Of their deceptive practices and efforts to fleece the Negroes she wrote:

A swarm of speculators hung about the freed people, to get away their lands. They used various means, chief of which was bad whiskey, treating the poor men to get them to give up their deeds, and treating them to clinch the bargain. No lands could be bought at this time excepting by colored people who were the heads of families, so the speculators contrived many ways to keep possession. They held the deeds "in trust," and "for safe keeping," and "as guaranty for payment of some debt."[61]

In the midst of the greedy activities of the economic vultures the government and "missionaries" earnestly tried to protect the Negro in the purchase of land. The greatest boon that came his way was the provision which enabled him to preempt certain lands for future purchase. He had the rare privilege of marking off twenty or forty acres of land, renting it for a few years, then buying it from the government at the ridiculously low figure of $1.25 an acre. What joy there must have been among these black people as they walked around over the familiar fields on which they had sweated as slaves to mark out their plots with small stakes. Surely, to them, the year of Jubilee had come, and they must have had great visions of operating large plantations as their masters had done. I do not

[60] Pearson, *op. cit.*, p. 316.
[61] Botume, *op. cit.*, pp. 220, 230, 259.

believe the Southern people, generally, condemned them in their high hopes of owning a little land. Certainly no reasonable man would do so today. Great rejoicing was everywhere. One Northern correspondent in a moment of enthusiastic approval indulged himself in the following *obiter dictum:* "Still it is the beginning of a great thing, negroes become land owners, and the door is thrown open to Northern immigration." But after the war the North apparently lost interest in the Port Royal Experiment, and her sons and daughters did not go thither on business ventures or humanitarian missions. Northern men are as scarce in the Black Border of South Carolina today as Puritans are in Boston. The prophecy of Northern immigration did not come true. The Negroes were properly advised by the Northern friends to pre-empt land and secure its possession. Philbrick wrote that on Sunday morning, at the church, after Parson Phillips had opened the services, "Mr. French followed, urging them to go ahead at once and locate their lots. General Saxton followed, saying but little, but urging them not to sleep till they had staked out their claims."[62] Again, he described a church meeting, in a letter dated January 20, 1864:

> Then a paymaster made a spread-eagle speech. Then Colonel Ellwell was called out by Mr. French. Then Judge Smith mounted the pulpit and explained to the negroes the meaning of preemption, how it was formed of two Latin words. Colonel Ellwell contrived to mystify the people a little as follows. After expatiating on the goodness of President Lincoln, he said he was so kind he had even offered pardon to the rebels, and perhaps we should see their old masters back here some day, with a whole country of scoundrels to swear they had always been loyal Union men, etc. The whole fandango lasted till nearly three o'clock and then we had the usual amount of shaking of hands, etc., outside.[63]

A government superintendent of freedmen, Reuben Tomlinson, of St. Helena Island and Ladies Island, wrote for the *Philadelphia Press* in April, 1864, a valuable account of the way the Negroes received the pre-emption privileges and of their success as independent farmers after the land had been acquired:

[62] Pearson, *op. cit.*, p. 244.   [63] *Ibid.*, pp. 244 f.

THE PORT ROYAL EXPERIMENT 329

When the "instructions" authorizing the "preemption" of land came down here, over eight thousand dollars were at once deposited, with parties appointed to receive it, by the colored people. This, of course, did not take in anything like all the money that would have been forthcoming had the people felt sure that by so doing they would have secured the land. They had been deceived too often, and, to use their own phrase, they "couldn't trust." At the sale of the town of Beaufort, a short time ago, a large proportion of the purchases were made by colored men, many of them paying the whole amount down, while others bought with soldiers' privilege, one-fourth down.[64]

Regarding their progress as farmers under the new regime, he wrote:

Last year four plantations were purchased and worked by the Freedmen for themselves. The "Reynolds" place produced over four thousand dollars worth of cotton, besides a plentiful provision crop. After paying all their expenses, the people on this place have a very handsome balance to commence the year with. The "James Fripp" place did proportionately as well, but I cannot trust my memory to give exact figures, and cannot get them in time for the steamer. I know that no person on the place received less than fifty dollars as his share, while most of the shares ran over one hundred dollars, and some as high as two hundred dollars. This, also, besides a large provision crop. The "Inlet" place, owned and worked by Harry McMillan, produced thirteen hundred and fifty-eight dollars worth of ginned cotton. The bulk of this cotton was raised by the labor of Harry, his wife, and two daughters, with the aid of a mule and plough. Harry pays for his plantation, buys necessary stock, including cotton gins, &c., and has left a handsome balance to [resume] the year with. . . .

Thus for those that worked for themselves. Now for those that worked for other people. Anthony and Venus, laborers on the "Capt. John Fripp [sic] Corner" place, St. Helena, received $194.80 exclusive of their provision crop. Anthony is over sixty, and Venus over seventy years old. Frank and two daughters, girls of sixteen and eighteen years, of the same place, received $184.55. Cato, wife and daughter, of the "Robert Fulton" place, received $180.00. The following amounts were received by persons on the "Coffin Point" place; Aaron and Judy, $136.48; Abel and family, $210.57; Amaretta and family, $335.24; Leah and Peter, $99.38; Hackliss and Phillis, $175.32; Frank and family, $181.93; George

[64] New England Freedmen's Aid Society, *Second Annual Report* (1864), p. 67.

and family, $174.60; Miller and family, $188.67. There are several other families receiving amounts ranging from $50.00 to $100.00.[65]

One of the most interesting characters connected with the coastal experiment was E. S. Philbrick, whose name has been frequently mentioned in this book. He was a strange combination of patriot, astute businessman, speculator, and humanitarian. When the call came for superintendents and teachers for the Carolina islands under the direction of Special Agent Edward L. Pierce, Philbrick was among the first to volunteer. Not only did he go without pay, but he made a contribution of one thousand dollars for the cause. He became the leader, among the laymen, in the Port Royal Experiment. His land deals were roundly condemned by some of his contemporaries and valiantly championed by others. He formed a corporation of fourteen men, all but one from Boston, which furnished the money for the eleven plantations purchased. "I got a letter," he wrote, "from Mr. Forbes who says he can raise the $12,000 for land, etc., to put in my hands, with the understanding that when I get tired of managing the thing, I shall close up and divide what shall be left. So I shall certainly buy that end of the island provided the lands are sold, which in Boston they feel very sure they will *not* be, and provided nobody else bids over one dollar an acre or so."[66]

One of Philbrick's plantation superintendents, writing of land sales, explained that on one "island two thirds were bidden in by the Government.... The other third was bought by Mr. Philbrick and two or three sutlers."[67] Another, speaking of Philbrick's purchases, remarked that the plantations were bought for "about $7000.00: three places for R., two for Wells; two for Hull on Ladies Island, six places within five miles of this place. I remain here, and shall probably assume Cherry Hill and Mulberry Hill, my old places; G. comes to Pine Grove, and takes that, the Point and Captain John Fripp Homestead."[68]

The question of the validity of titles naturally arose when the purchase of distress lands was contemplated. On this point

[65] *Ibid.*, p. 66.
[67] *Ibid.*, p. 177.
[66] Pearson, *op. cit.*, pp. 140 f.
[68] *Ibid.*, p. 172.

THE PORT ROYAL EXPERIMENT 331

the astute Philbrick wrote on January 2, 1863: "As to the title, the right of redemption expires at the end of two years in all cases, and fifteen per cent. interest must be paid by the redeemer before he can take possession. Now I never thought of paying more for these lands than the net value of two good crops, and don't undertake it for the sake of making money at all, but for the sake of carrying out a more satisfactory issue the present short-lived and unfairly judged experiment of free labor, and for the sake of keeping the people out of the hands of bad men."[69] Evidently the question of the wisdom of revealing to the public the extent of the Philbrick land deals arose among his superintendents. Writing to one of his employees, Philbrick declared: "I don't agree with you about avoiding publicity for our enterprise. I hold that the pecuniary success we are likely to meet with is the very best reason why the whole thing should be made public, for it is the only sort of success which can make our enterprise a permanent thing and take it off the hands of philanthropic benevolence, which, though well enough for a spurt, can never be relied on to civilize the four millions of darkies likely to be on our hands."[70] Not only were the buyers of land chafing under the criticisms from their Northern friends who charged that their philanthropic efforts were becoming degraded, but the news of the cheap lands they were buying whetted the appetites of economic adventurers who were now eager to move southward. A superintendent wrote: "Did you know we had long ceased to be philanthropists or even Gideonites? We are nothing now but speculators, and the righteous rail against us. A great crowd of our brethren have just come down to be present at the late sales. Mr. Philbrick and the purchasers of last spring paid about $1.00 or $1.25 per acre; now prices run from $5.00 to $27.00 per acre. There has been the most disgraceful squabbling among the tax commissioners, General Saxton, Rev. Mr. French, and other authorities. The people are the victims."[71]

The year 1862 was a good one for Philbrick. "The cotton crop," he explained, "will be worth, on this and Ladies Island, about $40,000. I have stored twenty-five thousand pounds stone cotton on my plantations which will be worth at least

[69] *Ibid.*, p. 135.
[70] *Ibid.*, p. 20.   [71] *Ibid.*, p. 254.

$4000."[72] Philbrick was generous enough to help those who had helped him. One wrote: "Mr. Philbrick has very generously offered to assist three or four of us poorer superintendents in buying plantations. If we do not buy, the occupation of most of us is probably gone."[73] The Edgerly plantation, on Port Royal Island, was bought for Negroes by the Reverend Dr. Peck. An interesting letter to the *Freedmen's Advocate,* New York, written March 22, 1864, reveals something of the way in which Negroes handled the lands they purchased or paid for in part. Excerpts from the letter follow:

> Having had a few days rest among home friends, I sit down to fulfill the promise made to you to give some account of the Edgerly Plantation of Port Royal Island, upon which I have resided, as a teacher, for the last seventeen months. I could relate much that would be interesting connected with the place, during the spring and summer of 1862, when I spent a few weeks there; but I wish more particularly to speak of the last year, during which time the people have been working for themselves.
>
> Last March (1863) the plantation, containing about 800 acres, was sold, and bought for them by the Rev. Dr. Peck, at the request of the people of Edgerly and those of the adjoining "Red House" plantation. They raised what money they could, (about $500), and the Doctor generously advanced the rest, which was repaid as soon as they received what was due them from the Government. If I remember rightly, the cost of the place was $710. . . .
>
> On Edgerly the purchasers comprised thirteen or fourteen families; the able bodied men being in the army or service of the quartermaster, so that the labor had devolved largely upon the females. . . .
>
> They had early vegetables of all kinds to eat and sell; large numbers of melons in their season; potatoes, corn, and rice enough to furnish them with food during the ensuing year. Besides this, they raised upward of 1,200 pounds of ginned cotton of the best quality. All this was done with the aid of a mule part of the time, the greater part being done with the hoe. They had no superintendent or overseer, one of their own number being called a foreman, having oversight only of what was owned in common. They worked their crops separately. . . .
>
> Our school comprises the children and youth of the two places of which I have spoken, and of three other plantations. Their prog-

[72] *Ibid.,* p. 109. [73] *Ibid.,* p. 137.

THE PORT ROYAL EXPERIMENT 333

ress has surprised me, but I must defer a relation of it, till I have more time to do them justice.[74]

As the war came gradually to a close and the glamour of military occupation began to dim, the social experiment turned into a drab affair. Most of the homesick Northerners were ready to sell their lands for a profit. Richard Soule, Jr., wrote in December, 1865: "Mr. Philbrick has made an effort to sell most of the plantations. As yet no purchaser has appeared.... Negroes continue to steal cotton, and we continue to be helpless against their depredations."[75] But better luck came the next year. Philbrick wrote that "C. F. Williams is busy sharing our land. He sells the whole of Fripp Point in small lots to the negroes of both places ... and the Captain John Fripp place is only four hundred and sixty acres instead of one thousand for which I bought it! By the way, the old man is dead, leaving three daughters in poverty, to earn their living as best they may."[76] Of the other sales, Philbrick explained to one of his partners: "In the morning I walked out with Mr. Wells and sold him both the plantations of which he has had charge for me, viz., the Jenkins place, where he lives, for $1600 or $10 per acre and Morgan Island $1200, or about $5 per acre, which is more than any one would have given a few weeks ago, when we couldn't get a negro to stay there for fear of the rebels. I daresay he may do very well with it now, but it is a vexatious thing to get rations to them in such an out-of-the-way place, and after all young Mr. Fripp may make them another visit, some night, and carry off some more negroes."[77] By the year 1866 losses were rapidly deluging Philbrick in his farming enterprise. In 1864 his company made a profit of $19,000, in 1865 they just about paid expenses, and in January, 1866, he wrote that he had "lost $2800 on the negro cotton ginned in New York, and paid over about $2800 on account of the cotton which they ginned there! I also lost some $2,000 on cotton taken from Mr. ——— in Beaufort, he turning out a knave."[78] "I advanced a dollar a pound," he added, "on the negroes' cotton, you know, and it has cost me about twenty-five cents a pound

---

[74] New England Freedmen's Aid Society, *Second Annual Report* (1864), pp. 68 f. M. A. Wright to C. C. Leigh, Natick, Mass., March 22, 1864.
[75] Pearson, *op. cit.*, p. 324.   [76] *Ibid.*, pp. 325 f.
[77] *Ibid.*, p. 296.   [78] *Ibid.*, p. 326.

more to gin it, etc., etc., while I am offered less than a dollar. Query: How much commission shall I get for doing the business?"[79]

Concerning the success of Northern farming ventures in the islands Richard Soule wrote disconsolately that "There is ground for hope, but the case is a pretty desperate one."[80] Another superintendent remarked that "Those who are to stay next year are all bemoaning their fate. . . ."[81] "There is a universal feeling of dissatisfaction, not to say, disgust, with our colored brethren . . . ," wrote Soule. "They are stealing cotton at a fearful rate." A few nights before they had stolen from a neighbor a whole bale. "We none of us feel secure against their depredations."[82] From the beautiful Coffin's Point plantation came this note of discouragement: "I expect my sojourn at Coffin's Point is nearly closed. The attractions of the place or the people are not sufficient to keep me here another year. The climate is bad enough, the general 'shiftlessness' of the people is disgusting enough; but when I see that the disposition to steal the crop is general, that the people have done and can do it with impunity, I am discouraged about cotton-raising here."[83]

One acquainted with the amiable and leisurely character of the coastal Negro, can scarcely read these letters without a smile. Why did the freedmen spend themselves for their Northern superintendents, even though they were paid? Were not the tidal creeks full of fish, even as they are now? Because of the mild climate little clothing is required in lower Carolina, and the coastal Negro demands little. This combination of circumstances has made of them one of the most leisurely and independent groups on earth. The Negroes clamored about the final payment of their cotton, wrote another, but when they were told there would probably be no further payments, "they think we have cheated them and so the world goes in South Carolina. Rather a thankless task."[84] Another, writing of their "slow, shiftless habits, and . . . general stupidity," made the following observation: "It is a very great trial to any Northern man to have to deal with such a set of people, and I am satisfied that if the Northerners emigrate to the South and undertake

[79] *Ibid.*, p. 310.
[81] *Ibid.*, p. 288.
[83] *Ibid.*, p. 323.
[80] *Ibid.*, p. 312.
[82] *Ibid.*, p. 322.
[84] *Ibid.*, p. 311.

THE PORT ROYAL EXPERIMENT 335

agriculture or anything else, here, they will be compelled to import white laborers."[85] A letter from St. Helena reveals a complaint: "nothing but tief, tief [thieve], all the time. We do not get more than one-fifth of the weight of seed cotton after it is ginned, and the probabilities are that they steal the balance; but we are perfectly helpless, for we cannot prove it against any of them."[86] Those who know the Negro and his difficulties will not condemn him too severely because of these charges. Such conduct had its origin in slavery and a primitive African culture. The Southern planter was not surprised that the Negro stole things about the plantation; in fact, in his best moments he knew in his heart that the slave had some right to the things he helped produce. At any rate, Southerners have not looked upon such conduct as despicable. They carried the cornhouse keys, to be sure, but allowed for a certain *shrinkage* which they knew was inevitable. And I doubt not that the Recording Angel turned his head when a poor Negro took something he needed. After all, it was not exactly stealing. It was just taking something illegally that one had a right to! And something of this tradition has come down to this day in the South, especially the Deep South. The Southern man, so often harsh in exterior, is lenient in his heart. And those who would hasten better race relations in America must build upon this foundation of good will and mutual understanding. The white man must be brought to understand that elemental justice is the least he can require of himself in his relations with the Negro. And the Negro must be wise enough to take into account the peculiar difficulties the white man encounters in his efforts to bring about a better understanding. And the best place for the consummation of this desired end is the South, where many ways for co-operation already exist. What a pity it would be if the South lost this great opportunity!

But the story must reach its end. The pampering of the Negro by his Northern friends produced a great deal of unlovely behavior in the black man. Elizabeth Botume, relating incidents of a steamer trip in 1868, tells the following story:

> We took a small steamer from Charleston to Beaufort. Here we found a decided change since we went North. Then no colored person was allowed on the upper deck, now there were no restric-

[85] *Ibid.*, pp. 315 f.   [86] *Ibid.*, p. 320.

tions,—there could be none, for a law had been passed in favor of the negroes. They were everywhere, choosing the best staterooms and the best seats at the table. Two prominent colored members of the State legislature were on board with their families. There were also several well-known Southerners, still uncompromising rebels. It was a curious scene and full of significance. An interesting study to watch the exultant faces of the negroes, and the scowling faces of the rebels,—rebels still against manifest destiny and the new dispensation. Until now we had but little understood these portentous changes, the meaning of which we study out for ourselves.

We were summoned to dinner. When we reached the table we found there only colored people occupying more than half the seats on each side. They were doing the honors with something of an air that said, "Receive this from me or go without." In all respects, however, they were courteous and attentive. There was no loud talking or laughing.

The stewardess came behind us, and leaning over whispered we has better wait a little while, as they were obliged to give the colored passengers the first table. The white passengers would come to the second. We thanked her, but preferred to keep our seats. A few Northerners joined us.[87]

The freedman was led to think more highly of himself than he ought. Put forward into places of prominence without the necessary qualifications for such office, he was greatly embarrassed in his impossible position. Like strong wine it went to his head. Against the great masses of colored people the Southern whites hold no indictment to this day. It was their misguided friends who caused the greatest trouble. Professor Le Conte, who felt the full blow of Reconstruction in South Carolina, declared that "The sudden enfranchisement of the negro without qualification was the greatest political crime ever perpetrated by any people. . . ."[88] The early Reconstruction government in South Carolina, let us admit, was fair and it was readily accepted. The issues were clear-cut. The South lost decisively and accepted the result. "But," wrote Le Conte, "when the permanent government was organized in the presence of bayonets, with a carpetbag governor, scalawag officials, and a negro legislature controlled by radicals, things were very different, and at last became simply intolerable." Professor Le Conte further explained that there was, at that time, a five per

[87] Botume, *op. cit.*, pp. 267 f.   [88] Le Conte, *op. cit.*, p. 238.

THE PORT ROYAL EXPERIMENT 337

cent income tax imposed by the scalawag government, and the amount of the tax on his salary of two thousand dollars was one hundred dollars, which he paid. "I subsequently learned," he wrote, "that I paid more tax than the whole legislature put together."[89] The tragedy that befell South Carolina, not only through loss of her best young men in war, but because of the blighting experiences of Reconstruction, made the state an inhospitable field for the pursuit of any of the sciences and arts. The dreary prospect drove from the state many of its best minds. Among them was the distinguished Le Conte, who declared:

> I bore the iniquities of the government as long as I could but when the negro legislature began to talk about what they were going to do with the University [of South Carolina], I thought it time to quit. Colonies were being formed to emigrate to Mexico and Brazil, and for a while John [a brother] and I thought seriously of trying our fortunes with Maximilian. But just then we heard through friends of the proposed University of California, and wrote immediately applying for professorships. We were elected, John in November and I in December, 1868, and this led to our removal to California in the following year.[90]

The bungling and errors of the Port Royal Experiment are nowhere more clearly revealed than in proceedings consequent upon the return of the land to the planters. When the heat of war and the desire for retribution began to wane, it was very evident that the former owners of land had been treated with gross injustice. President Johnson realized that the dispossessed planters had been wronged and put in motion efforts to set right some of the worst grievances. Again the Negro suffered because of the white man's blunders: hundreds of blacks were already settled upon their cherished forty acres and had begun, as they thought, a veritable Utopia. Soon after the close of the war General Saxton estimated that forty thousand Negroes had been provided with homes in the coastal country according to the provision of General W. T. Sherman's special field order setting aside the islands of Charleston for the exclusive use of Negroes.[91] In addition, he reported that over six

[89] *Ibid.*, pp. 237 f.
[90] *Ibid.*, pp. 239 f.
[91] Webster, *op. cit.*, p. 96.

hundred certificates of title to real estate were issued to Negroes by the tax commissioners of South Carolina.[92] The situation around Port Royal, Beaufort, St. Helena, and Edisto was such that the Negroes in these areas suffered keenest disappointment when they were required to give up the land. For it was here that the promise of free land was first held out and they had occupied the plantations since the early days of the war. After four or five years of living on the land as owners it was exceedingly difficult for them to understand why they should give it up. The feeling was particularly acute on Edisto Island. For some reason the Negroes got it into their heads that this territory would surely be given to them. All of these troubles, the adjustment of differences between the Negroes and the dispossessed planters, and many other problems of like nature were thrown into the lap of the newly organized Bureau of Refugees, Freedmen, and Abandoned Lands, commonly called Freedmen's Bureau. General O. O. Howard, its first commissioner, divided the duties of his organization into four general departments: "one of lands, embracing abandoned, confiscated, and those acquired by sale or otherwise; one of records, embracing official acts of the Commissioner, touching labor, schools, quartermaster and commissary supplies; another of financial affairs; and the fourth the medical department."[93] No doubt General Howard's most difficult problem in the early days of his administration was the adjudication of the tangled land affairs in the Carolina sea islands. The difficulty was immeasurably enhanced by General Sherman's field order. So acute was the situation along the Carolina coast that the commissioner felt it necessary to make a special trip there in person. Earlier in the war he had visited the territory and was interested in the experiment in rehabilitation conducted there. In his report to Secretary of War Stanton, Howard asserted: "I resolved to go to Edisto, as soon as the people could be convened at some central point . . . accompanied by several officers and the representative of the Edisto planters, Mr. William Whaley. I met the freedmen at a large church on the island."[94] Mary Ames, who was teaching the Negroes on Edisto at the same time, recalled that the meet-

[92] *Ibid.*
[93] *Executive Documents*, 39th Congress, 1st Session, No. 11, p. 2.
[94] *Ibid.*, p. 7.

THE PORT ROYAL EXPERIMENT 339

ing was held in the Episcopal Church and that scores of Negroes mounted on mules and horses of every sort and description rode down to Steamboat Landing to give General Howard and his assistant, General Saxton, a real military reception. General Howard explained "that the owners of the land, their old masters, had been pardoned, and their plantations were to be given back to them; that they wanted to come back to cultivate the land, and would hire the blacks to work for them." At first the people could not understand, but finally the import of Howard's mission was understood, and grievous dissatisfaction arose. At a tense moment, recorded Mary Ames, they were asked to sing, and the assembly burst forth into the old spiritual, "Nobody Knows the Trouble I See." Then they sang "Wandering in the Wilderness of Sorrow and Gloom." Two of the largest owners, former residents of the island, came with the officers. Mary Ames wrote: "Many of their old slaves were in the church. It was touching to see them saying, 'Howdy' to each other. The gentlemen also felt it. Tears were in their eyes."[95] This meeting General Howard described in an official telegram to Stanton: "I met several hundred of the colored people of Edisto Island to-day, and did my utmost to reconcile them to the surrender of the lands to former owners. They will submit, but with evident sorrow, to the breaking of the promise of General Sherman's order. . . ."[96] On the island "Meeting after meeting was held to reconcile them to the changed and difficult conditions. On one occasion, when explanations seemed to create greater antagonism, I ventured a remark, and was quickly told by Ishmael, their leader, that I had 'Better go into the house and attend to study. . . .' "[97] Concerning the Edisto Island meeting, General Howard added: "I explained what I believed to be the wishes of the President, as set forth in his interview with me just before leaving Washington. . . . The [Negro] people chose a committee of three of their number and to them I submitted the proposition to which the land owners were willing to subscribe." The committee found that the freedmen were unwilling to work for wages for their former owners under overseers, "but if they could rent

[95] Ames, *op. cit.*, pp. 90 ff.
[96] *Executive Document*, 39th Congress, 1st Session, No. 11, p. 8.
[97] Ames, *op. cit.*, p. 121.

the lands of them, they would consent in other respects to arrangements proposed." The Negroes readily left the final details of land restoration to Howard, who formed a board of supervisors, "in which the government, the planter, and the freedmen had each a representative for the adjustment of contracts and cases of difficulty. Each land-owner was required to sign an obligation, after which the order of restoration was to be issued."[98] Thus through the local committee and by the advice of General Howard and the influence of President Johnson, a great part of Edisto Island was restored to its former white owners. Mary Ames incorporated in her diary a pathetic document bearing upon this period—a letter of protest to President Johnson written by the poor Negroes of Edisto Island against the return of the land to the owners. Its faulty diction and pitiable spelling make its meaning obscure in places. The letter follows in part:

Wee the freedmen of South Carolina wish to address you with a few lines Conserning the sad feelings that is now restin upon our minds. . . .

Mag genrl howard has paid the freedmen of South Carliner a visit & caled a meating on Edisto Island South Carliner in the Centrel part of the island at the priskple Church thair hee beutifly addressed the freedmen of this island after his adress a grate many of the peple understanding what was said they got aroused & awoke to perfict sense to stody for them Selves what part of this law would rest against us, wee said in rafarence to what he said that nothing did apier at that time to bee very opressing upon us but the one thing that is wee freedmen should work for wages for our former oners or eny other man president Johnson of u st [*sic*] I do say . . . man that have stud upon the feal of battle & have shot there master & sons now Going to ask ether one for bread or shelter or Comfortable for his wife & children sunch a thing the u st should not aught to Expect a man (to do). . . .

"Here is Plenty Whidow & Fatherless that have serve you as slave now losen a home," and they beg that you "give Each one of them a acres & ½ to a family as you has the labers & the Profet of there Yearly [early] Youth.[99]

The adjustments on Edisto Island must have been generally satisfactory, for there appears to have been little trouble after

---

[98] *Executive Document*, 39th Congress, 1st Session, No. 11, p. 7.
[99] Ames, *op. cit.*, pp. 99-102.

THE PORT ROYAL EXPERIMENT 341

General Howard's visit. I. J. Mikell, who described the return of his father's family to the ancestral home on beautiful Peter's Point plantation, explained that while all of their buildings escaped the ravages of war, Negroes were in complete possession of the home and all Negro cottages. It, he wrote, "required the authority of the United States officer in command of troops stationed here to dispossess them. Once in possession, no further trouble as to claiming ownership was experienced."[100] Other landowners were not so fortunate as to find their homesteads intact, even though occupied by Negroes, when they returned after the war. Ambrose Gonzales described his family's sad return to the ashes of Oak Lawn plantation on Pon Pon, the ancestral home of the Gonzales family:

When it was all over we returned to the ruined low-country and to Reconstruction! Far worse than the poverty and privation was the constant realization in the minds of the boys of the physical and mental strain upon the grown-ups they loved. And the hopelessness of it all! We felt, young and old, like rats caught in a trap. We couldn't think our way out and could see no light ahead.

Back at the plantation the boys took up the new life under changed conditions. The sturdy English brick walls of the old house still stood but they were now green with ivy and wreathed with climbing roses. The only stick left standing on the place was the "wash kitchen," a servant's house, which the pleadings of an old caretaker induced the Federal colonel to leave for the Negro's occupancy. Before the family returned the weatherboarding had been stripped away and stolen but the framework and the chimneys remained, and about these a crude habitation was constructed that sheltered the family for years.[101]

The plight of the planters had its inevitable reaction upon the Negroes. They were all, both black and white, poor, but for the whites there loomed a desperate economic struggle, and in their hearts was the resolve that the Negro should never again get the upper hand of affairs and become a landowner and a political power, and especially that he should never be allowed to carry out Sherman's design. This, of course, was a serious blow to Negro progress, and thenceforth the Negroes were set over against the whites and the whites against the Negroes. In the meantime the Northern friends of the black people were

---

[100] Mikell, *op. cit.*, p. 124.
[101] Gonzales, *In Darkest Cuba*, from the Foreword by Ambrose Gonzales.

rapidly withdrawing from the field. Of all ways to help the Negro they chose the worst! After the war and the restoration of land to the whites the Negroes were still keenly desirous of owning property. Their utopian dream of forty acres and a mule was now replaced by the desire to buy a few acres of land so that they might be independent of their former masters. This wish was often gratified by the circumstance of the sale of plantations by white owners who preferred to try their fortunes in other sections. Many of them were eager to dispose of their holdings along the coast. A Port Royal letter writer of that time stated, "There are a large number of old planters who are offering their lands at very low rates, and so many tempting chances are offered to Northern men."[102] This correspondent might have added that the opportunity was offered to Negroes also. Howbeit, it was considered unwise to sell land to Negroes as such ownership increased labor problems for the whites. But the economic motive outweighed all other consideration, and, consequently, thousands of Negroes in the coast country today own their little tracts of land with their crude dwellings. On St. Helena and Ladies Islands alone, with a population of 4,785 in 1928, there were 1,201 Negro farms of over three acres, seventy-five farms of less than three acres, and only 266 of the total number were of more than twenty acres.[103] One is impressed with the great number of small Negro farms in the whole coastal area. Many of the titles could be traced back to Federal tax sales and confiscation proceedings of Civil War days. Ambrose Gonzales has left a vivid picture in his book, *The Captain*, of private sales to Negroes after the war. Mitchell plantation was divided into forty-odd ten-acres tracts and sold to Negroes. Old Cassius, one of the purchasers, obtained a plot situated on high ground and covered with virgin-growth longleaf pine. Suspicious of his treatment, at first he finally came to the conclusion that the young surveyor had done well by him and had selected for him a goodly land: "Uh t'engkful to me Gawd," declared Cassius, "cause Him tell Mas' Rafe en' de Suhweyuh fut pit me puntop shishuh good groun' lukkuh dis.... Dem *mek* me tek'um. T'engk-Gawd." Experienced axeman that he was, he "threw" a dozen saplings to be used in building his cabin. Working hard, raking, clearing, and digging, he

---

[102] Pearson, *op. cit.*, p. 317.   [103] Woofter, *op. cit.*, pp. 263, 271.

finally stopped to rest, "and Negro-like his spirit yearned for fire." From lightwood splinters Cassius kindled a small blaze. Crouching near and with his back against a great pine, the old man was soon asleep. When the surveying party arrived, Cassius was startled: "Jumping up, he rubbed his eyes, and then raked out the embers. 'Mas Rafe,' he said, 'Uh drap 'sleep en'—Uh binnuh dream [I've been a-dreaming]!'"[104] Cassius doubtless uttered the sentiment of thousands of disillusioned coastal Negroes, who, looking in retrospect upon the fanfare of war, uniformed soldiers, liberators, and fair promises which could not be kept, and awaking from those happy visions to face the stern realities of life, could say, not in desperation, but in fine Negro philosophy, "Uh binnuh dream!"

[104] Gonzales, *The Captain*, pp. 170-171.

BIBLIOGRAPHY

BIBLIOGRAPHY

Allen, William Francis (comp.). *Slave Songs of the United States.* New York, 1867. Reprinted, 1929.
American Freedman, The. New York, 1866-1869.
Ames, Mary (Clemmer). *From a New England Woman's Diary in Dixie in 1865.* Norwood, Mass., 1906.
Ballanta, Nicholas George Julius (comp.). *St. Helena Island Spirituals.* St. Helena, S. C., 1925.
Barnwell, Robert Woodward, Sr. *Dawn at Daufuskie and Other Poems.* Privately printed. Florence, S. C.: Florence Printing Company, 1936.
Bassett, John Spencer. *The Southern Plantation Overseer, as Revealed in His Letters.* Northampton, Mass., 1925.
Bellinger, Lucius. *Stray Leaves from the Portfolio of a Methodist Local Preacher.* Macon, Ga., 1870.
Bennett, John. "The Comedie Humaine of the Gullah Darkey," *The State* (Columbia, S. C.), Dec. 17, 1922.
Bennett, John. "Gullah: A Negro Patois," *The South Atlantic Quarterly,* VII, 332-347 (Oct., 1908); VIII, 39-52 (Jan., 1909).
Bolton, H. Carrington. "Decoration of Graves of Negroes in South Carolina," *Journal of American Folklore,* IV, 214 (July-Sept., 1891).
Botume, Elizabeth Hyde. *First Days amongst the Contrabands.* Boston, 1893.
Bremer, Fredrika. *The Homes of the New World; Impressions of America.* 2 vols. New York, 1854.
Bruner, Clarence Vernon. *An Abstract of the Religious Instruction of the Slaves in the Antebellum South.* "George Peabody College for Teachers, Contributions to Education," No. 112. Nashville, Tenn., 1933.
Capers, William. *Catechism for the Use of the Methodist Missions.* . . . Nashville, Tenn., 1876.
Chambers, William. *Things as They Are in America.* Philadelphia, 1854.
Christensen, (Mrs.) A. M. H. *Afro-American Folk Lore, Told Round Cabin Fires on the Sea Islands of South Carolina.* Boston, 1892.
Christian Advocate and Journal. New York, 1826-.

BIBLIOGRAPHY

Clark, Elmer Talmadge. *The Negro and His Religion.* Nashville, Tenn., 1924.

Davis, Henry C. "Negro Folk-Lore in South Carolina," *Journal of American Folklore,* XXVII, 241-254 (July-Sept., 1914).

De Bow's Review. New Orleans, 1846-1880.

De Saussure, Nancy (Bostwick). *Old Plantation Days.* New York, 1909.

Dett, Robert Nathaniel. *Religious Folk-Songs of the Negro.* Hampton, Va., 1927.

Dinkins, Charles Roundtree. *Lyrics of Love.* Columbia, S. C., 1904.

Doar, David. *A Sketch of the Agricultural Society of St. James, Santee, South Carolina. And an Address on the Traditions and Reminiscences of the Parish, Delivered before Society on 4th of July, 1907.* Charleston, S. C., 1908.

Dow, Lorenzo. *Life, Travels, Labors, and Writings.* . . . New York, 1881.

Educational Commission for Freedmen. *First Annual Report (May, 1863).* Boston, 1863.

Elliott, William. *Carolina Sports by Land and Water; Including Incidents of Devilfishing, etc.* Charleston, S. C., 1846.

Fickling, Susan Markey. *Slave Conversion in South Carolina, 1830-1860.* "Bulletin of the University of South Carolina," No. 146. Columbia, S. C., 1924.

Freedmen's Record, The. Boston, 1865-1873.

Fulton, Maurice Garland. *Southern Life in Southern Literature.* Boston, 1917.

Gonzales, Ambrose Elliott. *The Black Border.* Columbia, S. C., 1922.

Gonzales, Ambrose Elliott. *The Captain.* Columbia, S. C., 1924.

Gonzales, Narciso Gener. *In Darkest Cuba. Two Months' Service under Gomez along the Trocha from the Caribbean to the Bahama Channel.* . . . Columbia, S. C., 1922.

Harrison, William Pope. *The Gospel among the Slaves.* Nashville, Tenn., 1893.

Hawkins, William George. *Lunsford Lane.* Boston, Mass., 1863.

Hewatt, Alexander. *An Historical Account of the Rise and Progress of the Colonies of South Carolina and Georgia.* London, 1779.

Higginson, Thomas Wentworth. *Army Life in a Black Regiment.* Boston, 1870.

Hoole, William Stanley. *A Check-List and Finding-List of Charleston Periodicals, 1732-1864.* Durham, N. C., 1936.

Hucks, J. Jenkins. *Plantation Negro Sayings on the Coast of South Carolina in Their Own Vernacular.* Georgetown, S. C., 1899.

BIBLIOGRAPHY 349

Humphreys, David. *An Historical Account of the Incorporated Society for the Propagation of the Gospel in Foreign Parts.* . . . London, 1730.

Johnson, Guy Benton. *Folk Culture on St. Helena Island, South Carolina.* Chapel Hill, N. C., 1930.

Johnson, Guion Griffis. *A Social History of the Sea Islands.* Chapel Hill, N. C., 1930.

Johnson, J. Rosamond (comp.). *Utica Jubilee Singers Spirituals.* Boston, 1930.

Johnson, Robert Underwood and Clarence Clough Buel (eds.). *Battles and Leaders of the Civil War.* 4 vols. New York, 1884-1887.

Jones, Charles Colcock. *A Catechism of Scripture, Doctrine and Practice, for Families and Sabbath Schools, Designed also for the Oral Instruction of Colored Persons.* Savannah, Ga., 1844.

Jones, Charles Colcock. *The Religious Instruction of the Negroes in the United States.* Savannah, Ga., 1842.

Jones, Charles Colcock, Jr. *Negro Myths from the Georgia Coast Told in the Vernacular.* Boston, Mass., 1888. Reprinted by The State Company, Columbia, S. C., 1925.

Krapp, George Philip. "The English of the American Negro," *American Mercury,* II, 190-195 (June, 1924).

Krehbiel, Henry Edward. *Afro-American Folk Songs: A Study in Racial and National Music.* New York, 1914.

Laurens, Henry. *Correspondence.* Edited by Frank Moore. New York, 1861.

Le Conte, Joseph. *Autobiography.* New York, 1903.

Lowery, Irving E. *Life on the Old Plantation.* Columbia, S. C., 1911.

Lusk, William Thompson. *War Letters of William Thompson Lusk.* Privately printed. n.p., 1911.

McCrady, Edward. *The History of South Carolina under the Proprietary Government, 1670-1719.* New York and London, 1897.

McCrady, Edward. "Slavery in the Province of South Carolina, 1670-1770," *American Historical Association, Annual Report* (1895), pp. 631-673. Washington, 1896.

Massebeau, W. A. *The Camp Meeting in South Carolina,* Annual Address before the Upper South Carolina Conference Historical Society in Greenwood, S. C., November 4, 1919, and before the South Carolina Conference Historical Society, McColl, S. C., November 25, 1919. Published by the Order of the Societies. n.p., n.d.

BIBLIOGRAPHY

Mikell, Isaac Jenkins. *Rumbling of the Chariot Wheels.* Columbia, S. C., 1923.
Moore, Frank (ed.). *Rebellion Record.* . . . New York, 1861-1865.
Nation, The. New York, 1865-.
National Geographic Society. *The Book of Fishes.* Washington, 1924.
Negro Yearbook: Annual Encyclopedia of the Negro. . . . Nashville, Tenn., 1912-.
New England Freedmen's Aid Society. *Second Annual Report* (April, 1864). Boston, 1864.
News and Courier. Charleston, S. C.
O'Neall, John Belton. *The Negro Law of South Carolina.* Columbia, S. C., 1848.
Pearson, Elizabeth Ware (ed.). *Letters from Port Royal.* Boston, 1906.
Phillips, Ulrich Bonnell. *American Negro Slavery.* New York, 1918.
Phillips, Ulrich Bonnell. *Life and Labor in the Old South.* Boston, 1929.
Phillips, Ulrich Bonnell. "The Public Archives of Georgia," *American Historical Association, Annual Report* (1903), I, 439-474. Washington, 1904.
Phillips, Ulrich Bonnell, John R. Commons, Eugene A. Gilmore, Helen L. Sumner, and John B. Andrews . . . (eds.). *A Documentary History of American Industrial Society.* 11 vols. Cleveland, Ohio, 1910.
Pinckney, Eliza (Lucas). *Journal and Letters of Eliza Lucas.* Wormsloe, Ga., 1850.
Pringle, Elizabeth Waties (Allston). *Chronicles of Chicora Wood.* New York, 1922. Reprinted, Boston, Mass., 1940.
Proceedings of the Meeting in Charleston S. C. . . . on the Religious Instruction of the Negroes. Charleston, S. C., 1845.
Ramsay, David. *History of South Carolina, from Its First Settlement in 1670, to the Year 1808.* . . . 2 vols. Newberry, S. C., 1858.
Smith, Reed. *Gullah.* "Bulletin of the University of South Carolina," No. 190, November 1, 1926. Columbia, S. C., 1926.
Rice, James Henry. *Glories of the Carolina Coast.* Columbia, S. C., 1925.
Salley, Alexander Samuel (ed.). *Narratives of Early Carolina, 1650-1708.* New York, 1911.
Savannah (Ga.) *Morning News.*

BIBLIOGRAPHY 351

[Society for the Preservation of Spirituals.] *The Carolina Low-Country*, by Augustine Thomas Smythe, Herbert Ravenal Sass, Alfred Huger . . . [and others]. New York, 1931.
State, The. Columbia, S. C.
Stevens, Hazard. *Life of Isaac Ingalls Stevens*. 2 vols. New York, 1901.
Stoney, Samuel Gaillard and Gertrude Mathews Shelby. *Black Genesis*. New York, 1930.
Sunday News. Charleston, S. C.
United States Congress. *Congressional Record*. Washington, 1873-.
United States Congress. *Executive Documents*, 39th Congress, 1st Session, 1865-1866, No. 11, *Report of the Commissioner of the Bureau of Refugees, Freedmen and Abandoned Lands*. Washington, 1866.
United States War Department. *War of the Rebellion: A Compilation of the Official Records of the Union and Confederate Armies*. . . . 130 vols. Washington, 1880-1901.
Wallace, David Duncan. *Life of Henry Laurens, with a Sketch of the Life of Lieutenant-Colonel John Laurens*. New York, 1915.
Webster, Laura Josephine. *The Operation of the Freedmen's Bureau in South Carolina*. "Smith College Studies in History." Vol. I, No. 2. Northampton, Mass., 1916.
Weston, Plowden C. J. "Management of a Southern Plantation: Rules Enforced on the Rice Estate of P. C. Weston, Esq., of South Carolina," *De Bow's Review*, XXII, 38-44 (Jan., 1857).
Whaley, Marcellus Seabrook. *The Old Types Pass*. Boston, 1925.
White, Newman Ivey. *American Negro Folk-Songs*. Cambridge, Mass., 1928.
Wightman, William M. *Life of William Capers, D. D., One of the Bishops of the Methodist Episcopal Church, South; Including an Autobiography*. Nashville, Tenn., 1859.
Williams, John G. *De Old Plantation*. Charleston, S. C., 1896.
Williams, John G. "A Wedding on Combahee," *News and Courier* (Charleston, S. C.), Dec. 16, 1894.
Williams, John G. "Is Gullah a Corruption of Angola?" *Sunday News* (Charleston, S. C.), Feb. 10, 1895.
Woofter, Thomas Jackson. *Black Yeomanry; Life on St. Helena Island*. New York, 1930.
Wright, Joseph. *English Dialect Grammar*. Oxford, 1905.

www.ingramcontent.com/pod-product-compliance
Lightning Source LLC
Chambersburg PA
CBHW060511080526
44586CB00012B/457